Kissing Fish

Kissing Fish

christianity for people
who don't like christianity

Roger Wolsey

To order additional copies of this book, contact:
Xlibris Corporation
1-888-795-4274
www.Xlibris.com
Orders@Xlibris.com
72172

Contents

Praise for Kissing Fish

Kissing Fish is a unique blend of personal confession of faith and systematic theology. Roger Wolsey offers a manifesto for "progressive Christianity" that aims to break the seeming stranglehold that "conservative Christianity" has on the minds of many, both in and outside the official churches. He writes in a friendly, accessible manner that is deeply grounded in the best of Christian tradition, both old and new. For those young adults who know there is "something more" to life than the deadening drumbeat of empire but have doubts that "Christianity" is where to find it, this book offers a much needed invitation to discover the joy, love, and compassionate justice that lie at the heart of the Gospel of Jesus Christ.

Wes Howard-Brook, author of *Unveiling Empire: Reading Revelation Then and Now, Becoming Children of God, The Church Before Christianity,* and *Come Out My People!": God's Call Out of Empire in the Bible and Beyond.*

* * *

Roger Wolsey has bitten off a big chunk to chew on: a thorough comparison and contrasting of what is typically called "progressive" Christianity with more well-known forms of Christian expression, typically called "conservative evangelicalism" and "fundamentalism." In doing so, he exhibits great ambition and it is left to the reader to determine whether or not that ambition has been fulfilled.

What makes *Kissing Fish* attractive is not so much Wolsey's theological compare and contrast as it is his weaving throughout the whole work his own spiritual journey. After all, that is the story. It's not an academic tome, though it brushes up against that. Neither is it a philosophical/theological apologia for Wolsey's understanding of "progressive" Christianity. Rather, it is story; it is narrative; it is the journey of a young man who begins his story with the profound admission: "I probably shouldn't be a Christian." It is the journey of a young man, who being raised in typically mainline Protestantism, who is trying to construct his faith in the shadow of societal and cultural change, a change greatly informed by postmodernist thinking.

In the end, Wolsey views "progressive" forms of Christian thinking and being as the genuinely "conservative" ones; to wit, reaching back to the earliest Christian origins (pre-Constantine) to find itself.

While I might not share all of Wolsey's conclusions and characterizations (after all, I am an old man now at this writing and not in his target audience of Gen-Xers or Millennials), this is a thought-provoking, insightful work and we should all be grateful for his insight and his journey. Read it!

The Revd. David R. Gillespie, Progressive Christian Alliance Minister Director of Sacred Journeys: Pastoral Care & Spiritual Direction, Christ the King Lutheran Church, Greenville, SC

About the Author

Roger Wayne Wolsey is a free spirit who thinks and feels a lot about God and Jesus. He's a progressive Christian who identifies with people who consider themselves "spiritual, but not religious." A trumpeter, Roger grew up during the "Minneapolis Sound" era of the 1980s and '90s. These experiences contribute to a musical approach to his theology. Roger studied philosophy and political science, graduated *magna cum laude* and *Phi Beta Kappa*, from Macalester College in St. Paul, MN, and earned a Master of Divinity degree at the Iliff School of Theology in Denver, CO. Roger is an ordained pastor in the United Methodist Church. He has taught Introduction to Religion classes as an adjunct instructor at Graceland University in Lamoni, IA. He has served as a pastor for churches in Minnesota, Iowa and Colorado. He currently serves as the Director of the Wesley Foundation campus ministry at the University of Colorado in Boulder, CO. Roger was married for ten years, divorced, and co-parents a delightful child. He loves music, yoga, dancing, rock-climbing, motorcycling, trail running with his dog Kingdom, and hosting house concerts. Roger is also president of the board of directors of the Boulder International Fringe Festival and blogs for *Elephant Journal,* a magazine for the Buddhist and yoga communities.

Acknowledgments
& Dedication

I would like to thank the following individuals who read early drafts of this book and offered their insightful feedback and editorial suggestions: Andee Miller, Heather Warweg, Erika Usui, Laura Brewster Bowes, Carolyn DiBella, Sarah Cooke, Ashley Page Randall, Julie Kinsey, Jessie Nelson, and Sarah Schoonmaker. I am especially grateful to Cynthia Beard, Karen Melissa Stronglove Vuto, Hannah Walker, Linda Cummings, and Melissa McEver for their helpful insights and careful attention to my drafts. The many college students and young adults who I work with at the Wesley Foundation at the University of Colorado-Boulder who helped me to develop and test drive the ideas and material presented within have been a tremendous blessing. I'd also like to express my deep gratitude to all of my Facebook friends, some of whom I've actually met, who cheered me on each step of the way. Last but not least, a huge thank you to the wonderful staff at the IHOP restaurant in Boulder, CO—where much of this book was written. I couldn't have done this without your encouragement and your coffee! I dedicate this book to my son Andrew and to the world that his generation will inherit. May the Christianity that is around when you grow up offer a faith that is robust yet humble, makes sense, embraces mystery, pursues justice, helps you feel loved, and empowers you to love and serve *everyone* unconditionally.

Foreword

One of the great liabilities of life is that all too many people find themselves living amid a great period of social change, and yet they fail to develop the new attitudes, the new mental responses, that the new situation desires. They end up sleeping through a revolution. Martin Luther King, Jr.

Whether he is befriending a homeless man, berating a homophobic protester, helping heal a broken woman, comforting a sexually abused person, or speaking out for social justice and peace, Roger Wolsey seeks to incarnate the Christian faith that nourishes his spirit and propels him to love more deeply and live more meaningfully.

"Kissing Fish: christianity for people who don't like christianity" is a bold effort to reach across the growing chasm between Christian believers and non-believers. Alarmed that the rich diversity of Christian thinking has been hijacked by rigid conservative dogmatics, Wolsey advances a critical and creative presentation of progressive Christianity. His passion is matched only by his intellect as he explores the geography of faith and invites the reader to experience God the Extreme Adventurer, who takes great risks by encouraging human freedom.

An Inclusive and Winsome Faith

Though Wolsey might not be comfortable to be identified as a Christian apologist in a postmodern era, he certainly asserts a straightforward presentation of an inclusive and winsome Christian faith. He does not shirk from re-thinking classical doctrines, re-examining the historical traditions, and re-invigorating ethical teachings. Even as he appeals to those alienated, wounded and

13

rejected by religious teachings and people, Wolsey never hides his own profound spiritual nourishment that he drinks from the deep wells of Christian faith.

By challenging contemporary misunderstandings of Christian faith, Wolsey does not distort Christian teaching but draws upon often overlooked currents of theology that are too often besmirched by established religious leaders and missed by the media. A keen participant-observer of contemporary culture, he says that people:

> " . . . *today tend to embrace a more nuanced, experiential, paradoxical, mystical, metaphorical, and relational approach to faith and spirituality. We like it messy, down-to-earth, and real. Interestingly, this is the same kind of approach to Christianity that early Christians experienced and understood. Hence, what I'm referring to as 'progressive Christianity' isn't new or novel, in many ways it's a reformation of the Church to its earlier, pre-modernist and pre-Constantinian roots. Ironically, this implies that in reality, it is 'progressive Christianity' that is conservative—and that 'conservative Christianity' isn't!"*

A "No Pretensions" Author

Honest, blunt, and candid, Wolsey never pretends he is a saint. Often autobiographical, he dares to be open about his own faults and failures. Historically, Christian theologians piously proclaim that they, like all other human beings, are sinners, but instead of opening a window on their weaknesses, they often become self-righteous propagandists of a faith and an ethic by which they do not live. In contrast, Wolsey tends to over-amplify his sins, saying: "I suck as a pastor, I sucked as a husband, I suck as a father, I suck as a lover, and I might even suck as a human being." This is not exactly the language of the Pope, Karl Barth, the TV evangelist, or bishops of any denomination! Yet it is a frank acknowledgement of his own imperfection and need for God's unconditional love and unmerited grace. This candor helps him identify with other human beings and their quest for meaning, hope, and healing.

Wolsey also never pretends that he has all the answers. Like the old bumper sticker that reads, "Jesus came to take away our sins, not our minds," Wolsey's purpose is to prompt people to think, to argue, and to be in dialogue. Judgmental, closed minds, and churches trapped in exclusivist, rigid, and dysfunctional theologies will not welcome Wolsey's insights and ideas, but his vision and voice will be refreshing to a society where more and more people are proclaiming they are "spiritual but not religious."

Addressing the Contemporary Culture

This primer in progressive Christianity celebrates an all-loving God, a subversive radical Jesus, and a compassionate community of faith. Less concerned about doctrinal orthodoxy, and more concerned about how people live (*orthopraxis*), Wolsey yet outlines in detail the distinctions between conservative and progressive visions and versions of Christianity. Readers will find in his charts helpful ways to sort out the differing emphases within Christian theology.

Never fearing to address issues in contemporary culture, Wolsey, for example, directly confronts what many consider the "civil rights cause" of our time—namely issues of human rights posed by gay, lesbian, bi-sexual, and inter-sex persons around the world.

Since this book is targeted primarily, but not exclusively, at young adults, it is astonishing to note that 91% of non-churchgoers from the age of 16 to 29 think Christianity is anti-homosexual. Furthermore, 80% of the churchgoers in that same age group agree! Wolsey notes that, "Conservative Christianity has largely reduced sin to what happens in people's bedrooms. Namely, who they should love and how and when they should love them." He affirms that the condemnation, stigmatization, and discrimination of same-sex loving persons are contrary to the inclusive love of God expressed in Jesus' ministry and teachings.

Conservative Christianity's misrepresentation of the Gospel as being exclusive stands in stark contrast to Christianity's progressive perspective that God loves and accepts all human beings regardless of sexual orientation and practice. The spiritual faith, that Wolsey proclaims and lives, embraces all God's people and calls them to be transformed by God's amazing grace. Wolsey acknowledges that what he writes is neither new nor novel, but a message that needs to be re-asserted and re-claimed, lest the current generation miss the opportunity to experience Christian faith and life at its best.

Rev. Dr. Donald E. Messer

Author of numerous books including, *A Conspiracy of Goodness, Contemporary Images of Christian Ministry, and 52 Ways To Create An AIDS Free World,* Messer served the Iliff School of Theology from 1981 to 2006. He was president from 1981 to 2000. He currently serves as Executive Director of the Center for the Church and Global AIDS.

Preface

A prominent feature of today's "emerging" and progressive churches is an eclectic, mosaic approach to worship that draws from several sources and styles. As someone who is part of that movement, I realize that I have not one, but many voices and my writings in this book reflect this. You will notice that there are several "voices" and styles of writing that I have employed in the pages within—including, an informal, conversational, self-revealing voice; a playful and occasionally edgy voice; and a more philosophical, scholarly voice. While I try to maintain a conversational tone throughout, some readers will be drawn to the chapters and portions of chapters that come from one voice, while others will be drawn to those of another voice. **Feel free to read the passages that attract you and skip the others.** The initial printing of this book is a work-in-progress. Like a theatre company offering a preview test run to a circle of friends, peers, and colleagues, I'm intending this to serve as an incubator to further the development of this project. I also intend for it to introduce progressive Christianity to as wide an audience as possible.

Though I employed an editor to provide some professional services, she is in no way responsible for any mistakes or awkwardness within the text. Defects of any sort (from typos to heresy) are mine. I wanted to get this book out into the marketplace of ideas as soon as possible and didn't want to wait until everything within it is in a perfected form. I'm hoping that the feedback from you all, the first wave of readers, will help with that perfecting process. Please feel free to post comments and suggestions to the guestbook at **www.progressivechristianitybook.com.**

I chose Aimee Dansereau to help me edit the book because of her professional reputation and because she isn't a Christian.

She's a Buddhist. And I wanted feedback from a young adult from another faith tradition.

Notes to the Reader: Interspersed throughout the text are sections that I call "**Break It Downs.**" These are provided to allow us to go deeper into various subtopics and provide background information, or some of my musings, on a variety of topics. If you like going down rabbit holes of the mind, you might enjoy them. Feel free to skip them if you like. The **Footnotes** are a combination of more of my thoughts on certain subtopics, passages from other sources that provide further information, and references from works that I cite. **Feel free to skip Chapter 1** if you'd rather dig right into the meat of the text. It's just a bunch of stuff about me and the book isn't really about me—besides I'm a dork. **If you'd prefer to skip past the theology and focus more upon what progressive Christianity looks like** *in practice*, **you might wish to simply read the Introduction and Chapter 2 and then skip ahead to Section II and see Chapters 11-13 and the Postlude.** I alternate referring to God as "He" and "She." I speak to why I do this in Chapter 3. I sometimes refer to God with the pronoun *Who* intentionally capitalized. This is done to show reverence and to make it clear to whom I am referring.[1] Unless otherwise indicated, the Bible passages that I quote are from the NIV (New International Version) Bible (Zondervan, 2010). This is intentional as I feel it does a good job with the Greek in the New Testament, many conservative Christians favor it, and I'd like to help any conservative Christians who read this book to feel a sense of familiarity and hospitality. Due to legal issues regarding the quoting of music lyrics, I paraphrase them when I use them.

Because there are many varieties of Christianity and there is no way I could speak to all of them, I have limited my focus in this book to distinguishing progressive Christianity from the forms of the faith that are most prominently featured and discussed by the American media; i.e., conservative evangelicalism and fundamentalism. I employ a compare-and-contrast approach that may come across as dualistic or divisive. In the *Postlude* at the end of the text I make a point to reconcile and state that progressive

---

[1]   http://www.gotquestions.org/capitalizing-pronouns-God.html

Christianity isn't necessarily better than other approaches to the faith. I recognize the limitations of these approaches, but my intention is to help correct the current imbalance of conservative Christianity all but monopolizing the faith. The conservative evangelical approach isn't resonating with many of today's young people (or older people for that matter) and I have a heart to share the approach of progressive Christianity.

Introduction

The message of Jesus as I understand it, is contained in the Sermon on the Mount unadulterated and taken as a whole. If then I had to face only the Sermon on the Mount and my own interpretation of it, I should not hesitate to say, "Oh, yes, I am a Christian." But negatively I can tell you that in my humble opinion, what passes as Christianity is a negation of the Sermon on the Mount. Mohandas Gandhi

"Someone made a circle to keep me out, so I made a bigger one to include us all."
Native American Proverb

She loves her church and country and thinks they need some mercy. (paraphrased)
—Mercy Now, Mary Gauthier

I believe, help my unbelief! Mark 9:24

I probably shouldn't be a Christian, and if you're an early middle-aged Gen-X-er or a young adult Gen-Y "Millennial"[2] in America, you probably shouldn't be either. I say that I *probably* shouldn't be a Christian because the odds were against it. Few friends who went to high school or college with me, and even fewer of my more recent friends and acquaintances, identify themselves as being Christian, and yet somehow I do. Many of my peers who were raised in the church have shifted away from Christianity toward other religions—or increasingly, to no religion.

---

[2] Generation X refers to persons born between 1961-1981; Generation Y, 1982-2001.

This book is an attempt to understand and explain how I, a postmodern,[3] politically liberal Gen-Xer, have come to be an intentional follower of Jesus—who actually calls himself a "Christian."[4] My larger purpose is to share about progressive Christianity—the approach to the Christian faith that inspires and feeds me. I probably couldn't be a Christian if it were not for this approach to the faith. I conducted an informal survey of numerous young adults living in my community during the summer of 2007 to see how many people were familiar with the terms "progressive" and "conservative" in regard to Christianity. Without exception, the persons surveyed had all heard of conservative Christianity, yet only a small number had heard of "progressive Christianity." Based upon numerous conversations I've had with others in their twenties to early forties around the U.S. (at various conferences, via telephone, email, internet bulletin boards, chat rooms, as well as social networking sites) it is clear to me that this is true across the country.

The intended audience of this book is young adults in the West who don't currently identify as being Christian—or who do privately, but are hesitant to let others know because the word

---

[3]   Epistemology is the study of what and how much we know and postmodern thought is a critique of the epistemological arrogance of the modern era, specifically, the Enlightenment period (Descartes to Kant), Euro-centrism in general and the politics and philosophies of colonialism. The term *postmodernism* was first used in the 1870s (describing art). Postmodernism as philosophical approach originated in Europe in the 1920s and gradually permeated the arts, literature, and then in the late 20th Century, it started influencing Christianity. Postmodernism is a contemporary paradigm/worldview with the following characerics: skepticism toward claims of objectivity and absolute truth; wariness of alleged authorities; a rejection of rigid categories and dualities; an embracing of shades of gray; a tendency toward ethical relativism; and an emphasis upon how people's respective contexts (language, culture, class, etc.) impact their values and ways of perceiving reality and the world.

[4]   Many of the folks who've come across the things that I have about the origins of Christianity (several pagan roots, etc.) have opted out and have chosen instead to be atheists, agnostics, or "spiritual but not religious."

"Christian" has come to be associated with behaviors, stances, and attitudes that they don't want to be associated with. This book also seeks to speak to the multitude that go to church and yet feel a disconnect and a gnawing sense of discomfort or dissatisfaction because they don't agree or resonate with what's often said from their church's pulpit or in their Bible studies. People who are active within the Church and trying to relate and connect with today's younger generations will also benefit by exploring the ideas discussed within these pages.

I don't pretend to have all the answers but I do have a theological education. I've experienced, and thought a lot about, God and Christianity. I'm knowledgeable about the current trends in Christian ministries, books, and websites. I'm aware of what's working, what isn't, and I have some hunches about what might work better for a growing number of people whose minds simply don't "tick" the same way as those of previous generations.

If your only exposure to Christianity has been strident, greedy, or sunshiny televangelists, unwelcomed knocks on your door from people who want to "save your soul," or harsh judgment and exclusion from persons who claim to be Christians, it's no wonder you've not been drawn to Christianity. If your only experience of Christianity has been hearing about campaigns to support U.S. imperialism or wars, or to bring about a return to mandatory prayer in public schools, force public schools to teach "creationism" in science classes, remove references about Thomas Jefferson from textbooks,[5] or legally limit what people may do with their bodies and whom they should love, it's not a surprise that you haven't been an active churchgoer. If your only experience of Christianity has been with family members or neighbors who smother you with unsolicited religious pamphlets or cheesy forwarded email messages and tell you that they're praying for you for fear of you "going to hell" or being "left behind," it's no wonder you haven't been interested in Christianity. Unfortunately, these forms

---

[5]   Apparently, some folks don't care for Jefferson having advocated for the separation of Church and State, see: "Texas Conservatives Win Curriculum Change," James C. McKinley Jr., March 12, 2010, *The New York Times,* http://www.nytimes.com/2010/03/13/education/13texas.html

of Christianity have so dominated the media and our nation's attention that they've almost hijacked and monopolized Jesus, Christianity, and even the word "Christian" itself.

There are a lot of people who call themselves "Christians" who are judgmental and closed-minded. They're not the sorts of folks most of us want to sit next to on a long plane ride. There are a lot of people who claim to be Christians who seek to influence our political process with agendas that bolster our nation's march toward wars and corporate imperialism. There are a lot of Christians who've been promoting archaic agendas that are laden with patriarchy and homophobia. Numerous individuals who call themselves Christians seem to turn off their brains as they shun the truth and insights of contemporary science. Many folks who claim to be Christians don't give a damn about global warming, or taking care of the environment, or addressing issues of war and social injustice because they expect to be "raptured up" into heaven soon. Such persons apparently believe something along the lines that "since Jesus will be coming soon, there's no need for any of us to be concerned about what's happening on the earth."[6]

I've met plenty of Christians who come across as selfish, unloving, and judgmental and who don't seem to give a rip about the plight and needs of other people.[7] I'm guessing you have too.[8] There are a lot of those kinds of folks. So many, in fact, that as far as the media seems to be concerned, Christianity has come to be *equated* with those ways and those forms of Christianity—as if those sorts of Christians speak for all Christians and all of Christianity. If those were the only ways of being Christian, I wouldn't want any part of Christianity either.[9]

---

[6] And then there are those who believe that they shouldn't do anything to take care of the earth because "doing so would delay Jesus' return."

[7] Except perhaps for "the unborn"; i.e., fetuses that they don't want to see aborted.

[8] I can be selfish, unloving, judgmental, hypocritical, and a jerk too. But, with God's help, I'm striving not to be—and hey, at least I can admit this.

[9] Sadly, quite a few young people have come to think that those judgmental and exclusivist forms of Christianity are the only forms of Christianity. See, http://www.barna.org/barna-update/article/16-teensnext-gen/94-a-new-generation-expresses-its-skepticism-and-frustration-with-christianity

Happily, there *are* other ways of being Christian—*thank God!* This book explores a certain approach to the faith that a surprising number of people aren't familiar with and don't know about—the approach of progressive Christianity. Despite its name, this is not a "new approach" to the faith. In fact, reading the Bible in a literal manner is instead a recent phenomenon for the faith. Fundamentalism is a reactionary response to the rise of science, particularly evolutionary theory, during the modern era. Today's young adults aren't seeking to be convinced by logical or rhetorical evidence in order to come to Christ. They sense that faith isn't something that one comes to through debate, data, or arguments. Instead, they realize that faith comes by noticing the lives of people who do have faith and then living into it themselves. Young adults today embrace a more nuanced, experiential, paradoxical, mystical, and relational approach to faith and spirituality. We like it to be relevant, down-to-earth, and real. This is the same kind of approach to Christianity that the early Christians experienced and understood. Hence, what I'm referring to as "progressive Christianity" isn't new or novel. In many ways it's a reformation of the Church to its earlier, pre-modernist and pre-Constantinian roots.[10] Ironically, this implies that in reality, it is *progressive* Christianity that is conservative and "conservative Christianity" isn't! However, for the sake of consistency and using words as they are most commonly used, we'll keep using those terms as they are conventionally employed.

This book will have us exploring various key pieces of the Christian faith and noticing the differences between the

---

[10] Most all of the official dogmas and doctrines about Jesus were enacted during and shortly after the reign of the Roman Emperor Constantine. He had been persecuting Christians but had a dream telling him to have his soldiers paint the Greek letters "Xr" (*chi rho*) onto their shields before a major battle. He had his troops do just that, they won the battle and, in response (and in part due to the wooings of his Christian wife) Constantine ended Roman persecution against Christians and allowed it to be an allowed religion of the empire. It soon became the official religion of the empire (irony should be noted) and Constantine had his hand in helping to define and make official the boundaries of "official/ orthodox" Christianity.

progressive and conservative approaches to them. I'll also be weaving in some of my own story and how I've been finding a way to be a Christian in the 21ˢᵗ Century.

If you're someone who likes Jesus and his teachings but you don't really want to be associated with "Christianity" or "Christians" and so you've decided to check "Spiritual but not Religious" on your Facebook, MySpace, or Match.com profiles, or if you're someone who resonates with, or owns, any of the following bumper sticker slogans:

"Christian—not closed minded"
"I like Jesus, it's his followers who I can't stand"
"I'm for the Separation of Church & Hate"
"Lord protect me from your followers"
"Straight but not Narrow"
"One nation, many faiths"
"Prays well with others"
"Coexist"
"My Karma ran over your Dogma"
"Hate is not a family value"
"God bless everyone. No exceptions."
"I love my Church but I think we should start seeing
other people"

or if you like the idea of seeing the **Darwin fish and the Christian fish** emblems kissing each other on the back bumper of the same car,[11] or if you simply think Christianity might be more about accepting and including than judging and excluding, then this book and progressive ("Kissing Fish") Christianity are for you.

[11]   I say more about this in Break It Down XII in Chapter 8. For now, suffice it to say that progressive Christianity doesn't think that science and faith are incompatible or mutually exclusive.

Section I

Chapter 1

My Spiritual Journey

The wood of the boat is tired but reaching the destination isn't the point, it's about the journey. (paraphrased)—The Wood Song, Indigo Girls

Being religious means asking passionately the question of the meaning of our existence and being willing to receive answers, even if the answers hurt. Paul Tillich

Re-examine all you have been told . . . Dismiss what insults your soul. Walt Whitman

When I was a child, I talked like a child, I thought like a child, I reasoned like a child.
When I became a man, I put childish ways behind me. Paul, 1ˢᵗ Corinthians 13:11

I'm nothing special. I'm just some dude who's trying to make it in this world as best he can. I wipe out every so often, but I've come to have a sense of trust that with the help of others, and a little help from above, I'm able to dust myself off and get back up to try again. I'm just a beggar who has learned a few places to get fed and I feel that it's neighborly to tell others about those places so they can get fed too.[12] That's what this book is about. With that in mind I'll go ahead and share more about myself. I'm going to be specific as I tell my story in hopes that by doing so,

---

[12] My variation on the famed quote from the late Sri Lankan evangelist and ecumenical leader, D.T. Niles.

it'll speak to a larger, more universal story that other people in their twenties-to-mid-forties might commonly share. You might see some of your story, in my story, even if just in bits and pieces.

Let me be clear from the start. I'm a Christian who believes in God. I believe that God is good, alive, and well and that following Jesus is "the way, the truth, and the life."[13] However, I don't think that everyone needs to be a Christian or that everyone has to think about or experience Jesus in the same way. Nor do I think that there is one right way for people to come to know Jesus and let him become a part of their lives.

I do think that Jesus is one heck of a guy and that he's the most amazing, loving, radical, subversive, counter-cultural, revolutionary, compassionate, prophetic, healing, present, engaging, transformative, and godly person who's ever walked the face of the earth. I have felt far more inspired, purposeful, passionate, alive, and whole ever since I allowed Jesus to be an active presence and influence in my life. I wish more people could know the liberating power of Jesus in their lives too. I am convinced that other young adults can experience a profoundly enriched and transformed life that's packed full of meaning, adventure, purpose, passion, and joy if they try connecting to and relating to God by following Jesus and his Way.

Let me start at the beginning—well, my beginning. My parents were each raised as mainline Protestants (Methodists) and they met while they were in graduate school through a campus ministry called the Wesley Foundation at the University of Kansas. They moved to St. Paul, Minnesota in 1965, took teaching positions at a small college, and started attending Hamline United Methodist Church. My twin sister and I were born in the summer of 1968. We were baptized as Christians through that church soon after.

Mainline Christians tend to be somewhat reserved and private about their faith and they like to seek common ground doing ministry together "ecumenically" with various denominations within the Christian family. These denominations have a rather low-key, private, rational, even-tempered, and somewhat status quo approach to the faith. In fact, they were the most common

[13]   John 14:6

sorts of Christians (next to Roman Catholics) in the U.S. until the 1980s.[14]

I attended church services, went to Sunday School, took part in occasional church sponsored "Vacation Bible Schools" and summer camps, went through the confirmation program, and participated in the youth group. We weren't particularly zealous or "on fire" about God, Jesus, or the Church. It was more of a "this is what we do on Sundays" sort of thing, but I have fond memories of exploring the books on the shelves of the church lending library in the parlor room, gazing at an abstract wooden statue of Mary holding the baby Jesus in one of the side lobbies, and making paper airplanes out of the worship bulletins.

My family didn't really talk much about church, God, or faith outside of church, or even much *in* church for that matter. My parents did teach me to say nightly prayers before going to bed and we took turns saying table grace before eating dinner. This may have been a bit more of a religious upbringing than many people in my generation experienced, but overall, it was a pretty mellow and minimalist approach to the faith.[15]

I participated in my church's confirmation program when I was in seventh grade and I took those classes somewhat seriously—for a 13-year-old boy anyway. My pastor at the time, Rev. Dr. Bruce Buller, led a stimulating and highly informative

---

[14] Until about 1980 or so, the United Methodist Church was the largest Protestant denomination in the U.S., featuring more church buildings than U.S. post offices. Though they tend to be private about their faith, they have been very active in the public arena and they often serve as judges and officials for civic elections. A disproportionate number have served in Congress. It's a "big tent church" (both Hillary Clinton and George W. Bush are United Methodists). It's one of the few remaining avenues in our increasingly polarized country where liberals and conservatives get together and transcend their differences and break bread together.

[15] This is not to say that my church or my family had a "luke-warm" faith or were participants in "Churchianity." Those are pejorative terms employed by many evangelicals and fundamentalists (and even by some "relevant and emergent Christians") to dismiss the faith of liberal, moderate, or mainline Christians without really knowing them or the depth of their faith at all.

series of classes and I enjoyed reading the various workbooks and pamphlets he provided. It was a safe environment and I asked many questions. The more I learned about John Wesley, the founder of Methodism, the more I found myself resonating with his beliefs and that approach to the faith. Wesley was a preacher in the Church of England back in the 1700s. He grew frustrated with the Church because they were failing to reach out to the poor, and to help people deepen and mature in their faith. So he started a movement of young people who went out into the streets, town squares, and coal mines to share about God's grace and love. They literally met people where they were at. The movement held small group meetings in people's homes to help them become more intentional about their *discipleship* (living life with God and Jesus and putting their faith into action). Eventually, that "Methodist" movement took on a life of its own and evolved into denomination.[16] I recall proudly making the decision to "confirm for myself God's grace that first took place in my life upon my infant baptism." I remember putting on a suit and proudly sharing my membership vows before the congregation.

The following Sunday, I became an atheist. I found myself sitting in the pews looking at a bunch of stuffy hypocrites. I saw a church more concerned about people dressing up in formal suits and dresses, pouring lots of money into maintaining a grand building with colorful stained glass and a gigantic pipe organ, and going through the motions of religiosity rather than really "getting" and living out the radical message of Jesus and the passions of John Wesley. I felt like I was the victim of false advertising or the butt of some sort of cosmic joke that's been perpetuated for the last 2000 years. So, in a burst of adolescent rebellion, I decided to reject God and the Church. I didn't tell anyone about it at the time.

I continued going to church with my family. In time, I found myself softening the harshness of my earlier stance to the point where I shifted toward being an agnostic "seeker" who had a growing respect and reverence for God—especially through appreciating nature. Looking back on it, this was in part due to

---

16   Due in part to the American Revolution where everything "English" was shunned and the Methodist movement seemed to be a newer alternative the Church of England—so it was a hit.

enjoying lots of camping opportunities with my Boy Scout troop and lots of miles running with my cross-country team along the gorgeous banks of the Mississippi River.

Then something happened. Sometime in 1982, at the age of 14, I was introduced to the Irish rock band *U2*. I found myself being drawn to their uniquely gorgeous and haunting rhythms and melodies. I was drawn to the passion and spiritual, but not churchy, boldness of their lyrics.[17]

A few months later, I discovered something that rocked my world—these guys were Christians! I couldn't believe it. The coolest rising mega band in that decade was a bunch of *Christians?!* As much as I couldn't believe it, it also made sense. I felt *Christian* when I heard them. I felt inspired. I heard the voice of Jesus coming through in a far purer and more potent way than I tended to do in most church settings. Their music and lyrics poetically pointed to God's love and the Divine without being overt or preachy and there were underlying prophetic invitations and challenges to discern. Curiously, they were making a point *not* to bill themselves as "Christian artists" or contract with Christian record labels—which, with a few exceptions, were pretty dorky and hokey at the time. They were intentionally choosing to be part of the secular music scene. They weren't getting much play on mainstream radio stations at that time, but their albums were a hit with the growing "alternative music" subculture. They were rebels *with* a cause. A small, inner part of me wanted to jump on board!

Like many teenagers, my faith pretty much was only "switched on" when I was listening to music. During most of my life (sans *Walkman*)[18] I was just an ordinary dude who was into running, practicing my trumpet, and fantasizing way too much about naked women. My church wasn't up to speed with the U2 way of expressing Christian hope, vision, and ideals. In fact, there was a notable *lack* of passion and youthful energy in the mainline churches at that time. So, the portion of my soul that had been

---

[17]   For instance, *I Will Follow*, from their first album "Boy," 1980.

[18]   For the benefit of younger readers, a *Walkman* was a portable music listening device with earphones (not ear-buds) that was the predecessor to the iPod and MP3 player. The first generation played tape cassettes and the later versions played CDs.

turned on by hearing U2's music was relegated to a hidden place inside—but a seed had been planted.

It wasn't until my college years that I started to deepen spiritually. In the fall of 1986, I went to Coe College, a small liberal arts school in Cedar Rapids, Iowa. A close high school friend of mine had become active in a conservative evangelical campus ministry at the college she was attending in another state. It changed her—and I wasn't particularly sure it was for the better. Every letter she wrote to me was filled with all sorts of syrupy evangelical rhetoric about how much God and Jesus love me and she informed me that she was praying for me to come to realize this too. I found it all rather off-putting. "What exactly made her think that I wasn't aware of this?" And, "What *happened* to my friend? Is she in a cult?!" She had become born-again in a stereo-typically evangelical American style and apparently felt that unless I did too, I wasn't a real Christian. This point was further punctuated upon learning that she had been re-baptized. We both grew up in the same denomination so the unspoken message of that was that our infant baptisms weren't genuine—that I wasn't a "real" Christian. As much as I tried to be affirming of her, I was repelled and our friendship became a bit strained for a few years.

I decided to double major in philosophy and political science and prepare to become a statesman so that I might help make a positive difference in the world. However, that first year had me taking a lot of required classes from the broader academic disciplines. I remember walking across campus one day during the spring semester and seeing some rabbits and squirrels playing together among a bed of budding flowers. Something in me started clicking. Noticing the synchronicity of that moment in the small little ecosystem of campus with the fuzzy critters, the birds sing up above, and the beauty of the budding trees and flowers, removed a veil in my mind. I started seeing how the inter-connectedness of that little scene pointed to a similar inter-related connectedness among the various classes I'd been taking. Freshman Orientation; Intro to Humanities; Biology; Intro to Philosophy; The Nature of Science; American Government, and Chinese literature were all melding together in my mind in ways that caused me to see that everything is connected and what affects one discipline and area of life affects the others. Upon recognizing this, other veils were removed from my mind and my heart as it dawned on me that all of this is related to God and things of the Spirit. And then I felt something sublime and beautiful—a profound "oneness" with all that is.[19]

Then and there, I created my first official personal theology. It was in the form of concentric rings that ripple outward like a pebble dropped onto the surface of a pond. It went like this: "I am a person who seeks connection to the Source of Life and Love. Within this, I declare myself to be a monotheist (I believe in one God). Within that, I embrace Christianity as my primary vessel. And within that, I like the Methodist/Wesleyan approach to following Jesus, who points and embodies the Way to God."

Kind of nifty, I thought. Yet it was mostly a cerebral and private sort of declaration. I didn't do anything to feed or nourish it and it would've been challenging even if I'd wanted to.[20] Although Coe is a Presbyterian related school, it didn't have a campus chaplain at the time—or *any* campus ministries. This was typical during the late '80s and early '90s. Many church-related colleges had discontinued campus ministries and several denominations started shifting energy and resources away from young adult ministry—including college students.

---

[19] A mystical experience is often described as sensing the "one-ness" of everything, the connections between people and the earth, the relationships that hold all living things together in one web of life: or the sense everything is, in some way, alive—energetic, organized, and valuable.—William Cleary, *Prayers to an Evolutionary God*, p.117, Skylight Paths Publishing, 2004.

[20] I did co-found a peace group on campus, "Coe Action for Peace," but I didn't do it with a religious motivation—though I suppose it could be said that it was a fruit borne of my faith.

Break it Down I

For the past 20 years, membership in many traditional "mainline" Protestant churches[21] in the U.S. has been declining or stagnant while newer, conservative churches have been booming. That said, the largest growing "church" is "the church of the un-churched"—or as some refer to it, "the Church Alumni Association." A cover story titled "The End of Christian America" was published in *Newsweek* saying that the percentage of self-identified Christians in America has fallen by 10% in the past two decades[22] and only 18.5% of Americans now regularly attend church[23]. There are several reasons for this. The heyday of the mainline denominations was the 1950s and early '60s and upon reaching their zenith, many of these churches assumed that things would always be the same for them. Hence, they figured they could rest on their laurels and passively allow institutional momentum to keep things going. The focus shifted away from evangelism (reaching out to potential new members) and more toward developing massive bureaucratic structures involving lots of committees and cumbersome staffs with lots of people working on the national level—and fewer on the frontlines of the grassroots level. During the 1970's and '80s, less attention was given to campus ministries or camping ministries; i.e., to nurture and develop the spiritual lives of the younger generations—the future of the Church.

Since nature abhors a vacuum, newer, upstart groups rose up to fill in the gap. Evangelical ministries were started in empty storefronts, school auditoriums and movie theatres. Those churches, neighborhood youth groups, and campus ministries spread like wildfire. I suppose there were

---

[21]   Mainline Protestant denominations include, the United Methodist Church, the Lutheran Church (ELCA), the United Church of Christ, the Episcopalian Church, and the Presbyterian Church (PCUSA). Protestants used to mean all Christians who aren't Roman Catholics (inheritors of the Protestant Reformations of the 1500s), but these days, that term pretty much has come to refer primarily to the traditional mainline denominations. While they technically are Protestants (because they aren't Roman Catholics), many evangelicals, charismatics, and fundamentalists don't consider themselves as being "Protestants"—or at least they don't often use that word to refer to themselves.

[22]   Meacham, John, "The End of Christian America," *Newsweek*, April 4, 2009

[23]   http://thegospelcoalition.org/blogs/justintaylor/2007/03/01/how-many-americans-attend-church-each/

four main reasons for this. First of all, most of the mainline church buildings were built many years ago. During the era of skyscrapers, shopping malls, personal computers, new wave music, *Star Wars, ET, Top Gun,* and *RoboCop* people were drawn to more hip and contemporary digs and trappings. Many people were also feeling overwhelmed with the fast pace of change in society. There was a certain appeal to approaches to the faith that reduced it to bite-sized concrete, and literally interpreted, creeds and dogmas that avoid the messy gray areas of theology and life.

Additionally, in response to corporations being less loyal to their workers, young Americans became more distrusting of institutions and less loyal to particular denominations. A consumerist model of "church shopping" emerged and the older churches were structured like old establishment departments stores such as *JC Penney, Sears,* and *Montgomery Wards* while the newer churches were more like *Super Target,* and *Walmart.* The older churches, therefore, were coming to be viewed as antiquated dinosaurs. Perhaps most significantly, those ministries readily embraced electric guitars and music that better reflected the younger generations. They may not have embraced the progressive, social justice-oriented spirituality of U2, but they sure knew what time it was! Since then, many of those start up ministries have grown into massive mega-churches boasting thousands of worshippers. However, it's looking like the peak of the "big box" church era has happened and many leaders in the Church are scratching their heads about how to operate in the future.

None of the local churches in Cedar Rapids at that time were making efforts to reach out to the students at Coe. I went out of my way to walk a few blocks to visit a few of the local churches, but I wasn't particularly made to feel welcome. Note to churches: if the only person who greets and shakes hands with a college student, or a young adult, is the greeter assigned for the day, that is a problem—a tragic one. This is all further evidence to support my earlier assertion that "I probably shouldn't be a Christian."

In the fall of my junior year, I had a governmental internship in Washington, D.C. That experience led me to conclude that politics wasn't for me. In addition, the philosophy department at Coe fell apart while I was away, and when it became clear they had no plans to add new instructors to that department at that time, I transferred to Macalester College in St. Paul, MN. Coincidentally, "Mac" is also a Presbyterian-related institution and has an attractive, contemporary, very cool chapel. But again, during those years, the college didn't have a chaplain, nor were any of the local churches doing much to reach out to the students. There were, however, two Christian ministries on that campus both were minority groups at that largely secular school. One was a conservative "para-church" campus ministry called InterVarsity Christian Fellowship that met in a house off-campus. The other, smaller group, was an entirely student-led group called *Compline*. It was to this second group that I felt drawn.

Compline met on Wednesday nights at 10:00 p.m. (study-break time for nerdy Mac students) in the chapel. About a dozen of us would sit on the floor in a circle outside the actual sanctuary in the hallway near the main entry. We followed the same basic format and liturgy from week to week. It was based upon the medieval monastic service called compline, a contemplative evening service like vespers. We sang songs accompanied by acoustic guitar, checked in with each other to see how things were going in our lives, and then one of us would present something that we felt moved to share—a song, an experience, a poem, a passage of scripture that spoke to us, etc. We'd discuss, shift to a time of prayer, sing some more, and then go downstairs to eat cookies and drink apple cider.

It was a simple, gentle, relaxed, and welcoming ministry. It was also low key, unobtrusive, authentic, down to earth, and intellectually, emotionally, and spiritually satisfying. Come to think of it, we didn't even call it a "ministry"—that's how non-threatening it was. Compline also provided a safe space to be real, to doubt, to laugh, and to cry. It provided an intimate community and fellowship to share, stretch and grow with. Because we were such a small group in a sea of secularity, it often felt like we were early Christians subversively worshipping in secret in the catacombs beneath the streets of Rome. It was because of my involvement with that group that I came to value the importance of a shared, communal approach to the faith—instead of just trying to be some sort of "spiritual" person of faith flying solo. It was also because of my involvement in this ministry that I made the overt and intentional choice to be a Christian.

While I was at Macalester, I continued my double major in philosophy and political science and found myself taking courses in the religious studies department as electives. I enjoyed experiencing a scholarly approach to the New Testament and the letters of Paul—which involved learning quite a bit about Judaism. I also was thrilled to learn about Eastern religions and Islam and learn how they compare to Christianity. Taking those classes broadened my appreciation for other world religions while confirming my decision to be a Christian. From what I could tell, no other religion emphasizes grace, forgiveness, inclusion, peace, justice, joy, celebration, and unconditional love as much as Christianity does—*at its best.*

Break it Down II

Which brings up yet another roadblock that many people have with Christianity. Namely, we Christians have *not* always been at our best. During the past centuries, Christians have committed acts of injustice, war, slavery, genocide, and oppression—in the name of Jesus. However, as it's sometimes put, "It's not that Christianity has been tried and failed. It's that it hasn't been tried at all." Which I take to mean that even though a lot of people who claim the name Christian have committed monstrous acts, that does not mean that such actions are Christian. Indeed, they are most *un*-Christian. As one bumper sticker puts it, "*I love Jesus, it's his followers I can't stand.*"[24]

But not all Christians over the years have been oppressive, violent monsters. The vast majority of them have been simple, salt-of-the-earth people who've tried to do their best to love God and their neighbors as best they can. A good many of them have been rather exemplary in their love toward God and God's creation (sometimes called "saints"). I realize it's not as simple as saying "it's unfair to judge a whole religion because of the evil actions of a few of its members" as it's clearly been a lot more than a few who've engaged in acts of injustice and oppression. I won't claim that such persons who've been acting in those ways "aren't Christians," but I will say that they're misguided Christians—not very good at following Jesus. Far too many Christians over the years have confused love of country with love of God. Zealous nationalism and patriotism have sought to co-opt the Christian faith and harness it to bless imperialism and unjust socio-political status quos ever since the days when Christianity was domesticated by the Roman Emperor Constantine. This is all quite similar to what's been happening to Muslims lately. Many people are judging all Muslims by the actions of a relatively small, but incredibly violent, few. The current pope rightly took a lot of flack for his overstated remark that Islam "is a violent religion that is spread by the sword."[25] Pot meet kettle.

---

[24]   Based upon a quote by Mohandas (aka Mahatma) Gandhi, "Oh I do not reject your Christ. I love your Christ. It's just that so many of you Christians are so unlike your Christ." "Gandhi and Christianity," Rowland Croucher and Others, August 28, 2003, John Mark Ministries, http://jmm.aaa.net.au/articles/552.htm

[25]   "Pope's speech stirs Muslim anger," Sept. 14, 2006, BBC News, http://news.bbc.co.uk/2/hi/5346480.stm

Because of my enjoyment of my religious studies electives, I came to the point where I might have dropped my majors in political Science and philosophy and shifted to theology if that had been available at my college.

During the summer before my senior year (1989), I met up with a friend of mine. Peter and I grew up in the same neighborhood and we had been classmates and friends since elementary school. We had a lot in common: we were both white boys from professional, middle class families. We both played trumpet. We both were in Boy Scouts. We both were runners. We both were fairly studious, but known for being a bit zany. However, during junior and senior high school, we diverged politically. He was a strong supporter of Ronald Reagan and George H. W. Bush and I wasn't. Peter went to American University in Washington, D.C. and was active in ROTC. He, like I, had a major in political science with an intention to serve in public office.[26]

We knew we'd come to hold different political views and we wanted to meet to discuss this. We sat in his parent's backyard and shared our respective political views and philosophies. In the midst of our conversation, it dawned on me that our political differences were stemming from religious differences, yet we were both Christians! Peter was a conservative Presbyterian and I was a liberal United Methodist. We explored the roots of our political differences and we came to realize that we held dramatically different notions about God, Jesus, humans, and the Bible! While Peter viewed God as male and omnipotent, I saw God as more mysterious and enigmatic. While he viewed Jesus as having literally and physically risen and as one who will literally return to judge the living and the dead, I believed in the symbolic and spiritual importance of the resurrection. I saw Jesus' return as more present and ongoing than as a special, super-natural

---

[26] The parallels continued in that he is now a professor of Biblical Studies at an evangelical Christian university and seminary . . . and another, neighbor kid who grew up in our neighborhood became a Catholic priest—must've been something in the water.

"*Shazam!*" moment that'll happen sometime in the future.[27] While he viewed humans as being essentially corrupt and evil in nature, I viewed humans as being more neutral with capacities for good or evil. Where he read the Bible literally, I read it more metaphorically. I sensed Truth deeper than the "truth" of the details of the stories. I sensed that the lessons of some of those passages contain life-giving truth—even if the events in those stories didn't happen. While he believed that Moses wrote the first five books of the Bible, it made more sense to me to agree with the many scholars who indicate that it was written and edited by numerous people, with differing agendas, over the course of many years. Through this conversation with my friend I had an important realization: "these sorts of differences really matter and since I think my approach to Christianity is a darned good one, it's important to really live into it and to share it with others."

With renewed vigor, I became active once again with my family's church and I helped out with the junior and senior high youth groups. My involvement wasn't merely because of my being attracted to the cute youth director who worked there at the time (that was a bonus) I wanted to serve God and share my faith with others! Attending worship at my home church again as a young adult struck me differently than it did when I was a youth. I earlier stated that I became an atheist at age 13 immediately after becoming a confirmed member of the Church. I had once seen a bunch of people dressing up in nice suits and dresses, hypocritically acting as Christians once a week. I naively and self-righteously dismissed them as "not really being true believers." However, with the eyes of an adult, I realized how profoundly this community of believers has been living out their faith in some truly meaningful and real ways. They served hot meals regularly at a local soup kitchen: helped many marginalized Vietnamese, Hmong, and Laotian refugees resettle, learn English, and begin new lives in America; and they sponsored, supported, and were involved in all sorts of other meaningful ministries I simply wasn't aware of as a youth.

I realized that I hadn't been an "atheist" so much as an *a-churchist*—someone who believes in God but who isn't too

---

[27]   More on this in Chapter 10.

impressed with the people who worship Him. With more grace in my life, it dawned on me that the people who I'd written off as "hypocrites" were no more hypocritical than I am. They are ordinary people who are doing their best to gather once a week to be reminded of who they are as God's people and to "work out their own salvation with fear and trembling"[28] with communal love and support. They are fellow pilgrims who see the value of shared Christian fellowship, mutual accountability and community, instead of trying to be solo believers. They pooled their resources to make real differences in people's lives that disconnected, "unorganized," individuals couldn't possibly do on their own.[29]

Break it Down III

Losing my religion—REM

It turns out that this experience of being raised in the Church, rejecting it, and then coming back to it on my own terms is an entirely normal and even ideal one. It may well be argued that if the Church and its families are doing their job, a process of "Thesis, Antithesis, and Synthesis" occurs. The Church exposes children to the basics of Christianity. The children become adolescents whose job it is to rebel and reject what they've been taught. Then, as those teenagers mature into adults, they come to see the value and wisdom of what they were taught. Next, they come back to the faith, on their own terms, in their own way, reincorporating the things that make sense, discarding or reinterpreting the things that don't. And then they become the ones who share faith with the next generation. This concept is notably observed and embraced in the Amish rite of *rumspringa*. (Do a web search. It's pretty cool.)

---

[28] Philippians 2:12
[29] The very word *religion* comes to us from the Latin *religio* (reverence for the Divine), which comes from *ligare* (to bind/connect), and when the prefex *re* is added, *religare* means "to re-bind together" and "to reconnect." Curiously, the word *yoga* has similar connotations. It means "union/yoking." Societies function better if there is some force of common yoking and togetherness and at its best religion helps to foster this.

Two years after graduating from college, something happened. Let me first share the context for this happening. After college, I became active in the alternative dispute resolution community in Minnesota. I was a charter member of the Minnesota Council of Mediators and chair of its ethics committee, and I was employed as the ethics and legal fee arbitration administrator for the Hennepin County Bar Association. I did a lot of volunteer work as a community mediator and counselor at a 24-hour crisis-counseling center. I'd had a wide range of housemates from all walks of life, including an atheist Hispanic Jew, a Unitarian Universalist African American; and several gay men—including one who wore dresses and dyed himself blue. I seemed to have developed an ability to connect, click, and "go deep" with all sorts of people from different backgrounds, even upon meeting them for the first time.

I also took the Christian season of Lent (the 40 days of preparation before the celebration of Easter) seriously for the first time in the spring of 1992. I'd take the early bus from St. Paul to my office on Nicollett Mall in downtown Minneapolis and read passages from the Bible, along with a daily devotional booklet. Then I'd spend time in prayer. I wasn't doing this with a feeling of "I have to do this." Instead, I looked forward to this new morning ritual in my life with a feeling of I *get* and *want* to do this!

One night, I went up to the room I was renting in a house I shared with four others. At about 2:00 a.m., I sensed a presence in the room with me. I then felt myself being held, slightly gripped even, and the whole thing sort of spooked me. So I left the room and lay on the floor of another room at the top of the steps. Again, I sensed a presence in the room with me. I felt myself being held, yet this time it was softer, more like being lovingly cradled. As I surrendered to it, I heard a voice. Whether it was external or internal, I couldn't say. If there had been a tape recorder there I have no idea if it could have recorded it, but I heard it nonetheless. Neither male nor female, it was strangely familiar. The voice asked me: "Do you know who I am?" Without having to open my mouth to speak, I said, "You are God."

There was a brief pause during which I found myself wondering just what on earth I had for supper that night that could be causing such a weird experience to be happening to me—bad sausage on my pizza? Did someone spike my milk? I couldn't think of anything out of the ordinary. I sensed a profound "I Am," and then the voice continued with two messages to convey. The first was that God was pleased that I was coming to realize that my "abilities" in conflict resolution, crisis counseling, and interacting with diverse people weren't because of achievements on my part, but are instead were gifts from God. God was celebrating this awareness. Yet, God also was urging me to notice that in almost all of my interactions, I was doing everything *but* bringing my faith into things. I had been leaving God out of the loop. God was inviting and challenging me to be more intentional about sharing my faith with others.

That wondrously mystical experience was a pivotal moment in my life. God wasn't explicitly saying "Roger, my son, go ye and become an ordained United Methodist minister!" But when I shared this experience with my pastor and my congregation, they encouraged me to interpret it as a call from God to enter the ministry. Because of that profound experience, I can no longer say that I "believe" in God—I *know* God. It's no longer a matter of yearning to believe in various doctrinal assertions about some strange, potentially fictitious, deity—I've *met* (or at least had an encounter with) Him/Her! Yet, as true as that is, I've since experienced numerous periods where I've doubted what happened back then and I'm now back to a place of feeling like a regular person of faith again. I've experienced several dark days of the soul and seasons of doubt and I no longer walk in the robust certainty I had in the days immediately following that unique encounter. I intentionally have to choose to be a person of faith—to believe the story each new day. For this, I am grateful. I'd rather bumble along humbly in faith than to strut around with an arrogant air of elitist specialness, as if I were any holier than anyone else. I, and plenty of others, can assure you I'm not.

I turned in my notice at work, and visited the Iliff School of Theology in Denver, CO. I fell in love with that school at first sight, and started my graduate studies there in the fall of 1992. I had several internships and field education experiences during those years that confirmed my ease and sense of "rightness" about my path to professional ministry.

Iliff is one of the most theologically liberal seminaries in the country and, even though I was a tad more conservative theologically than many of the professors, I'm so grateful to have gone there.[30] I learned a great deal about Church history, early theologies, medieval theologies, Catholic theology, reformed theology, Wesleyan theology, Calvinism, social gospel, liberal, fundamentalist, neo-orthodox, and black, feminist, gay/lesbian, process, openness, narrative, post-liberal, and other contemporary theologies. I found my heart resonating as I learned about liberation theology, narrative theology, process theology, and openness theology—approaches to God which help capture Jesus' counter-cultural, radical, subversive, anti-imperialist political agenda and God's expansive and creative ways that make sense intellectually in light of the insights and discoveries of contemporary science and postmodern worldviews. During those four years, I found ways to celebrate God that spoke to me and wove together my intellectual, artistic, pastoral, and political sensibilities.[31] I felt like I could be me and yet allow myself to be transformed into more than I was before.

Then . . . *reality* hit. After graduating with my Master of Divinity ("M.Div") degree and becoming ordained, I started serving local churches back in the Midwest (Minnesota and Iowa) and experienced what many young pastors run into when they graduate from seminary. I discovered the disappointing gap between idealistic notions of what the Church can and could be—and the decidedly non-ideal, petty, political, conflicted, dysfunctional, beautiful messes that most of them are. Now I say this lovingly, because most people, including most Christians, and

---

[30]   Sadly, there are an increasing number of church affiliated "academic" institutions in the U.S. where the faculty have to sign documents stating that they believe a certain creed and doctrine statement in order to be employed. To my mind, this is more than incompatible with academic freedom and the spirit of a university. It's a form of *idolatry*—humans having the gall to limit God and theological discourse about God. Ironically, that's precisely what such mandatory statements are supposedly intended to guard against.

[31]   During those four years while in grad school, I also spent a fair bit of time exploring Quaker, Unitarian Universalist, Wiccan (neo-pagan), Evangelical, and Buddhist communities and worshipping with them. I learned a lot—most profoundly that God is at work in more places than many people give Him credit for.

myself, have some degree of dysfunction going on, so why would anyone expect things to be anything other than *more* chaotic when 30 or 100 or more Christians get together? As it's sometimes put, "The church isn't a museum of saints, but a hospital for sinners."

Even with that insight in mind, I felt a lot of frustrating dissonance because I wasn't feeling comfortable being fully myself. It was apparent that there were only a handful of political liberals in my first congregation, let alone theological ones. I feared fully speaking my truth and sharing my actual beliefs about God with the people I was serving. In time, I developed an ability to communicate in double-speak—conveying things in such a way that the liberals heard what they wanted and needed to hear and the conservatives did too. I suppose some might call that "learning to be pastoral," but I felt that my prophetic edge was being dampened. My ability to speak truth to power, criticize certain social injustices, and keenly articulate what I see as Jesus' and the prophets' key concerns were being held back.

On an even more basic level, it was hard to pray to God in public when my view of God is more mysterious and enigmatic and yet many of the people who were hearing me pray held a notion of God as being more like a giant, bearded old man in the sky who judges and micromanages our lives. My notion of prayer involves helping people to become open to God's mysterious nudging, invitations, peace, and creativity, whereas many people seek divine intervention from a giant Superman-type hero figure (or cosmic bellhop or waiter) who rushes in to rescue us and magically make everything hunky-dory in our lives because of our telling him what to do.

I also sensed that a lot of people come to church merely to be comforted and assured that everything's going to be okay. In terms of the Big Picture, that's true, and we need to be reminded of that. But *dang it*—we humans have a lot of work to do to help improve the lives of the poor and oppressed, including the environment. Part of a pastor's job is to afflict the comfortable, not merely to comfort the afflicted![32]

---

[32]   An old principle for preachers, adopted also by some journalists is that faithfulness to the truth calls us to "comfort the afflicted and afflict the comfortable." "The job of the newspaper is to comfort the afflicted and afflict the comfortable" is a 100-year old quote that

I was able to suppress and live with this ongoing dissonance and disharmony for several years, and could have probably done it longer, but then something else happened. My marriage of ten years ended. It didn't "just happen." Shandra and I participated in couples counseling even before we got engaged. We had about five years of marriage counseling off and over the course of the marriage, and we simply faced some irreconcilable differences. I was fully open to divorce and remarriage for *other* people—however, divorce wasn't on my radar as an option for my own life. I felt stuck and imprisoned. I didn't feel like myself. I didn't like myself. I felt dead inside. I was depressed. When we did decide to divorce, it was like a humongous weight was lifted. I became "Roger" again (with God's help in the forms of grace, medication and counseling). Shandra and I remain good friends and we're each thriving a lot more—proof that God really does redeem and transform things in our lives.

Ending the marriage wasn't an easy matter. I felt horrible about my part in allowing the marriage to fail. I was ashamed of some of the thoughts that came into my head during those last difficult years. While I knew in my heart that I was essentially a good person, I was forced to acknowledge that I have a darker shadow side.

A couple of years after we divorced, I had my shadows held up before me to gaze upon. I wrote the following piece as a blog a couple of years ago:

Break it Down IV

Ouch. It cuts like a knife. And wow does it hurt. I write this blog at a cruising altitude of 31,000 feet above sea level—somewhere above the snow covered fields of Nebraska. I caught a plane with my little boy this morning to visit my family back in Minnesota. I've been sick as a dog for the past few days and it was all I could do to get us to the airport.

Today's venture involved the usual comedy of errors: misplaced tickets, misplaced carry on bag, etc. and it also had the lovely added complication of my sharing some of my less than pleasant symptoms with people around me.

---

can be traced to the work of Finley Peter Dunne. It is not clear who coined the phrase first.

We sat down at the gate and I started farting up a storm. Unfortunately, it wasn't just passing innocent gas. It had to be the stinking, sulfury, rotten egg kind of farts. I could even smell them despite the fact that my sinuses and nasal passages were cram-packed with sinusitis phlegm and crud. *Sigh*.

While I was busy pretending not to notice, my mind raced with the possible source of this malodorous tirade. Were the antibiotics I'm currently on causing a biological imbalance in my bowels? Could be, but I think the real culprit was the small bottle of really cheap whiskey that I purchased yesterday at a local liquor store in order to make myself a hot toddy tea drink in hopes that that would help me get to sleep last night. I couldn't see spending a lot of money for a pricey brand of poison if it's just going to be mixed with tea. The guys at the store winced as they saw which bottle I decided upon. I suppose that should've told me something.

Anyway, as we stood to get into the line to board the plane, I noticed a man at the gate. What I noticed about him was that he had a massive scar that covered a good 80% of his face. It was red and fierce. I couldn't tell if it was a birthmark or the result of some sort of unfortunate mishap, but it was as nasty a disfigurement as I've ever seen before.

His scar matched the red sweater he was wearing—part of his uniform. His job is to provide wheelchairs to people who might need assistance when they board planes. My first thought was, how horrible it must be for this man to have such a scar—something that is literally a part of his life that he can't escape from.

Then, sometime after take-off, the farting resumed. I hate to be inflicting this on the woman sitting next to me, but there's no choice in the matter. "Fart happens," and on this day, a lot.

At any rate, at some point during one of these fumigating episodes, I emerged from the toxic fog with an awakening. That man with the scar on his face—is *me*.

I may not have a large unsightly blemish on my face, but I am scarred just as badly as he is—maybe even worse. You see, for all I know, that man may go home each night to a loving partner and kids who cherish him, and make him feel like the richest of kings. I on the other hand, have had a series of dysfunctional relationships and the common denominator in them is *me*.

I may not be on the pages of *GQ* or *Maxim*, but I've been told I have nice eyes (courtesy of my father) and a nice smile (courtesy of my parents who paid for braces). I've even been led, at times, especially in the past three years, to believe that I'm somewhat attractive, fetching, and reasonably handsome.

But my face is merely a mask. It's a mask for a far less attractive self underneath the surface. My scars are on the inside and they are deep and many. I have scars from feeling neglected by my parents as a child. They were both ivory tower academicians more than nurturing types. They weren't "touchy feely," and it was a bit of an emotionally repressed environment. On top of that, I was scared of my father and his leather belt. I have scars from both fearing and hating him. I have scars from feelings of low self-esteem, and of feeling undervalued and unloved. I have scars from feeling invisible, ignored, and unimportant. I also have scars from each of the relationships I've derailed —including a recent one that ended with a major face-plant.

I saw an image of a tree recently that relates to this. It was a naked tree, dark and without its leaves. Though it was majestic and grand, it had a major gash in its center—a gash that looked fatal. That tree's days are numbered. Like that tree, unless I change my ways, unless I repent, unless something happens—intensive therapy? massive soul-searching and examination? Divine intervention?—my days in the sun will be numbered too.

Luckily (I can't believe I'm using that word), a friend of mine (who I dated a year after the divorce) pissed me off royally the other day. Over the past few months, this friend has been seeking to hold a mirror up to me. The purpose of that mirror was to: tell me that I may not really be "all that"; to knock me down off my pedestal and cut me down to size; to tell it like it is; to be brutally honest in order to help me hear the painful truth—that I'm not a very whole, functional or loving human being. It wasn't until this friend made one particular comment the other day that I finally got it.

My first reaction was to be profoundly defensive. I issued a curt and indignant pink slip and fired that person from being my friend. I wanted to start the New Year dropping this "friend" because who really wants someone hanging around who criticizes, belittles, and attacks them instead of supporting them or making them feel good?

Then, after a few hours of allowing my knickers to get in a twist, I got quiet. I turned off my defensive shield, I ceased sending out my retaliatory nuclear missiles, and I shut up. I sat in silence and fell asleep. Which brings me back to the awakening I've just had while on the plane.

In the Middle Ages, one of the members of a king's court was the jester. Through the use of subtle or even sarcastically lampooning humor, the jester had the responsibility of putting a check to the king's ego, exploits, and escapades when it looked like things were getting a bit out of hand. Jesters were prophetically called to say, "The Emperor has no clothes." Needless to say, jesters had little job security and diminished life expectancies. They often found themselves suddenly separated from their heads. But wise kings granted jesters permission to do their jobs. Really wise kings listened to what their jesters had to say.

Off and on over the past decade, I've had moments where I've felt like I'm a fraud and a hypocrite. I've not always practiced what I've preached, and I've not even always been very good at preaching—at least, I've not reached my full potential. I'm a man of God who believes that God is love and that God's children are supposed to be loving and yet, I'm emotionally handicapped and have not always been good at loving or being loved.

I'm thinking of writing a book about progressive Christianity and it includes chapters on God, Jesus, Salvation, etc. Given my dysfunctional, emotional hang-ups, who the heck am *I* to write about God? Who the heck am *I* to write about love, wholeness, and salvation? I sometimes feel like I wouldn't know salvation if it bit me on the ass and like I couldn't love my way out of a wet paper bag. I say one thing, and do another. In sum, I suck. I suck as a pastor. I sucked as a husband. I suck as a father. I suck as a lover, and I might even suck as a human being.

I've had similar thoughts along those lines cross my mind over the years; I've just never had anyone else say them to me. Well, it's happened. 'Bout time huh? (To be fair to this friend, I'm overstating things a bit, but I'm needing to do this to help me drive the message home and to fully embrace it).

So, I suppose it's "welcome to the club" for me. Welcome to the club of egotistical blowhards who've had someone burst their bubbles. Welcome to the club of lions who've had a mouse *place* a thorn *into* their paw instead of removing it. Welcome to the human condition.

I'm still wincing a bit from what happened. I'm still in the wake of the storm. But, a shift has definitely taken place.

It's been said, "You can't be anything unless you've been nothing." Well, I must really be on my way to something now. I'm not done gazing into this mirror. I still have many insights and truths to discover and assimilate. And then there's all the work of rebuilding from the ground up that lies ahead. *Holy schnikes.*

Well, this is as good a way as any to start out a new year. I have hope that someday I might grow to be like one of the two trees in Gibran's famed parable, "On Marriage". I want to grow mightily along side another mighty tree—one who is independent of me, yet who supports me, one who doesn't strangle my roots nor rob me of the sun. I would be these things for her as well. In the meantime, I will keep things simple. I will eat. I will sleep. Parent. Work. Pray. Dream. I will fart.

In the spirit of holding me accountable to being the best I can be, if anyone sees me in a liquor store about to purchase a really cheap bottle of whiskey to make a hot toddy with, don't let me. For the love of God, and for the good of travelers everywhere, *don't* let me.

I'd preached about God's amazing grace and love before, but for the first time, I had to deeply allow it into my own life. It was easy to tell other people that God loves, accepts, and forgives *them* just as *they* are. It was another thing for me to accept this for *myself*. Thankfully, I did, and being a Christian and accepting the truth of the life, death, and resurrection of Jesus had everything to do with it.[33] Perhaps for the first time, I truly allowed Jesus to really be "Lord of my life." I more deeply took into my heart the gift that God loves me so much, even though I'm broken. How I came to know this is because of what I knew of Jesus and how he interacted with broken people. In our darkest hour, God is there. She really cares, and knowing this matters.

After some time of grieving the loss of my marriage, I came to feel that I wanted to remarry again someday. I realized this wouldn't happen if I didn't do some dating. By this point, I'd already shifted away from working as a pastor in the local church to serving as the director of a campus ministry at the University of Colorado in Boulder—one of the most liberal and secular cities in the country. I loved my new job and I finally felt like I was in an environment where I could really be myself and truly speak from my heart to the people entrusted to my care. Young adults tend to be open-minded and accepting of new ideas and alternative ways of looking at things. *Woo hoo!* I felt free to stretch my wings and soar. I was finally in my element. I found myself especially thriving as I learned more about a growing movement called progressive Christianity. This form of Christianity goes beyond the issues I had with both liberal and conservative theologies, and it somehow just felt "right" to embrace it. I had finally "come home."[34]

While my professional life was finally clicking, my personal life was very much up in the air. I met my ex-wife while we were

---

[33] That said, accepting that I am flawed but still totally worthy is an on-going challenge. I need reminders of God's grace and love from time to time. This is a big part of why I enjoy going to church.

[34] This book in part is a way for me to condense and share some of these progressive Christian insights and perspectives that have fed me—as well as to present my own take on things.

in our seminary graduate studies so we both knew what to expect for life as a clergy couple. However, trying to date as a Christian divorcee in Boulder, CO in the 21st century is a whole different matter. Many of the young adults in Boulder either identify as being atheist, agnostic, Buddhist, pagan, Sufi, New Age, or most commonly, as "spiritual but not religious." Curiously, many of the churches in the area are even more conservative in over-reactive response to the perceived secularism and "anti-Christianness" of the Boulder community. *Yikes!* I realized that being a progressive Christian, and a pastor at that, might present a bit of an extra challenge for me when it comes to dating. Happily, it wasn't long before I had a number of dates with some wonderful people who helped me to accept that I truly am a lovable person and that some women are drawn to and attracted to me.

However, as loved and as lovable as I was beginning to feel, I felt hesitant to tell people that I was a pastor right away. Sometimes I was even hesitant to tell people that I was a Christian. For example, I'm at a party surrounded by people I don't know. I'm talking with a group of people, and one of them asks me where I'm at spiritually or if I'm a Christian. I don't know what they *mean* by that word (what baggage they carry regarding that word). So I might say, "Well, I'm into Jesus and his teachings. How 'bout you?"—shifting the conversation away from me in order to share more with them later depending upon how they responded. Or, I might say something a bit vague like "Well, yeah, but I like other religions too." I don't want them to think that I'm one of "those" kind of Christians. I'm not one of the judgmental exclusivist types who are overly fundamentalist, and no fun to be around.

I also discovered that quite a few of my new musician and rock-climbing friends, as well as a large number of the women I was meeting for dates, were also hesitant to call themselves "Christians." I learned that several of the women who I met on computer dating services intentionally *avoided* clicking on "Christian" when they were filling out the criteria for who they were willing to date or be matched with. Some of these particular women did date me, but it was because I initiated things with them and because they were willing to meet and date me *in spite* of my being a Christian! The majority of these people had grown up in the Church but had made a point to flee from it when they grew up. This was because they were raised in homes where they were forced to go to church; or where the parents sent their kids to church but modeled[35] that it isn't important for *grown ups* because they didn't go themselves; because of some form of theological or pastoral trauma or offense that took place; or because they were simply repelled by exclusivist and judgmental forms of the faith.

It became obvious that a generation of young people who feel drawn to Jesus and his teachings, are really turned off by, or feel conflicted about being associated with, churches and Christianity. While there are some hard-core atheists out there who are opposed to God or faith in any way, I suggest that many of these people may not really be anti-*God* per se. They simply don't believe in the popular, and currently prevailing, understandings about God. Frankly, I've come to be atheistic about *that* God too. It's also clear that a lot of people really respect and admire Jesus, want to learn more about him and be like him, and might be open to Christianity if they knew that there were ways of practicing it besides the conservative, evangelical, fundamentalist approaches to the faith.[36] The next chapters will explore some of these ways.

---

[35] . . . and therefore actually *taught*, as what kids see their parents *do* teaches them more than what their parents tell them.

[36] As some put it, "Give me rules and I will flee. Give me Jesus and I am free."

Chapter 2

Two Ways

Pray to Gods out of fear, or because of love. (paraphrased)
—*Pray Your Gods*, Toad The Wet Sprocket

*One Sabbath Jesus was going through the grain-fields, and
his disciples began to pick some heads of grain, rub them in
their hands and eat the kernels. Some of the Pharisees asked,
"Why are you doing what is unlawful on the Sabbath?"
Jesus answered them, "Have you never read what David did
when he and his companions were hungry? He entered the
house of God, and taking the consecrated bread, he ate what
is lawful only for priests to eat. And he also gave some to his
companions." Then Jesus said to them, "The Son of Man is
Lord of the Sabbath." Jesus, Luke 6:1-4*

I contend there are two basic approaches to Christianity,
conservative and progressive, and this is true for both Catholics and
Protestants. However, before speaking to the differences, let's begin by
affirming what most Christians believe in common and agree upon.

Most Christians believe in God and consider this to be the
same God who Jewish people worship (YHWH aka *Yahweh*). We
most commonly understand God as being "one God in three
persons,"[37] a.k.a. the Trinity.[38] We agree that the founder of our

---

[37] At least since 325 A.D. as before that, many Christians held beliefs
more similar to the Unitarian position.

[38] The three persons of the Trinity are usually referred to as "the
Father, the Son, and the Holy Spirit."

faith is Jesus (*Yeshua*) of Nazareth. We typically refer to him as Jesus the Christ (anointed Messiah) and as our Lord and Savior.

It is interesting to note that the earliest Christians didn't refer to themselves as "Christians." Instead, they considered themselves as Jews, along with a few Gentiles, who believed that Jesus is the Messiah for whom the Jews had been yearning for years. They called themselves "people/followers of the Way."[39] Many progressive Christians prefer this original way the earliest Christians used to refer to themselves, that is, some progressive Christians prefer to call themselves "followers of The Way of Jesus" instead of "Christians." It helps keep the focus on what they think Jesus intended—off of Him and more on *the Way* and *the God* he was seeking to invite people to experience and follow. The way the term "Christian" is typically used anymore tends to take the focus off of the *way* of Jesus and instead places it on the *person* of Jesus, which potentially leads to making an idol out of him. It wasn't until the Christian message hit the Gentile city of Antioch that some of the people in that town began mocking Jesus' followers, calling them "Christ-ones" or "little Christs"—translated as "Christians" (Acts 11:26). Some of the leaders who were concerned about events taking place in the Palestinian portion of the Roman Empire started noticing the differences between regular Jews and the Jews who embraced Jesus. They started referring to this growing sect of Jews as "Christians." At some point, the early followers of Jesus came to embrace the label that was used to mock them. That new moniker stuck and it's the primary name still used today for referring to believers in, and followers of, Jesus.[40]

---

[39] See: Acts 9:1-2, 19:9, 19:23, 22:4, 24:14, 24:22, etc.

[40] As an aside, the early Christians often used abbreviated shorthand to refer to Jesus, Christianity, and followers of Christ. They used the Greek letters *Chi* and *Rho*—"Xr "—the first two letters in the word *christos* which is the Greek word for the Jewish concept of savior. Ironically, many of conservative Christians have forgotten this and this gap in their knowledge leads them to experience unwarranted heartburn and grief when they see people shortening Christmas to "Xmas," etc. That's all academic now as the term "Christian" eventually became the predominant word used to refer

Most Christians would agree that Christianity started around 30-33 A.D. in the Judean province of Palestine under the imperialist oppression of the Roman Empire. Christians of various stripes might even agree with the notion that Jesus didn't intend to start a new religion, but rather to introduce certain reforms and emphases within Judaism—but with the added emphasis of living life abundantly and fully in God's Kingdom and providing a way for non-Jews (Gentiles) to know and be in relationship with God. We'd also agree that the apostle Paul helped present the faith to the Gentiles and established and nurtured many churches.

Similarly, most Christians agree that we have one book of sacred scriptures—the Holy Bible, which was written over many years—originally in Hebrew and Aramaic (Hebrew Scriptures/Old Testament); and Greek (New Testament). There are 66 books in the Protestant Bible and seven more, the "Apocrypha," in the Catholic version. Some Christians read it literally, and others read it with more nuance discerning allegories, metaphors, symbolism, etc. Most of us view it as containing God's "revealed" truth and as "inspired by" God. We may mean very different things by this, however.

Christians tend to have in common certain basic worship, rites, and rituals. Most Christians value communal worship and growth together with others, usually in church facilities[41]. We don't believe in special, "secret" rites, secret knowledge, a rigid dualism between the Divine and the earthly, or in cultic practices—beliefs and practices that were part of the early heresy of Gnosticism. Baptism and the Lord's Supper (Holy Communion) are the two sacraments, "tangible means of God's grace," held in common by most Christian Churches. Mormons and Catholics each have seven sacraments, and some Christians view the stuff—"the elements" of the sacraments (water for baptism and bread and juice/wine for Communion)—as literally being God's actual flesh and presence while others view them symbolically. Most Christians encourage putting their faith into action through voluntary missionary efforts

---

to Jesus' followers and it is that term which has stuck and become the standard and norm.

[41]   But also sometimes in rented spaces like public school gyms and theatres, and increasingly, at coffee houses and in people's homes (like the early Christians used to do).

such as evangelism or humanitarian relief work and community service. Because Jesus said that his followers would be "known by their love," we share a common desire to provide tangible assistance to persons in need, especially the poor, widows, orphans, prisoners, and others who are downtrodden or oppressed. However, not all Christians emphasize, nor even condone, advocacy for the needy or the marginalized on the systemic, governmental policy, social justice level.

Most Christians engage in, or affirm the value of, certain other practices including Bible study, prayer, singing, fasting, community service, evangelism (spreading the faith to others), sharing testimonies of God's love in their lives, and enjoying fellowship and shared meals with fellow believers—especially those featuring coffee, doughnuts, casseroles, deviled eggs, hot-dishes, and fruit and vegetable-infused Jell-O salads. This is about as far as one can go with what the approximately 225 million Christians in the United States share in common—let alone the 2.5 billion Christians currently on the planet.

That common heritage and foundation has evolved[42] into several major branches with some 38,000 different Christian denominations within them. The major branches of the faith in the U.S. today include: Roman Catholic, Eastern Orthodox, Mainline Protestant, Evangelical, Fundamentalist, Charismatic, and the so-called non-denominational churches. Again, I submit that within most of those groups, there have come to be two basic approaches to the Christian faith today—conservative and progressive. The first of those two approaches is far better known than the latter.

Let's explore some of the differences between these two forms of Christianity. Conservative Christianity focuses on the religion *about* Jesus and getting people to agree with certain intellectual truth claims; for example, "people are sinners who aren't right with God" and "Jesus is their personal Lord and savior;"[43] and it asserts that it's important for people to believe

---

[42]   ... *devolved* into?

[43]   A concept invented by evangelicals. Those words aren't in the Bible, so the idea that all Christians *need* to believe it is highly problematic. I came across the following anonymous comment on the net re: how

these things here and now if they want to go to heaven when they die. Conservative Christianity often has wariness about the insights of contemporary science. Instead it finds solace in established, definable boundaries, including who God is; who Jesus is; the Bible; and doctrines, beliefs, and stances on morality. Conservative Christianity emphasizes praising God and "evangelism" which, for conservative Christians, basically means getting more people—ideally everyone on the planet—to become Christians who profess Jesus as their personal Lord and Savior and believe certain things about him.

Instead of getting people to agree with certain assertions about various dogmas, doctrines, or "truth claims," progressive Christianity focuses more upon following a certain, radical *way* of life; namely, following the countercultural, subversive, and life-giving teachings and example of Jesus. The focus is more upon the religion *of* Jesus,[44] his actual beliefs, teachings, practices, ways, and lifestyle, than on the religion *about* him. In other words, progressive Christianity focuses more upon *orthopraxy* (right behavior, actions and relationship) and less upon *orthodoxy* (right doctrines and beliefs).[45] This is not to say that progressive Christianity is not concerned about orthodoxy. It's a matter of emphasis. Progressive Christians would rather go to their graves having done their best to live rightly and follow the teachings and

---

a Catholic might respond when an Evangelical asks them if they have accepted Jesus as their personal Lord and Savior? "I always respond, "Of course!" This is often followed by the question, "When did you accept Him?" (the question I was waiting for). I respond, "There was not a real single point in time, but it a continual process of accepting and renewal in Him and His will." The best set up response I have ever received was by a Baptist minister, his response was, "That's ridiculous, that's like saying you continually re-marry your wife." To which the response is, "Well, kind of. We continually renew our marriage vows!" Many mainline Protestant and progressive Christians resonate with that perspective.

44   As opposed to "about" Jesus. (see the previous paragraph).

45   We do so following the lead of Jesus' brother James when he wrote, *But someone will say, "You have faith and I have works." Show me your faith apart from your works, and I will show you my faith by my works.* James 2:18

example of Jesus than to have "believed all the right things *about* Jesus" but fail to demonstrate or live out those beliefs. Progressive Christians prefer to hold various doctrines and beliefs loosely as they observe that it is extremely arrogant, and potentially idolatrous, for humans to think that any of our notions about God are without any degree of error.

Instead of seeking clear, black and white notions about God and theology, progressive Christianity not only tolerates but also appreciates and *embraces* ambiguity, paradox, mystery, doubt, and questioning. It is quite comfortable with being stretched by and incorporating the insights of various theologies and contemporary science. Where conservative Christianity tends to emphasize people's personal relationships with God, progressive Christianity remembers the Jewish (and Jesus') understanding of salvation by additionally focusing upon the broader pursuits of inter-human *hesed*[46] ("loving-kindness") and the societal Kingdom of God and striving for personal wholeness and social peace, justice and liberation from bondage and oppression.

When it comes to personal relationships with God, conservative Christianity tends to focus upon *conversion* as attempting to "convict" people of their personal sins, then asking them to repent of those personal sins and accept Jesus Christ as their personal Lord and Savior.[47] Progressive Christianity tends to view conversion more as helping people shift away from their self-defeating tendencies to follow the domineering and oppressive ways of the world and away from false notions of who they are—and to instead follow Jesus' alternative *way of living*. Jesus' way is liberating, counter-cultural and subversive to the worldly powers that be. Progressive Christianity also places more stress upon *sanctification*—the maturation, growth, and moral and spiritual development of Christian believers, especially as a community of believers, with the primary goal being social holiness that is not limited to personal morality and piety. Finally, unlike conservative Christianity, progressive Christianity openly acknowledges that God works through other major world religions

---

[46]   For example, Genesis 19; 1 Samuel 5:16; & 2 Samuel 9:1, 3, & 7.
[47]   See footnote 33.

and that Christians can benefit by learning the truths and insights they offer.[48]

It should be said that many Christians, myself included, probably identify and resonate with certain aspects of *both* conservative *and* progressive approaches to the faith. I've come to lean more toward the progressive approach and I feel called to help restore the balance by helping more people to become aware of the progressive approach to Christianity. What I will be referring to as "conservative Christianity," others have referred to as "popular Christianity, "traditional Christianity," "evangelical Christianity," "fundamentalism," "theism," "classical theism," or "supernatural theism." There are important distinctions among those categories, yet because they share much in common, for the purposes of this book I will have in mind all of those things when I say "conservative Christianity."[49] Most everyone has heard that

---

[48] While progressive Christianity is an open-minded approach to the faith, it is not to be confused with, or equated to, Unitarian Universalism. Most U.U. congregations offer a "cafeteria/ smorgasbord" approach to religion, effectively equating all religions, minimizing their differences, and encouraging people to pick and choose what they like from various traditions. Progressive Christians are intentional about following the specific religious vehicle of Christianity and going deeply into it. This said, many UU-ers will likely resonate with much that is said in this book. Progressive Christianity, despite its name, is not a "new approach" to the faith. Indeed, reading the Bible in a literal, fundamentalist manner, is instead what is a recent phenomenon for the faith; i.e., a modern era reactionary response to the rise of science, evolutionary theory, etc. Hence, what I'm calling "progressive Christianity" is what is *actually* conservative Christianity—but it's probably too late to fight that battle over terms.

[49] It should be said that the term "progressive Christians" has been used to describe persons involved in several Christian movements in the past. It has even referred to various churches and denominations that are now considered as being conservative. Examples of this include the Church of the Nazarene, the Free Methodists, the Wesleyan Church, and the Christian Missionary Alliance and certain other evangelical groups who, back in the 1800s were viewed as progressive for their opposition to slavery, their (then) egalitarian views about marriage, and their being among the first churches to

term. It's a broad umbrella for all of those sub-groupings and it provides an obvious contrast with "progressive Christianity."[50] Let's explore the differences and distinctions between these two ways of being Christian.

Conservative Christianity is identified by an approach to the faith that seeks to be "right" and to make and to heed to firm and fixed belief statements, dogmas, and doctrines to keep things "correct." Fundamentalism takes this to an extreme by declaring five "essential fundamentals of the faith":

1. The verbal inerrancy of Scripture (that there are no mistakes or false statements in the Bible)[51]
2. The divinity of Jesus Christ (that Jesus is God)
3. The virgin birth of Jesus (that his mother Mary was a virgin when Jesus was born)[52]

---

ordain women. These Christians based their "progressive" beliefs and actions upon their Christian commitments that frankly demand the pursuit of social justice. Since then, those groups have largely come to hold quite traditional beliefs about God, theology, marriage, and their approach to the Bible to the point where they are very much in the conservative camp.

[50] Progressive theology is similar to what is now known as "emergent/ing theology." There isn't a lot of difference but progressive theology pre-dates the emergent movement and it comes from mainline Christians. Though it started in an Anglican church in England, emergent theology primarily comes from young leaders in the evangelical community who are questioning the priorities and agenda of traditional evangelicalism. There is a bit more variety within the emerging community as some of their theologies in progress are pretty darned conservative. Progressive Christians are more uniformly open and accepting of homosexuality than emergent Christians are.

[51] ... and that any discrepancies in manuscript sources were "resolved" by God who guided man to select the "best, most perfect" manuscript sources.

[52] In the Roman Catholic Church there is the dogma of Perpetual Virginity (that Mary remained a virgin both during and after Jesus' birth, for the remainder of her life).

4. The substitutionary theory of the atonement (that Jesus' death, especially his blood, is what allow humans to be saved)
5. The physical resurrection and the bodily return of Christ

Fundamentalism originated in the late 1800s in the United States, soon after the teachings of Charles Darwin became known to the masses and it was created as a counter-movement to certain people's anxiety with modernity and the pervasive liberalism that went along with it. Because they felt liberal Christians held too high of an opinion of humanity, "progress," scholarship, and science, fundamentalists battened the hatches, solidified their core beliefs, and erected firm walls around them—effectively creating "holy huddles." Within the safe confines of their ideological shielding they reassured each other that they'd protected the faith by tightly holding on to their newly codified "right thinking." Those fundamentals became a sort of "shibboleth"[53] and litmus test (a term from the science that they reject) that determined whether you were of this "holy huddle" (a *real* Christian) or not.[54] (For more about fundamentalism, see Break It Down VII in Chapter 4)

In contrast, progressive Christianity is an approach to the faith that holds beliefs and doctrines loosely and is prepared to modify and even relinquish them if new information warrants it.

> *"Progressive Christianity is defined simply by its willingness to question and to be changed when it can be shown that change is necessary. It is willing to examine itself, to reform(ulate) itself in the context of the world in which it*

---

[53]   A "shibboleth" is a test to determine if someone is an insider or an outsider. It originates from the Hebrew *shibb leth*; from the use of this word in Judges 12:6 as a test to distinguish Gileadites from Ephraimites. Conservative Christians often have certan shibboleths to determine who are the "true Christians" including which version of the Bible someone prefers, where he (and it often has to be a he) went to seminary, what denomination someone belongs to, whether they're a Calvinist or not, whether they believe in infant or believer's baptism, and people's views on homosexuality, abortion, etc.

[54]   For a delightful exploration of this, see: Chad Holz's blog, Dancing on Saturday, "Why I am a FundaMergent," July 2, 2009, http://chadholtz.net/?p=867.

lives. Progressive Christianity lives; it lives and breathes; it grows and develops; it lives in the tension between valued and trusted historic, traditional formulations and the need to always express anew what the gospel means, and can mean, to the world."[55]

And it was Augustine, who said,

"In matters that are so obscure and far beyond our vision we find in Holy Scripture passages which can be interpreted in very different ways without prejudice to the faith we have received. In such cases, we should not rush in headlong and so firmly take our stand on one side that, if further progress in the search for truth justly undermines this position, we too fall with it."[56]

With those things in mind, this book operates with the following definition of Progressive Christianity—note that these are the beliefs and teachings that we "hold loosely"—although some more loosely than others (I'll be explaining the terms used here as the book progresses):

Progressive Christianity is an approach to the Christian faith that is influenced by post-liberalism and postmodernism and: proclaims Jesus of Nazareth as Christ, Savior, and Lord; emphasizes the Way and teachings of Jesus, not merely His person; emphasizes God's immanence not merely God's transcendence; leans toward panentheism rather than supernatural theism; emphasizes salvation here and now instead of primarily in heaven later; emphasizes being saved for robust, abundant/ eternal life over being saved from hell; emphasizes the social/ communal aspects of salvation instead of merely the personal;

---

[55] David Gillespie, Southern Fried Faith, "Seeking the Essence of Progressive Christianity," Aug. 23, 2010, http://david-gillespie. blogspot.com/2010/08/seeking-essence-of-progressive.html   used with permission.

[56] *De Genesi ad Litteram*, I, xxxxi. Modern translation by J.H. Taylor, Westminster, Md., Newman Press, 1982.

stresses social justice as integral to Christian discipleship; takes the Bible seriously but not necessarily literally, embracing a more interpretive, metaphorical understanding; emphasizes orthopraxy instead of orthodoxy (right actions over right beliefs); embraces reason as well as paradox and mystery—instead of blind allegiance to rigid doctrines and dogmas; does not consider homosexuality to be sinful; and does not claim that Christianity is the only valid or viable way to connect to God (is non-exclusive).

We'll explore what all of that means in the chapters ahead. Let's begin with God.

Chapter 3

God: Big Guy in the Sky?

Share all your thoughts about God (paraphrased)—Counting Blue Cars, Dishwalla

Now we see but a poor reflection as in a mirror; then we shall see face to face. Now I know in part; then I shall know fully, even as I am fully known. Paul, 1 Corinthians 13:12

Every child has known God-Not the God of names-Not the God of don'ts-Not the God who never does anything weird-But the God who knows only four words and keeps repeating them, saying: "Come Dance with Me." Hafiz

"You can safely assume you've created God in your own image when it turns out that God hates all the same people you do." Anne Lamott

God is love. Lenny Kravitz, Marvin Gaye & 1 John 4:8

My earliest memory of God is when I was laying in bed saying my nightly prayers.[57]

---

[57] My earliest experiences with God were when I was a very young child. The Wesleyan in me would say that God's "prevenient grace" (how God loves us even before we're aware there is a God or that we need God in our lives) was actively involved in my life from the moment I drew my first breath out of the womb and that all of the hugs and kisses my parents and family members showered upon me were subtle, yet tangible, ways that God was conveying His/

"Thank you God for my mom and my dad and for Carole (my twin sister) *and for Grandmom and Granddad and Annemomma and Andaddy (my pet names for my mother's parents). And thank you for Aunt Margaret and Uncle George, and Uncle Les and Aunt Pat, and for Uncle Red and Aunt Margaret and for my cousins, and for Aunt Carrie, Uncle Linwood, Aunt Beth and Uncle Harold, Aunt Bessie and Uncle Chandler. And thank you for my friends, and my school and for our church, and for our house, and for our food, and for all of the people in the world. And thank you for all the animals too. Amen!"*

I'd then break out into song, singing kiddie praises to God—*Jesus Loves Me, Deep and Wide, Away in a Manger*, etc. I'd also sing patriotic songs like *America*, and, since it had "God" in the title, and, especially, *God Bless America*.[58] Those bedtime moments were like little recitals I'd perform before God. It was quality time between Creator and creature, between "Father" God and one of His little children. It was truly precious, special, wondrous, innocent, and magical.

My childhood notions about God were pretty typical. I viewed God as a giant, elderly white man with a white beard in the sky Who loves us very much. He knows all that we do and He is someone we can reach out to for help when we're scared or in need. I was given an illustrated children's Bible. Through learning those stories and looking at the pictures, I acquired a sense that God is serious, that sometimes He gets really angry and that maybe people should be afraid of Him. Some might refer to that as a healthy and right "fear of the Lord,"[59] yet I found it

---

Her love for me even before I was aware that there is a God or that I need God in my life.

[58] This shows how insidious Civil religion is in our culture and how readily it weaves itself into and waters-down authentic Christianity. See Appendix VI

[59] Proverbs 1:7 states "The *fear* of the Lord is the beginning of all wisdom." The Hebrew word here really means "respect/honor/ revere." The Old English word *fear* used to mean those very things.

troubling. It didn't really connect with the intimate warmth and unconditional love of my nighttime experiences with God. I had an intuitive sense that the Bible was written by a lot of different people over many years and that they didn't all think alike. I knew that some of the other kids in my neighborhood were being raised in Catholic, Lutheran, Presbyterian, and Jewish families, and I came to an early awareness that not everyone understands God in the same way.

There's a parable from India that describes six blind men feeling different parts of an elephant—a strange creature that none of them knows about. One of the men has his hands on the animal's thick side and declares, "This creature is a wall." The second man has his hands on one of the sharp, smooth tusks and declares, "No, it is a spear!" The third man has a hold of the creature's squirming trunk and says, "No, it is a giant snake!" The fourth man is feeling one of the beast's thick, sturdy legs and says, "Not at all! This is a *tree!*" The fifth man has his hands running along the elephant's wide ear and says "Nope. It's a fan!" And the sixth man has his hands around the animal's rough tail and says, "You're all wrong, this *clearly* is a rope!" While each of the men was keenly familiar with the part that they were feeling, none of them had a full or accurate insight about the whole of the creature that they were describing. So it is with theology.

Theology comes from two Greek words that mean "God" (*theo*) and "the study of" (*ology*) and this chapter is focused on just that. Christian theology shares much in common with Jewish theology and is just as varied. Despite the claims from some quarters, there is no such thing as "The" Christian theology. There have been, and remain, numerous Christian *theologies*. However, certain Church Councils met during the formative years of Christian evolution and their resulting creeds sought to establish certain basic guidelines, known as "orthodoxy," in order to distance Christianity from certain teachings that were deemed heretical, including the teachings of groups that didn't embrace the Trinity or the "fully human and fully Divine" natures of Jesus, as well as

---

Fear has come to be associated with that which is "scary" and we should be "afraid" of. It is unfortunate that many contemporary Bibles still employ the Old English word here.

Gnosticism and Docetism.[60] Those movements in particular held teachings of a special "secret" knowledge that is not available to the masses. Both groups held rigid dualisms between the spiritual and the earthly realms. In the extreme, those dualisms meant that Jesus wasn't a real human being but more of a non-human illusory spirit or ghost-like apparition.[61] This idea denies the Gospel—the good news of the very real life, death and resurrection of Jesus.[62]

Even with those heretical notions ruled out, there's still an incredibly wide range of theological latitude and variance among Christians even "faithful" ones. Most Christian theologies claim to be biblically based, and I'd agree that most of them are—they're just based and grounded upon different parts and interpretations of the Bible. Just as there is no "one" or "right" Christian theology, there isn't a single biblical theology either. Indeed, there are numerous theologies within the Bible. The Hebraic notions of God evolved from being more a provincial, tribal warrior god to being the sole creator of the universe. Along the way, their views of God shifted from being a judge; a compassionate, assuring and forgiving leader; a jealous lover; a vindictive wrathful ruler;

---

60 Note, the primary intention of those Councils, and their resulting creeds was not to define Christianity, but rather to assert what sorts of beliefs *aren't* included in the Christian ballpark; i.e., to assert what Christianity isn't, not what it is.

61 Sort of like the hologram of Princess Lea in *Star Wars* or Luke Skywalker's encounters with Obi-Wan Kenobe (as a "Force Ghost") in *The Empire Strikes Back*. Gnostics and Docetists held rigid dualistic beliefs about a strict separation between the Divine and worldly realms. As enfleshed creatures, humans are corrupt, fallen, and wretched and there's no way that God could or would stoop to being enfleshed in human form. With such a notion, there is absolutely no way that Jesus could in any way be of God, let alone God incarnate.

62 One of the virtues of Gnosticism was its embracing of Jesus' radical egalitarianism concerning relations between men and women. Sadly, it appears that Christianity was "Romanized" by the Emperor Constantine (co-opted and adapted to Roman culture) and the Church began to revert to more traditionally patriarchal ways—at least until the 19th Century when certain Protestant groups started ordaining women.

one who will present a messiah to rescue Israel from oppression, and raise it to its former glory; as an intimate, loving parent who was uniquely present in the life of Jesus; and finally, as the One who will make all things new by destroying and displacing all the bogus, ungodly powers and rewarding the faithful at a future global judgment and reckoning day.

Many Christians would say that the God we seek to worship is the same God that our Jewish and Muslim friends worship[63] though we emphasize certain qualities and notions about God. Most of us commonly understand God as being a relational and mysterious "Trinity"—one God in three Persons—not three different gods. We typically refer to God as "Father, Son, and Holy Spirit" or as "Creator, Savior, and Sustainer." St. Patrick supposedly used the three leafed clovers that were indigenous to Ireland to help explain the concept of the Trinity to the Irish—one entity with three different parts. I prefer the metaphor of water, which occurs in three forms: liquid, solid, and vapor.[64] It's all still water. All three exist on the earth simultaneously. It's present everywhere, and we need it to live.

In contrast to the detached and dispassionate god of Deism,[65] Christianity views God as being concerned about, and actively involved with, all of God's creation including all people. Most Christians agree that God is a spiritual being without a physical body. Most Christians also would agree, on the record, that God isn't actually male or female. However, in common practice it's probably safe to say that many Christians think of, and refer to, God as being male.

---

[63]   Judaism, Christianity, and Islam are all "Abrahamic" religions "of the Book." We all claim to believe in the God of Abraham and trace our roots to him and his family line. *Allah* isn't a different God, it's merely the Arabic word for God.

[64]   According to my father, Wayne C. Wolsey, a chemistry professor emeritus at Macalester College, these three forms of water are in co-existing equilibrium at the triple point—0.01 C and 4.58 torr pressure.

[65]   The Enlightenment era theology held by several of our nation's founding fathers which basically posits a generic God who created the universe like a watchmaker and then dispassionately watches as it gradually ticks and winds.

Most Christians would also agree that God is *like* a loving, protective, just, and merciful parent. By referring to God as "Abba," (the Aramaic word for *papa*) Jesus introduced the notion that God is like an intimate and loving parent. Curiously, not many Christians follow Jesus' example in doing this ourselves. While Jesus prayed to God and distinguished himself from God the Father (for example Mark 13:32 & John 14:28) Christians consider Jesus as being a manifestation of God, "the 2nd person of the Trinity," and the *incarnation*—"enfleshment"—of God on earth. Most Christians would agree that Jesus' life, death, and resurrection exemplify God's nature. There are, however, significant differences in how we interpret and understand Jesus' life, death and resurrection.

For much of its history, Christianity has treated God as being eternal, changeless, *immutable* (unchanging/unchangeable), *impassible* (dispassionate, unaffected by the influence of others), *omnipotent* (all powerful), *omniscient* (all knowing), and *omnipresent* (everywhere). However, the earliest Christians didn't think of God in quite those ways. While they largely seem to resonate with some of the biblical treatments of God, most of those qualities attributed to God were originally pagan Greek ideals. These ideals were woven into the faith by some of the early Christian theologians who were influenced by their study of ancient Greek philosophy—especially Augustine of Hippo.[66] With this awareness in mind, some contemporary Christian views (for example, process and openness theologies)[67] deny or redefine some of those terms,

---

[66]   I refer to these as "pagan" Greek ideals with a bit of sheepish delight. I don't normally use the word pagan—it's usually judgmental conservative Christians who wield that term—and they use it in a dismissive manner. I appreciate the irony of pointing out a truth that they aren't likely to either be aware of—that what has become traditional Christian theology is greatly borrowed from non-Jewish and non-Christian sources. See: Daniel W. Graham and James L. Siebach, "Philosophy and Early Christianity," 210-220; Cook, "How Deep the Platonism," 269-286 in *Farms Review of Books*, vol. 11, no. 2 (1999).

[67]   Process theology is an approach to God that is popular in certain, mostly mainline Protestant, traditions. It is based upon certain passages of the Bible and is inspired by the process philosophy of Alfred North Whitehead and believes that we should hold all of our beliefs loosely and conditionally and allow them to evolve as

but the belief that God is compassionate, caring, active, and present in our lives is maintained.

Most Christians would agree that the Holy Spirit is the third Person of the Trinity who fills, comforts, confronts, guides, teaches, intercedes for, and advocates on behalf of God's children.[68]

With all of that said, there are dramatically different ways that various Christians understand and experience God. Indeed, there are many different "Christianities." In a playful, yet perhaps insightful way let me suggest that the motto of what I'm broadly calling conservative Christianity is *"God is awesome and He's the same yesterday, today, and tomorrow."* Worded another way: *"Our God is an awesome God, He reigns from heaven above,"* which is from a popular praise song. That sort of theological imagery is perhaps an unconscious reason why so many Christian conservatives supported President George W. Bush's war of "shock and awe" with Iraq. Societies base their policies and actions upon the view of God that they embrace. A god described with the words, *"When He rolls up His sleeves He ain't just putting on the Ritz . . . There's thunder in his footsteps and lightning in his fists . . . Our God is an awesome God"*[69] is a god who's prepared to kick some butt. People

---

new information comes in. It maintains that God is all-present, but suggests that God is mostly knowing, not all knowing; and that God very powerful, but not all powerful. This takes God off the hook in matters of theodicy—why bad things happen to good people. Openness theology is similar but comes more from the evangelical community and maintains that God is all-powerful (I address the subtle differences between process and openness theologies in Break It Down XIII in Chapter 9).

[68] There are theologically unitarian Christians, but there aren't many left in the world. Even in the denomination that goes by that name. They've largely become polytheists and/or inter-faithists upon their (American Unitarian Association) merger with the Universalist Church in America in 1961. There are other sects which also embrace a unitarian view of God including the Ebionites and Nazarenes, the Jehovah's Witnesses; and the Church of Jesus Christ Latter Day Saints (Mormons).

[69] *Our God is an Awesome God*, by Rich Mullins, BMG Songs, Inc., 1988, see: http://www.lyricsmania.com/lyrics/rich_mullins_lyrics_33372/other _lyrics_64277/our_god_is_an_awesome_god_lyrics_758740.html

strive to emulate the god they adore and if the popular view of God is vengeful and violent, then the people of that society will naturally be vengeful and violent as well.[70]

Conservative Christianity asserts that "unlike other religions," the Christian God provided unique knowledge about Himself for people—knowledge that can only be found in "the special unique revelation" of the Bible. In my opinion, besides arrogantly asserting that God didn't speak through the texts of other major world religions, this viewpoint denies the messy variety and inconsistencies in much of that biblical revelation. Again, there is no one consistent presentation of God in the Bible. As I see it, the God that many conservative Christians embrace is far more similar to the anthropomorphized ancient Greek god Zeus, or even an angry volcano god, than the more mysterious and compassionate God "in whom we live, move and have our being" (Acts 17:28). Conservative Christians seem to support such a view of God as a stoic, independent, sovereign, majestic, Spartanesque, retributive, kick-ass king using certain passages of Scripture that they read literally.

While official Christian orthodoxy ("the official stances and doctrines") asserts that God is both *transcendent* (God is separate from God's creation and dwells in a realm utterly removed from the earthly one) and *immanent* (God is everywhere throughout creation and there's nowhere we can go where God isn't present), conservative Christianity emphasizes God's transcendence from the world. This phenomenon is observed in most of the sermons preached on Christian radio stations and by most contemporary praise songs. If one scans the lyrics from most conservative hymns or songs, one can readily observe a particular theology—that God is all-powerful, kingly, male, transcendent, up in heaven, judgmental, and wrathful. That theology asserts that God determines, or even pre-determines, the things that occur in the earthly realm. There are songs that point to God's amazing love, grace, and compassion, yet a good number of them carry the reminder of God's legitimate right and ability to be wrathful and to give us what's coming to us.

---

[70]   René Girard suggests that much human behavior is based upon *mimesis*—essentially, "monkey see, monkey do." See his book *Violence and The Sacred*, The Johns Hopkins University Press, 1979.

A strong influence on several forms of conservative Christian thought is Calvinism, which gets its name from John Calvin,[71] a French Protestant leader from the Reformation movement in the 16th century. There are five tenets of Calvinism—oftentimes described with the acronym "TULIP": Total Depravity; Unconditional Election; Limited Atonement; Irresistible Grace; and Perseverance of the Saints. Those beliefs don't work for me—and a whole lot of others. As a United Methodist, my understanding fits better with that of John Wesley, who adopted the beliefs of the Dutch theologian Jacobus Arminius *(who was perhaps influenced by the prior insights of Pelagius—who also might have influenced King Arthur, at least according to Hollywood).*[72]

---

[71] One of the most troublesome phenomena within certain forms of Christianity is legalism. In addition to my disagreeing with the 5 tenets of Calvinism, I'd also suggest that Calvinism tends to bolster a legalistic approach to Christianity. It comes as no surprise that John Calvin was a lawyer, and that colored (and arguably handicapped) his understandings of the Christian faith. After all, he legalistically imposed mandatory worship attendance. He banned swearing, gambling, fornication, and dancing, and even had a man burned to death (Michael Servetus).

[72] Pelagius, ca. AD 354—ca. AD 420/440, was a Christian ascetic who denied the doctrine of Original Sin. Movie lovers might recall references to Pelagius in the movie, *King Arthur* (2004) with Clive Owen. A subplot of that film was that Arthur was a Roman follower of the teachings of the Christian monk Pelagius who embraced the concept of human free will instead of the Augustine's dogmas of Original Sin and God determining what humans do in life. In that movie, when Arthur learns that Roman Church/Empire (which were wedded at the time) had Pelagius killed, he switches allegiances to the native Brits and helps them to fight off the Romans and Saxons (echoes of Kevin Costner in *Dances With Wolves*.)

Break it Down V

Calvinism vs. Arminianism (Determinism vs. Free Will):

One of the age-old "in house/intermural" issues of controversy and division within Christianity is the matter of to what extent God determines and/or pre-determines things and to what extent humans have free will. Methodists, and possibly most progressive Christians, are followers of the tradition established by John Wesley. Wesley was a vigorous opponent of the tenets of John Calvin. He instead favored the understanding articulated by Jacobus Arminius.

The **Five Points of Calvinism** are:

1) **Total Depravity:** Humans are so affected by the consequences of original sin that we're simply incapable of being righteous and are always and unchangeably wretched and sinful. Human freedom is enslaved to sin so we can only choose evil. Put simply, humanity is essentially evil.

2) **Unconditional Election:** God unconditionally elects that people are destined (either before they were born or after) to be saved or unsaved. And since humans don't have the ability to choose this for themselves, God by His sovereign (and apparently capricious) will decrees that some persons will be counted among the righteous, without any conditions being placed on this election. Certain humans have been chosen as "the elect" and there's nothing neither they, nor those who aren't the elect, can do about it. You're either saved or you aren't.

3) **Limited Atonement:** Only some humans—"the elect whom God has chosen"—are forgiven for the sins of humanity and saved by the atoning work of Jesus Christ.

4) **Irresistible Grace:** The grace that God provides to the chosen persons to allow for their election cannot be resisted, refused or rejected, since it has been determined and decreed by God. If one is of the elect, they will be saved by God's grace. They're unable to resist this or say no to it.

5) **Perseverance of the Saints:** Because God has determined and decreed who the elect are (those who are chosen to be saved), and because they're unable to resist God's saving grace, such persons are unconditionally and eternally secure in that status of election. Once people are saved, they're unable to become unsaved or lead an ungodly lifestyle. "Once saved, always saved."

Calvinism also embraces the notion that God is immutable and impassible.

In contrast to these, John Wesley articulated five tenets of his own using the theology of Jacobus Arminius as his basis. The **Five Points of Arminianism:**

1) **Free Will:** As part of how we were "created in God's image," all humans have true free will and can choose good or evil. Our nature is more neutral than wretched—though we have a propensity to sin. We are depraved, but not totally so. Our tendency to sin makes us incapable of being fully righteous without God in our lives. However, we're not irredeemably sinful and we can be transformed and renewed.

2) **Conditional Election:** God has chosen that all humanity will be righteous by God's grace, yet God has called us to respond to that grace by exercising our human freedom as a condition for fulfilling election. People are saved/made elect contingent upon their accepting the gift of salvation which God intends for them. Arminians would say that it doesn't make much sense to preach or tell people about Jesus if people are incapable of choosing to accept God's gift of grace.

3) **Universal Atonement:** The effects of the Atonement are freely available to all those who choose it. God wants all humans to be saved, but He knows that not all will be as it's up to them if they choose to accept the gift or not.

4) **Resistible Grace:** God's grace is free and offered without merit on our part. We don't do anything to earn it. However, human beings have been granted freedom by God and can refuse God's grace based upon our free will. We have the ability to say yes or no to God's grace in our lives.

5) **Assurance:** There is security in God's grace that allows assurance of salvation, but that security depends upon our continuing to be faithful. We can still reject God if we wanted to. There is "falling from grace," once a person is saved/elect, that doesn't make them immune to succumbing to future temptations in their life. They may still sin from time to time. Our assurance doesn't mean that we will perpetually stay in a saved/elect condition. We may indeed slide down a slippery slope of falling back into our former wayward ways. Arminians also deny the notions that God is immutable (never changes His mind) and impassible (not subject to suffering or changes of mood).

Calvinism was a major doctrinal perspective of the Presbyterian Church, but in the U.S. (a land of people who embrace independence and free will), many of them have now moved toward the Arminian perspective. However, many conservative Christians, especially from the Reformed, Baptist and Presbyterian denominations lean toward Calvinism.

To my mind, the Arminian perspective is far more compelling: logically and experientially. As I experience it, faith is a human-Divine joint endeavor and relationship. It's a mutual thing as "it takes two to tango." God dances with each of us and when two persons dance together, they're *really* engaged with each other, one party doesn't control and determine everything—even if one of them is leading. However, to loosely quote Forrest Gump (at the graveside scene at the end of the film) *"Some folks say that the things that happen in life are all fixed and determined and some say that things just sorta happen by chance like the wind blowing, or because people choose things—maybe it's both."*[73]

If the conservative Christian slogan about God is *God is awesome and He is the same yesterday, today, and tomorrow*, the mottos of progressive Christianity are *The God that can be named is not the real God* and *God can't be put into a box*. These mottos show the greater comfort with mystery, ambiguity, and paradox that progressive Christians have, as well as their openness to the insights of other major world religions. The primary Taoist sacred text, the *Tao Te Ching*, begins with these words *"The tao that can be told is not the eternal Tao. The name that can be named is not the eternal Name."* Early Christians wrote similar descriptions about God. Saint Gregory of Nyssa said, *The simplicity of the true faith assumes God to be that which He is, namely, incapable of being grasped by any term, or any idea, or any other device of our apprehension, remaining beyond the reach not only of human but of angelic and all supramundane intelligence, unthinkable, unutterable, above all expression in words, having but one name that can represent His proper nature, the single Name being 'Above Every Name.'* Saint Nicholas of Cusa wrote: *As Creator, God is three and one; as infinite, He is neither three nor one nor any of the things which can be spoken. For the names that are attributed to God are taken from creatures, since He in Himself is ineffable and beyond everything that can be named or spoken.*[74] Mystical and otherwise not overly defined notions such as these jibe well with today's postmodern mindset.

---

[73]   It could be argued that Forest Gump was an example of a late 20th Century postmodern, emergent Christian—a forerunner of non-dualistic, paradox-embracing Emergent & Progressive Christianity.

[74]   From p. 49, *Four View of Salvation in a Pluralistic World*, Dennis L. Okholm, et al, Zondervan, 1996.

Progressive Christianity isn't based upon Taoism though—[75] it's based on the Bible, supportive voices from within the varied traditions of Christian theology, and upon people's experience and relationship with God and the risen Christ. Progressive Christians look at the biblical texts and affirm the following key insights about God:

- God is the Creator of Creation, implying that He's the one true God (Genesis 1 and 2).
- This God is mysterious and beyond full human comprehension, referring to Herself as "us" (Genesis 1:26-27); as "I Am" (Exodus 3:14); and appearing in burning bushes that aren't consumed by fire (Exodus 3:2-4) and winds that rush in (Acts 2:1-4). The Hebrew word for God's name is YWHW—a.k.a. the "Tetragrammaton," pronounced as *Yahweh*. The ancient Jews considered the name too holy for humans to dare to pronounce so they deleted the vowels. This wording (YWHW) conveys the ineffability of God—that ultimately, God is indescribable and incapable of being expressed.
- God is both transcendent from us and as close to us as our breath (Genesis 2:7; 1 Kings 19:11-13; Job chapters 40-41).
- God desires personal relationship with humanity and hopes we'll follow Her ways instead of our own (1 Samuel 8:6-7; Luke 14:27).
- God cares about us and is upset by human oppression, exploitation, and injustice (Exodus, Deuteronomy, the Prophets, the Gospels—all of the Bible really).
- God uniquely revealed Herself in the person of Jesus (the New Testament).
- Nothing we do can separate us from God's love (Romans 8:39) and that God has incredible powers of transformation and renewal.

---

[75] . . . and Christianity certainly doesn't jibe with the Taoist goal of "wu-wei"—the path of least resistance. If anything, progressive Christianity follows the path of *most* resistance—the Way of the Cross.

God: Big and Small, Far and Close

Earlier I stated that conservative Christianity emphasizes God's transcendence from the world—that He literally resides "up there," "in heaven." Such an understanding fits in with the ancient and medieval understandings of the universe and its cosmology. Prior to the advent of science, it was typically thought that the world was part of a multi-tiered order. With this notion, the earthly realm was seen as flat. Above the flat earth was the sky. Above that was heaven. Below the earth was an ethereal and nebulous underworld called *Sheol* or hell.

We now know that the earth is round. That it is one of *many* planets, in one of *many* solar systems, in one of *many* galaxies, in an expanding universe.[76] Likewise, contemporary science suggests to us that there isn't a literal heaven (at least not in the physical realm of creation in the sky above the earth) and that there isn't a literal hell (at least not below the surface of the earth). However, that change in cosmological understanding doesn't mean that God doesn't exist. What it does mean is that our understandings about God need to shift. So, if God isn't sitting on a throne up in the sky, then where is He?

Consulting the Bible is helpful here. According to the Bible, God is indeed distinct from God's creation. There is a difference between Creator and Creation. This means that God transcends the world. Much conservative Christian theology is based on an amplified interpretation of this concept—that there is a massive gap, distance and estrangement between God and humanity. Conservative theology has stressed the need for a priestly mediator who bridges that chasm between people and God. Roman Catholics believe that priests bridge that gap, but it's ultimately based upon the notion that Jesus serves as this mediator on behalf of humanity—primarily because he is "an unblemished sacrificial lamb" and "His blood is shed on the cross."

Progressive Christianity doesn't deny that there's a difference between Creator and Creation, or that people can become estranged

---

[76]   See: Universe 101, National Aeronautics and Space Museum, http://map.gsfc.nasa.gov/universe/uni_expansion.html

from God. However, it gives equal attention to the reality of God's *immanence*[77]—God's constant presence in our midst. In numerous places, the Bible indicates that God is quite close to us. In Exodus, we see how the ancient Hebrews understood God as traveling and camping with them in the wilderness. In Deuteronomy, we see how God is like a mothering eagle protecting her brood with her wings. In 1 Kings, we see how God speaks to us in the still small voice. And in Jonah, we learn not only that God cares deeply about what's going on in human societies, She can call people to act on Her behalf to help others get back on track. There's no place that we can go to flee from God since God is always present wherever we are. In many places in the Bible, we see how God's *ruach* (breath) is as close to us as the air we breathe. In the Gospels, we see how God effectively came to dwell among us, live life with us, teach us, love us, and share in our common suffering, in the form of Jesus. In the Book of Acts, we see how Paul described God as *"the one in Whom we live, move and have our being."*[78] That's close.

Even though historic Judaism and Christianity officially embrace both God's transcendence and His immanence, because traditional theism tends to exclusively emphasize God's transcendence, and because traditional Christian theism has tended to become equated to Christian theology altogether, a newer word has been created to describe the form of theism which embraces and gives equal emphasis to both God's transcendence *and* God's immanence—*panentheism*.[79] Progressive Christianity commonly embraces this understanding of God.

---

[77] Immanence should not be confused with *imminence* (which means "something just about to happen very soon"). Immanence refers to God's presence in and among us. To distinguish, one might say that Jesus' 2nd coming is imminent.

[78] Acts 17:28. In part, the basis of theologian Paul Tillich's referring to God as "the ground of all being."

[79] The term *panentheism* was coined by the German philosopher Karl Christian Friedrich Krause in 1828 but the concept goes back to several aboriginal Native American tribes and the ancient Greeks. The concept was popularized by philosopher Alfred North Whitehead—whose writings have influenced numerous process theologians. He referred to this as a "bi-polar" God.

It should first be said what panentheism isn't. It's not *pantheism*—the notion that creation *is* God or that God is simply the earth or the whole universe. In contrast, panentheism maintains that there's a difference between the Creator and Creation (that God is fully transcendent from the world) but it also emphasizes God's immanence—that God is fully *within* all that is. Traditional theism asserts that God is the sole Creator. Panentheism suggests that creation, especially humanity, is a "co-creator" with God. Saying that humans are co-creators with God implies that God doesn't have all of the agency, will, or control about what happens in the world. Panentheism affirms this and its implications.

Instead of presenting God as a dictator or monarch who calls all the shots, panentheism understands God as more like a dance partner or a jazz composer and musician who creatively and perfectly introduces beautiful things into the world, and yet empowers the rest of us to respond on our own terms and to improvise on His dance and tune.[80]

Panentheism suggests that God intervenes and engages with the world not by the means of coercive power, but by persuasive power. God doesn't brutishly force Her will on anyone. Instead, God gently courts, woos, prompts, and nudges us.[81] God wants authentic and genuine relationship with His people. We're free to accept or to resist God's nudges in our lives. This implies that God changes.

That last sentence will cause some folks a certain degree of heartburn, but when two living beings interact with each other they necessarily affect each other. One cannot have real relationship with anyone without being changed in the process. If God nudges us to help some poor stranger by the side of the road, and if we respond by ignoring that person or by kicking him, God will no doubt be affected by that. God's mood may change. Yet, it goes beyond affecting God's emotions. The things we do and the choices we make influence God's strategies and choices for dealing with us and the rest of humanity.

---

[80]   For more on this, see the "Groovin' with God" sermon at the ending of Chapter 8.

[81]   Most Christians would attribute this wooing capacity of God to the Holy Spirit aspect of the Trinity.

God's character may be consistently steady (perfect, loving, compassionate, gracious, merciful, just, good, etc.) but having one's emotions and one's strategic choices being influenced implies that He's affected, moved, and changed. Biblical examples of this include: Abraham negotiating with God in Genesis 1:16-23; Jacob wrestling with God (Genesis 32:23-34); Moses negotiating with God when he was resisting being called by God to demand the release of the Hebrews from Pharaoh (Exodus 3-4); God hearing the grumbling of the wandering Israelites during the Exodus, and responding by providing them food (Exodus 16); Moses interceding on behalf of the people and God responding by helping Moses to spring forth water from a rock (Exodus 17); Moses intervening on behalf of his people and persuading God to change his mind about punishing them, when they rebelled against God by worshipping a golden calf (Exodus 32:11-14); and God sparing the people of Nineveh in response to their repenting (Jonah).

Two biblical passages are especially compelling and supportive of the suggestion that God changes. The prophet Jeremiah presents God as saying:

> *"At one moment I may declare concerning a nation or a Kingdom, that I will pluck up and break down and destroy it, but if that nation, concerning which I have spoken, turns from its evil, I will change my mind about the disaster that I intended to bring on it. And at another moment I may declare concerning a nation or a Kingdom that I will build and plant it, but if it does evil in my sight, not listening to my voice, then I will change my mind about the good that I had intended to do to it"* (Jeremiah 18:7-10).

This passage doesn't make sense if God knows from all of eternity what He's decided to do. If the future were completely determined, could God sincerely desire to bring something about and then actually change His mind and not bring it about? In 2 Kings 20:1-6, King Hezekiah is informed by the prophet Isaiah that he will die from his current sickness. However, after Hezekiah ardently prays, God reverses Himself and extends the king's life by another 15 years. If what's become known as the "traditional" view of God is correct (that God doesn't change—not even His mind), then God was being insincere or even deceitful when he initially told Hezekiah that he wouldn't recover.

Still other examples include: God responding to Samuel's prayer concerning the people's yearning to have a king of their own "like all the other nations have" (my paraphrase of 1 Samuel 8:5). God allowed it, but indicated that the people were rejecting Her by doing so and that there would be grave consequences for this choice—namely, the King commandeering their sons and their daughters for his purposes. Another example is Jesus being swayed by a Canaanite woman to extend God's grace and love to her and her daughter even though they aren't Jews (Matthew 15:21-28).[82]

To the extent that Jesus *was* "God on earth," His actions clearly point to a God Who is deeply moved by human suffering. God's character doesn't change. On numerous occasions, Jesus took pity, felt compassion, and reached out with mercy to persons afflicted with disease and social estrangement. Indeed, Jesus' life indicates a God Who was deeply moved, troubled, and cried upon seeing Lazarus' sister in grief (John 11:33-35); Who wept when looking upon wayward Jerusalem (Luke 19:41); Who angrily knocked over tables and chased out money lenders from the Temple courtyards (Matthew 21:12); Who cried out with feelings of forsakenness upon the cross; and Who responded to being rejected and killed by offering understanding and forgiveness (Luke 23:34).

Panentheism doesn't embrace traditional understandings of the "omni" qualities attributed to God by some of the early Christian theologians who were influenced by pagan Greek philosophical

---

[82]   Some might suggest that Jesus was testing this woman's faith. That is sheer speculation. If one reads the text plainly (he went from effectively calling her a female-dog to commending her faith), it may very well be that Jesus was truly transformed by his interaction with this woman. Either way, given that the passage immediately before this one deals with "what is clean and unclean"—not external things but only the things which come from the heart—the author's focus appears to have been to demonstrate to Jesus' disciples, and to his post-resurrection followers, that God's work through Jesus wasn't intended only for the Jews.

ideals. God isn't understood as *omnipotent* (all powerful). Rather, God is viewed as *very* powerful—as powerful as God can be, and be in authentic relationship to us. It might be said that in creating humans, God relinquished some of Her power to us to allow for the possibility of real and genuine relationship.

Similarly, in the panentheistic view, God isn't understood as *omniscient* (all knowing) either—at least not how that's traditionally been understood. If God has given us free will and agency, then we're free to introduce novel, new things into the world on our own—including things that aren't in God's will. If we have *real* will and agency, and genuine relationship with God, then God *can't* know everything that we will do from moment to moment—let alone in the future. Instead, God is fully aware of all that *has* happened, all that *is* happening, and most all of what is *likely* to happen in the future. In other words, God knows all that is *possible* for Her to know given that She's turned over some of Her power and agency to humanity. This is still an awful lot of knowledge. It is with this knowledge of the past, the present, and the likely and probable future that God seeks to influence us through the Holy Spirit toward the most ideal and beautiful options in each and every moment.

I can't speak for all of progressive Christianity, but I would like to introduce a new "omni" quality for God, perhaps to override the "omnis" that have been displaced or reinterpreted—"*omniamo*" (or *omniamore*)—all loving. If there is one essential and consistent theme throughout the whole of the Bible it is God's love. We see that God loves us unconditionally like a protective parent, like a wooing lover, and like a committed lover. God loves us incarnationally, down to earth and relationally. God loves us like a friend. In sum, God loves us like a God *worthy* of humans loving Her! We also see that God calls *us* to love in these same ways, to love ourselves and to love others, as God loves us. Indeed one of the shortest verses in the Bible is one of the most profound: "God is love" (1 John 4:8).

Progressive Christianity tends to endorse this form of theism because it corresponds better with the fullness of the biblical text, the writings of the earliest Christian theologians and mystics, the insights of contemporary science, and with many people's lived experiences of God.

In the interest of being inclusive and politically correct (and avoiding heresy), some liberal and progressive Christians have referred to God in generic, impersonal ways. Examples of this include avoiding the use of personal pronouns by referring to God only as "God," or encouraging people to think of God as some vague, abstract, ethereal being. I suggest that this is a mistake. One simply can't have a deep, intimate, personal and life-changing relationship with someone/"thing" if s/he merely considers an it and generically refers to it as "Mystery," "The Source," "The Universe," "Spirit," "Deity," "Wisdom," "Parent." Hence, my use of *He, She, Father, Mother, Abba,* and *Ama.*[83]

Jesus is the model and example for those who seek to follow him, and he had an incredibly intimate relationship with God. He referred to God as "Father," and even more intimately as *Abba*—Aramaic for "papa." Those terms are metaphors, but they are deeply personal ones that meet a real human need. Some of the great Christian mystics such as Teresa of Avila and Hildegard of Bingen employed other metaphors that referred to God as "lover" (based in part, I think, on the biblical book Song of Songs/Song of Solomon. Others might speak of God as "Mother" or *Ama* (mamma).[84] These personal terms necessarily require the supplemental use of "He" or "She" and "Him" or "Her." All of these are helpful terms that serve to endear God to us. Jesus encouraged his disciples not to see themselves as his "servants"—dispassionate and disenfranchised pawns—but as his *friends* who know God's business and have a close relationship with Him (John 15:15).

After reading what I've shared about God in the paragraphs above, a careful reader of the Bible and of this book might want to ask, "But what about those towns mentioned in the Bible that God is said to have destroyed? Or those people turned into pillars of salt, or attacked by bears? Are you saying that God didn't cause

---

[83]   And yes, I actually refer and pray to the "amoeba/womb image of God" that I described before, as "Abba" or "Ama." See also this song by Moby, *Lift Me Up*, http://www.youtube.com/watch?v=Dw17-BEFb3Y

[84]   For example, Moby in his song, *Lift Me Up*.

those things to happen?" In a word, yes. I would say that many of
the things that are "recorded" in the stories of the Bible, did not
happen. Or if they did, it wasn't necessarily God's will that made
them happen. If a town were destroyed by fire or earthquake,
it would only be natural for people to look back on that event
afterward and to try to make sense of it. I'd say that many of the
remarks in the Bible which appear to say, "X tragedy happened
to Y community because it was God's will" are simply instances
of people theologizing in hindsight. People try to make sense
of various traumas after they occur. Just because some of these
stories might not have actually taken place doesn't mean that they
don't convey truth and aren't worthy of being in the Bible. (More
about this in Chapter 8)

Another question the reader might ask is, "You say that God
changes and evolves. Doesn't that mean that God was imperfect
before and still isn't perfect?" Answer: No. But I suppose it might
depend on what one means by perfection. It's perfect that God
is perfect in each new moment. He seeks to influence everyone
toward the most beautifully ideal choice at each and every
opportunity. If people fall short of actualizing that preferred ideal,
then God regroups in the next moment and seeks to once again
perfectly nudge us toward a new set of ideal possibilities. It's not
that God wasn't or isn't perfect. God keeps on being perfect in
new ways.[85] Perfection can be defined by a consistent evolution.
If one stops changing and growing, one ceases to be perfect. As
God continues to shift, grow, adapt, and change, God maintains
and enhances Her perfection.

Another question the reader might want to ask is, "You seem
to be presenting a really nice and lovable sort of God, but what
about all of those passages in the Bible about God's wrath and
anger?"

Answer: I don't mean to suggest that God doesn't get upset with
us. In fact, I think it's rather clear that God has a lot of righteous ire
and outrage at seeing how badly we humans treat each other and
how poorly we're serving as stewards of His creation. The prophets
were vessels who conveyed God's anger about seeing His chosen

---

[85]   Perhaps including on a supernatural level that humans simply aren't
       aware of.

people, the Hebrews, repeatedly falling away from His plan for them by engaging in idolatry and seeking to follow worldly leaders in worldly ways. A bluntly stated bumper sticker that was popular among political liberals during the George W. Bush era said, "If you aren't outraged, you aren't paying attention!" One aspect of Christian peace and social justice work has involved conveying prophetic anger about racism, sexism, militarism, imperialism, homophobia, and various forms of oppression. Parents often get angry with their children but that doesn't mean that they don't love them. Likewise, God may get royally pissed-off at us from time to time but, metaphorically, God's skin is thick, Her shoulders are broad, His hugs are warm, Her tears are sweet, and His love and mercy are deep and eternal. God absorbs the tantrums, violence, and grief that we throw at Him. God's response is not to lash out at us, but instead to woo and nurture us back into right relationship. Sure, God may allow us to fall flat on our faces and to experience the consequences of our wayward actions, but that doesn't mean that God intends punishment.

One of the key emphases of a progressive Christian understanding of God is the avoidance of rigid dualisms and instead embracing the notion that things of the spirit are more "both/and" and less "either/or." It isn't a case of *either* God is transcendent or immanent. He is *both* transcendent and immanent. God isn't either all-powerful *or* impotent—God is *very* powerful. God isn't either angry and wrathful *or* nice and loving. God loves us zealously, vigorously and passionately. When we have a loving authentic relationship with God, sparks fly a bit from time to time. Instead of seeking to find a fully revealed, fully knowable God in a comfortable intellectual box, progressive Christianity embraces the holy paradox, ambiguity, and mystery of God. In C.S. Lewis' *The Chronicles of Narnia*, the Christ figure Aslan inspires awe and trembling among the animals. As one character says, "He's not a tame lion." Progressive Christianity bows before the wild lion that is our God.

In my experience, progressive Christianity doesn't speak much about visualizing God, but most of us would say that our visual images of God have changed significantly since our first childhood notions. Several progressive Christians, myself included,[86] currently imagine God as being like a cosmic, amoeba-like womb.[87] Well, at least the womb part. The amoeba bit is my own variation.

The Hebrew word for womb, *rehem*, has the same root as the word for compassion—*rahamim*. In the Jewish understanding, it is from the womb that compassion and mercy emanate and God's compassion and mercy are a constant theme throughout the Bible. Employing metaphors and similes, God is like a giant womb that encompasses and envelops all that is. God's womb is warm, safe and nurturing. The tissue of God's womb is protective, strong and muscular. God's womb expands and flexes as we kick, stretch, grow, throw tantrums, and move about throughout life. God's womb nourishes and sustains us with the strength to grow. It gives us the grace to forgive when we hurt our siblings or God. And yet, the skin of God's womb is like the permeable membrane of an amoeba.[88] Humans are able to pull away from God, perhaps not physically, but at least energetically and relationally with our intentions. I think of the person I saw one day saying "F-you!" to God.[89] God is immanently within each of the cells of our bodies too, but She's always able to re-envelop us. There's no place we can go that God can't gather us back into Himself.

An amoeba is a distinct living being that is neither male nor female. It has boundaries, indicating transcendence, but they are permeable—conveying immanence and being able to be impacted and influenced by Creation. I picture the created universe as surrounded by this womb-like God who is filled with an "embryonic fluid" that offers the nourishment of God's grace, wisdom, and indicators of God's will and preferences. However, while all is *in* God, there are no forced links (no umbilical cords) to this nourishment. We are able to choose not to accept this

---

[86] Marcus Borg also embraces this metaphor in several of his writings including *The Heart of Christianity*. We came to this metaphor independently of each other—which suggests the universality and potency and attractiveness of this visual concept.

[87] (Though perhaps a wild, lion-like one!)

[88] . . . My variation on the womb metaphor.

[89] I suppose in my own way, I've done that too. I can recall a few times when I flipped the bird "to the universe."

connective empowerment. Of course, this metaphor breaks down when it comes to relationship. It's hard to imagine relating with an amoeba or a womb. However, I didn't say that God *is* an amoeba or a womb. That's simply what I envision when I imagine what God might look like.

I offer this image as a gift for others to consider. I'd love hearing about how you currently visualize or imagine God. Please feel free to describe your image of God at **www.progressivechristianitybook.com.**

One Progressive Christian's notions about God:

It strikes me as idolatrous to assert our views of God as proven, actual, or literal. However, I affirm many biblical references to God including: *Adonai/Kyrios* (Lord), *Elohim/El Shaddai* ("God/almighty"), *Immanuel* ("God with us"), Yeshua/Jesus ("God saves"), and especially, "I Am"—as in "I am Who I am and will be what I will be" (Exodus 3:14). I agree with Augustine (something I do less and less these days) that God is the Most Beautiful, the perfection of perfections, and the breath beneath existence. This is a wonderfully appropriate use of the language of worship and devotion. Theological language is metaphorical, not literal. Although they are metaphors, they are powerful, even dangerous. If we exclusively refer to God as "Father" or read the Bible with male bias or other myopic lenses from the context of privilege, we risk oppressing women and committing other forms of idolatry and oppression. Metaphorically, I often refer to God as "He" or "She" (or "S/He").

I am influenced by the process and openness theological understandings of God.[90] In my interpretation of these lines of thinking, God is the original creator of everything. He is actively present and involved in the world. It is through the "person" of the Holy Spirit

---

[90]   I don't agree with either of these theologies completely. For instance, to the extent that Process theology says that God *needs* the world and creation, I disagree. That doesn't mean that there aren't helpful insights that theology has to offer. Key Process theologians include: Charles Hartshorne (1897-2000), John B. Cobb, Jr., David Ray Griffin, and several rabbis including Harold Kushner. Key Openness theologians include: Gregory Boyd, Clark Pinnock and William Hasker.

that God acts by persuasively luring and wooing us toward actualizing the best and most beautiful possibility (the "initial aim") in each and every moment. I understand these initial aims (preferred intentions) of God as being the *Logos* (word/reason) and *Sophia* (wisdom) of God that are available to all humans if we are open to them.

In this respect, God is the external standard and judge for all that we think and do. However, I'd say that God is less like a hyper-vigilant school hall monitor or an overly picky professional sports referee who is quick to boot players off the field. Instead, I'd say that God is more like a head coach (the Father) or a team's captain (in the person of Jesus). The main priority of a coach or a captain isn't to punish or whittle their team down to one or two "perfectly saintly" players—as if there are *any* of us who are perfect. Coaches and captains are primarily concerned about helping their team to be the best they can be, and to play to their highest potential and excel. Sure, some reprimanding and switching out of players may need to take place from time to time, but there is a marked difference between a judging referee and an inspiring and instructing coach or captain. Coaches and captains passionately live with, work with, and play with their team. They show up, lace up, and put all that they have into every game. They attempt to model what they're seeking to manifest from their team and they're biased in favor of their team. So it is with God.

In my view, God is all-powerful, but chooses to limit His agency by delegating a significant portion of power to His creation. God has structured things such that God will not, and perhaps cannot, recall this delegated power. Metaphorically speaking, God has chosen to restrain Himself and to tie one arm behind His back. The living material of creation effectively act as co-creators with God. This is especially true for human beings who have the greatest amount of free will and agency among God's creation. God is not all knowing in the sense that He knows all of what will happen in the future. Like a masterful chess or poker player,[91] God is all knowing of the past, of all present moments, events, patterns, tendencies, and possibilities. He knows which future

---

[91]   Perhaps even as one who counts the cards to give Him an even greater advantage. ;)

possibilities are most likely to come about or are most likely to be actualized at any given moment.

I consider God to be an extreme adventurer.[92] By limiting Herself, God is able to more richly enjoy Her creation as we are capable of freely following God's aims and intentions, and being in celebratory Communion with God and each other. However, God takes great risk in allowing us such freedom. We are just as able to choose not to seek this connection to Her. When creation doesn't follow God's aims and intentions, both God and creation suffer—often greatly. The analogy of a parent works well here. A good parent doesn't wish to be a dictatorial puppet-master. S/he is willing to let children be themselves, make mistakes, leave home, possibly return, and hopefully freely reflect back the love received from the parent.

As I said before, I currently visualize God as being like a giant amoeba-like womb. I realize that most people "see" God in human images. God can be understood as Creator, Leader, Friend, Lover, Companion, Partner, Parent, and so on. We humans need to perceive that God is with us and cares for us. An anthropomorphic metaphor (referring to a non-human entity as if it were human or human-like) is acceptable here—but not necessary for me. Anthropomorphism (especially a "Superman" image) can lead to the problematic notion that God acts as a coercive intervener when we're facing tough circumstances or crises. I don't think that God typically acts in this way. Moreover, that approach doesn't deal with the issue of *theodicy*—why bad things happen to good people—in a satisfying way (more in Chapter 9).

To use some theological jargon, I feel that God is best understood as personal, dialogic, and agential. Dialogic means that God speaks and we respond. There is an "I-Thou" relationship between us and the Divine.[93] While this position might focus upon human sin, guilt, and forgiveness, this doesn't mean that God is indifferent to the natural and social worlds. In fact, as the biblical prophets point out, God tells us to care for each other and our Earth! As I mentioned before, I experienced God talking to me one evening back in 1992.

---

[92]   Perhaps because I'm a Gen-Xer who is into "X-treme sports." I came up with this image for a paper on process theology I wrote in seminary in November, 1996—"God: The Adventure of a Lifetime."

[93]   A concept made famous by the Jewish philosopher Martin Buber.

However, aside from that profound experience, my communication with God is more whisper-like and felt within my gut. When I say that God is agential, I mean that She is an agent Whose intentions are realized in history. I merely note that God attempts to realize these intentions through a cooperative synergy with humanity—more about this in Chapter 5. Ultimately, I agree with the prophet Jeremiah and Jesus that to know God is to boldly help the poor and the needy (Jeremiah 22:15-16 & Matthew 25:31-40).[94]

Concerning the Trinity, I can see that God does indeed act in three distinct manners in the Bible and in our lives. I am open to these ways being described as "Father, Son, and Holy Spirit/Ghost" but I'm also comfortable with "Creator, Redeemer, Sustainer," "Mother, Child, Holy Spirit," "Creator, Created, and Nurturer," as well as other metaphors. I value the concept of the Trinity as the demonstration of God's very self as healthy, loving, and in an inter-connected relationship[95]—this is exactly what we're all called to know and experience with God and each other. I do not think that attempts to understand the Trinity in literal, metaphysical, or ontological manners is fruitful, helpful, or necessary. It's a mystery, and progressive Christianity is okay with that.

A word about The Holy Spirit

While it's probably fair to say that most charismatic,[96] "spirit-filled" churches lean toward conservative Christianity, not all of them do and I don't think that there's a significant

---

[94] This is also affirmed by Jesus' brother James, see: James 1:27.

[95] For terrific treatments of this notion of the inner-relationality of the Trinity, see *Faith Seeking Understanding: An Introduction to Christian Theology*, by Daniel L. Migliore and also a recent novel called *The Shack* by William Young.

[96] Like all Christian churches, charismatic churches trace their origins to the birth of Christianity as a distinct new religion upon the "Pentecost experience" of the early Church described in Acts Chapter 2. They emphasize the "gifts of the spirit" that they feel are essential to authentic Christianity; for example, speaking in tongues, interpreting tongues, being "slain in the spirit," faith healings, etc. The Pentecostalists and the Assembly of God are the most prominent. There are a growing number of Charismatic Catholics too.

difference in how conservative and progressive Christians view and understand the Holy Spirit.[97] Both types of Christians agree that the Holy Spirit is the "counselor, comforter, advocate, and helper" who Jesus promised God would send to comfort the early Church after Jesus' resurrection and ascension (John 14:16). This refers to the third person of the Trinity. For me, the Holy Spirit is God's vehicle or agent for offering wisdom, guidance, and grace to humanity. Part of God's grace for us is His nudging and wooing us towards certain choices and actions. This grace is, however, resistible and we need to freely choose to receive and accept it (Calvinists might differ from this point of view). Grace is a manifestation of God's inviting love for us. The Holy Spirit works as an aid for all of creation today and we may choose to seek Her guidance through intentionally being open to God's *Logos* (Word) and *Sophia* (Wisdom) in a wide variety of forms including the Bible, the sacraments, life experience, and through the actions of fellow believers—and even through nonbelievers.[98]

Instead of being a passive vending machine that dispenses grace to us in the elements of water, bread or wine; the Holy Spirit is more dynamic, wild, and free according to progressive Christians. She is untamable and unfettered. I view Her as an infinite pool of creativity, options, and potentials—perhaps a bit like a toolbox or a paint palette—but with a mind of Her own. We can "tap into" this

---

[97]   Though the Greek word for Spirit, *pneuma*, is gender netural, the Hebraic basis, *ruah*, is feminine and means, "air, wind, breath." Ruah is sometimes referred to as "the breath of God within us."

[98]   Clearly, God is at work through all sorts of people who don't claim to believe in Her. Examples that come to my mind include many singer-songwriters, artists, musicians, scientists, world leaders, and more. Some unbelieving singer-song-writers and poets are obvious vessels of light, truth, and love and I would say that they are tapping into the Holy Spirit as a Divine Muse and are receptive to Her nudgings, even though they aren't necessarily aware of it. It makes sense that they'd likely be even more effective and amazing at their craft and as vessels of light and love if they were to become intentional believers, but I'd say that some people who aren't believers clearly have a "God radar" that works very well indeed. For more on this, see *The Artist's Way: a Spiritual Path to Higher Creativity* by Julia Cameron.

resource as well when we are faced with challenging circumstances. For instance, in hostile conflicts, we can find healthy resolutions. Individuals and collective groups may seek the aid of this Spirit. For more than 2000 years, the Church has sought Her guidance. I feel that the Holy Spirit is active in the formation of progressive Christianity—even in this book.

Progressive Christianity differs from conservative Christianity in its tendency to embrace the Holy Spirit as a feminine aspect of God. Conservative Christians who read the Bible literally believe that the Holy Spirit wasn't actively present in the world until the day of Pentecost—50 days after Jesus' resurrection according to a literal reading of Acts 2:1. However, progressive Christians contend that the Holy Spirit has always been actively involved with all of creation, including the creation of creation, and it was actively present among humanity even before the time of Jesus. As God's active presence in the world, the Holy Spirit was no doubt involved in the choosing of when, where, and how to intervene in and engage the world through the person of Jesus. To the extent that God is "unchanging," it makes no sense to think that He somehow was once be a "binary/dyad," the Father and the Son, and only at a later point became a Trinity with the introduction and inclusion of the Holy Spirit. Likewise, if the Holy Spirit has in fact always been one of the three persons of the Trinity, then it makes little sense to think that the Holy Spirit would not also have been active and involved with creation from the beginning. Jesus was simply informing his disciples about how God would be tending to them and guiding them after he finally departed from their presence (John 14:16). Progressive Christians also point out that the Christian tradition has tragically largely forgotten about a key feminine aspect of God that once was part of our Judeo-Christian heritage—*Shekinah*. Like many Christians, I'm not as familiar with this concept so I will defer to the words of another to explain the concept (from what appears to be a Kabbalistic perspective.[99]):

---

[99] Kabbalah is an esoteric, mystical branch of Judaism akin to Sufism in Islam.

Break it Down VI

Shekinah: The Presence of Divinity

Shekinah—also spelled Shekhina, Shekhinah, Shekina, and Shechina—is known in the Qabalah, an ancient form of Jewish mysticism, as one of the emanations of God and the actual Presence of God. The belief was that one could not see God in Its fullness, but could see the emanation of God, Shekinah. When Moses asked to see God, it was Shekinah that he saw. Shekinah is also the consort, or Bride, of God. As such, she is Mother to us all, just as God is our Father.

In earlier times, God was seen as either dwelling in the clouds or in high places like mountains or very high hills. With the construction of the Ark of the Covenant, and then the construction of the Temple, a part of the Godhead came to dwell in the Ark and then in the Temple. This could not be the male God, the God of the Sky and of High Places. So Shekinah, formerly known as Asherah, a Goddess of Earth and Sea, came to dwell in the Ark of the Covenant and then in the Temple.

Originally it was Asherah who dwelled in the Temple as the Bride of God, His representative there. But after the "reforms" of King Josiah, Asherah worship was forbidden in the Temple. Still, the Jews knew that their Lady was still living there as their Queen and the representative of *El [as in El Shaddai (God is Great) or Elohim "God the mighty one," El is the ancient Cannanite word for God appropriated by the Hebrews]* their God. So Asherah evolved. She began to be seen as the presence of God, and less as a separate entity. She became Shekinah, which means something like She who dwells (from the Hebrew shakhan, which means the act of dwelling). However, Asherah did not really change. She was always the representative of Her Husband, just as He was always her representative. She, an Earth Goddess, was also Queen of Heaven. He, as Sky God, was also Ruler of Earth. This occurred only through their marriage. So, it was not really that Asherah worship ever changed much within Judaism, or that Asherah Herself changed; only, it was made to look like it had changed to fool the patriarchal priests.

Unfortunately, Shekinah has been all but lost to Christianity. Elements of Her remain in Mother Mary, who was perhaps Shekinah's incarnation. Mary Theotokos *["Mother of God"]*, as She is called, actually held the presence of God *([Jesus] Yeshua)* within Her. She is known as the Queen of Heaven, but she is the representative of God to us and delivers our prayers to Him, according to Catholic tradition. Her apparitions are much more frequent than the apparitions of Yeshua, and the Father never appears. It seems that She is truly His representative to us, because (as we know) She is His Bride.

The union of Shekinah and El was never more evident than in the Sabbath. She is known as the Sabbath Bride, or the Sabbath Queen. Each week on the Sabbath, God and Goddess, El and Shekinah, act out the Song of Songs. One rabbi called that holy book the "Holy of Holies" of the Bible![100]

. . . Aside from my remarks in [brackets] above, I simply remind us that the Bible refers to God with female imagery in other places as well, including: as a protective mother bird (Deuteronomy 32:7-12 & 18) and as a mother bear (Hosea 13:8).

Progressive Christians, especially mystically and contemplatively oriented ones, are often inclined to embrace and emphasize God's Wisdom (*Hokmah* in Hebrew, *Sophia* in Greek) as a particularly feminine aspect of the Divine. In the book of Proverbs, for instance, God's Wisdom is personified as Sophia. This feminine word is not merely the Greek word for wisdom. As a woman's name, Sophia expresses this personification better than the more neutral and abstract sounding "Wisdom." Some people suggest that Sophia is the female aspect of God. This might be implied in the creation story of Genesis in which God says, "Let *us* make humankind in *our* image . . . So God created humankind in his own image, in the image of God he created them, *male and female* he created them." (Genesis 1:26-27 NRSV, emphasis mine). Such Christians are often inclined to suggest that it is this early biblical feminine aspect of God that was later suppressed as the Church became influenced, and co-opted, by the patriarchal Roman culture.

There cannot be a "last word" about God, but in order to close this chapter, l want to lift up something about God that I celebrate. God specializes in transformation and renewal. As some of the folksy sayings put it, God has an amazing knack for "turning lemons into lemonade" and "making a way when it seems like

---

[100]   See: http://www.northernway.org/shekinah.html, Esoteric Interfaith Church, Inc. Bishop Katia Romanoff, Esoteric Interfaith Theological Seminary (used with permission).

there's no way." Whenever and wherever people are oppressed, exploited, wronged, rejected, or stuck in seemingly impossible jams, God puts His "nudging and wooing" powers of influence into overdrive in order to sway things toward release, freedom, liberation, safety, peace, justice, forgiveness, and reconciliation. There are many examples of this including, the nonviolent Civil Rights Movement in the U.S.; the fall of the Berlin Wall; the peaceful, non-retaliatory end of Apartheid in South Africa; and the efforts to foster reconciliation in Rwanda after the genocide.

Whenever people forgive and reconcile with those who've wronged them; when would-be offenders are swayed not to harm someone; when prisoners feel free even though they're behind bars; when people rally to help a struggling widow or single parent; when people break free from addictions; when people release their shame, worries, and grudges and begin to sleep well through the night; when people recover from a broken heart or any sort of trauma and move forward in life with renewed hope; and when a way opens up when it looked like there was no way—people have seen God.[101]

---

[101] A powerful example of this is what happened in Atlanta, GA on March 12, 2005. A man on a murderous rampage was converted by a woman who read *The Purpose Driven Life* to him when he broke into her apartment. That book, by evangelical pastor, Rick Warren, doesn't embrace progressive Christianity, but it is written in an accessible and relatable manner and it has been quite popular among conservative Christian Baby Boomers. See: "Hostage Reads 'Purpose-Driven Life' to alleged Atlanta Killer," Erin Curry, BP News, *Christian Examiner*, April 2005, http://www.christianexaminer. com/Articles/Articles%20Apr05/Art_Apr05_15.html

Chapter 4

Jesus
Wanted: Dead or Alive

*Christianity is purportedly about Jesus of Nazareth, but
unfortunately, it more usually reflects the values of the people
who killed him.* John Petty

*Dear little baby Jesus, who's sittin' in his crib watchin' the
Baby Einstein videos, learnin' 'bout shapes and colors . . .*
Ricky Bobby in *Talladega Nights*

Who do you say that I am? Jesus, Matthew 16:15

My earliest recollection of learning about Jesus was when I was a small child. This was probably through a combination of hearing Christmas carols and seeing the porcelain figure of the little baby Jesus that my mother would lay in the manger in the nativity crèche scene beneath the family Christmas tree. Jesus was a cute babe in a manger and he was many times smaller than I was. Jesus was nice, quiet, calm, innocent, still, and domesticated like the cows and the sheep in that manger scene—Jesus was *safe*.

Then as I grew, I started to notice the pictures in my children's Bible and it became clear that Jesus didn't remain a tender babe in swaddling cloths. Most of the pictures were of a grown man with a full beard and a determined look on his face. Jesus was always on the go, purposefully walking on land, walking on water, riding on boats, riding donkeys, calming storms, healing people, teaching people, preaching about the Kingdom of God, inviting himself to dinner in people's homes, blessing children, arguing with angry

religious leaders, knocking over tables, and then getting whipped
and nailed to a cross. It was apparent that Jesus was a serious man
on a mission. He was a man of action. I didn't understand why he
was driven, why he looked so loving and also so serious, why some
people didn't like him healing the sick, why religious leaders
argued with him, or why those Romans killed him. I wanted to
know why.

Two Stories:

The answers to those questions were readily available in
popular American Christianity. According to this widely held
conservative, traditional perspective, the reason for all of these
questions and concerns I had about Jesus can be found in the
following description:

About 6,000 years ago, from his home in up in heaven, God
created the world and it was good. Then, just a few days later,
the first humans, Adam and Eve, screwed everything up (but
mostly Eve) when they ate from the forbidden fruit in that idyllic
garden. Ever since then, people have been wretched sinners who
do horrible things. God created a special race of people called
the Jews. The Jews worshipped Him—but they didn't really
understand Him and they constantly messed up their covenantal
relationship. About 2,000 years ago, things became so bad that,
according to His Divine plan, God provided a way to help people
escape the consequences of their actions. That way was by Him
coming down to earth in the form of Jesus. This Jesus was born
of an actual virgin, who was possibly immaculately conceived
herself[102]—and hence, he was untainted by "the genetic birth
defect" of human sinfulness.[103]

---

[102]   This is a Roman Catholic dogma.

[103]   Some conservatives provide very specific logic and reasoning
concerning the circumstances of Jesus' birth. Oftentimes, it may be
worded something along these lines: *In Bible times, it was common (and
expected) that a girl was a virgin before she got married. Mary was most
certainly a virgin. The first reason was for genealogical purposes. The second
reason was that the Messiah had to be born of a virgin, since man's seed is
the genetic carrier of sin and defects. Jesus couldn't have genes from Adam*

Jesus grew up, was baptized by His prophetic cousin John, went out to the wilderness to be tempted by the devil, resisted the temptations, and gathered a band of disciples and followers and taught them about God and God's Kingdom. However, His true and primary purpose was to die for people's sins, so God (according to God's plan) had Him killed through the means of the human rulers. He was nailed to a cross, His blood was shed, and He died—thus saving all of us who believe in this version of the story. To sweeten things for Jesus' grieving followers, and to help people know that provision of salvation is what took place, God resurrected Jesus from the dead to show us that death (the "wages of sin") and Satan had been defeated and that God's power is greater than human sin. We therefore have hope for whatever we may face in life. We know our sins have been forgiven by what Jesus did. He died for us as a proxy or substitute for us so the rest of us wouldn't have to get what we deserve—being killed. A "just God" requires retributive justice and punishment. If Jesus hadn't been killed, *we* would have been (or we'd all go to hell after we die of natural causes and/or after the Second Coming of Jesus).

Now this traditional and popular version of Christianity has indeed given meaning, life, hope, motivation, inspiration, and encouragement to millions of people over the years. Part of

---

otherwise Satan would be his relative and Jesus couldn't defeat him. The Bible said clearly that the Messiah must be born as seed of woman, not of man. This logic leads to a curious glitch regarding Jesus' messiahship. Hebraic prophecies indicated that the messiah would be of the lineage of King David. Joseph was supposedly a descendent of David, but, according to tradition, Joseph wasn't the biological father of Jesus, so a fudge-factor was introduced—Joseph "adopting" Jesus. One wonders what people who assert this sort of logic make of the possibility of Jesus being born via parthenogenesis (the phenomenon in nature where females who haven't been fertilized by males spontaneously conceive). What do such persons make of mitochondrial manipulation or cloning? Do they really think that a human child born of such means would be any different than the rest of us? That s/he wouldn't sin? Really? Literalism doesn't hold up to such scrutiny. This may be partly why conservative Christians tend to oppose cloning—to avoid having to face the limits of their theological premises. I'm opposed to it too, but for different reasons.

the selling point for this story is that it supposedly fulfills the prophesies about the Messiah that are found in the Hebrew Scriptures—referred to by many Christians as the "Old Testament." The author of the book of Matthew appears to have had these prophesies in mind. A major part of the author's agenda, it seems, was to help persuade fellow Jews that Jesus meets the criteria for being the Messiah by finding passages from the Hebrew Scriptures, and "proof-texting"[104] and spinning things so that it would be as obvious as possible that Jesus is the Messiah. Perhaps the reason this effort was so intentional was because Jesus didn't exactly meet the most commonly held expectations about the Messiah—that he would be a powerful military leader who would overthrow the worldly powers that be, kick the oppressive Roman "heathens" out of Israel, and reestablish a powerful and independent Kingdom of Israel.

However, that form of "apologetics" (defending the faith and explaining it to others) no longer works well in this new day and age. The last great death-throe for this using-scripture-and-legal-reasoning-to-prove-that-Jesus-is-the-Savior approach was Lee Stroble's book, *The Case for Christ*[105] (1998)—and it has sold many

---

[104]   Proof-texting refers to selecting various passages of scripture out of their original context and using them to "prove" some theological assertion (liberal and conservative Christians are both guilty of this). An obviously liberal-like interpretive approach was employed by the early Christians (though conservative Christians may deny this). The early Hebraic prophesies about how the messiah would die indicate that he would be hung from a tree, not nailed to a cross (Deuteronomy 21:23, see also Joshua 8:29; 10:26 & 10:27). Since crosses are made out of wood, and since being nailed to one is a bit *like* being hung from a tree, well, you do the math. Executions by nailing people to crosses was an invention of the Roman Empire. It was a punishment that was reserved for persons found guilty of political subversion, rebellion, or terrorism. The Roman Empire wasn't in existence when Isaiah was written so the notion of being nailed to a cross wouldn't have been on that author's mind.

[105]   Though Strobel contends that he had been an atheist until he did some "research" on Christ, his research was from a legalistic perspective and it is not a small coincidence that Strobel has a law degree. Efforts to try to "prove" a "case" for religious belief by

copies (as well as a few newer variations on that original text). However, I'd hazard a guess that most people who have purchased that book already believed that popular, traditional interpretation of Jesus, and if they gave a copy of it to someone who isn't a Christian, it likely went unread.[106] The problem is that the times have changed. The era of modernity has ended and we've moved into the postmodern era.[107]

Break it Down VII

The over-arching worldview and paradigm of modernity (around 1890-1960—though it maintained dominance in the Church until the 1990's) was hyper-rational and this affected all areas of our culture, including Christianity. A theological movement known as liberalism emerged which sought to understand Jesus and the miracles he performed by utilizing science to help pursue and discern the "historical Jesus" (as opposed to the post-resurrection "Jesus of faith"). Liberalism sought to explain the miracles Jesus is said to have performed using scientific explanations in order to help those fanciful tales correspond better with "more rational" modern sensibilities.[108] Stated more succinctly, modernism held that truth can be known objectively and science is valued as a means for pursuing it. Modern era Christianity believes the creeds more concretely and embraces science to the extent it helps confirm biblical accounts, etc. (In contrast, postmodernism "deconstructs" modernity and holds that truth is subjective and so is science, religion, ethics, and well, everything).

In response to the modernist liberal movement emerged another movement, fundamentalism. Fundamentalist Christians felt that science

---

appeals to legalistic rhetoric (especially to one-sided rhetoric as he failed to interview people with dissenting opinions) fall flat in our postmodern era. Just because that book has sold like hot-cakes, doesn't mean that many people are coming to Christ because of it.

[106] Based upon the number of obviously unread copies of that book that I've seen at garage sales and thrift stores.

[107] To be sure, that book (and ones like it) is still selling, but this is because we are living the transition between two worldviews—with older generations being more steeped in modernity and a higher percentage of younger individuals identifying with a postmodern perspective.

[108] For example, http://news.blogs.cnn.com/2010/09/21/where-did-waters-part-for-moses-not-where-you-think/?hpt=C2

was over-rated, probably "of the Devil," and that appealing to it was watering down the faith. They were particularly alarmed about seeing other Christians embracing Darwin's theory of the evolution of the species. They felt it directly went against the truth of "what the Bible says." These fundamentalist Christians introduced something new to the faith—reading the Bible literally.

Fundamentalists shared the liberal's hyper-rational modernist mindset, but they used this "rationality" to reject the insights of modern science, new scholarship, and knowledge. They created an approach to Christianity that read the Bible literally, and sought to discern and operate out of the "logic" of the Bible (especially when it comes to predicting Jesus 2nd coming and the apocalypse). Though fundamentalism was a backlash to modernity, fundamentalists also ironically embraced it as well. They employed the modern era's invention of history, science and "historical and scientific facts"[109] in their efforts to "prove" how most everything that's in the Bible actually happened just as it's written—"The Bible says it, I believe it, that settles it." The early Jews and Christians didn't do this as they were

---

[109] The word [*history*] entered the English language in 1390 with the meaning of "relation of incidents, story." In Middle English, the meaning was "story" in general. The restriction to the meaning "record of past events" arises in the late 15th century. In German, French, and most Germanic and Romance languages, the same word is still used to mean both "history" and "story". The adjective *historical* is attested from 1661, and *historic* from 1669. *Historian* in the sense of a "researcher of history" is attested from 1531. In all European languages, the substantive "history" is still used to mean both "what happened with men," and "the scholarly study of the happened," the latter sense sometimes distinguished with a capital letter, "History," or the word *historiography*. W.D. Whitney, *The Century Dictionary: an encyclopedic lexicon of the English language*, The Century Co., 1889. However, it should be said that the concept of history (and the self awareness of the history of history) didn't really bloom until the Enlightenment era (late 1700s). As I understand it, the term *science*, and *scientific fact/truth* can only be said to go back as far as 1021 A.D.—due to Alhazen's use of an obvious scientific method in his optical experiments reported in his *Book of Optics*. Alhazen was a Muslim who lived in what we now call Iraq. The scientific method of the Modern era can be said to have arrived in 1637 when René Descartes' outlined its exact method in his *Discourse on Method*.

largely an oral culture and they were able to discern nuances, metaphors, hyperbole, exaggerations, humor, and the larger Truth of a story without getting caught up in the "factual/historically true" specifics of the details. Ironically, theological liberalism and fundamentalism are two sides of the same modernist coin.

Trying to use a modern era, historical, scientific, legalistic, "proof-texting" approach in this postmodern culture falls flat, as the basic premises for those approaches are no longer held by the masses.[110] The liberal modernist approach to "evangelism" (getting others to become Christians) is basically an effort to invite people to join the Church in spite of all of those far-fetched miracle stories. It takes one of those inconvenient stories as the Hebrews crossing the Red Sea and posits a scientifically based explanation such as "quick-acting drought" or "an intense bout of sheer line winds" took place, parting the waters to allow them to flee from the Egyptians. This is an unbecoming, overly apologetic (pun intended) approach that smacks of a used-car salesman trying to persuade you to buy an old "grandfather's car" despite its obvious flaws.[111] Likewise, the modernist approach of conservative Christian evangelism and apologetics wrongly assumes that people grant authority to the Bible and that if they do read it, they do

---

[110] To remind us, the notions of history, historical fact, and science and scientific proof and facts are inventions of the late middle ages and the early modern era of humanity; i.e., those concepts weren't around in Biblical days or in the life of the early Church. The earliest Christians weren't concerned with determining if Jesus really ever existed, or which, if any, of the words attributed to him in the Gospels were actually said by him, or if he actually was born to a virgin, or if he actually performed all of the miracles attributed to him. The pre-modern mindset heard Truth beyond the truth of any of the details. They *saw* the forest for the trees (as opposed to "missing the forest for the trees").

[111] A progressive treatment of those miracle stories is that they are just that—stories. Godly Truth is in them for us to be inspired and challenged whether or not they actually occurred.

so in a literal manner. This conservative modernist approach also wrongly assumes that the "substitutionary atonement" model of the atoning work of Jesus is the only valid, right, and true one—it isn't (more on this in Chapter 6).

Another problem with the modernist approach of conservative Christianity is that it operates out of a narrow, *transactional* understanding of the faith—"If people believe x, y and z now, then they'll be right with God, be saved, and get into heaven." Increasingly, today's generations of seekers gravitate less to approaches to faith that hinge upon agreeing with certain dogmas and truth claims. Young adults today tend not to be compelled or persuaded by approaches that seek to provide allegedly scientific or historically verifiable "evidence" about Jesus or the content of the Bible. This is true whether these "facts" are provided by liberals or conservatives. Both approaches operate from an out-dated modernist mindset. Liberals do this with their quest for the "historical Jesus" (trying to make sense of Jesus and his miracles by appeals to science). Conservatives do this when trying to prove that Jesus really is the messiah by appealing to cherry-picked, literally interpreted, passages of the Bible as the primary source of historical authority. For example, the assertions that "Jesus fulfilled these prophesies," "these archeological digs prove that such and such town really existed and it has the remains of an ancient pool so this shows that Jesus could've really performed that healing by the pool," or "Jesus is either who he said he is, or he's a madman or a liar."[112]

---

[112]   Of course they base this largely upon the words attributed to Jesus in the Gospel of John. Many scholars have concurred that John was the last gospel to be written (after 70AD and perhaps 90AD); the least historically accurate; and that there's no way any of Jesus' original disciples wrote it. They point out that its style, vocabulary, and agenda clearly show that it was written for a different audience; i.e., as a devotional text instead of an historical account. Most conservatives don't realize that even before Jesus was born, the Roman Caesars had been referring to themselves as "God, Son of God, Lord, Prince of Peace," etc. They don't like to admit that Jesus never overtly said, "I am God." They forget that the very first Christian creed—"Jesus is Lord"—was as much a political claim as a theological one for it carried with it the obvious implication, "... and Caesar isn't!" They

Postmodern young adults who are into Jesus accept that he really existed and recognize that his teachings were genuinely radical and full of truth. I've seen this first hand in my work with college students at a large university. They recognize that Jesus was especially authentic and real and relatable. Whether, and how, he performed miracles isn't really an issue for them, as they resonate more with a "narrative theology" where they hear the story of Jesus, sense its truth and feel it piercing and inspiring their lives. That is what matters. Postmodernists who accept Jesus as their savior do so with an intentional choice to align themselves with Jesus and his countercultural ways—not so much because they believe x, y, and z (doctrine and beliefs) about Jesus. They do it because they love what he stood for. They do it because they see their own story reflected in his life and in the rough-and-tumble, doubt-laden, lives of his first followers.

As I suggested before, there are two basic stories about Jesus—a conservative one and a progressive one. In order to speak to their differences, allow me to restate the conservative story again, worded a bit differently:

The Conservative view:

Jesus is Lord, God, the Son of God, the Prince of Peace, the King of Kings, God with us, the second person of the Trinity. As God the Son, Jesus has always existed and wasn't created. He is fully God and fully Man (the two natures joined in union—not mixed). As the second person of the Trinity, Jesus is co-equal[113] with God the Father and the Holy Spirit. In becoming human, God, as Jesus, was begotten through the Holy Spirit and born of the Virgin Mary (Joseph wasn't involved except that it was helpful for him to adopt Jesus as that connected Jesus to the line of King David). Jesus is the only way to God, salvation and eternal life.

---

don't like to acknowledge that Jesus' most prevalent way of referring to himself was as "the son of Man"—not as "the son of God." Think about it. How often do you hear conservative Christians referring to Jesus as the Son of Man? Not very.

[113] The Council of Nicea (325 A.D.) declared that Jesus is "co-equal" with God,

Jesus died on a cross according to God's plan as a perfect sacrifice and payment for our sins. His spilt blood provided for our salvation by washing away our sins. Jesus rose from the dead on the third day, and is now spiritually and physically immortal. For the next 40 days, more than 500 witnesses saw Him. His wounds were visible and He ate meals of fish and bread. He then physically ascended to heaven. Jesus will come again visibly and physically at the end of the world to judge us and forcibly establish God's Kingdom. Jesus is the Jewish Messiah promised to Israel in the Old Testament and is the savior of the world.

A Progressive view of Jesus:

Progressive Christianity is aware that most of the conservative Christian historical fact. Progressive Christians are mindful that neither the letters of the apostle Paul nor the Gospel of Mark (the first Gospel to have been written) mention anything about a virgin birth or a literal, physical resurrection. We're aware that the writers of the gospels wrote in a Hellenistic and Middle Eastern milieu. We realize that part of their agenda was to sway people of those societies to come to believe in Jesus as their savior. And we recognize that they intentionally appropriated various "god-man myths" from those pagan sources in this effort. Examples of this include: Jesus being "god incarnate"; born of a virgin,[114] in a cave or a stable; the son of a god; a savior; his followers being born again through baptism; his turning water into wine at a marriage ceremony; walking on water; dying as a sacrifice for sins; descending to the place of departed spirits and rising to heaven on the third day; his followers awaiting his return in glory to be the judge of mankind at the last days; and his followers celebrating his memory through a ritual meal of bread and wine representing his body."[115]

---

[114] And in time, well after the Gospels were written, the assigning of the date of Jesus' birth to December 25 was an intentionally political move as several of the ancient gods and demi-gods were said to have been born around that time of the Winter Equinox. The hope was to Christianize those holidays of their pagan rivals. It worked.

[115] For instance, many of those things were attributed to Mitrhas, the son of Zoroaster, Horas, Osiris, Asclepius, Empedocles, Attis,

Progressive Christianity asserts that Jesus was a radically loving and profoundly wise Jewish prophet, teacher, healer, and mystic who had a profoundly intimate relationship with God such that he and God shared the same mind, character, values, emotions, passions, and priorities. God and Jesus were so tight and simpatico that they were effectively "one and the same." That is what is meant is when the Gospel of John has Jesus saying, "the father and I are one" (John 10:30) and "anyone who has seen me has seen the father" (John 14:7-10). It's like a lieutenant saying to his troops, "I represent the General and whatever I say is as if it were coming from the General," or a Hollywood-style mob boss conveying that he represents the Godfather by saying, "You've seen *him*, you've seen *me*"—while holding his hand up in the air with the pointer finger and middle-finger held tightly together. "We're like *this!*" It's like the expression, *Mi casa, es su casa*, in which my house isn't literally, legally, or actually your house—but for all practical purposes, please make yourself at home. *Capiche?*

This metaphorical understanding may be interpreted by some folks that progressive Christians deny the traditional Christian view that Jesus was God.[116] While many progressive Christians

---

Orpheus, Dionysus. Several of those attributions were even asserted by the Roman cult of the emperor starting with Caesar Augustus. For more about this, see: *The Mysteries of Mithras: The Pagan Belief That Shaped the Christian World*, Payam Nabarz. See also: http://www. religioustolerance.org/symes02.htm; http://www.religioustolerance. org/chr_jcpa3.htm, http://www.religioustolerance.org/chr_jcpa6. htm & http://www.religioustolerance.org/chr_jcpa.htm; Martin Luther King's observations about this, http://mlkkpp01.stanford. edu/index.php/kingpapers/article/volume_i_13_september_to_23_ november_19491/ ; www.amazon.com/God-Empire-Jesus-Against-Rome/dp/0060843233 ; and John Dominic Crossan's book, *God and Empire: Jesus Against Rome* which shows how the first Caesars called themselves God, Son of God, Prince of Peace, Lord, Savior, etc. It should be said that the ancient Hebrews had already assimilated many of these pagan god-man myths into their prophesies about a coming savior.

[116] "Most Christians believe that Jesus was God. Of course, many Christians do not believe this. The Palestinian Jewish Christians who followed the brothers of Jesus, first James and then Jude

have a "low Christology" and may even leave open the question of Jesus' divinity, they resonate with the idea that God was somehow uniquely and especially present in the person of Jesus. Jesus himself appears not to have viewed himself as God. He never overtly stated that he was God. When someone called him "good teacher," Jesus replied, "only God is good" (Luke 18:19). When teaching about the end of the earth, Jesus said, "No one knows about that day or hour, not even the angels in heaven, nor the Son, but only the Father" (Matthew 24:36). Jesus told Mary Magdalene "I am ascending to my Father and your Father, to my God and your God" (John 20:17). Jesus prayed to God—not to himself (for example, Mark 14:35-36). Paul, or whoever it was who wrote Timothy,[117] apparently didn't think Jesus was God. He wrote, "For there is one God, and there is one mediator between God and men, the man Christ Jesus" (1 Timothy 2:5).

Progressive Christians typically refer to Jesus as Lord, Savior, and Christ, and believe that he was effectively God on earth. We say that Jesus was a person of God whose "God-radar" was especially, accurate, sensitive, and tuned. He lived his life more in sync with God's will than anyone else. We say things like "God uniquely breathed His/Her love into Jesus and permeated his being" and, metaphorically, that "Jesus is all of God that could fit into human form." Jesus prophetically taught, modeled, and invited us to live life abundantly in deep, communal, and mutually

---

[Judas], never accepted Paul and his teachings, but formed their own church called the Ebionite Church. They did not believe in the divinity or virgin birth of Jesus. Other Christians who didn't believe that Jesus was God include, the Arians, Nestorians, Copts, Christadelphians, Jehovah's Witnesses, Unitarians, Universalists, Iglesia ni Cristo, most Friends [Quakers], many Methodists, and many members of the United Church of Christ. Many individual Christians have taken this position as well, such as Martin Luther King, Jr. (Baptist), Albert Schweitzer (Lutheran) and Bishop Pike (Episcopalian)." From, *The Divinity of Jesus* by Mike Nassau, http://www.geocities.com/bicolagnostics/divinityjesus.htm

[117] A consensus of many Biblical scholars contend that Paul didn't write all of the letters/epistles in the Bible that are attributed to him. They believe that Paul didn't write what are known as the "Pastoral Epistles"; i.e., I & II Timothy, and Titus.

sacrificial relation to God and each other instead of being in bondage to the ways of the world/empire. Christians are called to follow and imitate these abundantly life-giving, "Kingdom" ways of Christ. We're to claim *Jesus* (and The Way of Jesus) as Lord of our lives instead of worldly, imperialistic forces and powers, and invite others to do the same. Jesus calls us to live fully and abundantly in God's Kingdom instead of merely surviving a bleak and depressing existence under the oppressive ways of the world and empire—including patriarchy, racism, materialism, militarism, and hetero-sexism.

In 6-4 B.C.,[118] Yeshua[119] of Nazareth was born into a humble peasant family, in a tiny town, in the backwater hinterlands of Palestine territory on the eastern edge of the Roman Empire. It doesn't really matter if Jesus was born to an actual virgin or not—or even if he was born in Bethlehem for that matter. The point is moot. Either way, he grew up to be our savior. In fact, if Jesus wasn't born to a virgin, being born as a bastard[120] to an unmarried teenaged peasant from the sticks on the far eastern fringes of the Roman Empire would have only *further* highlighted God's amazing and empowering ways.

---

[118] One might wonder why I didn't say that Jesus was born in 1 A.D. The reason for this is that it is known that a monk employed by Pope Gregory made a mistake. When the Western world switched from the Julian calendar to the Gregorian one that we now use, the dating for when Jesus was thought to have been born was inadvertently altered by 4-6 years. That monk, Dionysius Exiguus (the inventor of Annos Domini—"A.D."), forgot to factor in that Jesus was born under the reign of King Herod and Herod is known to have died in 4.B.C. So, in reality, you need to add 4-6 years to whatever year it happens to be when you read this book; i.e., if you read this book in 2011, it's actually 2015-2017 A.D./C.E.!

[119] *Yeshua* (Jesus is the Latinized transliteration of that Hebrew word) was a common name in Israel at the time Jesus lived. Because so many of his contemporaries shared that name, it made it very down to earth and relatable. Yeshua literally means: "God is a shout for help." So, when people say, "God help me!"—they're actually saying "Jesus!"

[120] A human-made concept and label which societies look down upon and view as "illegitimate."

Jesus demonstrated a truly faithful and liberating way of life which included loving and giving to others, nonviolent direct action, and rejection of oppressive powers. Jesus introduced what has become known as the "Way of the Cross." It is the way of living that rejects the status quo and the dominion of worldly powers. It may lead to getting executed but it's so much better than living a dominated, timid, conventional life under the authority of the worldly powers that be! By living such a life, Jesus proved that it is possible for *others* to live this way through relationship with God and with God's help. I refer to this as the "*Via con Dios*"[121] (the way with God). Jesus is indeed the Messiah promised in Scriptures but he's not the violent, large and in charge, ass-kicking "Rambo/ Braveheart/Neo (from *The Matrix*), knight in shining armor" type that many expected.

Progressive Christians believe that it's not the specific means of Jesus' death that matters. He could have been hung from a tree, nailed to a tree, nailed to a cross, stoned, hung, shot by a firing squad, or strapped to a gurney to receive a lethal injection. It's not the specific means of his death that matters. What matters is that he led a life that challenged and subverted the dominant worldly powers that be—the ones competing with God. They executed him by whatever means they chose, and God redeemed that hateful, humiliating tragedy by resurrecting Jesus to show us that nothing can separate us from God's love, not even that.

Progressive Christians believe that the notion that Jesus' death had to occur by him being nailed to a cross in order to fulfill scriptural prophesy arose when the early Jewish Christians tried to convince their fellow Jews that Jesus was the messiah by finding any passages from the Hebrew scriptures which could in any way be linked to Jesus—including his death. They were proof-texting.[122]

---

[121] A mix of Latin and Spanish, not to be confused with the Spanish "Vaya con Dios" which means "go with God." *Via* is Latin for 'way'.

[122] The Roman Empire was not in existence when Isaiah was written so the notion of being nailed to a cross would not have been on the author's radar. See footnote 98 for more about proof-texting and its relation to Jesus' cross.

Progressive Christians aren't particularly swayed by the efforts of the early Jewish Christians to try to link Jesus to ancient Jewish texts, which might have bearing on Jesus' messiahship. We accept Jesus as Lord, Savior, Christ, and Messiah more as a matter of faith, not due to a need for scriptural evidence that he met certain ancient Hebraic notions about the messiah. Instead, we find ourselves compelled by evidence of the belief that Jesus is Lord and "Caesar"[123] isn't. We put our trust and reliance upon God through our effort to follow the radically bold yet vulnerable way of Jesus.[124]

We grant Jesus that sense of authority in our lives not because we're told to accept or "believe in" certain dogmas or doctrines nor because we're persuaded by supposed scriptural "evidence" that Jesus is the Messiah. We bestow that sense of authority and messiah-ship to God through Jesus because *we experience* God working effectively in the world through the way and teachings of Jesus and through people who claim to follow Him, the "living body of Christ."

Conservative Christianity overly emphasizes Jesus' death to the point where one would think that his radical teachings in the Sermon on the Mount and his political confrontations with the worldly powers don't matter, and what matters is that he was killed in order to save us. By that logic, Jesus' three years of ministry was wasted time. He may as well have been killed by Herod as an infant or actually pushed off that cliff in Nazareth when he started his ministry as that would've been far more efficient.[125] Conservative Christianity emphasizes Jesus' death to such a high degree that one might wonder if His life and resurrection matter—especially his life. The vast majority of the songs played on Christian radio

---

[123] *Caesar*, is a title much like "king" that was bestowed upon the Roman emperors. Christians have long used that word as a metaphor for any worldly system or power, especially oppressive ones.

[124] In other words, we grant Jesus the role and status of Savior, Christ, Lord, and Messiah to the extent that we come to trust and find life-giving transformation, peace, and life-enhancing robustness and wholeness in our lives because of putting our trust and reliance upon God through the way of Jesus.

[125] See: Matthew 2:16 & Luke 4:29

stations and those sung in most evangelical and fundamentalist churches confirm this. Here's how one influential conservative Christian put it, *"Christ was born to die. He wasn't born to teach, heal or show the way: He is the Way. And He was born to die—not pointlessly, but purposefully, so that we could live."*[126]

One Progressive Christian's thoughts about Jesus:

Instead of speaking in vague generalities, it may be helpful for readers to see how a particular someone who identifies as a progressive Christian describes their personal understanding of Jesus. I'll now share my personal views and understandings of Jesus. After seeing God's people continually go astray,[127] God revealed Herself to humanity through the life of a real living human, *Immanuel*.[128] God did this to call us into right relationship with our God, our planet, each other, and ourselves. I believe that Jesus of Nazareth, the Jewish son of a young peasant girl and a common laborer, was and is the Messiah, Christ and Lord. I believe Jesus was the anointed agent of liberation and salvation for humanity, for whom the hopeful and expectant Israelites were waiting. I believe he was an inconvenient, unexpected and surprising sort of Savior.

I think God's grace[129] however, was available before the life of Jesus. Numerous people received God's grace in their lives before Jesus lived and died. His death simply heightened our awareness to the incredible depths and magnitude of God's grace and love.

I agree with the orthodox Christian doctrine that Jesus was both fully God/Divine and fully human. Yet, I also agree with the Protestant Reformers that we should focus our attention to the benefits of faith in Christ, and minimize technical deliberations concerning the "two natures." The important thing isn't a correct theory[130] concerning

---

[126] Waitsel Smith, "The Passion of the Christ," http://www.christianmovies.biz/Passion_Review.html

[127] . . . worship false gods, submit themselves to oppressive worldly powers, and lead empty, broken, and disconnected lives—the price one pays as an "adventuring risk-taker" or a "loving parent!"

[128] *Immanuel* means "God with us." See: Matthew 1:22-23

[129] Grace is the freely given means of inviting us to connect to God.

[130] Metaphysical or ontological

Christ's nature, but the conviction that through Jesus, God was revealed as gracious, loving, merciful, liberating, reconciling, and redemptive. Even though God chose to reveal Herself through Jesus, Christ still had free will and the ability to refuse and reject God's guidance and leadings in his life. For example, Jesus resisted various temptations in Luke 4:1-13, and he chose to go ahead and allow himself to be arrested and face a grim fate in the garden of Olives in Luke 22:39-46. For some wonderful reason, Jesus didn't refuse God's leadings. He allowed himself to be a channel and vehicle of God's love in a way more fully than anyone else ever has. When I say that Jesus is Divine, I don't mean that his DNA or his birth was any different than other people's. I use that term in an honorary, worshipful and devotional way to celebrate his close connection with God. Technically, it might be considered idolatry but given that God wanted to work through Jesus, it seems to me that God isn't offended in any way by my worshipping Her through Jesus—or even *as* Jesus. In fact, I think God is delighted about it. However, I don't pray to Jesus. I pray to the God Who Jesus prayed to.[131]

Through the Gospels, we remember the events of Jesus' life, death and resurrection. This allows us to feel connected to him and his mission. He lived a real human life. He suffered in many ways, and the rest of us can relate to this. Jesus also rejoiced and wined and dined (for example, Luke 7:34 & John 2:1-11). We know times of joy and celebration as well. Jesus led a bold and holy life that was unusually sin-free and faithful. Jesus exemplifies the possibility for humans, with God's help, to be able to connect with God in such a way that we may rise each day knowing that we are unconditionally loved, forgiven, and accepted by our Creator. With God's help, and following Jesus' example, we can move forward in life with joyful and hope-filled confidence to meet the struggles, sorrows, and beauty of every new day and be able to support, confront, and graciously forgive ourselves, and others, in the process!

The actions of God in Jesus demonstrate that God's love for humanity reaches to all people, regardless of ethnic group/race, illness

---

[131] When praying in public, progressive Christians will often end prayers with "In Jesus' name we pray, Amen." I don't do that. When it comes to my personal prayer life. I just say "Amen." In fact, I don't even always say that. I just pray.

or physical ability, occupation, class rank, social status, sex/gender, sexual orientation, and any other category. God sends us a message through Jesus that She will always forgive and love us unconditionally. He accepts us for who we are—His children. We're always welcomed back into relationship and covenant with Him. However, we still feel the tendency to indulge in the ways of our own limited agendas and fail to do what is right. Luckily, we can work toward repentance.

Jesus' primary focus wasn't getting individuals to repent from their personal sins *per se*—at least not as an end unto itself. He focused on helping human societies break free from their enslavement to unjust worldly systems and powers of domination. Jesus invited people to repent from oppressive worldviews,[132] and to move toward God and God's ways.[133] When Jesus healed individual persons, his larger purpose was to use such healings as object lessons to the larger society who had been alienating and excluding individuals who were blind, lame, or diseased. Jesus had a passion for holding mirrors up to the imperially-beholden, Temple-based, religiosity of the day to show how corrupt and misguided it was. He performed healings to provide signs and evidence that he was the Messiah so that people would pay attention to his larger teachings about living in God's Kingdom.

As a faithful Jew who cared about his people, Jesus had real problems with what the Jewish religion had been reduced to under the oppression of the Roman Empire. As a dominated member state of that empire, Israel had Roman-approved puppet leaders installed to govern them. Their religion was reduced to being a Temple-based, transactional, institution in which people came to purchase birds and other animals to have temple priests sacrifice on their behalf in order to help them get right with God. The sense of salvation being a societal, corporate, group concern and yearning was replaced with a focus solely on the personal, individual level. It became an opiate for the masses to placate them with a reduced sense of their Jewish heritage while being safe and non-threatening to the powers that be. Some patriotic

---

[132] For example, "Might makes right," "Get them before they get you," "Keep up with the Jones'," "He who dies with the most toys wins," etc.

[133] The life-giving ways of God's Kingdom are humble, just, forgiving, inclusive, compassionate, hospitable, respectful, and loving.

Jews took matters into their own hands by zealously exacting vengeance upon their Roman oppressors by assassinating Romans and Roman-sympathizers. They were known as "Zealots."

Jesus provided a far more holistic sense of salvation to people. After being baptized by his cousin in the Jordan, and after his 40 days of preparation and being tested in the wilderness, Jesus returned to his hometown of Nazareth and went to the synagogue on the Sabbath day.[134] He boldly read from the scroll of Isaiah, saying: *"The Spirit of the Lord is upon me, because he has anointed me to preach good news to the poor. He has sent me to proclaim freedom for the prisoners and recovery of sight for the blind, to release the oppressed, to proclaim the year of the Lord's favor"* (Isaiah 61:1-2—notice that Jesus intentionally edits out a portion of verse 2, . . . *and the day of vengeance of our God, to comfort all who mourn*—rejecting the notion that God is vengeful and that there is anything redemptive about violence). Then, he sat down (that's how rabbis preached back then) and said, *"Today this scripture is fulfilled in your hearing"* (Luke 4:14-21).

This passage of scripture is the key to properly understanding all of the New Testament. This was "Jesus' manifesto." These words set the tone and agenda for his work for the next three years. These words are what it's all about. Notice that the notion of salvation described here is as much communal and societal as it is personal and individual. Jesus' reference to the "year of our Lord's favor" refers to the ancient Jewish honoring of "Jubilee"—whereby every seventy years, all debts were forgiven.[135] Lands that were claimed by lenders were restored to their families of origin to allow a fresh start and to ensure social justice. Jesus was claiming that the year of Jubilee (which hadn't been honored for quite some time) was being restored and it begins *now*. It isn't any wonder that the people who heard that sermon tried to kill him in response (Luke

---

[134] Saturdays is the Sabbath day for Jews because it is the 7th day of the week and the day that God rested according to the Genesis creation story. The Sabbath actually begins at sundown on Fridays but Saturday is the day that people come to worship.

[135] A direct link to the Lord's Prayer, the prayer that Jesus taught his followers to pray; i.e., to ask God to help have our debts forgiven and an instruction for us to forgive those who are beholden and indebted to us.

4:28-29). This passage speaks to religious, social, and political powers and institutions that oppress and lead to injustice and to God's intention for liberation and justice.[136]

As part of his offering of salvation, Jesus also provided healing for broken, busted people. On numerous occasions, Jesus came across people who needed healing. In most of these instances, the healing that they needed was ostensibly physical (blindness, leprosy, bleeding, seizures, mental illness or "demon possession," and so on). In each case, Jesus healed them of their afflictions. Progressive Christians suggest that Jesus' primary intention in those healings was to restore those individuals to communion with their larger society. In those days, people with physical maladies were considered as being ritually unclean and impure. As such, they weren't allowed to participate in religious functions and they were shunned because others didn't want to become unclean themselves from physically interacting with such persons. Those persons were as afflicted (or more) from being shunned by society than they were of their particular physical maladies. In most every case, Jesus instructed the people he healed to immediately go and show themselves to the religious leaders so that they might be reconciled and restored to the community. I submit that Jesus did this so that those religious leaders might be transformed to be who God was really calling *them* to be—which would in turn, transform that nation. This is the larger salvation that was really needed.

Jesus also offered healing salvation to persons who suffered from nonphysical afflictions. They too were estranged and alienated from society and from their true selves. In many of the reported instances of Jesus' healings, the person who was healed (or a relative or friend of that person) had faith in Jesus' healing abilities. Jesus commended them for their faith thus indicating that salvation is, in part, a fruit of personal belief. Yet, on several other

---

[136]   To those who might say that I'm presenting Jesus too politically, I remind them of a) the overtly political framing of the beginning of Luke's Gospel (Luke 1:5 & 2:1-7) and b) the radically subversive "Magnificat" of Mary, the song that she sings in response to her being praised by her cousin Elizabeth for being the one to bear the savior, Luke 1:46-56). If you think these treatments are "too political," your beef is with Luke—not with me.

occasions, Jesus healed and restored people who didn't have faith or who weren't seeking to be healed. Examples include the demon possessed mad-man who villagers had chained outside of their community in Garasene; Lazarus, who Jesus resurrected from the dead; and Zacchaeus, the tax collector in Jericho, thus indicating God's intent to provide salvation to His people even if they aren't overtly seeking out salvation or healing. Several of those healings were of people who weren't Jews, but gentiles, thus demonstrating God's universal sense about who Her children are—*all* of us.

The Christian gift to the world is the audacious proclamation (*kerygma*) of the good news for humanity that Jesus is Lord, Christ and Messiah—and "Caesar" isn't.[137] Part of this *kerygma* is the awareness that God is *Immanuel, with* us in all of our joys, doubts, and sufferings. Nothing can separate us from Him.[138] Popular American Christianity asserts that the good news is that Jesus "took upon himself a punishment properly due to fallen humanity in order to satisfy God's justice." That notion makes no sense to progressive Christians. Christ lived and died *for* us—not *instead* of us. Atonement means a reconciliation ("at-one-ment") that restores the incomplete and estranged relationship between humanity and God, yet progressive Christians believe that humanity isn't all that estranged from God. God made us. God loves us. And God dwells within us all. To the extent that we are estranged, we see the *entirety* of the life, death, and resurrection of Jesus Christ as serving as the catalyst for this deepening re-union. It isn't "just about the cross." While I believe that Jesus did live, die and was resurrected, I don't believe the literal events or details of Jesus' death didn't cause this reconciliation. The resurrection wasn't a cosmic *"Presto!"* moment that magically forced itself onto people's lives. Its power takes effect when we come to accept and live as if it were true—as new creations who aren't defined by our pasts, who allow ourselves to be transformed, and who have an entirely free, expansive, and abundant future ahead of us. Coming to such a realization and awakening can be said to "rock our worlds."[139]

---

[137]   Again, *Caesar*, here means dehumanizing, dominating, and oppressing worldly powers in whatever manner, shape or form.

[138]   Matthew 28:20 & Romans 8:31-39

[139]   If you're curious what a progressive Christian Easter sermon might look see Appendix I.

The resurrection really has God as the central player. It is a prime example of God's *"agape,"* unconditional and freely given love. The power of it is a gift that we may choose to accept. The atonement occurs when people believe that Jesus lived, died, and was resurrected as he did. It informs us that we are unconditionally accepted by God. We're invited to participate in the great banquet and party of the Divine life in the Kingdom of God. Rejecting, and even killing God's agent in the world doesn't end God's love for us. God will always have the last word and that word is love.

The good news of the life, death, and resurrection of Jesus isn't a dogmatic teaching. It's a call to live a new life in utter Communion with God. It calls for our repenting from all that binds us and holds us back from the fullness of who we can be as individuals and as a people. It promises that the Holy Spirit will help us as we seek to live this new "Kingdom-living" way. The *kerygma* is an appeal for us to give up our former self-understandings, and to accept ourselves as lovingly accepted, fully worthy, children of God.

The resurrection is the disclosure of God's power over the powers of sin, the powers of oppression and injustice, and our fear of death. It is the basis for our confidence in the possibility of a life free from the dominion of these powers. This awareness is saving for us. Christians are people who have had, spiritual experiences that lead us to accept this proclamation and/or are engaged in a lifelong process whereby this *kerygma* is revealed.

Growing up as a United Methodist, my understanding of the atonement is naturally influenced by the theological perspective known as Arminianism.[140] Here, God's actions establish the principle that "whoever believes in God through Jesus the Christ will experience salvation." The atonement is intended for all persons. This doesn't necessarily mean that all people will inevitably experience salvation. It's simply available to all people. Sadly, there have been many people who have lived their lives and gone to the grave as bitter, broken souls. It is the Christian hope that this pattern will cease. The way that we believe this will be accomplished is by God working through us as we live according to Jesus' way, and

---

[140]   Methodism was founded by John Wesley and Wesley sided with the free will teachings of Jacob Arminius instead of the predestination teachings of John Calvin.

invite others to do so too. In Christ, we are "a new creation." In Christ, we are glorious, amazing, and victorious, and yet, we're also broken, busted, and vulnerable. The more we acknowledge those shadow parts of ourselves with others—the more saved and whole we are, and the more effective we will be in bringing others on board too. Though it seems counter-intuitive, it is a blessed truth that our weakness is our strength (2 Corinthians 12:7-10).

Ever since Jesus' resurrection, people who celebrate Jesus as Lord and Savior are the *living body of Christ*—the Church. We are called to recognize Christ in ourselves and in each other and especially in those who are suffering, oppressed, or alienated by society (Matthew 25:34-40). I close this chapter with a poem written by a fellow Gen-Xer, while she was in her twenties, named Maggie (last name not provided) that conveys this idea beautifully:[141]

Do you know
do you understand
that you represent
Jesus to me?

Do you know
do you understand
that when you treat me with gentleness,
it raises the question in my mind
that maybe He is gentle, too.
Maybe He isn't someone
who laughs when I am hurt.

Do you know
do you understand
that when you listen to my questions
and you don't laugh,
I think, "What if Jesus is interested in me, too?"

---

[141] An anecdote, ironically, from a sermon preached at Willow Creek Community Church, an evangelical mega-church in Illinois in the mid 1990s. Note: I do not contend that nothing good can come from a conservative church. http://www.geocities.com/lauho08/ do_we_understand_that_we_represent_jesus_to_others.html

Do you know
do you understand
that when I hear you talk about arguments
and conflict and scars from your past,
I think, "Maybe I am just a regular
person instead of a bad, no-good little girl
who deserves abuse."

If you care,
I think maybe He cares—
and then there's this flame of hope
that burns inside of me
and for a while
I am afraid to breathe
because it might go out.

Do you know
do you understand
that your words are His words?
Your face, His face
to someone like me?

Please, be who you say you are.
Please, God, don't let this be another trick.
Please let this be real.
Please!

Do you know
do you understand
that you represent
Jesus to me?

For more about a progressive view of Jesus, see: The Last Week
by Marcus Borg and John D. Crossan, Meeting Jesus Again for
the First Time, by Marcus Borg, and Jesus and Empire: The
Kingdom of God and the New World Order, by Richard Horsley.

Chapter 5

Humans, Sin & Morality

Why must he be like that and chase cats? Perhaps it's just the
dog in him. (paraphrased)
Atomic Dog, George Clinton & P-Funk

Some people blame a woman, but he knows it's his fault.
(paraphrased)
—Margaritaville, Jimmy Buffet

"Human history becomes more and more a race between
education and catastrophe."
H.G. Wells

For I do not do the good I want to do, but the evil I do not
want to do—this I keep on doing.
Paul, Romans 7:19

I mentioned earlier about a conversation that I had during my college years with my friend Peter. In that discussion, it dawned on me that the reason we chose different political allegiances was due to our differing understandings of God and theology. A key component of any systematic theology is anthropology—how one views and understands humanity. Over the ages, perceptions of the human condition have shaped political, ethical, and religious doctrines and the cultural manifestations of those beliefs. The great Chinese scholar Confucius[142] had a largely neutral view

---

[142] (*K'ung-fu-tzu*, Confucius is a latinization of that name in the same way that Jesus is a latinization of *Yeshua*)

of humanity positing that people were capable of being either "superior" or "inferior." Two major students of Confucianism however, came to diverging notions about humanity. Mencius (*Meng Ke*) believed in the innate goodness of all people whereas Hsun-Tzu thought that people were essentially evil. As a result, depending upon the direction of the prevailing political winds, and who was in charge at any given time, the leadership of China has been more or less legalistic and oppressive—or creative and free—depending upon which of those two schools of thought the reigning political powers subscribed to.

There are similar diverging understandings of humanity within Christianity. We touched on this earlier in our treatment of Arminianism and Calvinism. According to conservative Christianity, humans are fallen, wretched, and utterly depraved. It bases this notion upon a literal understanding of the "fall" story in the book of Genesis. If Adam and Eve (mostly they blame Eve) hadn't eaten that fruit from the Tree of Knowledge in the Garden of Eden, then humanity wouldn't know suffering, death,[143] or even work. But since they did, we were booted out of Eden. We know suffering, death, and have to work to provide for ourselves. Women now have pain in childbirth, and we're supposedly in a perpetual state of war with snakes (Genesis 3:14-19).

To be fair, conservative Christianity also bases this understanding not merely on the creation myth in Genesis. They also ground it in the actual experience of humans being at their worst. Indeed, this was the basis of Karl Barth's dialectical "Neo-Orthodox" theology. He taught theology in Switzerland and Germany during World Wars I and II and he saw that the liberal Social Gospel (the theology that was in vogue prior to WWI) held an *overly* high esteem and regard for humankind which failed to recognize how monstrous and evil we can be toward one another.

If one holds that humans are essentially evil and wretched, then it would make sense for society to have many harshly enforced laws that proscribe how we should interact with each other. Such a view also implies that our justice system should

---

[143]   . . . the "wages of sin" being death (something Paul wrote in Romans 6:23).

be retributive—as restorative justice wouldn't make sense if people have no hope of changing their ways. Draconian, fascist, dictatorial, and otherwise strongman forms of governance would be natural and logical given that premise.[144] Another natural result would be requiring citizens to be submissive, blindly loyal, law-abiding citizens. The masses should be kept in line via the stick (punishment) instead of the carrot (reward). If humans are *utterly* wretched, they don't have the capacity to be motivated by positive reinforcement.[145]

According to this logic, since humans don't really have the ability to pursue the common good of their fellow man, then efforts to improve society are to be considered in vain. The ethical focus instead becomes trained on the personal. This has frequently meant condemning personal laziness, specifically, the perceived lack of drive of indivuduals to pursue their personal good. That matter aside, for some reason[146] conservative Christianity has largely reduced sin to what happens in people's bedrooms: whom they should love and how and when they should love them as well as sex and abortion. It was recently reported that 91% of non-churchgoers ages 16-29 describe Christianity as being "anti-homosexual." 80% of churchgoers ages 16-29 agreed.[147] Progressive Christians ask, "Is that really what Jesus had in mind?"

---

[144] This is ironic considering that Barth's theology was based upon his experience of the extremes of German fascism.

[145] An exception to this is seen in the political liberals who feel that certain humans (capitalists) are incapable of self-regulation. For instance, the corruption of the CEOs of the banking, mortgage, and investment industries in 2007-9. Political liberals are advocates of regulated markets; i.e., they advocate the stick when it comes to this segment of the population. Philosophical consistency is not a human strong suit—but progressives at least are willing to admit this.

[146] (Subconscious infection by the body-hating and sex-avoiding Gnostics and being overly influenced by the Victorian era, I'd guess)

[147] http://healtheland.wordpress.com/2007/10/16/barna-survey-says-young-people-are-rejecting-christianity/

Break it Down VIII

Conservative Christians oppose homosexuality because of their interpretation of the Bible. Progressive Christians interpret the Bible differently than the conservative do. For many conservatives, even though the Bible only speaks to homosexuality on 6 occasions (though even that is debatable), and even though Jesus *never* spoke about it, condemning homosexual behavior trumps all other moral matters. Progressive Christians read those 6 passages of scripture in their original time and setting, their context within their particular book of the Bible, as well as in their context within the Bible as a whole. In almost every case, those prohibitions are listed among other behaviors that are prohibited for the ancient Hebrews who were trying to live differently than the rest of the world. These were all concerns about ritual purity and keeping kosher. These included things such as not eating shellfish, not eating pork, not having sex during a woman's menstrual period, not wearing clothing of mixed fibers, etc. All of these were *equally* "abominations" according to that Levitical code (the laws in the book of Leviticus).

The progressive Christian perspective holds that non-Jews (gentiles) aren't bound by those ancient Hebraic laws. And what was being prohibited wasn't anything like homosexuality as we know it today. Instead, what was being prohibited was engaging in the fertility rites of the Canaanites, temple cultic prostitution, and pedophilia. But, for the sake of argument, even if it were the case that homosexual behavior is a sin, progressive Christians remind us that it would be far less important of a sin than greed, consumerism, poor stewardship of the environment, nuclear weapons, unjust wars, and exploiting the poor are—things we don't often hear conservative Christians rallying against. Aside from the fundamentalists, most conservative Christians make allowances for divorce and remarriage (things which Jesus clearly spoke against). This is hypocritical. It is also scape-goating.[148] They are allowing for something which affects 50% of today's society (divorce) while condemning an activity which affects only 5-8% of our population—homosexuality.

Progressive Christians also do allow for divorce and re-marriage, as marriage today is different than it was in biblical days. Women are now considered full persons instead of as chattel (the property of fathers and husbands). Women today, at least in the West, are financially empowered

---

[148] The practice of singling out one child, employee, member of a group of peers, ethnic or religious group, or country for unmerited negative treatment or blame.

and aren't likely to be reduced to begging on the streets if they get divorced. Divorced women are no longer considered "damaged goods" (because they aren't virgins) by most Western men. Women can also initiate divorces now, not just men. The average lifespan in developed nations today is 80 years of age versus the 40 years of age back then. It's much harder for a marriage to last 50-60 years than for it to last 10-20 years. "The biblical" teaching about marriage isn't exactly what today's conservatives claim it is—one husband with one wife until death do they part. Polygamy was clearly allowed for, and apparently God-blessed, in the Bible. Indeed, it is nowhere condemned in the Bible.

This matter has become highly politicized, with the conservatives seeking to impose their religious views upon the rest of the citizenry, specifically, banning gay marriages. However, from a truly biblical point of view, banning civil marriages for homosexual couples makes about as much sense as is does to do what we're currently doing—allowing heterosexual couples to divorce for reasons other than adultery. Also, in several states, heterosexual couples that live together for a certain period of time can opt to be recognized as legally married (for example, "common law marriage" in Colorado and Texas). From *a* "biblical" perspective, legally denying homosexual civil unions makes about as much sense as legally allowing divorced straight persons to remarry.

Alas, we live in a *hypocritically* "Christian" nation. Since the majority of Bible readers are straight people (with a good many of them being conservative), they rationalize their "sinful" behaviors (re-marriage, divorce for reasons other than adultery, premarital sex, etc.) by focusing the attention upon the 5-8% of our population who are homosexual. Straight conservatives make homosexuals scapegoats in order to allow them (straight conservatives) to fool themselves into thinking that they are "righteous" while "those others" are not. Yet, Christianity is supposed to be about love, compassion and grace. Due to life experience and societal change, many denominations (including ones that are not overtly progressive) now allow couples who are living together before marriage to get married in their churches; many denominations now allow their members to divorce for reasons other than adultery; many denominations allow their members who've been divorced to remarry. They do this not because they "dismiss" the Bible. They interpret it as Jesus did—graciously, compassionately, and non-legalistically.

Progressive Christians point out that the so-called sin of "sodomy" has nothing to do with homosexuality. The sin of the town of Sodom was extreme inhospitality and lack of loving-kindness (*hesed*). That town behaved very poorly toward strangers and foreigners. This hit a climax in their desire to

rape (a power act, not primarily a sexual one) two foreigners in their midst
(angels from God—*not* men and therefore no homosexuality involved).
The prophet Ezekiel later interpreted that story about Sodom saying,
*'Now this was the sin of your sister Sodom: She and her daughters were arrogant,
overfed and unconcerned; they did not help the poor and needy. They were haughty
and did detestable things before me. Therefore I did away with them as you
have seen* (Ezekiel 16:49-50). The focus is clearly upon the sins of being
selfish and indifferent, and abusive toward others. Jesus interprets things
the same way when he says to His disciples, *"When you enter a town and
are welcomed, eat what is set before you. Heal the sick who are there and tell
them, 'The Kingdom of God is near you.' But when you enter a town and are not
welcomed, go into its streets and say, 'Even the dust of your town that sticks to
our feet we wipe off against you. Yet be sure of this: The Kingdom of God is near.'
I tell you, it will be more bearable on that day for Sodom than for that town*
(Luke 10:8-12). That passage is clearly in the context of people offering
compassion and hospitality, or failing to do so, and has *nothing* to do with
sexual behavior.[149]

Abortion is the other issue that conservative Christianity lifts up as "the
other major sin of humanity"—though it primarily affects women. While,
most Christians feel that abortions happen too frequently and aren't the ideal
form of birth control, conservative Christianity has pegged it as one of the
two worst things that humans can do. Equating it to murder, they consider
it "genocide" against innocent persons. They look at the issue in black and
white terms, ignoring nuance and shades of gray. Progressive Christians *care*
about those gray areas and feel that there are significant differences between
abortions during the first trimester of pregnancy and ones that occur after
a fetus is in a stage of development where it may viably live outside the
womb. Progressive Christianity also takes into account other factors such
as if a woman became pregnant due to rape; if the pregnant female isn't
a woman, but rather a minor under the age of 18; if a fetus has a severe
disorder; e.g., a cephalic condition; or if giving birth to a child would likely
cause harm or death to the mother. Since abortion is never addressed in the
Bible, progressive Christians find it problematic to say that it is "clearly
sinful." Many progressive Christians resonate with the traditional Jewish
understanding that a fetus is not a human life, a person, until it draws its

---

[149]   It's also helpful to observe that Jewish traditions and texts do not
        emphasize the homosexual aspect of the attitude of the inhabitants
        of Sodom as much as their cruelty and lack of hospitality to the
        "stranger." The Inhospitable Sodomites, Rictor Nelson, A History
        of Homophobia, http://rictornorton.co.uk/homopho2.htm

first breath of God's breath (*ruah*) into its lungs out of the womb.[150] Granted, not all Jews or progressive Christians think the same way.

For an outstanding essay on the Bible and homosexuality see Rev. Dr. Walter Wink's "Homosexuality and the Bible," http://www.soulforce.org/article/homosexuality-bible-walter-wink

A Progressive view of Humanity & the need for Divine Grace:

With the advent of human beings from the long processes of evolution and natural selection, a species was created that: is aware that it exists; has high critical thinking and tool making skills; is capable of humor and self-reflection; can work as co-creators with God; can choose to worship God and be awed by Him; and who can choose paths of great self-harm and destruction. We are potentially moral beings. We can decide to act in accordance with the needs of one another, our planet, and our God. When we opt to not act in accord with God's will, we sin. Sin means, "missing the mark." It's like when an archer shoots an arrow and it fails to hit the target. The further away the shot lands, the greater the degree of sin. Though neutral or good in nature, we're busted and broken. We're cracked pots. We're imperfect vessels. We're beautiful messes and paradoxes. We're selfish and selfless. We're a loveably, consternating amalgam of sinner and saint.

Because of our free will, we humans have a real propensity to screw up. Sinning is a bit like getting frostbite. Once you've experienced frostbite on the tip of your nose or on the tips of your toes or fingers, those areas become more likely to become frostbit again in the future. Each new instance of frostbite increases the likelihood of new experiences of frostbite. It's also a bit like trying to eat just one *Pringles* potato chip or one spoonful of *Ben & Jerry's* ice cream. Once you've had a taste, it's awfully hard to not eat more. Sinning is very much like an addiction.

---

[150]   See: http://www.rossde.com/editorials/edtl_abortion_religion.html, and http://www.religioustolerance.org/abo_biblh.htm

The more you do something, the more it becomes a habit, and a pattern deepened "deer trail" in the brain becomes established. In time, those deer trailed neuro-pathways become widened to become neuro-superhighways, which become our default way of being. Progressive Christians view Christianity, in part, as a way to break apart those dysfunctional superhighways that lead us off self-sabotaging cliffs. It provides a way of repenting and reorienting to establish alternative neuro-pathways, ones that with enough nurturing and practice can become such a dramatically different way of being that we can say that we have been saved and are "born again."

In Jesus' day, sin had become reduced to legalistic notions about being ritually impure and "dirty," and unworthy of participating in Temple practices. Jesus subverted that notion. Instead of treating sin through the lens of retributive law books, "if you commit x transgression, you deserve y punishment," Jesus embraced restorative justice. He saw that when sin is committed, it harms both the sinner as well as persons his/her actions may have wronged. Jesus emphasized restoration and reconciliation of relationships—not the doling out of appropriate punishments that only further alienate people from one another and God. There is a Christ-centered call for us to curb much of our evolutionary processes and oppressive natural selections. Examples of this include a call to not to abandon the elderly, infirm, or infants who are born with handicapping conditions;[151] to not resort to violence or vengeance when dealing with conflict; and for straight men to practice monogamy. The early Christians were known by the Romans for their deep love for each other, how they tended to the dying, sick and the lame; how they took pains to provide burials for paupers, and how they sought to forgive each other and restore broken relationships. Tertullian, an ancient Roman scholar, is famously reported to have said, "Look at that those Christians! See how they love each other!"

---

[151] Infanticide was a common Roman practice where children born bith birth defects or deemed weak were killed. It was also employed as a form of birth control. See: http://www.christiancadre.org/member_contrib/cp_infanticide.html

With humanity's freedom of choice comes substantial risk and great potential for suffering. People are not easily able to choose and act in complete accordance with God's preferences and aims. We are only able to do so in varying degrees. On our own, none of us is able to fully satisfy God's callings. Sinfulness is part of our human nature. Like the rest of creation, we humans have inherent value but we are neither the peak, nor are we necessarily "the goal," of God's creative energies. It is "from dust" that we came and it will be to dust that we shall return (Genesis 3:19). Progressive Christians contend that humans never experienced any "original state" that entailed a harmonious Eden. The idea of a Golden Age in our past is a beautiful, but nearly universal, human myth. Humans haven't "fallen" from some idealized status or state of being, and there was no literal "original sin"—at least not in the sense that that term is often used, specifically, that because of Adam and Eve's eating a piece of fruit, human genes have carried a collective guilt from generation to generation such that all humans are born as sinners even before they've committed their first sin.[152] Instead, progressive Christians simply suggest that from the beginning, humans are born into the world not as sinners, but as loved children of God have both propensities to seek union with God as well as tendencies to attempt to do things our own way.

Genesis 1:26-27 proclaims that humans are created in "the image of God." Numerous doctrines have been generated in response to this "*Imageo Dei.*" We don't need to understand this to mean any sort of "original spiritual possession" that we "lost in the fall." Nor do we have to accept the notion that we ever had any Godly supernatural endowment (*Similitudo Dei*) of original righteousness—after all, according to the story of Adam and Eve, we are capable of acting out of sync with God's will—they sinned. Like God, humans have creative free will. It is this quality that makes us similar to God. It is what it means to be "created in His image." Progressive Christians agree with theologian Karl Barth, who also rejected the idea that the first humans "had a natural basis" for knowing God more fully. Barth held that our being created in "the image of God" should be held

---

[152] Interestingly, there is no doctrine of original sin in the Jewish faith (and they're the ones who wrote the book of Genesis!).

as an eschatological goal; that is, as an ideal for we are striving to attain and achieve.

We've earlier outlined how God attempts to lure us toward following Her best possible choices in every given instance—the "initial aims." Humans are endowed with creative souls that receive these preferred "aims" from God. The soul is where we struggle with how to perceive, interpret and respond to God's nudges and callings. We can leave open the question as to whether the soul is merely an "appropriate metaphor," or if it has a particular ontological, physical, or supra-natural existence. To be sure, we are not merely spirited souls. We are *embodied*.[153] Sinning doesn't take place by disembodied souls, it occurs in the thoughts and bodies of embodied souls—by human beings.

I will discuss sin in further detail in Chapter 9. For now, I offer this working definition of sin: **Sin is disconnection from God and from whom we are meant to be. It is falling short of the mark of God's initial aims for our lives. Sin is the extent to which we do not follow God's initial aims or accept Her grace—choosing instead to go our own way out of communion with God. Sin means doing what we shouldn't do and failing to do what we should. It means acting without love. It means living falsely and contrary to reality.**

Some progressive Christians suggest that when we sin when we are not seeing things the way they truly are thus we do not understand the full consequences of our actions in our "unreality." If we did, we would not do them, because we would realize that we are only causing suffering to ourselves and others (including the fact that any time we cause suffering to others, we cause ourselves to suffer). Others contend, however, that we have it within us, to knowingly do harm—even when we do realize that we are harming others or ourselves.

Either way, sin is a way of life that is readily ingrained through the negative role modeling of our families, leaders, and peers, and the inertia of the past. With repetition, it becomes a destructive habit of the heart—both on the personal level and societal levels. It is equally sinful for us to fail to live up to our potential grandness

---

153   For more on this see *The Body of God: an Ecological Theology* by Sallie McFague.

(being overly humble, meek and subservient to corrupt persons or powers) as it is for us to act beyond our proper place (being overly selfish and prideful). This phenomenon has historically been a gendered one. Because of patriarchy and sexism, many women have been socialized to be overly timid, quiet, and submissive, while many men have been molded to be too self-assured, independent, and arrogant. There are, of course, exceptions on both sides.

This isn't to say that God is the only one who makes the decisions and that our only options are to follow or not to follow. That wouldn't allow for full human agency—merely blind obedience. We have true creativity. We can initiate wondrous things of our own. We can adapt or improvise upon God's actions and callings. Sometimes, our collaborations with God result in much beauty and goodness. However at times, we really botch it—sometimes *big* time. Human history is rife with examples of both. However, progressive Christianity suggests that we'd do well to reject Calvinistic doctrines that focus exclusively upon the shortcomings of humanity as "totally depraved" or "worm-like." We are able to connect to God, and yet none of us does so readily or fully. We aren't doomed wholly to sin. Transformation is possible! However, we need help, and this is most effectively done through accepting the freely given grace in resurrection of Jesus Christ. The acceptance of this atoning *kerygma* is the Christian way, and we are called to share with others (Matthew 28:16-20).

All humans have experienced brokenness and "dis-ease"[154] of some sort in themselves and in the world. As Christians, we realize that there is more to life than alienation and suffering. We also know about and experience God's grace, forgiveness, acceptance, and love. God offers us the power to reduce, minimize, and heal future brokenness in ourselves and in others. Faithful Christians will continue to stumble. We're still humans. We care about all people and seek to demonstrate the value of our Way. We lovingly remind the world that "the Church isn't a museum of saints, it's a hospital for sinners,"[155] and that Christians aren't perfect. We're simply people who realize that we're forgiven and have sufficient

---

[154] Not necessarily actual disease, but dis-ease of various kinds for sure.
[155] Attributed to both Abigail Van Buren and Morton Kelsey

hope to arise every morning (every moment in fact) knowing that, in Christ, we have a fresh start, a second chance and a new beginning. As the Apostle Paul put it,

> *"So from now on we regard no one from a worldly point of view. Though we once regarded Christ in this way, we do so no longer. Therefore, if anyone is in Christ, he is a new creation; the old has gone, the new has come! All this is from God, who reconciled us to himself through Christ and gave us the ministry of reconciliation: that God was reconciling the world to himself in Christ, not counting men's sins against them.* (2 Corinthians 5:16-19)

Ultimately, progressive Christianity shifts the focus from "avoiding sin" to "focusing on love." We manifest what we place our intentions and energies upon. If we focus on avoiding sin, we may end up caught up in the mires of it. Put another way, a Christian "campaign to stamp out sin" will always bring about less light, love and wholeness in the world than a "campaign to live in love." So, instead of focusing solely on not sinning, progressive Christians emphasize following Jesus' over-arching teachings that God is love, God loves us, and we are called to love ourselves and our neighbors in response. It's more positive, which is important for anyone who is recovering from the scars of a judgmental church upbringing.[156] We'll never be able to love perfectly, but there are practices and disciplines that can help us to love the best that we can (see Chapter 12).

I close this chapter by offering a unique sort of "beatnik sermon" that I wrote back in 1995 during my years in seminary. I delivered it as part of a chapel worship service at the Iliff School of Theology. I think it captures the understanding of sin that we've been exploring. You might want to snap your fingers and make soft, high-hat cymbal sounds as you read this: *"t-ttsss tt, t-ttsss tt, t-ttsss tt, t-ttsss tt, t-ttsss tt . . ."*

---

[156]   On a related note, as Mother Theresa put it, "If you judge people, you have no time to love them." This is true even you're the one judging yourself.

Groovin' With God[157]

Our Creator God does *indeed* create. *Mercy* and how!

But She is not the *only* one who makes the decisions about *what* will be created.

If that were the case, blind obedience . . . would be our only mission we would merely be *puppets* who could only do things when *God* pulls our strings.

Dig this. As children of God who've been called to groove, let's groove on the metaphor of "Jazz Music." In jazz there is an *imperative* for listening to, and respecting the composer and director. However, for *truly* beautiful and *creative* music to flow, there must be room for the musicians to play *off* the score.

We need,   to *improvise.*

Now *God* is the composer and lead musician of *all* creation.

He sets the beat and the main melody lines, and we humans, well we're asked to apply *our* gifts and graces and to playfully *experiment* and create *variations* on the themes.

Check it out! When we open-up and listen . . . we can hear some cool and kickin' riff floating in from above . . .

"Dom diba dooba, dom diba dooba."

We can groove on that wave for a while . . .

Dom diba dooba, dom diba dooba!

—then, one of us gets an idea of her own, d*oobie doobie dooba, doobie doobie dooba . . . s*he tries it out and adds a little bit of this . . . *zoobie*

You can hear me preaching this sermon here, http://progressive christianitybook.com/Roger_Preaching.html

dee dom, zoobie dee dom, . . . and brings in some of that . . . *zip zip zoi, zip zip zoi . . . a*nd before too long, something **new** has been created something that can only come from the dynamic synergy

of God

and God's People,

jamming   *together*!

However, we need to carefully listen to, and work with, God and each other otherwise . . . all we have . . . is *noise*.

The fool notion that "there are no wrong notes in jazz" is musically—false.

We *can* monopolize the act and not allow God or the others their turns to play.

. . . we can play out of tune or in the wrong chords . . . we might play too weakly when it's *our* turn to solo. or try to "hide-out" by meekly playing behind the others . . . or we might play in an inappropriate style, straight—when it should be *swung*,

Dixie, when its supposed to be *Cool*. . . Be-bop, when it oughta be *Smooth*, . . . and so on, and so on, etcetera, etcetera . . . *Man!*

None-the-less, God *desires* this creativity on our parts—you dig?

And She *risks* the sour notes. She always attempts to make beautiful *whatever* we come up with.

Humph. . . Sometimes, well, sometimes He has to work *harder* than others! But no matter what, God is inviting us to make beautiful music together.

It's up to us.

Are we willing to open up our ears?,
    To release the energies of our minds?,
        To let *loose the passion* in our
            hearts, souls and bodies?!

Now, Listen Up you Cats!
    Let's let God know that we've
        tuned our horns, freed our souls,
            and that we're *ready*
                to *groove* with the Lord!   Amen!?

Chapter 6

Salvation: When & Where?
And what's up with all the Blood?

Redemption Song, Bob Marley
Salvation, The Cranberries

People, even more than things, have to be restored, renewed, revived, reclaimed, and redeemed; never throw out anyone.
Audrey Hepburn

But Zacchaeus stood up and said to the Lord, "Look, Lord! Here and now I give half of my possessions to the poor, and if I have cheated anybody out of anything, I will pay back four times the amount." Jesus said to him, "Today salvation has come to this house, because this man, too, is a son of Abraham. For the Son of Man came to seek and to save what was lost." Luke 19:8-10

For God so loved the world that he gave his only begotten Son, that whoever believes in him shall not perish but have eternal life. For God did not send his Son into the world to condemn the world, but to save the world through him. Jesus, John 3:16-17

. . . work out your own salvation with fear and trembling.
Paul, Philippians 2:12

"Are you saved?" and it's corollary, "When were you saved?" are perhaps the most dreaded and off-putting questions that non-Christians encounter as they go about their business and living their lives. Both questions are loaded and those who ask them have a certain agenda—one that springs from conservative Christianity. That perspective makes certain assumptions including: a) that salvation is primarily a personal matter; b) that salvation means that someone has accepted Jesus Christ as their personal Lord and Savior; and c) that people remember and celebrate the date of when they made that decision. I sometimes refer to this as "the morning glory" type of Christians. The petals of Morning Glory plants stay in their buds a long time until one day, when the temperatures are just right—*Pow!*—they just burst open all at once. Powerful to witness! Indeed, there are people who know when and where they were when they accepted Jesus as their Savior. The thing is, Morning Glories aren't the only kind of flower and their way of blooming isn't the only way that flowers bloom. In fact, most flowers bloom through a low key, gradual, unfolding that doesn't involve much fanfare or attention. I would suggest that is the way most people come to faith in God through Christ and the sense of wholeness that goes with it. Instead of asking "Are you saved?" progressive Christians are more likely to ask "How are you doing?"; "How's it going with your faith life?"—or if they're old school, "How is it with your soul?" These are different sorts of questions based upon different ideas about what salvation is all about.

For certain readers, likely, those from a more conservative perspective, this chapter is the main event and the heart of the matter. What does Wolsey say about salvation and the atonement? How a theologian speaks to these matters tends to be the basis for whether or not they're considered a heretic (by those who go around considering such things). I don't want to be flippant. These are serious matters. We humans really are a pretty screwed up lot. We know less than we think we do. We don't know what's in our best interests. Even at those rare times that we do, we often self-sabotage. Our attempts to make the world a better place and improve things have a long track record of less than desirable consequences—frequently making things worse. We're exploited, used, and oppressed and we exploit, use, and oppress others. Left to our own devices, we tend to make a hell of a mess. Those who deny these realities are gravely deluded. We need help. Christians refer to this help as *salvation*. Let me begin by describing the typical conservative take on these matters.

A Conservative view: Salvation is by God's grace, not by an individual's or a community's good works. Salvation must be received as a gift by faith and it is by faith alone that people are saved. People must, accept with their mind, believe in their heart, and profess from their lips that Jesus suffered, bled and died for their sins. He physically rose again, which is the assurance of forgiveness and resurrection of our own bodies. This is God's loving plan to forgive and be reconciled with sinful humanity.

Break It Down IX

Some may find it ironic that conservative Christianity's approach to salvation is largely an intellectual one; i.e., when a person uses their mind to decide to agree with certain "truth claims." These claims include: that Jesus is Lord, their personal savior, that he's God, that he was literally born to a virgin, that his death saves us, that he literally and physically rose from the dead, and that he's about to return soon to judge everyone, and that how we're judged determines if we'll go to heaven or hell. God's saving grace is an unmerited gift—there's nothing we can do to deserve or earn salvation.

Such claims are based upon certain passages of the Bible, or at least certain interpretations of those verses. However, it is interesting to notice that the same conservatives who read those passages in a literal manner tend to not read certain other passages in a literal way; i.e., passages which suggest and imply that salvation is in part something that humans have a role in achieving. I think of the passage in 1 Timothy which states that women are saved by giving birth to children: *But women will be saved through childbearing—if they continue in faith, love and holiness with propriety.* (1 Timothy 2:15)

Curiously, many of those same conservative Christians have no problem with what was stated in the verses prior to that verse (11-12): that *"A woman should learn in quietness and full submission. I do not permit a woman to teach or to have authority over a man; she must be silent."* And thus, they endorse patriarchal family structures and giving women limited roles in the Church. I think also of Paul's instructions for people to *"work out their own salvation with fear and trembling"* (Philippians 2:12). Conservatives sometimes minimize that remark with the adage "Work as though it all depended upon you, but pray as though it all depended upon God." That's probably a healthy attitude, but the point remains, they minimize passages that deviate from the assertion that salvation is something that only God does for us.

Jesus' parable about the separation of the sheep from the goats makes it fairly clear that our salvation significantly involves certain human acts in the world (feeding the hungry, visiting the prisoners, clothing the naked, giving water to the thirsty, etc., Matthew 25:31-46). Jesus' brother James crystallized it further when he wrote *"What good is it, my brothers, if a man claims to have faith but has no deeds? Can such faith save him? Suppose a brother or sister is without clothes and daily food. If one of you says to him, "Go, I wish you well; keep warm and well fed," but does nothing about his physical needs, what good is it? In the same way, faith by itself, if it is not accompanied by action, is dead. But someone will say, "You have faith; I have deeds." Show me your faith without deeds, and I will show you my faith by what I do."* (James 2:14-18)

It's no wonder that Martin Luther considered the book of James an "epistle of straw" for it undermined his Protestant notion that salvation has no role for human effort whatsoever. Progressive Christians appreciate the book of James and celebrate the co-creative process of humans and God working together to bring us to our highest selves. We also affirm the primary role that grace plays. As Fr. Richard Rohr puts it, "Our struggle, our desire, our "yes" is significant and necessary. But in the end it is always grace that carries us up the staircase."

Conservative Christianity, which has become the predominant form of American Christianity, is significantly colored and influenced by its American context. This is seen in the most commonly held notions about theories of Jesus' atonement and its resulting understanding of salvation.

The United States of America is a new experiment in the world—one in which rights are granted to individuals and a spirit of hyper-individualism has been nourished and fostered. There are significant merits and benefits to such a political worldview. That individualistic political ideology affected our nation's religiosity. Many of the early Quakers and evangelical American preachers were ardent abolitionists (people opposed to slavery) and women's suffragists (advocates of emancipating women by giving them the right to vote). Their individualist-oriented reading of the Bible led them to conclude that they could not deny rights and liberties to African-Americans or women who were fellow children of

God—or at least as *potential* children of God.[158] And it was certain American denominations that were the first to ordain women as clergy.[159]

This emphasis upon the personal and individual became an *over*-emphasis upon the personal and the individual such that salvation was reduced to an individual's personal beliefs; his or her sense of a personal relationship with Jesus; and whether or not s/he will be going to heaven. Since the American ethos was hyper-individualistic, this naturally impacted our theology. As the U.S. embraced (minimally regulated) capitalism, it tended to allow rich persons to amass power through the exploitation of the poor and disenfranchised, with slavery being the most egregious form. The wealthy elite justified this injustice[160] by teaching (exploiting) the masses—and especially the slaves—that their *individual* rewards will be in heaven, not in this life.[161] This is

---

[158] Conservative Christian theology does not consider people who aren't actually self-avowed, practicing Christians as fellow children of God; e.g., http://www.gotquestions.org/all-God-children.html

[159] See footnotes 36 & 47.

[160] It is not an accident that the southern states are referred to as "The Bible Belt." This term is backed up by studies that have determined the states with the area in which Baptist denominations are the predominant religious affiliation; the region dominated by 24 fundamentalist Protestant denominations; and the greatest audience for religious television. I hold a pet theory that the reason that the southern states in the U.S. tend to be the most religiously conservative with the highest degree of Christian fundamentalism is because of exactly this phenomenon. They had to read the Bible in a literal manner in order to come up with a theology that condoned the practice of slavery. "The Bible allowed for slavery here, here, and here. And Paul told slaves to obey their masters!" Perhaps some grad student might consider exploring this for a thesis?

[161] One might argue that the American emphasis for the pursuit of civil rights (for women, people of color, people with handicapping conditions, homosexuals, etc.) springs forth from our emphasis upon individualism and individual rights—and this would partially be true. It has largely been Christians who embrace a liberationist, collective and communal view of salvation and social justice. Martin Luther King Jr. is a prime example, for example, *"The marvelous new militancy which has engulfed the Negro community must not lead us to distrust of all*

apparent in the lyrics of certain early African American spirituals and gospel songs.

America's geo-political history also played a role in this developing influence upon its theology. The United States is a land rich with a lot of fertile soil and a deep supply of natural resources. The nation was originally birthed via a war of independence and it was able to maintain its independence by being so far away from Europe and by its borders being protected by two massive oceans. The economy of the United States was artificially accelerated beyond its youth through the use of slavery for many years. For the first half of our nation's history, we largely adopted an independent, isolationist foreign policy. Coupled to that policy was disdain for the ways and teachings of the "old country"—ways and teachings that tended to be more familial, communal and collective in nature.

The theology of getting into heaven as the primary concern of Christianity had some of its roots in the medieval theology of Peter Abelard[162] whose teaching about Christ's atonement emphasized a notion of personal salvation.[163] This heaven-oriented theology

---

white people, for many of our white brothers, as evidenced by their presence here today, have come to realize that their destiny is tied up with our destiny and they have come to realize that their freedom is inextricably bound to our freedom. This offense we share mounted to storm the battlements of injustice must be carried forth by a biracial army. We cannot walk alone." (I Have a Dream speech); and *"All men are caught in an inescapable network of mutuality. Injustice anywhere is a threat to justice everywhere. Whatever affects one directly, affects all indirectly. I can never be what I ought to be until you are what you ought to be. This is the interrelated structure of reality; If we do not learn to live together as friends, we will die apart as fools."*

[162] A Medieval French theologian, famed for his work "Sic et Non" (Yes and No). Ironically, Abelard also demonstrated the non-dualist and paradoxical, "both-and," thinking of postmodernism and his view of the atonement also suggested the "moral influence" theory that is favored by many progressive Christians. This is ironic because while he was one of the first theologians to introduce the "personal" notion of salvation (which is the basis of modernist conservative Christianity) the rest of his theology lends itself far more toward today's postmodern sensibilities.

[163] Curiously, while that particular teaching of Abelard's doesn't jibe with progressive Christianity, he also embraced the "Moral

is also rooted in the teachings of John Calvin who emphasized individual salvation instead of societal/communal. In his teachings, the "elect" are merely the combined sum of the select individuals who were capriciously chosen by God to be saved and eventually reside with Him in heaven.

This theology also has roots in the French philosopher Blaise Pascal's famous "wager."[164] Using probability theory, Pascal suggested that even though the existence of God cannot be determined through reason, a person would do well to bet as though God exists, because one has everything to gain, and nothing to lose. Effectively, it's a form of spiritual life insurance—"Believe now for the sake of heaven later."[165] This is the basis of Billy Graham's[166] evangelical zeal and ministries such as Campus Crusade for Christ.[167] Helping people get to the point of accepting this saving grace—to convict people of sin and to get them to accept Jesus as the answer to their wretched, hopeless predicament—has been the m.o. (*modus operandi*) and the bread and butter of American evangelical Christianity.

Influence" theory of the atonement. He also embraced paradoxical thinking—both of which appeal to progressive Christians.

[164] This is ironic as Pascal rejected Calvinism for being contrary to the goodness and justice of God.

[165] One wonders about the depth of such a "wagered faith."

[166] In case you aren't aware of him, Billy Graham was the most famous Christian evangelist in the 1970s-1990s. He was a personal consultant to many U.S. presidents and at one point he was one of the most well known people on the planet.

[167] Campus Crusade for Christ is a conservative evangelical para-church campus ministry that seeks to convert as many young people around the world to Christianity as possible. That they have "Crusade" in their name hints at the aggressive tactics they employ. Most recently, they were able to get most all of the miners who were trapped in that mine in Chile for over 90 days (Fall of 2010) to wear t-shirts promoting their *Jesus* movie over their jumpsuits as they were being pulled up from that rescue shaft for the world to see. That said, it is wonderful that those miners were ministered to and were given hope and encouragement by this ministry. And, those t-shirts weren't merely promoting a movie. By wearing them the miners were expressing thanks to God.

If you couple this drive with the belief that if people don't have a chance to hear about the Gospel they are doomed to spend eternity in the fires of hell, this creates zeal to hold enormous "crusades" in order to get "the Word" out to as many people as possible. If you add the fundamentalist notion that Jesus' "second coming" won't happen until the entire world has been exposed to the Gospel, and combine that with a numbers-oriented American entrepreneurial spirit, you've got quite a force to reckon with.

As I understand it, one of Graham's favorite techniques for evangelism was a simple drawing of a canyon with a stick figure of a person representing humanity on one side of it and a drawing of a cloud with a "G" in it representing God on the other side. There is no way for that person and God to get together so He has provided the way. Enter the drawing of a cross in the middle of that chasm. The cross serves as a bridge and allows connection between God and Man. It's simple, short and sweet. So is the theology that goes with it. It's basically an approach to substitutionary atonement theology.

There are two forms of this approach to the atonement that can be found within conservative Christianity. A softer form simply states that God provided a way for us to reconcile our estrangement from God via believing that Jesus died for us and by so doing served as a substitute for us, providing a necessary ransom.[168] He took upon himself punishment that was originally meant for us—perhaps based upon Paul's remark in Romans 6:23, "the wages of sin is death."

A harder form of this theology is seen in Mel Gibson's movie *The Passion of the Christ*. This perspective seems to suggest that the more Jesus suffered; the more he was beaten, lashed, and twisted in agony; and the more blood which gushed from his body, the more saved we are. Aside from finding that to be really bizarre and twisted, progressive Christians point out that there's no way an actual human being could have sustained the beatings inflicted upon that character in Gibson's movie without

---

[168] *Ransom* here means a debt needed to be paid to right the cosmic order and balance the heavenly ledger books.

passing out and/or dying *before* being nailed to that cross.[169] That film struck me as a gore-fest designed to meet some people's vicarious and sado-masochistic to witness suffering inflicted upon someone in order to absolve them of their sense of wretchedness.[170] Apparently, Jesus being hung, shot, drowned, lethally injected—or even crucified *without* also being whipped,

---

[169] Biblically, when victims were whipped, they were to receive no more than 39 lashes as more than that killed them (Deuteronomy 25:2-3 & 2 Corinthians 11:24). In Gibson's film, Jesus is whipped 78 times. Granted, there was no limit to the punishment doled out by Romans, and victims of whipping often died from that alone. They certainly wouldn't have been able to carry a cross afterward. The idea that Jesus received an excessive amount of corporal punishment may've started with Augustine. "St. Augustine concluded that since every sinner deserves many blows, Christ, the bearer of all our sins, must have received an uncountable number of stripes . . . It is commonly thought that Christ's scourging especially atoned for sins of sexual impurity." http://users.netnitco.net/~legend01/scourge.htm

[170] Gibson is a passionate member of the Catholic Traditionalist movement [and Opus Dei], a minority Catholic sect that rejects the reforms of the Second Vatican Council in 1964-65—in particular the abolition of the Latin Mass. Overlooked in much of the criticism of The Passion is the fact that it is not actually based on the Gospels so much as on the visions of a forgotten 19th century mystic and stigmatic, Anne Catherine Emmerich. She claimed to have the gift of being transported back in time, which enabled her to supply details missing from the biblical accounts of the Passion. These were then written down and published in several best sellers by the German poet Clemens Brentano. Very probably, Brentano embellished her account. For example, in the Gospels, Jesus is shown praying in Gethsemane, but the devil is not mentioned. But in Emmerich's visions, the devil tempts Jesus as he prays. In Gibson's movie, the devil also tempts Jesus in Gethsemane. "The extreme religious sect which fuelled the passion of Mel Gibson," originally from, *The Scotsman*, March 20, 2004, George Kerevan, http://www.rickross. com/reference/general/general645.html

scourged, and stabbed—wouldn't have sufficed for folks who buy into this morbid line of thinking.[171]

But this isn't the *true* passion of the Christ. Christ's passion *wasn't* marching into Jerusalem that last week in order to allow his flesh to be whipped. His passion wasn't to be killed. It wasn't to die from tortured asphyxiation and hemorrhaging. No! Instead, Jesus' *passion* was to tend to the needs and the plight of the least, the last, and the lost. Jesus' passion was to restore the Jewish religion to how it was supposed to be. Jesus' passion was declaring the arrival of the God's Kingdom for all of God's people. Jesus' passion was to invite people to live life fully in God's Kingdom following Kingdom ways—instead of eking out a bleak and depressing existence under the oppressive ways of the world (imperialism, patriarchy, racism, materialism, and militarism). The passion of the Christ was to live his life fully for the sake of all.

Granted, Jesus eventually made peace with the distinct possibility that he'd be strung up for living life in that liberated and free manner, but that doesn't mean he wanted that to happen to him. *"My Father, if it is possible, may this cup be taken from me. Yet not as I will, but as you will."* (Matthew 26:39) and *"My God! My God! Why have You forsaken me?!"* Mark 15:34, exclamations mine, but I'm sure Jesus' too.

---

[171] E.g., "The men who teach the story of just 39 stripes have no idea, no concept of the torturous scourging of our Lord and Savior Christ Jesus, nor do they appreciate the extent of His suffering for *our* sins. I will not go into the full story of His scourging, but I will say that it went far beyond any human effort to endure. It took God the Son to endure the torture of the Calvary experience." http://www.ais-gwd.com/~cdevans/stripes.htm; see also: "Why Did Jesus Suffer?" http://executableoutlines.com/top/suffer.htm; "Did Jesus have to Suffer and Die?" http://www.sspeterandpaul. net/new_evangelization/RCIA/Handouts/did%20jesus%20 have%20to%20suffer%20an.pdf; and "Did Jesus have to Suffer and Die to Save Mankind?" http://www.agapebiblestudy.com/ documents/Did%20Jesus%20Have%20to%20Suffer%20to%20 Save%20Mankind.htm.

Break it Down X

A Wesleyan take on things . . .

As a transition between my treatments of the conservative and the progressive approaches to salvation, I offer the following articulation of my understanding of a Wesleyan understanding of salvation. Notice that salvation is understood as an ongoing process with this view:

I resonate a bit with the semi-Pelagian[172] concept that humans may choose faith, but that God grants us the grace to continue this new life. I affirm John Wesley's notion of a "three-fold flow of grace." Here is understanding of Wesley's theology: God loves and invites us to Him even before we consciously believe. This is God's freely given prevenient grace (*prevenient* means "before knowing"). Even before we know that there is a God, She's already loving us and wooing us to Her in all sorts of ways, through the beauty of nature, through music, through our families, possibly through church and Sunday school, etc. At some point in our lives we experience God's Justifying grace which is the grace that helps us realize that there is a God, and that there has come to be some disconnection between us and God and that the way to re-connect, and to become at-*one*-ed with God is by accepting God's love for us through the Good news of the life, death, and resurrection of Jesus. When we accept this grace, we become "justified sinners."

Once people have accepted this Good News (accepted Jesus into their lives), they begin to receive God's Sanctifying grace that helps them to grow toward "Christian perfection"—an ideal state of being where all of

---

[172]   Semi-Pelagianism is a weaker form of Pelagianism, a heresy derived from Pelagius who lived in the 5th century A.D. and was a teacher in Rome. Semi-Pelagianism (advocated by Cassian at Marseilles, 5th Century) did not deny original sin and its effects upon the human soul and will. But, it taught that God and man cooperate to achieve man's salvation. This cooperation is not by human effort as in keeping the law, but rather in the ability of a person to make a free will choice. The semi-Pelagian teaches that man can make the first move toward God by seeking God out of his own free will and that man can cooperate with God's grace even to the keeping of his faith through human effort. This would mean that God responds to the initial effort of person and that God's grace is not absolutely necessary to maintain faith . . . Semi-Pelagianism was condemned at the Council of Orange in 529. Christian Apologetics and Research Ministry, http://www.carm.org/semi-pelagianism

one's actions and thoughts are motivated solely by God. Persons receiving this grace experience the ongoing process of conversion and salvation. Salvation, in a truly biblical sense, means *wholeness*, both spiritually and physically. It means this on the personal level and on the larger corporate/societal one. Salvation doesn't necessarily mean the curing of illness, mending of bones, the growing back of amputated limbs, the breaking of addictions, or the erasure of past abuse. It means being aware that one is an unconditionally loved, accepted, and forgiven Child of God. It is the sprouting and consummation of a more full, more complete, and more satisfying relationship. It is a decisive change in the heart. Salvation may lead to a healthy acceptance of certain predicaments (disabilities, imprisonment, etc.) in this life and inspiration to continue our journeys. Salvation also implies the hope-filled inspiration to challenge other kinds of oppressive circumstances. To the extent to which we begin to realize these aims, we may discern assurance of our salvation. I also believe that a "saved" person can backslide into a miserable and tortured state. We do have free will after all. We make decisions every passing moment. It's possible to get off-track and derail as a consequence.

Once we perceive that we are experiencing salvation and wholeness, God's love doesn't end. In order to more easily achieve the acceptance of our lot in life and to become empowered to Christian *praxis* (putting one's faith, ideology, or worldview into action) we are blessed with God's Sanctifying grace. As we accept this grace, we grow in the knowledge and love of ourselves, our world, and our God. Good works and social justice will then naturally flow from us leading us to struggling with others and prophetically seeking liberation. This way of life is counter-cultural. Along with good works, I feel that an attitude of humility, respect, awe, gratitude, praise, and worship also naturally flow from us as we proceed in our newly recognized way of life in Christ. This grace allows us to begin to move toward sanctification, which I understand to mean as the state where more and more of our desires, motivations, thoughts, and actions flow from being fully in sync with God's will. It means being solely "in Christ" and having the "mind of Christ" (1 Corinthians 2:16).

This is the process of living a "regenerated" new life, with the Holy Spirit empowering us to love God and serve others, and releasing us from the compulsive powers of sin and guilt. I'm not sure if a state of actual Christian perfection or entire sanctification is possible for anyone of us to fully attain. Even it were, we'd be humble and modest about it and likely not tell anyone. Due to the realities of the vulnerable human condition, we would likely not be capable of remaining in such a state for long—perhaps no more than a few minutes. I think the Church of the Nazarene's traditional take on it, that we can achieve perfection in this life, is problematic. Methodists believe it is something that happens to us as we mature in the faith.[173] It'd be nice if more ministries gave more attention to the further nurturing of believers after they've "come to Christ."

I find it healthy to weave in some Jungian[174] (and arguably, Pauline)[175] notions too, particularly, embracing our shadow sides and not repressing them as we pursue sanctification. Repression always leads to dysfunction. Knowing, owning, befriending, and embracing our shadow sides is healthy and, well, *perfect*.[176]

A Progressive view of Salvation:

If salvation isn't primarily about Jesus dying on a cross, and if it isn't primarily about getting into heaven when we die, then what is it? I spoke to this in part in Chapter 3 so I'll try to avoid repeating myself. Most progressive Christians would claim that the salvation that the Jewish Jesus of Nazareth promoted and provides is closer to a Jewish notion about it than what has become "the" Christian take on

---

[173] Wesley's approach to sanctification is largely based upon the concept of *deification* of the Eastern Orthodox Church.

[174] Jungian refers to the analytical psychology introduced by Swiss Psychiatrist Carl Jung.

[175] Pauline refers to the theology of the apostle Paul, in this case, I'm referring to passages such as Romans 7:19-21 and Ephesians 5:7-14.

[176] A glaring example of what happens when we fail to admit and embrace our shadow sides is what happened to the Ted Haggard in 2006. Haggard was the senior pastor of a mega-church in Colorado Springs, CO and he was the president of the National Evangelical Association. He was forced to resign in utter humiliation when news reports were released about his engaging in extra-marital sex and taking illegal drugs with gay prostitutes in Denver. Note, I don't feel that homosexuality is a sin, rather, this incident point to the lengths that humans will go to deny and repress real parts of themselves—even to the point of hypocritically preaching against them. Although Haggard referred to this as "giving into his dark side," from a Jungian perspective, it might well be argued that he actually was allowing his golden shadow to come forth. See: "Haggard admits 'sexual immorality,' apologizes," Associated Press, Nov. 5, 2006, http://www.msnbc.msn.com/id/15536263/

it. It has as much of an emphasis upon societal/communal concerns as it does upon the personal. It is just as much or more about providing wholeness, liberation, and physical wellbeing here and now as it is about a potential future bliss we may experience in heaven after we die. Moreover, it is as much about being saved *for*, and not merely saved *from*. It's about being set free to be who we really are, not just about being saved from negative things like hell. To the extent that it *is* about being saved "from," it is as much about being saved from oppressive systems and social evils as well as being saved from our personal sins and shortcomings. As Bible scholar Dennis Bratcher puts it in his remarks about the Christian season of Advent,[177]

> *The anticipation of the Coming of the Messiah throughout [Judaism and the Hebrew scriptures] is not in connection with remembrance of sins. Rather, it is in the context of oppression and injustice, the longing for redemption, not from personal guilt and sin but from the systemic evil of the world expressed in evil empires and tyrants. It is in that sense that all creation groans for its redemption as we witness the evil that so dominates our world (Romans 8:18-25).*
>
> *Of course, there is the problem of longing for vindication from an evil world when we are contributors to that evil. This is the power of the images of Amos when he warns about longing for the "Day of the Lord" that will really be a day of darkness (Amos 5:18-20). Still, even with Amos' warning the time of Advent is one of expectation and anticipation, a longing for God's actions to restore all things and vindicate the righteous. This is why during Advent we as Christians also anticipate the Second Coming as a twin theme of the season. So, while some church traditions focus on penitence during Advent, and there remains a place for that, the spirit of that expectation from the Old Testament is better captured with a joyous sense of expectancy. Rather than a time of mourning and fasting, Advent is celebrated as a time of joy and happiness as we await the coming of the King.*

---

[177] *The Season of Advent Anticipation and Hope*, Dennis Bratcher, http://www.crivoice.org/cyadvent.html used with permission.

We need saving from the oppression, victimization, and injustice inflicted on us by outside others. We also need saving from ourselves. However, the emphasis on our own transgressions isn't primarily about our sexual choices or smoking habits, etc. The emphasis is on our complicity in contributing to systems that oppress others.

Progressive Christianity points out that this salvation comes to humans by God's grace and can be received by us, with or possibly even without, our awareness.[178] People who are aware of this (who've been "born again") make an overt decision to accept the free gift of the life, death, and resurrection of Jesus and all that He means in their lives—including a commitment to follow His teachings and in His ways. There are biblical instances where Jesus stated that salvation was provided to the members of entire households merely because of the conversion of one of its members. Progressive Christians believe that God is at work in "saving" ways through other religious traditions. We believe that people such as Gandhi, who weren't overtly Christian in their beliefs, were notably so in their actions—even to saintly degrees. Progressive Christianity points out that even *before* he was executed, Jesus provided atonement, at-*one*-ment—reconnection with God and social reacceptance, to hurting souls via his gracious interaction in their lives. This indicates that salvation isn't solely due to Jesus' death.

Examples of Jesus providing salvation to people before he was killed include: Jesus saving Zacchaeus, a tax-collector (and apparently all the members of his household) with Jesus saying, *"Today salvation has come to this house, because this man, too, is a son of Abraham. For the Son of Man came to seek and to save what was lost"* (Luke 19:9-10); Jesus healing a blind man *Jesus said to him, "Receive your sight; your faith has saved you,"* (Luke 18:42[179]); Jesus healing a

---

178   An example here might be of the Roman centurion's servant who was saved by Jesus from across a great distance without the servant even being aware of Jesus or what he was doing for him (Luke 7:10).

179   The Greek word *sozo* is translated as "saved" in the KJV and as "healed" in the NIV. I suspect the conservative editor's of the NIV wanted to prevent readers from thinking that Jesus saved people before he died. But clearly, he did. This is also a good place to remind us that the original Jewish notion of salvation referred to physical, relational, and mental/soul (*psyche* means both mind and soul) health and wholeness here and now—and had little to do with where we go when we die.

leper, *"Then he said to him, 'Rise and go; your faith has made you well [saved you]."* (17:19); Jesus healing a woman's bleeding, *And he said to her, "Daughter, your faith has healed you [saved you]."* (Mark 5:34); and Jesus healing a Roman officer's servant, *And they that were sent, returning to the house, found the servant whole [saved] that had been sick* (Luke 7:10).

The salvation that Jesus provides is just as much (if not more) about restoring people to right relationship with their community as it is about relieving their physical or spiritual maladies. Notice the people who come to Jesus in these stories—blind persons, lepers, tax collectors, bleeding women, Roman soldiers, etc. These are all persons who Jesus' society relegated as being second class, lesser, impure, infectious, and therefore to be shunned. The people whom his society thought were closer to God were the ones who *resisted* the salvation that Jesus was offering; for example, the rich young ruler who refused what Jesus offered (Luke 18:18-23) and the wealthy and well-to-do who refused to attend "the great banquet" (Luke 14:15-24).

Even though not everyone Jesus interacted with accepted his invitations of healing and wholeness, progressive Christians believe that Jesus intended salvation for everyone. This "universal salvation" offered by Christ is radically offered in two forms. The initial teaching was that it isn't just for Jews, but also for non-Jews (gentiles) as well—a concept that was quite radical at the time. Biblical examples of this include the instances where Jesus provided healing salvation to various non-Jews including, the demon possessed man in Gerasene (Mark 5:1-20); the Canaanite woman's demon-possessed daughter (Matthew 15:21-28); and a Roman officer's servant (Matthew 8:5-13).

The concept of universal salvation evolved to the perception that it is not just for overtly Christian believers, but also for all humanity. Universalism has come to mean the belief that *all* humans can be saved through Jesus Christ and eventually come to harmony in God's Kingdom. A stronger form is *apokatastasis*, the belief that all mortal beings *will* be reconciled to God, including Satan and his fallen angels.

Universalism was a widely held view among early Christian theologians. In the first 5 or 6 centuries of Christianity, there were six known theological schools, of which four (Alexandria,

Antioch, Caesarea, and Edessa) were universalist, one (Ephesus) accepted *conditional immortality* (that only those who are saved will live forever in heaven, the wicked get annihilated), and one (Carthage/Rome) believed in *endless punishment of the lost* (that persons condemned to hell stay there forever).

The two major theologians opposing universalism were Romans, Tertullian and Augustine. Progressive Christians suggest that the influence of those two theologians distorted the original intentions and understanding of early Christianity. Unfortunately, many of their teachings came to be adopted as "orthodox." In the 17th and 18th Centuries, several Christian reformers came to believe in a universally loving God and felt that God would grant salvation to all humans. They became known as the "Universalists."

Break it Down XI

The most famous 20th Century proponent of Universalism was William Barclay, a widely respected theologian and preacher in the Church of Scotland who died in 1978. He was Professor of Divinity and biblical Criticism at Glasgow University and the author of many biblical commentaries and books, including a translation of the New Testament, "Barclay New Testament," and "The Daily Study Bible Series." Barlcay wrote a powerful essay that solidly presents the biblical basis for this perspective, "I am a Convinced Universalist."[180] In the essay, Barclay shows how two of the early great Christian thinkers, Origen and Gregory of Nyssa, embraced a Universalist understanding of salvation. He then states four reasons that he shares that view himself:

He presents passages of the New Testament that support this view:

- "I, when I am lifted up from the earth, will draw all men to myself" (John 12:32)
- "God has consigned all men to disobedience that he may have mercy on all" (Rom. 11:32)
- "As in Adam all die, so also in Christ shall all be made alive" (1 Cor. 15:22)
- Paul's looking to the final total triumph when God will be everything to everyone (1 Cor. 15:28)
- "who desires all men to be saved and to come to the knowledge of the truth," and of Christ Jesus "who gave himself as a ransom for all" (1 Tim 2:4-6)
- *[I'll add another one: "For God did not send his Son into the world to condemn the world, but to save the world through him." (John 3:17)]*

---

[180] For the full essay, see: http://www.auburn.edu/~allenkc/univart.html

Barclay then discusses Matthew 25:46 where it is said that the rejected go away to eternal punishment, and the righteous to eternal life. He does a word-study on some of the Greek words used in that passage and shows how the form of punishment that's being referred to here is *remedial*; i.e. not something that will last forever.

He then asserts that it is impossible for humans to set limits to God's grace.

Fourthly, he defends his belief in "the ultimate and complete triumph of God, the time when all things will be subject to him, and when God will be everything to everyone" (1 Cor. 15:24-28). For Barclay, this means that, **"If one man remains outside the love of God at the end of time, it means that that one man has defeated the love of God—and that is impossible."**

He then describes how God is more than a King or a Judge, He's also a Father and "No father could be happy while there were members of his family forever in agony. No father would count it a triumph to obliterate the disobedient members of his family. The only triumph a father can know is to have all his family back home."

Barclay closes by asserting, **"The only victory love can enjoy is the day when its offer of love is answered by the return of love. The only possible final triumph is a universe loved by and in love with God."**[181]

I've put in bold the sentences that I think present the crux of the Universalist perspective on salvation. That perspective basically says that no matter what, love wins. This is essentially the same as a saying of the U.S. Marine Corps, "No one gets left behind." Not all progressive Christians subscribe to Universal Salvation in this sense, but many, do. It primarily addresses the state of our souls after we die. If you think about it, it's a rather "high Christology"[182] as it means a high degree of God's power through Jesus. I embrace the Arminian perspective when it comes

---

[181] Quoted from *William Barclay: A Spiritual Autobiography*, pg 65-67, William B. Eerdmans, Grand Rapids, 1977. See: http://www.auburn.edu/~allenkc/barclay1.html

[182] *Christology* is that area of Christian theology that speaks to the role and nature of Jesus the Christ. A high Christology typically means a belief that Jesus was fully Divine and God. A low Christology typically means that Jesus wasn't God, but rather, a uniquely blessed

to salvation while we are alive in the world, and the Universalist view for after people die.

Again progressive Christianity asserts that through Jesus, people are saved *from* the ways of the world, including from the worst parts of themselves and their self-destructive tendencies. They are saved *for* the ways of God's Kingdom when they accept and live-out this truth. Salvation is both personal and political/ societal. It is experienced here and now, and also later in heaven. If one's faith is real and authentic, then one can't help but *respond* by engaging in service to a world in need. Therefore, our hands can serve as God's hands in spreading salvation-wholeness into the lives of others.

The over-whelming momentum and volume[183] of what salvation has come to mean in popular American Christianity is that it really is about Jesus' death and his blood. It would be irresponsible to not address that perspective seriously. Most Christians have come to accept the notion that Jesus dying a violent death upon a cross is essential to "God's plan" for salvation. This *Substitutionary* or *Penal* theory of the atonement states that God's mercy replaces his wrath after Jesus' *sacrifice* (notice the intentionally theological choice of wording instead of saying "execution") on the cross.[184]

An example of this line of thinking is found in the following words from a conservative Christian website addressing the matter of Jesus' death and atonement:

> *Some people argue that since Jesus did not suffer eternally in hell, therefore suffering eternally in hell cannot be the penalty which sinners will receive. This argument is based on the assumption that Jesus, as our Substitute, took the exact same punishment that we should have received. But as we have seen, that is a faulty assumption. For example, imagine that I have*

---

and gifted human whom God used as a prophet who helped people know who God really is and how much God loves them.

[183] *Volume*—both in terms of amount of sermons, books, tracts, songs, etc., and in terms of decibels of said sermons and songs.

[184] It's interesting to note that the Penal Substitution theory does not draw heavily on the words or attitudes of Jesus himself in the gospels.

*a 4-year-old daughter who disobeys me one day, so I tell her
that she will be spanked. Imagine that I also have a teen-age
son who steps forward and offers to be her substitute and to be
punished in her place. I agree to the substitution, and I punish
him by grounding him for 2 weeks. At that point, punishment
has been done and I am satisfied. Notice that my son did not
become a person who had disobeyed me, and in the same way,
Jesus did not become a sinner on the cross. Also, notice that my
son made a substitutionary sacrifice in place of my daughter,
yet he did not receive the same punishment that I had planned
for her. Instead, he received a punishment that I felt was
appropriate, and which was satisfactory to me. In the same
way, Jesus made a substitutionary sacrifice in our place, but
He did not receive the same punishment which the Father has
planned for sinners. Instead, He received a punishment which
the Father felt was appropriate and which was satisfactory to
the Father.*[185]

Progressive Christians find several of these premises and
conclusions problematic. The analogy of a parent punishing his/
her child breaks down when it comes to God. If God punished His
son (or the rest of humanity by taking it out on Jesus) by killing
him, then as some theologians have observed, God would be guilty
of Divine child abuse no matter how noble the cause. It would
be an example of a utilitarian "the ends justify the means" kind
of ethics. Ironically, conservative Christianity typically condemns
utilitarianism as an "atheistic, secular" form of ethics. Yet here
they embrace it. The author of the above passage seems to feel
that spanking a child, a form of physical violence, is appropriate
and the right thing to do. It isn't. The author's premise is that
God requires punishment for sins and transgressions. Progressive
Christianity suggests that God doesn't operate that way. Why do
humans believe that God requires punishment and "satisfaction"
whenever we screw up? Is it perhaps because so many of us were
spanked by our parents? Is it because our society has largely been
influenced by a certain view of God as prone to violence and

---

[185]   http://www.layhands.com/HowDidJesusBecomeSin.htm

punishment? Or is it perhaps because of both because they work to reinforce and manifest each other?[186]

What if we viewed God as loving us like a loving parent who doesn't have a need to dole out punishment? Certainly, parents do not *have* to spank their children. I have a ten year old son whom I have never intentionally harmed in any way, including verbally or spanking, and all who meet him (at least so far) find him to be a sweet, respectful, well-behaved lad. Sure, he doesn't always do as I'd please or want, but if he sees "the look" on my face that I'm not pleased with him because of something he did or failed to do, that's all it takes. He's a sensitive little guy and his sensing that I'm disappointed with him is all it takes for him to straighten up. There's no need for punishment, let alone physical violence or the infliction of pain.

As theologian Walter Wink has pointed out, the pagan Myth of Redemptive Violence was one of the first meta-narratives to pervade human civilization.[187] The myth states that the perceived

---

[186]   One of Jesus' main messages was that we must love our enemies, forgive those who injure us, and overcome evil with good. These teachings are completely contrary to the idea that God demands the blood and a tortured death of an innocent man. Fr. John Mabry views the Penal Theory as "an oppressive theology, and inauthentic in light of Jesus' teaching." He asks: "how can a God who in Jesus told us that we were never to exact vengeance, that we were to forgive each other perpetually without retribution, demand of us behavior that God 'himself' is unwilling or unable to perform? . . . why can God not simply forgive as we are instructed to do, rather than mandating that some 'innocent and spotless victim' bear the brunt of 'his' reservoir of wrath? The ability of humans to do this when God will not or cannot logically casts humanity as God's moral superior. This is of course absurd!" The Christian Concept of the Atonement, "The Narrative Christus Victor Theory," by B.A. Robinson, April 12, 2005, Ontario Consultants on Religious Tolerance, http://www.religioustolerance.org/chr_atone14.htm

[187]   The myth of Redemptive Violence is a meta-narrative and a, if not *the*, major archetypal theme in literature, particularly in imperial cultures. The oldest known version of this story is the Creation myth of Babylon (the *Enûma Elish*) ca.1250 B.C. Walter Wink created the phrase as part of an analysis of its impact on contemporary culture

good guys need to kill or physically punish the perceived bad guys in order for things to be right with the world. This myth has become so thoroughly fused to humanity that it is fair to say that it is our dominant story. It is the basis of much of our culture from plays, operas, art, and songs, as well as comic books, movies, and our wars with al-Qaeda and Iraq. It is interesting to note that both sides of both of those wars, and all wars for that matter, perceive themselves as the good guys and the other side as the bad guys. All sides are buying into the myth of redemptive violence and having it dictate their policies and tactics. The dominant story of popular American Christianity is a story of Divinely sanctioned violence (Jesus dying on the cross for our sins) that results in justifying the majority of us being oppressed by worldly domination systems.

Progressive Christians submit that God "sent Jesus into the world,"[188] in order to attempt to subvert that old story and replace it with a new one—one that leads to abundant and eternal life. Yes, there may be some verses in the Bible that suggest that "chastening" a child, or a wife, with a rod, "no thicker than one's thumb," is allowed and even commendable. And yes, some parents, and husbands today may feel that spanking or physical punishment is okay.[189] This simply shows how pervasive and insidious the ancient myth of redemptive violence was and is. It has found its way into our sacred texts and it's still employed by many parents, husbands, and governmental leaders today.

This doesn't mean that God condones this myth or its resulting applications. Progressive Christians don't think that God wanted Jesus to be executed, or that God needed him to be killed in order to satisfy some bizarre need for transactional "Cosmic/Divine Justice/

---

and its role in justifying oppressive power structures in his book *The Powers That Be*, Three Rivers Press, 1999. See also, Walter Wink, "Facing the Myth of Redemptive Violence," http://www.ekklesia.co.uk/content/cpt/article_060823wink.shtml.

[188] Or alternatively worded, "sent nudged and wooed that man from Nazareth . . ."

[189] To remind us, wives and children were not considered full persons in Bible days. They were considered and treated as chattel—as the property of the husbands and fathers. While not many husbands in America today spank their wives, tragically, some beat their spouses.

Economics" or for God's "honor" to be restored. It makes more sense to suggest that as circumstances and tensions during Jesus' last week in Jerusalem came to a head, God allowed the inevitable collision with the worldly powers to run their course.[190] God saw that the best course of action was to let the Roman Empire and their Hebraic puppet powers dish-out the worst they could. They executed Jesus in the most painful and most shameful manner possible.[191] God demonstrated His amazing love and redemptive powers through the resurrection.[192] Christ's resurrection shows us that *nothing* can separate us from the love of God, not even doing

---

[190]   For more about this profound collision of powers, see *The Last Week* by John Dominic Crossan and Marcus Borg. You'll never think about "Holy Week" (Palm Sunday-Easter Sunday) in the same way. This "Passion week" is so fascinating—there is a sense of urgency and impending doom as the week progresses. I'm not sure that many people today know much about what happened between Palm Sunday and Good Friday. It's a time when Jesus becomes more intimate, withdrawn, contemplative, and aware of his own mortality—and simultaneously chooses to bond with his disciples. We can learn a lot about how to live our lives by looking at how he lived that week.

[191]   In a way, this provides a profound *inclusio* (framing bookend) if paired with the perception that Jesus was born as an illegitimate bastard to a common peasant girl in the hinterland fringes of the Roman Empire. Crucifixion was reserved for the worst of the worst, political insurrectionists and for persons who committed the most base and heinous of crimes. Being killed and hung up naked for all to see was, and probably remains, the most shameful thing a human can experience. So, perceptually at least, through Jesus, God entered the world and left the world in the most humble and shameful manners possible in order to show that God suffers with us and has compassion for us, thus making Him accessible and relatable to all humanity. (Notice also the extended *inclusio* if one considers the potentially similar humble birth of Moses; i.e., regarding his being born either out of wedlock or from an incestuous marriage between nephew and aunt, and a story about an order for newborn Hebrew boys to be killed).

[192]   Notice how that way of putting it is quite different from the conservative view that "God intended Jesus to be killed as a sacrifice to satisfy his wrath and/or need for Divine justice/retribution."

the worst thing that humans could possibly do.[193] The resurrection shows us that ultimately the worldly powers of this world are false and impotent. We can indeed trust Jesus' invitation to follow His loving, self-sacrificial, servant-hearted ways—ways that appear to be risky and foolish to the eyes of the world.[194] The resurrection also provides assurance that even if the worst were to happen to us, even if we were to be brutally and unjustly killed—perhaps even being shamefully crucified ourselves due to our daring to live by these Kingdom ways, that even *that* won't separate us from God. God will redeem, transform, and make everything right in the end.

Progressive Christians don't feel that God needed or intended Jesus to be executed. Instead we suggest that part of how God redeemed that horrible tragedy of what happened to Jesus, was to convey that Jesus' death on the cross would be the last "sacrifice." While God didn't want Jesus to be killed, since it was inevitable, and actually happened, God wants for us to view it as the *last* instance of religiously condoned violence. We think God wants Jesus' death put an end to sacrificial and retributive violence. Jesus' ministry was primarily a one of reconciliation and restoration—not judging or punishing.

Countries that consider themselves "Christian nations" would do well to remember this and enact social and governmental policies accordingly. Killing people is not simpatico with Jesus and his way. Progressive Christians agree with the numerous Catholic, mainline and Anabaptist[195] denominations that are opposed to capital punishment. One of God's chief commandments is to not kill. Efforts to reach out to save people's souls and rehabilitate them are pointless if they're dead. It is also oxymoronic to have a

---

[193] Though I can totally see how that may be considered an offensive over-statement by our Jewish friends who remind us that things like genocide of entire people groups is about the worst thing that humans can do.

[194] To the extent that we believe in and live-out these nonviolent, self-giving, reconciling ways—this "Way of Christ"—we experience and know salvation. God's work through the life, death, and resurrection of Jesus enable and empower us to be able to do those things.

[195] Anabaptist churches include the Quakers, Amish, Mennonites, and the Church of the Brethren.

policy of killing people in order to teach other people that killing people is wrong.[196]

Instead of focusing upon the gory details of what the Roman soldiers did to Jesus in killing him, progressive Christianity puts the emphasis upon what Jesus did that caused the Israelite and Roman officials to react as they did. Progressive Christians lift up Jesus' prophetic and subversive radicality. We suggest that Jesus emphasized this at the start of his public ministry. After being baptized by his cousin John, Jesus went into the wilderness for 40 days to ponder his purpose and course in life. He found himself tested and he had to face some profound temptations. Having defeated his demons, he went directly to his hometown:

> *He went to Nazareth, where he had been brought up, and on the Sabbath day he went into the synagogue, as was his custom. And he stood up to read. The scroll of the prophet Isaiah was handed to him. Unrolling it, he found the place where it is written: "The Spirit of the Lord is on me, because he has anointed me to preach good news to the poor. He has sent me to proclaim freedom for the prisoners and recovery of sight for the blind, to release the oppressed, to proclaim the year of the Lord's favor." Then he rolled up the scroll, gave it back to the attendant and sat down. The eyes of everyone in the synagogue were fastened on him, and he began by saying to them, "Today this scripture is fulfilled in your hearing."* (Luke 4:16-21)

This was Jesus' manifesto. With this bold declaration, Jesus states what he's going to be about for the next three years of his public ministry. He's here to say enough's enough! It's time to usher in God's Kingdom here and now. This included reasserting the year of Jubilee ("the year of the Lord's Favor," Leviticus 25:11)—which meant to void the debts of those who owed them, to release people from indentured servitude, and for the "haves" to give property back to the "have-nots!" Talk about rocking the

---

[196] Why the United States, a nation that many conservative Christians consider as being a "Christian nation" is the only Western nation in the world to still employ the death penalty is beyond me. It would be funny if it weren't so gravely tragic.

boat. It's no wonder that the people of his hometown nearly killed him right after he preached that short sermon! (Luke 4:28-29) If salvation was only about Jesus' blood being shed, it would've been far more efficient for him to have been killed right then from the get go—or even earlier by Herod when he was still a toddler along with those poor boys aged two and under living in Bethlehem (Matthew 2:16-18). We point out how Jesus' mother foreshadowed this radical manifesto while she was still pregnant with her equally radical "Magnificat":

> *And Mary said: "My soul glorifies the Lord and my spirit rejoices in God my Savior, for he has been mindful of the humble state of his servant. From now on all generations will call me blessed, for the Mighty One has done great things for me—holy is his name. His mercy extends to those who fear him, from generation to generation. He has performed mighty deeds with his arm; he has scattered those who are proud in their inmost thoughts. He has brought down rulers from their thrones but has lifted up the humble. He has filled the hungry with good things but has sent the rich away empty. He has helped his servant Israel, remembering to be merciful to Abraham and his descendants forever, even as he said to our fathers." (Luke 1:46-55)*

Progressive Christianity also points out that what Jesus talked about most wasn't himself. If one goes through all of the words that have been attributed to Jesus in the Gospels (in some Bibles, they're highlighted by being in red print), one will see that the overwhelming topic that Jesus spoke about most was God's Kingdom—with special emphasis upon its inbreaking into the here and now. The progressive Christian approach also reminds us that the *second* most frequent subject that Jesus talked about wasn't himself either. It was money and our relationship to it. Jesus repeatedly criticized greed, materialism, and striving for worldly successes. But one would hardly learn this in the many conservative churches which condone the U.S.' largely unregulated, "scarcity-based" capitalist economic system, and its resulting gap between the haves and the have-nots. Instead, what one hears most about in many churches across the land is that "God wants you to thrive financially, to have a nice car, and a fat checking account. The more you give to the church, the more God will bless you with such riches." This gospel of wealth and prosperity is a *false* gospel. It isn't the gospel of Jesus Christ.[197]

Let's return to addressing the conservative emphasis upon Jesus' bloody death as being the means of our salvation. Throughout the Bible, blood (*dam*) is identified with life (women know this intimately). According to Leviticus, *For the life of a creature is in the blood, and I have given it to you to make atonement for yourselves on the altar; it is the blood that makes atonement for one's life* (17:11). This is the only verse in the Hebrew Scriptures that suggests that the taking of life is related or necessary to providing atonement. It is found within the context of a passage speaking about ritual purity and dietary laws (keeping kosher—nothing to do with atonement). It provides the reason that the ancient Hebrews were not to consume blood because it is identified with life. Whether or not this is literally true, for Jews, it is true spiritually, and they, historically at least, acted as if it were literally true.

> ... '*Any Israelite or any alien living among you who hunts any animal or bird that may be eaten must drain out the blood and cover it with earth,* [14] *because the life of every creature is its blood. That is why I have said to the Israelites, "You must not eat the blood of any creature, because the life of every creature is its blood; anyone who eats it must be cut off* (Leviticus 17:13-14).

This use of the word *blood* in the Hebraic texts also relates to the Jewish celebration of Yom Kippur, the Day of Atonement—*atonement* conveying covering, cancellation, reconciliation, and pardon. In ancient Israel, Yom Kippur was the only day of the year when the High Priest could enter the Holy of Holies and call upon the Name of Yahweh (YHVH) to offer blood sacrifice for the sins of the people. The "life for a life" principle is the basis of the Temple sacrifice system. The root of

---

[197] Indeed, its teachings that "If you please God, you will be rewarded and if you are ill, down-on-your-luck, or otherwise suffering, it's because you have done something wrong" are very similar to the dysfunctional religiosity that Jesus was seeking to counter—ironic and tragic.

the word "kippur" is *kafar*, which is derived from the word, *kofer* meaning, "ransom." This is similar to the word *kipper*, meaning, "remove." Both are similar to the word "redeem" (Psalm 49:7) meaning "to atone by offering a substitute." Most of the usages of this word in the Hebrew Bible concern making atonement by the priestly ritual of sprinkling sacrificial blood to remove sin and defilement. The life-blood of the sacrificial animal was required in exchange for the life-blood of the worshipper—a symbolic expression of exchanging innocent life for guilty life. This symbolism was further demonstrated by the action of the worshipper in placing his hands on the head of the sacrificial animal and confessing his sins over the animal (Leviticus 16:21, 1:4, 4:4, etc.). Then the animal was killed or released as a scapegoat.

All this said, there is reason to think that God may not have actually approved of the Hebraic system of blood offerings. According to Isaiah, God says, *"The multitude of your sacrifices—what are they to me?" says the LORD. "I have more than enough of burnt offerings, of rams and the fat of fattened animals; I have no pleasure in the blood of bulls and lambs and goats.* (Isaiah 1:11)

But again, the idea of Jesus' death being a substitutionary sacrifice has certain basis in scripture. Jumping forward to the New Testament, the author of the book known as Hebrews, a Jewish Christian presumed by conservatives to be Paul, intended to show his fellow Jews how Jesus was the Messiah and how his blood provided the necessary sacrifice to atone for our sins. The author of Hebrews appears to have *not* been running with this concept as a *metaphor*. Instead, he actually *believed* that blood sacrifice *was* required by God to deal with human sin. "Without the shedding of blood there is no remission" (Hebrews 9:22). This writer apparently believed that there is no atonement without blood and that the substitutionary shedding of blood, the "life for life" notion, was essential to atonement with God. He understood Jesus as being the new High Priest (Hebrews 9:11) who offered his own body as "perfect, unblemished sacrificial lamb" (9:23) and as a "once and for all sacrifice for all of our sins" (9:28). The author believed that by the shedding of Jesus' blood we were atoned and reconciled to God (9:14 & 15).

Many Bible scholars do not believe that Paul authored Hebrews, however, but instead someone writing in the name of Paul.[198] This potentially gives that book a bit less authority. Though that book was canonized as part of the Christian canon, there are other biblical passages that lend themselves to supporting other views of the atonement that Jesus provides for us, for instance, Mark 10:45, 1 John 3:8; 2 Corinthians 5:18-19; Colossians 1:20-22; Acts 13:38; Ephesians 1:7; 1 Peter 2:24; and Romans 8:2-16 support the *Christus Victor* model of the atonement, and Ephesians 5:1-2 and 1 Peter 2:21 provide basis for the Moral or Exemplary model.[199]

It's clear that some of the writers of the Christian Gospels intended parallels between Hebraic atonement rituals and Jesus by placing the events of Jesus' last week of life during the festival of the Passover. Passover is when Jews celebrate God saving their ancestors from the angel of death that swept through Egypt.[200]

---

[198] "The book of Hebrews quotes extensively from the Old Testament. Paul, as a Pharisee, would have been familiar with the Scripture in its original Hebrew language. In other letters, Paul either quotes the Masoretic Text (the original Hebrew) or paraphrases it. All of the quotes in this epistle are taken out of the *Septuagint* (the Greek version of the Old Testament), which is inconsistent with Paul's usage. Paul was an apostle who claimed to receive his revelations directly from the risen Lord Jesus (1 Corinthians 11:23; Galatians 1:12). The writer of Hebrews explicitly says that he was taught by an apostle (Hebrews 2:3). "Who Wrote the Book of Hebrew?," http://www.gotquestions.org/author-Hebrews.html

[199] For more information on these alternative theories of the atonement see: "To what extent can a presentation of the Atonement that rejects 'penal substitution' and favours other models of the Atonement be a valid form of Christian gospel?," Jonathan Appleby, May 2007, http://www.appleby.org.uk/pdfs/Is%20Penal%20Substitution%20a%20Necessary%20Part%20of%20Atonement.pdf; The Christus Victor View of Atonement by Doulos Christou, September 16, 2009, http://loveacceptforgive.com/2009/09/16/the-christus-victor-view-of-atonement/; and Various Christian theories of the Atonement, http://www.religioustolerance.org/chr_atone5.htm

[200] According to the story, in the Book of Exodus, as a sign from God to tell Pharaoh to release the Hebrews held there in captivity as slaves (Exodus 12:7-22).

According to the Exodus saga, the Hebrews were spared because they followed God's instruction to put lamb's blood on their doors to signal the angel of death not to kill the people inside those dwellings marked by that blood. They were "passed over." If one thinks of the elements of Jesus' last supper with his disciples in that upper room as being a Passover meal (see Mark 14:12-25), this provides rich symbolism with the breaking of the bread and the sharing of the wine that represent Jesus' broken body and his blood. These lend themselves to being seen as metaphorical equivalents to the lamb, bread, wine, and other elements of the *Seder* meal that reminds Jews of God's saving their ancestors in the faith by liberating them from captivity and into freedom. Their partaking in those elements could potentially be interpreted as a new ritual for believers to partakein in order to have "the angel of death pass over" them (to be "saved").

Additionally, the name of the first person mentioned in the Bible, *Adam*, comes from the Hebrew word for "blood" (*dam*). The name *Adam* can be interpreted as "I shall become blood," an allusion to the power to draw the *nefesh* (soul) into the body by means of the blood. God created Adam from the earth and the word *adama* means "red soil/dirt." A portion of the name Adam, *dam*, is the Hebrew word for "blood" and *adom* is "red" in Hebrew. These root words are related. According to the Judeo-Christian creation myth, Adam represented all humanity and he was created from the earth. His spirit, the second part of his being, comes to him directly from God. God gave him a spirit (*ruach*) through a breath of life.and Adam became a living soul. In his letter to the Romans, the apostle Paul teaches that death and sin entered the world through the sin of Adam. It took the death of Jesus, as "the new Adam" (the new proto-human, Romans 4:25-5:1-21), to remove sin and death from fallen humanity—the "wages of sin" being "death" (Romans 6:23).

Progressive Christianity points out that that the wording employed by both the authors of Genesis and Paul are clearly metaphorical. Paul's letters, including Romans, are rife with metaphors and analogies.[201] There is no reason to think that he

---

[201]   Examples of this include: his metaphor of the Christian life as "slavery," in Romans 6 & 7 (where he subverts the oppressive

abstained from employing those in Chapters 4 and 5. While the implication of Paul's beautiful words is that sin and death have been abolished, in reality, sin and death still take place in the world—even in the lives of faithful Christians who still sin and die. The primary thrust of Paul in his letter to the Romans is articulating the teaching that Christians are justified and saved by faith. That essential teaching is in no way diminished if we realize that Paul is speaking metaphorically and sharing spiritual truths—not literal ones.

Going back to the discussion of the creation of Adam in Genesis, few Christians today believe that humans were literally created from actual red dirt. Instead, many understand that creation story as being just that, a story. It is a very specific story about who and Whose we are. The stories in Genesis were originally told as campfire tales long before they were ever written down. Their purpose was to entertain, foster group identity (in particular, for the Jewish peoples), and to inspire. Their purpose wasn't to give literal historical accounts or scientific explanations. If we accept that Adam was merely the name attributed to the first human to evolve onto the scene, we find no need to literalize the details of the story—let alone find ourselves bound to cultic practices of the Levite priests[202] as the underpinnings for our thoughts about salvation.

If we take seriously that primary passage in Leviticus[203] we may notice something. We may observe something inconvenient to conservative Christianity's assertion about Jesus' death and

---

experience of chattel slavery in the Roman empire with the choice between being a slave to sin or a slave to God); his metaphor of being grafted to an olive tree for helping understand how gentiles can be linked to the Jewish chosen people and their covenant in Romans 11:11-32; and his numerous forensic/judicial metaphors where he discusses various aspects of Christian belief to civil law—adoption, slavery, inheritance, financial agreements, etc.).

[202] (. . . to the practices and reasons behind the Temple sacrifices practiced by the ancient Hebrew priests, the Levites who wrote the book of Leviticus)

[203] Namely, the passage that is the cause of all of these mental gymnastics by Christians over the years about "Jesus' blood being the agent of our atonement to God."

blood causing our salvation—that the blood of a sacrificed animal is to be placed upon the altar in the Temple. *"For the life of a creature is in the blood, and I have given it to you to make atonement for yourselves on the altar; it is the blood that makes atonement for one's life"* (Leviticus 17:11). There is absolutely no indication, however, that Jesus' blood was ever placed upon the altar in the Temple. It is poor exegesis (critical interpretation of a sacred text) to take a verse out of context and then to focus only upon part of that verse, especially if one is interpreting the text literally. When we consider this total verse and do not ignore the fact that it is part of a passage that prohibits the consumption of blood, we see that it explicitly states that the blood of the sacrifice must be placed "upon the altar to make atonement for your souls." According to Leviticus, the only way in which blood can bring atonement is if it is placed on the sacrificial altar in the Temple. This is a necessary condition if one cares about the integrity of that verse. If one is going to appeal to Leviticus, and base his/her notion of Jesus' atonement upon, the entire verse from that text must be considered. Not just part of it.

In the Bible, impurity is often associated with death. The remedy for death is life, so blood (which the Hebrews thought of as the life force) is needed to cleanse. Yet, it's a *metaphor*. Jesus "gave his life for us." Yes, but it wasn't literally the spilling of his blood that was needed. Jesus poured out his life for humanity. He gave his all for us. He "bled out his life-force" so that we might truly live. He poured everything he had into his efforts to help us feel God's love—and he ended up being killed for it. Jesus lived and died *for* us, not instead of us. He didn't seek to live and die on our behalf as our proxy, as our "substitute." He hoped to wake us up into realizing who we really are as God's children and embolden us so that *we* might truly live as God intends!

The point is, even though we Christians remain mortal and continue to sin, we can experience a *spiritual* new life, a *spiritual* resurrection, and salvation! It should be remembered that Saul (Paul's name before his dramatic conversion experience)[204]

---

[204] Prior to his conversion, Saul of Tarsus was a self-imposed protector of the Jewish faith who went around serving as the heresy police. He zealously worked to persecute the early Jewish Christians—even to

didn't encounter a physically resurrected Jesus in the flesh on his famed horse ride to Damascus (Acts 9). Paul interpreted his experience as a spiritual rather than a literal one. While very real, he never said that he could touch the physical body of Jesus. Jesus appeared to him *spiritually* (1 Corinthians 15:1-50). While Paul firmly argues that the resurrection of Christ was real,[205] his actual experience of the Risen Christ was as a spiritual being. Likewise, Paul's experience of being born-again as a new creation is about his spirit, not his flesh. Paul asserts that when we are resurrected, we'll have spiritual bodies, not physical ones.

Progressive Christians realize that if instead of dying upon a Roman cross, Jesus had instead been executed by poisoning, suffocation, lethal injection or water-boarding, the writers[206] of the New Testament still would likely have poetically spiritualized the interpretation of Jesus' execution. In fact, they probably would've even included references to the "shedding of his blood," whether understood as being metaphorical, fabricated, redacted, tacked on, or spiritualized. That would be perfectly understandable considering the Judaic context in which they were living.

When progressive Christians sing *The Old Rugged Cross; When I Survey the Wondrous Cross; Victory in Jesus!;* and *Nothin' but the blood*[207] we sing them as the profound symbols and metaphors that

---

their deaths (Acts 26:10-11). After he was converted to Christianity, the change in his life was so dramatic that he changed his name to Paul.

[205] And Jesus' resurrection as being the basis for our own resurrections.

[206] Many of the Jews in ancient Israel in the decades leading up to and including when Jesus lived, were emphasizing the earlier texts and prophecies about the arrival of the Messiah (anointed savior Christ). Jesus' disciples and all of the early Jewish Christians are examples of Messianic Judaism. Today, "Messianic Jews" refers to both a certain denomination of Christianity that is comprised of Jews for Jesus who, like other Christians, believe that Jesus was the Messiah and who await for Jesus' Second Coming/return; and it can also refer to Jews who don't think that Jesus is the Messiah and so they are waiting for the first coming of the Messiah.

[207] Although to be honest, many progressives choose not to sing those songs to avoid the confusion of people interpreting the song too literally instead of metaphorically—to prevent people from thinking that we endorse a literal interpretation of those hymns.

they are. Hymns use poetic language to celebrate and convey the truth of the great gift that God has given to us in the life, death and resurrection of Jesus. We're not literally celebrating his being nailed to a cross and bleeding out. We celebrate how much Jesus loved us, how far he was willing to go to demonstrate that love. We celebrate that God redeemed the tragedy of that day on that city dump by raising Jesus from the dead inside people's hearts so that we can know that evil doesn't have the last word, and that nothing will separate us from God's love (Romans 8:37-39).[208]

Knowing this, we can live boldly and courageously. With confidence and assurance we can face the challenges that each new day brings. We're liberated when we can "let go" of our own agendas and our tendencies to follow the ways of the world and be willing to symbolically "drown" in a river,[209] and rise again to engage life as only "dead men walking" can—fully alive with no fear or inhibition. In such a state, we have nothing to be afraid of. We see the pettiness of our normal worldly hang-ups. We're free to admit and deal with our struggles. We're free to face our oppressors, our own demons, and our shadows. This releases us from their power and allows us to move forward.

An object lesson may be helpful. In Southeast Asia they developed an ingenious method to catch monkeys alive and unharmed. They call it the "Monkey Trap." It's very simple. A pot or a gourd with a wide bottom and narrow opening is buried in the ground so that the opening of the vessel is just above the ground. Pieces of fruit, nuts, or meat are placed in the vessel. The heat of the day causes the rising odors to attract monkeys to the delicious treats. A monkey smells the treats and reaches down into the narrow opening of the pot to grab hold of the treat. As the monkey attempts to extract the bait from the pot, the

---

[208] It is for this reason that Protestant churches display an empty cross (instead of a crucifix with Jesus still nailed to it) as we focus upon the resurrection and that death didn't have the last word. That said, there is deep meaning to be seen in a crucifix because it reminds us that Jesus suffered with us and that provides hope to many impoverished, struggling Christians around the world.

[209] Even if that "river" is water being poured over heads above a baptismal font.

monkey finds that its fist, full of food, will not fit through the narrow opening. The monkey, excited and frustrated, will scream as it continues to hold onto its food, and attempts to remove it from the pot. When its hollering is heard, the trapper strolls over to the monkey to retrieve the animal. Even as the monkey sees the trapper approaching, instead of letting go of the food, it holds on to the food tighter. It tries even harder to dislodge its fist of food from the pot. We humans of course realize that to escape, the monkey simply has to let go of the food and it'll be able to remove its arm from the pot and be free. All it has to do is let go!

While we may be brighter than other primates, we aren't all that different from our monkey friends. Out of concern for self-preservation and survival, we ardently hold onto what we perceive to be the sweet juicy fruit that we need in our lives; for instance, the hoarding, dog-eat-dog, competitive, vindictive, retributive, keeping up with the Joneses, "law of the jungle" ways of the world. We fail to realize that grabbing onto that fruit (those worldly ways) is self-defeating. The harder we hold on, the closer to ruin it brings us.

To the extent that we believe, trust in, and live out the reconciling "Way of the Cross," this "Way" of Jesus, we experience and know salvation. God's work through the Holy Spirit and the life, death, and resurrection of Jesus enable and empower us to be able to do those things and live in such a way. Salvation is found in deep faith, in surrender, in "letting go and letting God." This also applies to situations where people are holding onto distorted self-images or ideals, dysfunctional behaviors, and self-defeating patterns or traditions. Indeed, my writing of this book is in part an invitation for the Church to let go of *its* distorted and self-defeating images, ideals, ideas, behaviors, and patterns.

The salvation that Jesus invites the world to experience is not primarily focusing upon getting people to cease engaging in certain personal sins. Rather, it is one of restoring people to right relationship with society, a proper sense of who and Whose we are, and transforming oppressive and alienating systems.[210]

---

[210] That said, a person who is no longer being exploited, victimized, or treated poorly is less likely to treat others poorly or to self-medicate

I'd like to invite us to take a look at a famous passage from the Bible, Jesus' parable of the Good Samaritan (Luke 10:25-37):

> *On one occasion an expert in the law stood up to test Jesus. "Teacher," he asked, "what must I do to inherit eternal life?" "What is written in the Law?" he replied. "How do you read it?" He answered, "'Love the Lord your God with all your heart and with all your soul and with all your strength and with all your mind'; and, 'Love your neighbor as yourself.'" "You have answered correctly," Jesus replied. "Do this and you will live."*
>
> *But he wanted to justify himself, so he asked Jesus, "And who is my neighbor?"*
>
> *In reply Jesus said: "A man was going down from Jerusalem to Jericho, when he was attacked by robbers. They stripped him of his clothes, beat him and went away, leaving him half dead. A priest happened to be going down the same road, and when he saw the man, he passed by on the other side. So too, a Levite, when he came to the place and saw him, passed by on the other side. But a Samaritan, as he traveled, came where the man was; and when he saw him, he took pity on him. He went to him and bandaged his wounds, pouring on oil and wine. Then he put the man on his own donkey, brought him to an inn and took care of him. The next day he took out two denarii and gave them to the innkeeper. 'Look after him,' he said, 'and when I return, I will reimburse you for any extra expense you may have.' "Which of these three do you think was a neighbor to the man who fell into the hands of robbers?" The expert in the law replied, "The one who had mercy on him." Jesus told him, "Go and do likewise."*

The salvation that Jesus invites us to know isn't about legalistically following the letter of the law (as the religious leaders were trying to do). It isn't about being rigid about the way religion is "supposed" to be. And it isn't about simply believing certain things. As Jesus put it at another time, *"Very truly I tell you,*

---

by smoking, drinking, or promiscuity—especially if they're intentionally following a spiritual path such as Christianity.

whoever believes in me will do the works I have been doing" (John 14:12). Salvation is about showing loving kindness (*hesed*) to people in need. It's about realizing that the people who we prejudicially write-off as lesser (the "Samaritans"), may have a thing or two to tell us about how we miss the point of love.

A contemporary appropriation of that parable might have us seeing that the illegal immigrant from Mexico who stops to help a beaten-up victim of a carjacking by the side of the highway is a neighbor. To drive the point home even further, the drug-addicted, HIV+, domestically-beaten, welfare-receiving, lesbian single mother who helps a mugging victim in downtown Dallas is a neighbor to that person—not the thousands of fellow citizens who indifferently fly on by in their SUVs, gabbing on their cell phones with copies of *Left Behind*[211] on their laps, and Christian music blaring from their car radios ("the righteous priests" who passed by the victim on the road in the original parable).

The salvation that the carjacking and mugging victims need are found in the loving care provided by the socially marginalized illegal immigrant and single mother. The salvation the rest of us need[212] is to realize that we should embrace the foreigners and strangers[213] among us and to the plight of struggling immigrants, single parents, and homosexuals in our midst. We need to remember that *"Religion that God our Father accepts as pure and faultless is this: to look after orphans and widows in their distress and to keep oneself from being polluted by the world"* (James 1:27). This line of thought is further confirmed in Jesus' encounter with the rich

---

[211] The *Left Behind* series of pseudo-religious novels was widely popular among evangelical Christians in America in the 1990s during the Clinton administration. Based upon a literal reading of the Book of Revelation and a pre-millennial dispensation interpretation of the end-times, the premise is that mainline Churches have become too liberal and wayward and that Jesus returns to the earth and a whole lot of folks (mostly liberals) are damned to hell. I would suggest that it was their way of escaping into a parallel reality while Clinton was at the helm (liberals tended to do the same during the George W. Bush era with the TV show *West Wing*). More on this in Chapter 10.

[212] And we're all deserving of salvation—no matter what the Calvinists may think.

[213] See: Exodus 22:21, 23:9; Deuteronomy 10:18.

young man where Jesus instructs him to sell all that he has and give it to the poor as part of following him (Luke 18:18-23) and in Jesus' altercation with priests who were trying to catch him in a heresy where Jesus asserts that loving our *neighbor* is loving God (Matthew 22:34-40).

One of Jesus' favorite ways of describing the Kingdom of God is that it is like a dinner party or a great banquet. A case in point is Luke 14:15-24 where Jesus points out how those one might normally expect to attend such a banquet find excuses not to partake in it, while those one might least expect to participate in such a grand function show up in droves. The aim of Jesus' salvation is more upon reconciling marginalized people with society and calling society to transform and repent from its selfish, alienating, dehumanizing, divisive, exploiting, life and love-rejecting ways.

I realize that some of what I am saying in this book will be new and threatening to certain readers. To address those fears I would like to offer my paraphrase of a parable penned by Richard Bach. It might help us to "let go and let God."

There once was a group of creatures that lived at the bottom of a mighty river. All of the creatures clung tightly to the rocks that lined the bottom of that riverbank. Holding fast and clinging tightly was their way of life. Doing what they can to fight the current was how they were raised. But then one day, one declared, "I'm going to let go and see where this current takes me. I trust that it knows where it's going. Just clinging here isn't living, letting go is the way to live!"

The other creatures mocked him saying, "You Fool! If you let go, that current that you trust will smash you against the rocks and you'll die!"

But that one ignored their taunts. He took breath, let go, and was indeed smashed a bit by the current against some of the rocks. But before long, as that one continued to trust and resisted clinging, the current raised him from the bottom, and he was no longer banged and bruised. He was free.

The creatures who lived downstream of where he started didn't know him but when they saw him float by they declared, "Look it's a miracle! There goes a creature just like us yet he floats gently on top! It's the Savior, come to save us!" But the

one who was being carried in the current said, "I'm no more of
a savior than you are. This river wants to free us and lift us
up, we just need to let go!"

  But other creatures kept clinging to the rocks and instead
of letting go, made legends of a Savior.[214]

"The one" in this parable is similar to Jesus. There are differences of course. Jesus wasn't an underwater creature, nor do we have any record of him having once "clung to the ways of the world" before daring to let go and live a different way. Jesus really *is* our savior but he is only effectively so to the extent that we let go of the ways of the world and start following his ways and example. Otherwise, his life, death, and resurrection were largely in vain.

Conservative Christianity may celebrate deathbed conversions believing that what matters is whether one's soul will go to heaven or hell. Although progressive Christianity sees them as nice, it is really a tragic shame for folks to miss-out on living a full, whole, abundant life—salvation here and now.

---

[214] Richard Bach (author of *Jonathan Livingston Seagull*), from the prologue of his book *Illusions*, Dell, 1977.

Chapter 7

Heaven & Hell & what about all those other religions?

Sheep go to heaven . . . Cake

"He will reply, 'I tell you the truth, whatever you did not do for one of the least of these, you did not do for me.' "Then they will go away to eternal punishment, but the righteous to eternal life." Jesus, Matthew 25:45-46

Oh, my God, I want to love you not that I might gain eternal heaven nor escape eternal hell, But, Lord, to love you just because you are my God. Ignatius of Loyola

"Many Christians believe that Christianity is the "right" religion. This is what some say. The reality is, it matters not what religion you confess. If it isn't helping the rest of us poor bastards, who cares what you call yourself." T. Marquis Ramsey

A man dies and goes to heaven and was being shown around by St. Peter. As they went from cloud to cloud they came to various doors which St. Peter would open. One showed a large group rolling on the floor and talking in tongues. "Our Pentecostals" he said. Next was a serious ritual. "Our Jewish persuasion" he replied. Then another ritualistic service, "Our Catholics." At the next cloud, he didn't open the door but instead put his forefinger to his lips in the hush motion and they both tip toed past. Once past, the man asked, "What was *that* was all about!?" "Those are the Baptists," Peter explained. "They think they are the only ones up here."[215] While perhaps overstated, that joke is funny because it is based on a certain degree of truth.

Many conservative Christians hold rather exclusive ideas about which of their fellow humans gets to go to heaven. Allow me to briefly share the basic conservative take on this.

A Conservative view: "I can't wait for heaven!"

According to the typical conservative Christian perspective, after their death, all people await the final Judgment. Both saved and unsaved persons will be resurrected on the judgment day upon Jesus' return. Those who are saved will live *eternally*[216] with Jesus in heaven. Those who aren't will suffer the torment of eternal separation from God and damnation to hell. Jesus' bodily resurrection ensures believers that they too will share in a physical resurrection where they'll go into literal rooms in God's grand mansion in the sky. Literalist conservatives will point out that biblically people don't go to heaven, or hell, immediately after they die. Instead, the lay "asleep" in their graves until Jesus' second coming—and only then will they be resurrected, judged, and then sent to heaven or hell. So much for warm and fuzzy thoughts of recently deceased loved ones being with God, Jesus, and the rest of the family who've already gone on "to be with God." According to this perspective, they haven't. They're still in their graves.

---

[215]   That joke unfairly paints all Baptists with the same broad brush. The largest segment of Baptists is the Southern Baptist Convention and that denomination was hijacked by a fundamentalist take-over in the 1980's, but there are many moderate and even liberal and progressive Baptists—especially in the American Baptist Convention.

[216]   When conservatives say "eternal," "eternally," or "eternal life" they almost exclusively use it to refer to a sense of time; i.e., living with God in heaven forever and ever. In the original Greek, "eternal" life also refers to a markedly abundant and vibrant quality of life here and now.

A Progressive view of Heaven: "Heaven can wait"

Many progressive Christians aren't particularly concerned about going to heaven after they die. In fact, many are openly agnostic about whether or not there is a heaven. Our concern is more upon living and loving in God's Kingdom right now, and faithfully helping to manifest it all the more. We don't really know if there is an actual heaven, but if there is, none of us know who will be there and who won't be. Only God determines this, and God's inclusive mercy and grace far exceed human capacities. It could be that God intends all persons to be with Him in heaven but that some hardened individuals may still reject, or somehow not feel worthy of (or bitter about),[217] God's unconditional love and grace even after death.[218]

Jesus sided with the Pharisees (against the Sadducees) in believing in a resurrection and, apparently, a heaven. On two occasions he seems to have conveyed this:

> *Then the Sadducees, who say there is no resurrection, came to him with a question. "Teacher," they said, "Moses wrote for us that if a man's brother dies and leaves a wife but no children, the man must marry the widow and have children for his brother. Now there were seven brothers. The first one married and died without leaving any children. The second one married the widow, but he also died, leaving no child. It was the same with the third. In fact, none of the seven left any children. Last of all, the woman died too. At the resurrection whose wife will she be, since the seven were married to her?"*
>
> *Jesus replied, "Are you not in error because you do not know the Scriptures or the power of God? When the dead rise,*

---

[217] One perhaps thinks of a disgruntled soul like Jonah who was upset about God forgiving and sparing the people of Nineveh. One can also imagine that Adolf Hitler might have some major issues feeling welcome in Heaven, tormented by issues that only God can address—and he might not want, or be ready to, avail himself of that help.

[218] Effectively putting *themselves* into the corner, relegating themselves away from the warmth and love of the great party of heaven.

they will neither marry nor be given in marriage; they will be like the angels in heaven. Now about the dead rising—have you not read in the book of Moses, in the account of the bush, how God said to him, 'I am the God of Abraham, the God of Isaac, and the God of Jacob'? He is not the God of the dead, but of the living. (Mark 12:18-27)

"Do not let your hearts be troubled. Trust in God; trust also in me. In my Father's house are many rooms; if it were not so, I would have told you. I am going there to prepare a place for you. And if I go and prepare a place for you, I will come back and take you to be with me that you also may be where I am. You know the way to the place where I am going." (John 14:1-4)

This was clearly not a priority of Jesus' teachings and agenda. He only spoke to it twice—and even then, rather vaguely. Moreover, this is an aspect of our religious tradition that few of us have direct experience with.[219] Hence, progressive Christians are often inclined to consider this matter as a "non-essential of the faith"[220] that believers are free to have differing opinions about. We appreciate the Neo-Reformed movement's suspicion about Christian assimilation of the pagan Greek notion of the immortality of the soul as this can easily lead to Gnostic-like depreciation of the body and bodily experience.[221] However, many of us also leave open the questions

---

[219]   Aside from occasional reports of "near-death-experiences."

[220]   Progressives suggest that non-essentials of the faith include such things as: which translation of the Bible is read in worship; whether a person is baptized via immersion or via pouring water over their head; whether women can be ordained or not; whether one believes in the virgin birth literally or not; whether one uses wine or juice or leavened or unleavened bread for Communion; or whether one believes in free will or predestination, etc. To be sure, a progressive Christian's listing of non-essentials may well be longer than a one written by a conservative Christian.

[221]   Yes, there are passages in the Bible which may suggest or imply the immortality of the soul, yet the ancient Hebrews and early Christians lived in a thoroughly Hellenized context. Their culture was greatly influenced by Greek culture including their myths, ideologies, religions, and philosophies.

of whether there will be a resurrection for ourselves, body and soul, after we die and/or if we will go to heaven. There are few scriptures that speak to these matters and the ones that do, do so in a cryptic and enigmatic manner—which many suggest is metaphorical.

Progressive Christianity doesn't need the notions of a cushy cloud in the sky for deceased souls to relax upon, or our being reunited with previously deceased loved ones, as inspiration to be good or faithful in this life.[222] We're motivated more by the call of the prophets; the teachings and example of Jesus; and by the example of certain followers of Jesus such as John Wesley, Dorothy Day, Martin Luther King, Jr., Mother Teresa, Oscar Romero, Clarence Jordan, Jim Wallis, Daniel Berrigan, Anne Lamott, etc. We leave this all up to God and instead strive to live life as faithfully as we can here and now.

I sometimes picture that after we die we experience a profound *"A-ha!"* or *"Ohh!"*[223] moment where we're all brought up to speed and finally get what life and love are all about. Perhaps something along the lines of C.S. Lewis' vision about what happens to us when we die:

> *When we die we will not say: "Lord, I could never have guessed how beautiful you are." We will not say that. Rather we will say, "So . . . it was you all along. Everyone I ever loved, it was you. Everyone who loved me, it was you. Everything decent or fine that ever happened to me, Everything that made me reach out and try to be better, it was you all along."*

I then envision that we are absorbed back into our Source (God)—effectively having *fullest* Communion.

I'm not particularly concerned about my afterlife. It's my life here and now that matters most to me. I try to live as faithfully as I can and trust that whatever happens when I die will take care of itself. The blessings of faithful, Kingdom-living here and now are reward enough. As Episcopalian Bishop and Bible scholar, N.T. Wright puts it, *"The point of following Jesus isn't simply so that we can be sure of going to a better place than this after we die."*

---

[222]   Though I suspect most of us are open to this as a potential "bonus."

[223]   And I suppose for some of us, a *"Doh!"* moment (a la Homer Simpson).

Jesus appears to have given mixed messages on these matters. For example, Jesus tirelessly promoted unconditional love, forgiveness and even loving our enemies. Yet he also referred to hell and punishment for those who don't shape up. What are we to make of Jesus' famed story about the separation of the sheep from the goats?

"When the Son of Man comes in his glory, and all the angels with him, he will sit on his throne in heavenly glory. All the nations will be gathered before him, and he will separate the people one from another as a shepherd separates the sheep from the goats. He will put the sheep on his right and the goats on his left. "Then the King will say to those on his right, 'Come, you who are blessed by my Father; take your inheritance, the Kingdom prepared for you since the creation of the world. For I was hungry and you gave me something to eat, I was thirsty and you gave me something to drink, I was a stranger and you invited me in, I needed clothes and you clothed me, I was sick and you looked after me, I was in prison and you came to visit me.' "Then the righteous will answer him, 'Lord, when did we see you hungry and feed you, or thirsty and give you something to drink? When did we see you a stranger and invite you in, or needing clothes and clothe you? When did we see you sick or in prison and go to visit you?' "The King will reply, 'I tell you the truth, whatever you did for one of the least of these brothers of mine, you did for me.' "Then he will say to those on his left, 'Depart from me, you who are cursed, into the eternal fire prepared for the devil and his angels. For I was hungry and you gave me nothing to eat, I was thirsty and you gave me nothing to drink, I was a stranger and you did not invite me in, I needed clothes and you did not clothe me, I was sick and in prison and you did not look after me.' "They also will answer, 'Lord, when did we see you hungry or thirsty or a stranger or needing clothes or sick or in prison, and did not help you?'" He will reply, 'I tell you the truth, whatever you did not do for one of the least of these, you did not do for me.' "Then they will go away to eternal punishment, but the righteous to eternal life."
(Matthew 25:31-46)

First of all, it should be noted that it's just that, a story. When read in context, it is evident that it is the third of three stories in a row that Jesus told pertaining to the same concept—that we need to be ready to meet our Maker, to live our lives on the ready and to do the things that are expected of us (the prior ones being the parable of the ten virgins and the parable of the talents). Among those expectations are being watchful, keeping vigil, practicing good stewardship, and loving the people that Jesus loved in the ways that he loved them. It should be noted that *not* listed among those are right thinking, right believing, right orthodoxy, or right dogma. All of them are verbs, things we are to *do*—not things we are to think or believe.

Also to be noted are that each of those three stories ends with a threat or warning, and that the threats increase in magnitude. In the parable of the ten virgins, the warning is that those who fail to be prepared for the arrival of the bridegroom (by not having enough oil for their lamps) are locked out of the house and shunned. In the second story, the irresponsible steward is thrown out into the darkness where there will be weeping and gnashing of teeth. And at the end of the third story, the King judges his servants based upon their actions. The ones who do not visit "him" (in the person of the hurting people in the world) when he's incarcerated, clothe him when he's naked, tend him when he's sick, feed him when he's hungry, or give him drink when he's thirsty, etc., are cast away to be eternally punished. That pattern of increasing warning via stories has a name. It's the rhetorical device called *hyperbole*. Hyperbole is exaggeration that increases to drive home a point and convey a message. The story of "the little boy who cried wolf" is a famous one from the Western folk-tale tradition.

It should also be noted that the Greek word that we translate as *eternal*, doesn't necessarily have to do with time, and more likely has to do with a supreme quality. When Jesus spoke of his coming to give "eternal life," many Bible scholars believe he was referring more to an abundant, meaningful life, and wholeness than to living with God in heaven forever after we die. Similarly, when Jesus speaks of "eternal" punishment, he's referring more to a sense of supreme (rather than endless) punishment. Jesus used hyperbole in numerous other places in the Gospels so it can be understood that he didn't mean to convey an actual supreme punishment literally, but rather, as a means to really drive home his point.

This is similar to how even the most loving of parents may at times feel exasperated with their children in the midst of long road trips in the family car across the country. If children are squabbling in the backseats and incessantly asking, "Are we there yet?" more than a few parents have yelled back something like, "If you don't knock it off, I'm going to pull this car over and tie you to the top of the car and we'll drive the rest of the way with you up there!"[224]

I can certainly recall similar words being hollered back at my sister and me on various treks across the Badlands of South Dakota. My sister and I knew that our parents would never actually do that to us, but we could tell that they were really upset and meant business. Similarly, my mother used to threaten to give me *the hyjimakafluks and the spankuels*" when I was misbehaving at home. I never knew what they were and when I asked her, she'd say, "Well if you don't shape up by the time I count to ten, you'll find out!" I imagined it as being the worst form of spanking possible. I never had the guts to let her get past 9 ½. It was an idle threat, but one a hell of a persuasive one!

These hyperboles were deviations from Jesus' otherwise consistent messages of nonviolence, compassion, and unconditional love. The stories never led to actual harm or violence, merely the warning of it. Some folks seem to need that sort of thing. Jesus met their need if that's what it took to get them to live rightly. I like this very human part of Jesus. He wanted us to consider God as a loving parent, our ultimate *abba* (daddy). Sometimes dads get a bit worked up for their children's own good.[225]

An astute young adult friend of mine reports that,

---

[224] The Linn family presents a wonderful treatment of Jesus' use of hyperbole, including this reference to parent's threatening to tie unruly kids to the roofs of cars in their book *Good Goats: Healing our Image of God.*

[225] Note: there is no intent to condone or bless actual child abuse by parents, it's just an accurate description of the way it is when raising children (especially in families where there are several children).

"It never ceases to amaze me that in every conversation I have with critics of [Progressive Christianity], Emergent [Christianity], or even [ordinary] mainline [Christianity], I am never asked if I believe whether or not Jesus is Lord but whether or not I believe in hell and eternal damnation. Given the sort of questions that are asked it would seem that one is saved by faith in hell rather than faith in Christ."[226]

Progressive Christians don't typically have hell or the threat of it as a part of their beliefs. Progressive Christians are mindful of the gradual evolution of the notion of hell in the Bible and in human theologies from: *sheol/hades* (a neutral, ethereal, netherworldly, grave-like state of suspension for souls to dwell in just below the crust of the earth); to *Gehenna* (named after a valley outside of Jerusalem, a neutral temporary holding place for souls to dwell and/or be purified in before they are judged); to the metaphor of Gehenna as the burning garbage dumps outside of ancient Jerusalem in the valley of Gehenna;[227] to an actual, literal place of torture and punishment "down there" complete with a devil with horns, hooves, and a pitchfork (some of those ideas came about long after the Bible was written).

Progressive Christians tend to either not believe in the existence of hell, or understand it more as a desperate state of being that people can experience while they're alive on the earth (war zones, rape-infested refugee camps, living with domestic abuse, etc., or as a potential state of existence after we die). Some of us have speculated that certain tormented souls might still fail to accept God's grace and love even after death. Perhaps they feel ashamed and unworthy. So they effectively relegate themselves away from the glowing warmth of God and the company of the saints. Instead they enter dark, cold corners in isolated and lonely solitude.

A Word about Other Religions . . .

A Conservative view: Conservative Christianity is exclusivist, claiming that there is no other truth than the truth revealed by

---

[226]   Chad Holz—adapted from his Facebook page
[227]   This is the metaphor Jesus used most, see:Matthew 5:20-30.

God through the Bible. People who practice any other religion are deceived. They are heathens, pagans, and worshippers of false gods, and will likely be damned to hell. They may couch it in nicer language, and there may be bit more nuance, but not much.[228] That pretty much sums it up.

A Progressive view:

There isn't any one official stance about what to make of other religions that is shared by all progressive Christians. There is a range of options. On one end of the range is *Exclusivism*—that there is only one right, and true religion, Christianity. All other so-called religions are false and destructive. Progressive Christianity rejects exclusivism. A slightly more generous view is *Triumphalism*, which asserts that, while there are other valid religions out there, Christianity is the best and/or most true way. An alternative version of this perspective is the claim that all people around the world, no matter what religion they practice, are saved because of the Cosmic and Universal Christ at work in their lives (whether they know it or not, and by whatever, if any, name they call Him/Her). A few degrees more open than that stance is *Pluralism*, which holds that there are a variety of viable paths, and practitioners of each religion are entitled to consider their way as being the best way. An even more gracious version of Pluralism is what I'll call "Devotional Pluralism," where practitioners of given religions overtly realize that when they say "their religion is the best," that they do so in a loving way using the language of devotion—like a parent saying that their newborn baby is "the sweetest and most beautiful baby in the world." They mean it, but not literally, merely devotionally.

A perspective that is a notch more inclusive still is *Perennialism*, which says that all religions are pretty much the same. This view embraces the idea that there is one mountain with many paths that lead to the same peak. A Christian expression of this can be found in the claim that Jesus is one manifestation of the Cosmic

---

[228]   Namely, how long such damned souls will spend in hellfire; i.e., eternally or merely for a long time and then simply being removed from existence along with hell itself.

and Universal Christ (and that the Buddha, and others, were other such manifestations). On the far end of the continuum is *Syncretism*, which effectively treats all of the world's religions as a giant smorgasbord buffet which people are free to pick and choose from indiscriminately. At its worst, syncretism is shallow and culturally insensitive—condoning disrespectful cultural co-option and exploitation.[229]

I suspect that most progressive Christians fall somewhere between triumphalism and perennialism and it's probably fair to say that most progressive Christians are pluralist or perennialist. Progressive Christianity's attitude toward other religions is far more than a patronizing "tolerance" of them. We deeply appreciate how God is at work through other religions and we encourage Christians to learn about other paths—and even to learn *from* them. Progressive Christians believe that salvation is available to people who are outside of the Christian faith. We're also aware that "salvation" isn't a goal or even a concept in many religions. For example, the Hindu goal of *moksha* is not similar to the Christian goal of salvation. It is more accurate to say that there are *many* mountains with many paths to the peaks of those mountains. There are also many oceans, jungles, valleys, and plains, *each* with many paths or routes! Despite a certain amount of overlap and common ground, there are *different* salvations, different goals and means toward those goals among the world's religions—and perhaps even within them.

I was quoted in Denver's *Westword* magazine as saying, *"I view the major world religions as wells, and each well, if you go deep enough down into it, taps into the same aquifer. But if you try to go down several wells at once, you won't get very far into any of them and you'll never reach the source"*[230] While that remark might convey perennialism, I'm not a

---

[229]   At its worst, New Age spirituality does this to Native American and Eastern religions.

[230]   Here's the full quote in context: . . . *His other infamous question—and to Greg, the climax of Gospel Journey Maui—was: "Can everyone be right?" At the time, Emma agreed with Greg that they couldn't all be right, that either one religion is right or no religions are right. But since returning to Colorado, she's adopted a quote from the Reverend Roger Wolsey, who directs the Wesley Foundation United Methodist Campus Ministry at the*

perennialist. I'm more of a pluralist. I believe that God is powerfully at work in many other religions, yet I feel that Christianity, at its best, may be the most effective way for God's people to connect with God and to live life rightly in response. It's the best "well" for tapping into the "aquifer." When I refer to Christianity as the "best" and "most effective" vehicle or path, I am employing the aforementioned "language of devotion and adoration."

At its best, Christianity's emphases upon unconditional love, unmerited grace, forgiveness, reconciliation, inclusion, compassion, mercy, fellowship, and joy, and its pursuit of peace and social justice surpass all other religions as far as I've discerned.[231] While I say this here, I don't feel a need to go around saying that when I'm out and about interacting with others. That would likely come across as arrogant and off-putting and it's admittedly based upon my limited knowledge and experience.

If Christians truly have faith in God and in their views of God, then there's no reason for them to fear or put down other religions. That sort of anxiety and intimidation demonstrates a notable *lack* of faith and conviction. People of faith should let God be God and allow the proof to be in the pudding. Admittedly, the Christian pudding is more than a bit mixed with a lot of weeds growing

---

University of Colorado at Boulder: "I view the major world religions as wells, and each well, if you go deep enough down into it, taps into the same aquifer. But if you try to go down into several wells at once, you won't get very far into any of them and you'll never reach the source." "I like that," Emma says. "Because I can do my path and my well, and that doesn't mean I can't be with . . . someone in another well." Cover story, *"Gospel Journey: Teens Dare 2 Share*—Greg Stier is raising an army of adolescents to help save your soul," Jessica Centers, July 3, 2008, *Westword Magazine,* http://www.westword.com/content/printVersion/826270

[231] Unlike many of my fellow Christians, I'm not afraid to admit that many of the teachings and ways of Jesus are strikingly similar to those of certain Essenes as well as the Jewish Rabbi Hillel the Elder's—then again, most of my fellow Christians have never heard of him and would probably not want to. Hillel pre-dated Jesus by only a few years and his teachings clearly impacted Jesus—who, arguably, took them to the next level. See: http://www.ipl.org/div/farq/bestsellerFARQ.html

among the wheat. It's so messy that I've mixed metaphors to convey this. I can understand why many people choose not to be Christians and I feel no need to get them to be. What I do feel called to do is to help people make a fully informed choice. I feel called to ensure that they've at least heard about and explored the option of progressive Christianity. I sense that this is among the cutting edges of where God is up to new things in the world.

I encourage people to go deep with the well of Christianity because I know it works. I suspect the other wells do too. I've certainly met a lot of loving people of other faiths who have loving hearts, good values and integrity, but I know the Christian well works. It's the one that I grew up with and was formed by. It's the one that gives me hope and courage to face each new day. It's the one I continue to tap into, and it's the one that I am called to invite others to drink from.

But even though I'm a passionate advocate for Christianity, I'm one who fully believes that God is passionately at work through other religions too. Out of my progressive Christian sensibilities, I feel little compulsion to try to convert people who are active with other religions to becoming Christians. In fact, I celebrate them just as they are. They are loved, forgiven, and accepted children of God—whether they know it or not. If someone is a Jew, Muslim, Hindu, or Buddhist, I hope that they'll be the best Jew, Muslim, Hindu, or Buddhist they can be. I celebrate them and the paths they're on. For example, here's a piece I wrote for *Elephant Journal* (a Buddhist magazine):

Turning religious turds into lemonade[232]

Every religion seems to have its "crazy uncle Larrys." My own family of faith, Christianity, certainly has its fair share of them. For the past few years, Fred Phelps and his infamous Westboro Baptist Church have held the status of being our nuttiest relatives. Until . . . our crazy uncle Terry Jones and his not so aptly named Dove World Outreach Center (big name for a church of only

---

[232]   http://www.elephantjournal.com/2010/09/turning-religious-turds-into-lemonade/

50 people) usurped that role by their threats to burn copies of the Qur'an on Sept. 11, 2010.

Uncle Terry and his curious throng have found a way to get their 15 minutes of fame. It's not every backwater Protestant pastor who has the Vatican or 4 Star U.S. Generals calling them.

I don't like Uncle Terry and what he stands for. Frankly, I'm not all that thrilled about sharing the planet with him and I sorta just wish he would go away—or, convert to some other religion so some other group would have to deal with him (or that he'd more deeply convert to Christianity).

But there he is, a fellow member of the Church, the living Body of Christ, who apparently got himself a bit overly snookered on the Communion wine and is making an utter fool of himself. Even though it is Uncle Terry who is babbling loudly with a lampshade on his head, he's making the rest of us look bad. So, I have to deal with him.

Happily, I'm not doing so alone. In the midst of the media circus that he's created with his outrageous antics, some notable blessings have come to pass.

The first thing that transpired was the creation of a Facebook page, "People of Faith Opposed to Burning the Qur'an." Thousands of people *liked* it (became a "fan" of). Then some similar knock-off ones were created too such as, "Burning the Qur'an does not Illuminate the Bible;" "Americans Against the Qur'an Burning." Various Christian leaders, then starting with those of us on the progressive end of the spectrum, and began making statements condemning such an action. Soon after, leaders from our more mainline, evangelical, and Catholic brothers, sisters, and cousins joined in declaring that burning Qur'ans is most certainly *not* "what Jesus would do." It's rare for those various parts from within the Church to issue joint decrees and affirmations about much of anything these days—no small miracle.

While that ecumenical goodness was happening, several Christian leaders were joining forces with leaders from other world religions issuing statements with similar sentiments in an inter-faith way.

In addition, several Christian, and secular patriotic groups, have invited citizens to join them in everything from a) buying a Qur'an on Sept. 11; b) reading the Qur'an on Sept. 11; to c) donating money for them to give away 1-2 copies of the Qur'an in Afghanistan for every Qur'an that Jones burns—among them a major American Bible Society (*not* typically known for distributing Qur'ans!). Moreover, d) a Facebook page for Christians and Muslims seeking peace was created; and e) a friend of mine is promoting this terrific invitation for citizens to practice radical hospitality—the Million Meal Month (a call for American Christians to invite a Muslim person to their home to have dinner with them over the course of the next year).

What's really cool is that an edict was released by Grand Ayatollah Sistaani not only condemning Terry Jones's plans to burn Qur'ans but also asking all Muslims not to retaliate and to respect Christians and the Bible in case the Qur'an burning takes place!

And if that weren't enough, Uncle Terry's sideshow has single-handedly increased public sympathy for Islam, increased public scrutiny of religious extremism, and put a halt to the ridiculous allegations that President Obama is a Muslim.

The good Lord works in mysterious ways.

Christians have often said (at least since the invention of lemonade) that, "God's speciality is turning lemons into lemonade." It seems She's also in the practice of transforming turdish-idiocy into blessing.

—Brother Roger

The day after I wrote that blog, I had the chance to say "'Eid Mubārak!" (*Blessed Eid*)[233] to a Muslim family. It happened late

---

[233] The expression Muslims say to each other upon the end of Ramadan—a 30-day period of prayer and fasting that is the holiest time in the year for Muslims.

one night at the local IHOP. The father sent the little girl after me to bring me back to the table. He couldn't believe a random white dude would say that to them and lengthy discussion ensued. I shared with them that I'd been reading up on Islam that week and they truly felt that my saying that to them was a consequence of the hype about Terry Jones and his threats to burn Qur'ans. I think they're right—it's some of that "holy lemonade."

I close this chapter with a word about mysticism. Mysticism is an approach to spirituality that can be found in several of the major world religions. Rather than primarily employing the intellect to try to know about God by writing about God, mysticism involves nurturing and fostering one's direct consciousness and experience of the Divine rather than have it be mediated through prescribed corporate institutions and forms. There are strands of mysticism and contemplative spirituality to be found within Christian tradition. The Desert Fathers and Mothers emphasized practices similar to what are known today as centering prayer (essentially Christian meditation) and *Lectio Divina* (a contemplative approach to pondering Scripture). The Eastern Orthodox, Quaker, and Wesleyan traditions stress the importance of nurturing our inner lights, fostering direct experience with the Divine, and pursuing certain practices that foster deification and sanctification. Even the première scholastic theologian, St. Thomas Aquinas, famed for his extensive *Summa Theologica*, experienced a mystical communion with the Divine. Immediately after, he ceased writing and simply said, "All that I have written seems like straw."[234]

Mystics and contemplatives from Judaism (Kabbalah), Islam (Sufism), Christianity (e.g., Quakerism, Taize, and various forms of contemplative Christianity), and Hinduism (Vedanta), share notable common ground, including values, practices, and perspectives. These mystical traditions contend that humans can experience their true nature, the Divine within and/or outside of them, and feel a contented sense of oneness with all that is.[235] As Carl McColman puts it, "Mysticism is, ultimately, simply the art

---

[234]   See: http://www.chitorch.org/index.php/in-context/aquinas/

[235]   I had a mystical experience while snowshoeing outside of Nederland, CO on New Year's Day, 2011. I describe it poetically: back from snowshoeing. one word: divine two words: touched divine three:

of going to heaven before you die—or perhaps better said, the art of letting heaven emerge within you now."

Mystic approaches suggest that anybody can do this, regardless of previous religious background or education, by following certain practices, typically including: meditation/centering prayer; fasting; chanting/repetitive singing; intentional breathing; intentional silence; contemplative approaches to reading scripture, and various exercises which seek to expand the heart and our innate compassion. Music and dancing often play a role in these paths. Mystics from the world's various religious traditions may have more in common with each other than they do with the majority of the people from their own religions.

While not being the same as mysticism, progressive Christianity celebrates and affirms it. A bumper sticker that mystically oriented progressive Christians might resonate with reads *"Religion is for people who are afraid of going to hell. Spirituality is for people who've already been there."* Karl Rahner, one of the most renowned Catholic theologians of the 20th Century, once remarked, "The Christian of the future will be a mystic or will not exist at all." Progressive Christians are open to the possibility that he is right.

---

touched the divine five: i touched the divinity that   more: the i
that is you and me experienced us fully today.

Chapter 8

The Bible: Book of Science, Rules, Facts, Myths, or Life?

Yes, Jesus loves me, yes, Jesus loves me, Yes, Jesus loves me!
The Bible tells me so! Jesus Loves Me, traditional
American Christian folk hymn

There's nothing more radical, nothing more revolutionary,
nothing more subversive against injustice and oppression
than the Bible. If you want to keep people subjugated, the last
thing you place in their hands is a Bible. Desmond Tutu

Everything in the Scriptures is God's Word. All of it is useful
for teaching and helping people and for correcting them and
showing them how to live. 2 Timothy 3:16

No book has had a greater impact on humanity than The Holy Bible. It is the best-selling book ever published.[236] Children receive Bibles as gifts. Bibles can be found in drawers in hotel rooms. Evangelicals hand them out in public places. People at major sporting events hold signs quoting from it. Musicians and artists have drawn inspiration from it. People have placed their hands upon it when giving oaths and pledging to tell the truth. Families use them to keep records of their genealogy and stash special mementos. And, from time to time, people actually read it.

---

[236] . . . and published in the most languages and dialects—http://www. ipl.org/div/farq/bestsellerFARQ.html

The Bible is an integral component of Christianity and is embraced by Christians of different perspectives. These perspectives about the Bible range from understanding it as literally being God's actual words, as being a written record for how our ancestors in the faith experienced God and attempted to live faithfully, and even simply as beautiful poetic literature that inspires and comforts. The more literal approaches to this great book are troublesome to progressive Christians. The popular evangelical description of the Bible as "B.I.B.L.E: Be Instructed Before Leaving Earth" or "Basic Instructions Before Leaving Earth" coupled with the adage, "The Bible says it, I believe it, that settles it," rubs many of us the wrong way.

There are numerous ways to read and interpret the Bible, hence the many and varied translations of them on the market. But before we get into all of that, let's explore some of the basics of the Bible. Most Christians agree that we have one book of sacred scriptures—the Holy Bible, which was written over many years, originally in Hebrew, Aramaic, and Greek. Christians often refer to the Hebrew Scriptures, the Jewish Bible, as "the Old Testament" and the writings of the early Christians[237] as the "New Testament."

The word Bible comes to us from Latin and Greek words that mean "book" or "books." The Bible is actually an anthology, a collection of many books. There are 66 Books in the Bible.[238] Some Christians read it literally and legalistically, while others read it with more nuance discerning allegories, metaphors, and symbolism. Most of us view it as containing God's truth, and as "inspired by" God, though we may mean different things by this.[239]

The books of the Bible are of various types and genres including: creation myths, law, history, genealogies, writings/narratives, songs, poetry, wisdom sayings, apocalyptic visions, gospels, and epistles (letters). Jews refer to their canon of scripture, 24 books, as the

---

[237] Who were Jews, it should be remembered.

[238] . . . at least in the Protestant version of the Bible. There are seven more books in the Roman Catholic and Eastern Orthodox versions. Protestants consider those books to be less authoritative as none of the books in the New Testament quote from any of those books. They're referred to as "the Apocrypha."

[239] I discuss the various meanings of "inspired" later in the chapter.

Tanakh (*tan-ahk*). Tanakh is an acronym for the three parts of the Hebrew Bible. The first part is the *Torah* (teaching/law). Because these are the first five books of the Bible, the Torah is also known as the "Pentateuch" (meaning "the five"). The Prophets (aka the *Nevi'im*) comprise another portion of the Hebrew Bible. The "Writings" (aka the *Ketuvim*) make up the rest.

Those facts may be about all that can be stated that most Christians agree with about the Bible. Everything else is debatable and controversial.[240] These differences revolve around the following topics: origins, translation, interpretation, and authority. Conservatives believe that Moses wrote the first five books of the Bible, the Torah, whereas progressives assert that numerous authors wrote those books over many years. Many progressives are swayed by scholarship that suggests that many of the stories within numerous books found within the Hebrew Scriptures (the "Old Testament") were originally oral tradition long before they were ever written down. In Hebrew, the first five books of the Bible are referred to by the first few words that start them out. For example, the book of Genesis is known as the "*In the beginning.*" One can imagine an early Hebraic tribal elder being asked to "Tell that 'In the beginning' story!" during the waning hours after a meal while the listeners ponder life while gazing at the burning coals and embers of a campfire. With this perspective in mind, it is natural to think that those stories were told by different storytellers and then compiled years later when they were finally written down. This would also account for the two different creation stories found within the first two chapters of Genesis.[241] People probably loved both of them and didn't want to see either excluded.

I'd earlier stated that many progressives don't think Moses wrote all of the Torah. Similarly, many progressive Christians do not think that the first Gospels were likely to have been written by the disciples whose names are attributed to them. The average lifespan of humans back then seems to have only been 25-40

---

[240] Which goes a long way toward explaining why there are now some 38,000 different Christian denominations! http://christianity.about. com/od/denominations/p/christiantoday.htm

[241] Genesis 1:1-2:4a and Genesis 2:4b-2:25.

years.[242] Mark, the earliest Gospel, wasn't likely written until 60 A.D. at the earliest (and perhaps closer to 70 A.D.). The other Gospels were likely written between 70-95 A.D., with John being the last. Assuming Jesus' disciples were between 20-30 years of age at the time of Jesus' death in 33 A.D., it would be highly unlikely for many of those disciples to have written those texts—especially if they were persecuted and spent much time in prison. In that culture, it was a common practice for people to write documents in the name of well-known persons to demonstrate the "school of thought" that they are said to spring from and to help enhance their authority and progressive Christians don't understand why conservative ones make the Bible exempt from that practice. It is reasonable to assume that the Gospels were written for specific purposes. One reason may have been to address the mounting tensions between Jews who didn't accept Jesus as the Messiah, Jewish Christians, and the rising numbers of gentile ones. A second purpose was to help all of the early Christian followers to continue to believe that Jesus really is Lord and the Savior after the Temple had been destroyed by the Romans in 70 A.D. and Jesus hadn't returned soon afterward as they'd expected.[243] And a third purpose may've been to help present the good news of the life, death, and resurrection of Jesus to future generations of believers—in case Jesus' delay in returning would be a long one.[244]

The apostle Paul's letters were clearly written to help instruct, encourage, correct, and celebrate the fledgling early Christian churches—as well as to help stimulate fundraising for the mother Church in Jerusalem. The "Pastoral Epistles," the letters attributed to Paul but weren't likely written by him, were written to resist certain Gnostic teachings and, arguably, to curtail the role of women in the leadership of the church. The book of Revelation appears to have been written either to help provide

---

[242] See: http://danielle-movie.com/forums/archive/index.php?t-562. html. This is somewhat debatable, see: http://christiancadre.blogspot. com/2007/09/what-does-life-expectancy-tell-us-about.html

[243] See, http://www.christiandeistfellowship.com/4gospels.htm

[244] Though the early Christians, including the Gospel writers, all appear to have truly thought that Jesus would return in glory within their lifetimes.

encouragement and stimulate perseverance to early Christian communities who were being persecuted by the Roman Empire or to help encourage early Christian communities who were no longer being persecuted to avoid accommodating to the ways of the world in the midst of empire.[245]

Conservative Christians may wonder how or why progressive Christians give the Bible any sort of authority. Progressive Christians don't believe that Moses wrote the Torah or that the first disciples or eyewitnesses of Jesus wrote the Gospels. We believe the consensus of scholars who indicate that several of the epistles (letters) attributed to Paul weren't written by him, and that several of the books in the New Testament weren't originally written with the intention for them to be understood as scripture. We believe the scholarship that suggests that numerous editors and redactors altered and modified the scriptures over the years.[246] We emphasize the human role in the creation of the Bible. We do not read many of the biblical texts literally, and don't think a fair number of the "events" described in the Bible actually happened.

Progressive Christianity does, however, value and grant authority to the Bible. Progressive Christians affirm that we are "people of the book" and consider the Bible as being the charter documents of our faith. The books of the Bible provide the stories that ground us and give us identity. They inform us that we are loved, forgiven, and accepted children of God. The Bible is our primary source for who Jesus was and how we can commune with God through him. It provides information about the origins and organization of the early Church and how it grew and blossomed in spite of violent persecution. It also models for us how our early Christian and Jewish ancestors wrestled with concepts in their holy books, and with God. It invites us to do the same.

Though progressive Christians don't think everything that "happened" in the Bible actually took place, we find much truth

---

[245]   For more on this view, see *Unveiling Empire: Reading Revelation Then & Now* by Wes Howard-Brook & Anthony Gwyther, Orbis Books, 1999. This is one of my favorite books.

[246]   It should be said that there is no "official/original" manuscript of the Bible that exists in the world today. Instead, multiple manuscripts exist for many of the books of the Bible—and those manuscripts differ.

in those stories, truth that transcends the modern era's notion of truth as being merely what is historically or scientifically factual. Progressive Christianity sees that there are numerous contradictory passages and varying theologies within the Bible, but doesn't feel this is a reason to dismiss the Bible. In fact, we see it as reason to take the Bible seriously. If there *was* some sort of conspiracy to force people to believe a certain way about God and Jesus, when the books of the Bible were created (and edited), the authors and editors surely wouldn't have retained passages that didn't advance their agenda.[247]

The Bible is gloriously diverse, frustratingly enigmatic, and even outright contradictory in places. Since humans also have those tendencies, this suggests that numerous people really did put it together over the years without the over-controlling micro-managing of powerful elites hiding behind closed doors (at least without too much of that). Progressive Christians see that over the past 2000 plus years, billions of people of faith have been moved toward increased wholeness because of their interacting with the Bible. It has served as the basis for lifting up the value of all of God's people and therefore has helped to birth the notion of individual rights and liberties and has served as a powerful corrective to people who would oppress others. The movements to end slavery, empower women, establish worker's rights, and enact civil rights found considerable basis and support from the Bible. It has authority because it "works." It effectively helps many people to connect to God and to live in a more compassionate and loving way. I quote from the Bible extensively throughout this book—it is not peripheral. Christians are called to engage and interact with it and we cannot do that if we're not familiar with it.

Okay. That was a lot that I just put out there. Let me unpack it and explain things a bit further. First of all, progressive Christianity views the Bible as a collection of written texts that were compiled over many years. Much of it, in both the Old and New Testaments, originally started out as oral tradition. The creation stories in Genesis and the stories of how the early Hebrews were liberated from bondage in Egypt and fled into the

---

[247]   And, as was stated before in the chapter on God, there are numerous theologies found within the Bible.

Promised Land first began as folk tales and myths that were told by the Hebrew tribal elders around campfires. Now that sentence will cause major heartburn for many conservative Christians. For them, the idea that the biblical texts didn't somehow miraculously appear as "a revelation" from out of the blue and that they were all but written by God Himself is verboten. Heck, it's beyond forbidden, it's unfathomable. But if they were to stop to think about it, they'd have to admit that this is likely the case. Few conservative Christians would deny that much of the information contained in the Gospels was conveyed and passed along in other ways before it was written down. Between the time of Jesus' death and the time the Gospel writers put pen to paper, stories about Jesus as Lord and Savior spread across the masses orally—technically speaking, in the form of *gossip*.[248] The musical *Jesus Christ Superstar* conveyed this well with the lyric, "What's the buzz? Tell me what's a happenin'!"[249] It therefore shouldn't be troubling to realize the same is true for the origins of several of the texts in the Hebrew Scriptures.

The other piece that induces heart palpitations in many conservative Christians is referring to certain biblical stories as myths. To some, when something is referred to as a "myth" it means that it isn't true, that it was made up, and therefore has no authority. They fail to truly understand the nature of myth. In the field of religious studies, *myth* refers to a genre of literature that uses metaphorical stories to convey deep essential truths. In the case of Genesis, the creation myths don't seek to convey "facts" about how the universe was created. Instead they tell us Who created and why. Those myths give us identity. They aren't scientific treatises that seek to explain literally how creation took place. They give us meaning and purpose. As Mike Leaptrott conveys in his critique of Leslie Newbigin's book, *Proper Confidence,*

. . . *He further illustrates this point by making the classic false dichotomy of modernist theology* . . . "The only possible responses to the claims the bible [sic] makes are belief or unbelief." p. 55

Newbigin falls victim to the modern presupposition that in order for the Bible to have any value, it must be read the same way we read a

---

[248]   The sometimes scandalous word on the street.

[249]   Click here and enjoy, http://www.youtube.com/watch?v=_qxy4V605KY

history book or science textbook. He assumes the point of the bible [sic] is to believe its stories are facts or reject them as fiction. This view of the bible [sic] is precisely what fed fundamentalism and lured science into a war that it never intended to wage.[250]

Perhaps an analogy of my own may help here. In the world of professional sports, there are two sorts of commentators that are often at work describing a televised sporting event. A "play-by-play" commentator focuses on the facts of the game. For example, how many RBI's (runs batted in) this baseball player has, what the ERA (earned run average) of that pitcher is, and what the exact rules of the game are. The other sportscaster, the "color commentator," provides a different role, adding the background story, color, poetry and meaning to the experience. For instance, "This batter surely has a lot on his mind today. What, with just signing that new contract, the recent passing of his father, his wife just gave birth to his first child yesterday, and he's trying to get out of the slump he's been in for the last month! But, if he gets a solid hit, he'll break the record for a rookie with the most runs batted in! This is a man facing destiny." Neither approach is the "right" one nor are they in conflict with each other. They simply have different aims and bring different things to the experience.

When it comes to creation, none of us were there when it took place and yet here we are. Humans have a need to know our purpose in this big universe. The statistical, "just the facts ma'am" sort of commentator can't speak to that need. The metaphorical-narrative commentator can speak to it, hence the creation of the Bible. We also have a need to know how we got here—and the field of science came along to address those matters. However, science and religion are neither mutually exclusive nor need to be seen as at odds with each other. Simply put, there are two kinds of truth—factual truth, and meaningful truth. Curiously, it may be argued that over the years, factual truth is what tends to change and be less reliable. It used to be an established fact that the "flat" earth was the center of the universe. It used to be a fact that there are no exceptions to the laws of Newtonian physics. It

---

[250]   "Proper Confidence," Progression of Faith blog, Mike Leaptrott, Oct. 4, 2004, http://www.faithprogression.com/

used to be the case that there are no exceptions to the principles of Quantum mechanics, and so on.

But the truths conveyed by myths seem to transcend the ages. Let's consider an example. A young Cherokee brave once went to his tribal elder saying, "I can't figure out what's going on inside me! I want to do right but I end up doing wrong. I want to love but I end up hating. Can you help me?" The elder paused for a moment and then responded saying, "Inside every brave are two dogs that are always at war. One of them is the dog of love, compassion, and kindness. The other is the dog of selfishness, violence, and vengeance." The brave pondered this and said, "Which dog wins?" The elder said, "That depends upon which dog you feed."

Did this event really take place? Was there really such a brave or an elder? Was he really a Cherokee or was he a Lakota? Did they say those exact words? Were they dogs or wolves? Are there literally dogs living inside of us? Is that true? Those are questions from a modern era mindset. Asking such questions is an exercise in "missing the forest for the trees."[251] It misses the point. As I understand it, people in antiquity wouldn't have asked such questions. Instead, they would have received the story, seen themselves in it, and found it to meet a need in their life. Mythically speaking (which is to say, biblically speaking), yes, it is true. Another way of putting this is to say that there is capital "T" Truth and lower-case "t" truth. Capital T Truth is what myth conveys and provides. Lower-case t truth is the domain of science and forensics.[252] C.S. Lewis once described how this works saying that one time he pointed toward a bone and said to his dog, "Look at that!" The dog didn't see what he was pointing at. Instead, the

---

[251] The same could be said about Jesus' parables. They are lessons intended to teach us larger truths through metaphor and other rhetorical devices.

[252] One use of the word forensics refers to the science of determining how someone died or was killed. Ironically, forensics also refers to the art of legalistic debate, the domain of the aforementioned *The Case for Christ* series of books; i.e., it focuses on lowercase t truth (though not very well for it fails to consider evidence to the contrary) in spite of its intention to focus on capital T truth.

dog looked at the end of the finger he was using to point with. That's how many people have come to take the Bible. They fail to understand that the Bible serves to point them to God, not to itself.[253]

Let's apply this to some specifics within the Bible and look at the age-old question "Was Jonah really swallowed by a giant fish?" This question misses the point of that story—that God desires justice and wants Her people to repent. God provides prophets to warn Her people, even if those prophets would rather not be in that role. There's nowhere we can go where God isn't. The same is true with questions such as, "Were the ancient Hebrews really ever slaves in Egypt? Did Moses really part the Red Sea? Did Joshua really have the people march around the walls of Jericho blaring trumpets? Was Jesus really born to a virgin? Did Jesus really walk on water or feed 5,000 people with a few fish and loaves of bread?" The trouble is conservative Christians try very hard to force "factual truth" onto those stories. Shifting away from a literal interpretation of the Bible causes anxiety. It's as if their faith were a giant house of cards. If someone were to come along and pull one of those cards from below, they fear the entire house might collapse.

Progressive Christianity offers a way of being Christian and taking the Bible seriously without such anxiety. It suggests that the Bible is a human-Divine co-creation. We don't think that God wrote the Bible, or that God dictated its words to the authors.[254] Instead, like everything that humans create, it is a co-creation between God and His people. Some things that we produce are more of God than others. While God is surely at work in the lives of the people who put together our telephone directories and the want ads in our newspapers, God was much more actively at

---

[253]   Observation from Christian writer, Steve McVey, "The Bible As A Barrier," Sept. 14, 2010, http://gracewalkministries.blogspot.com

[254]   Although Muslims *do* believe that about the Qur'an; i.e., that God told Muhammad what to have his scribe write down as conveyed to him by the angel Gabriel. Similarly, Mormons believe this about the Book of Mormon; i.e., that Joseph Smith used some special "seer stones" to help him transcribe some golden plates that came directly from God.

work in the creation of sacred texts. Much in the way that artists seek to tap into the Muse, the people who wrote those texts were especially turning on their "God radars" and seeking to be open to Divine inspiration and guidance.

Since we're aware that imperfect humans were involved, progressive Christians don't share the fundamentalist Christian claim that the Bible is "inerrant"—without mistake or flaw. One can simply read the various accounts in the Gospels describing Jesus' last week to realize that they can't all be "true" (in the modern sense). They blatantly contradict each other regarding many details as to what happened and when. Does this mean that they don't convey some factual truth? More importantly, does this mean that those accounts aren't true mythically or meaningfully?

Progressive Christians freely acknowledge that mistakes and flaws are surely possible in the Bible because it was written by many writers over many years and was copied, edited and re-edited numerous times. But that doesn't cause us to dismiss the Bible. In fact, it endears the scriptures to us. If God can convey a fairly consistent message of unconditional love that encourages us to love each other that way, *despite* all of that, then that message is powerful indeed. Many of us would say that pop-fiction author Dan Brown went too far in his book *The DaVinci Code* that fictitiously suggests a massive conspiracy took place to corrupt the Bible in order to politically suppress certain groups and to amass power by the Roman Catholic Church. We don't deny that some amount of that may have occurred, but the Bible still contains many threads of beauty, love, justice, meaning, and truth. Sure, it is also flawed. But to progressive Christians that makes it perfect—as humans can only learn from those who are flawed. It could just as easily be said that portions of the Bible were actually *improved* over the years of editing. No one faults musicians for taking a given song and tweaking it with various creative modifications and adaptations of their own. In fact, many say that other people's covers of songs first written and sung by Bob Dylan or Leonard Cohen are better than the originals.

Another key dynamic is the matter of interpreting the Bible. Conservative Christianity, especially the fundamentalist variety, reads the Bible in a wooden, literal manner.[255] Their motto seems to be—The Bible says it, so it must have happened exactly that way—or, as it's often put, "God said it, I believe it, that settles it." Conservatives think this is the way the Bible has always been read but it is a rather recent phenomenon for people to read sacred texts in that sort of way. The ancient Hebrews didn't operate out of a modern era mindset with its concerns for secular historicity and scientific, factual truth. Indeed, the scientific method and its application toward history didn't come along until the modern era. As I understand it, when people in antiquity heard a biblical text (few of them read) they didn't spend time pondering if something really happened or how it happened. They focused upon the points and essential messages of the stories and how their lives related to them. Hearing sacred stories (how they were intended to be conveyed and received)[256] is a different experience than reading or studying a text—developments of the modern era. It may well be argued that there should be less reading of the Bible, and more telling and *hearing* of it. People are more likely to get caught up in stories they hear. They are more willing to grant artistic license and freedom to orators and oral storytellers than to writers.

Another dynamic within the topic of interpreting the text is to what extent readers should let the text speak for itself, and to what extent we should bring ourselves to the text as we read and try to make sense of it. In the worlds of Bible scholarship and homiletics (the study and art of preaching), *exegesis* refers to the attempt to explain what a given text means and *eisegesis* is what various readers *read into* the text that may or may not have been intended to be conveyed.

---

[255] Ironically, that's how many atheists read it too, which of course, also makes it easier to reject it.

[256] "How, then, can they call on the one they have not believed in? And how can they believe in the one of whom they have not heard? And how can they hear without someone preaching to them? And how can they preach unless they are sent? As it is written, 'How beautiful are the feet of those who bring good news!' But not all the Israelites accepted the good news. For Isaiah says, 'Lord, who has believed our message?' Consequently, faith comes from hearing the message, and the message is heard through the word of Christ." (Romans 10:14-17)

Preachers and theologians try to objectively exegete texts and to avoid eisegesis. With the dawn of postmodernism, it has become clear that such objectivity is illusory and it is even suggested, "All exegesis is eisegesis."[257] This means that there is in reality no such thing as an "objective reader." We cannot help but bring our past, upbringing, and social location, status, and experiencees to bear to anything we read. There is no such thing as reading without interpretation. As Anaïs Nin noted, "We don't see things as they are, we see them as we are." With this in mind, if 1000 people read the same passage, there may be 1000 different interpretations.

That sounds like anarchy and chaos—and I agree it could be. Progressive Christians aren't advocating chaos however. We contend that some interpretations are better than others based upon the standards of whether they correlate and make sense within the larger biblical context and whether or not they promote justice, peace, inclusion, acceptance, reconciliation, and unconditional love. We see those as the biblical themes and values that Jesus championed. They are the standards by which one ought to read the Bible and be Christian. That would be known as our *hermeneutic*—the "theological lens that we use to see through" and the school of thought by which we operate.

Some portions of the Bible were not written from that perspective of love. Those are passages that progressive Christians reject, avoid, or openly wrestle with. However, many progressive Christians, myself included, do not advocate rejecting any part of the received text. We consider all of it to be a mirror for us to gaze into as we allow God to prophetically and pastorally speak to us, and for us to see our beauty and where we fall short.

Jacob was a major founding figure in Judaism. Part of the reason why he is celebrated is because of his willingness to wrestle with God (Genesis 32:23-34). Progressive Christians claim "the wrestling spirit of Jacob" as we encounter and grapple with our sacred texts. There may be some within the progressive Christian family who feel that the Bible, a work written in different

---

[257] This is especially true for interpreting the Bible as in most of the ancient manuscripts, there are neither chapter nor verse numbers. Nor are there spaces between the words or punctuation marks! One simply cannot avoid engaging in interpretation as one reads those texts!

languages, in a different time, by a different culture, is so difficult for today's people to make sense of, and it takes so much work that it's not worth the effort. For such persons, the Bible is an antiquated, peripheral vestige that holds us back more than it empowers us and meets our needs. However, those voices seem to be a minority within progressive circles. Most of us couldn't imagine going to church and not hearing a passage from the Bible read aloud, discussed and applied to our lives.

Though it involves work, most progressive Christians love wrestling with the Bible. Many of us do so with the tools of the aforementioned "hermeneutic of love"[258] as well as by seeking to interpret the Scriptures in a participatory, communal manner. Since we embrace the postmodern perspective that suggests our environment and our limited understandings condition us, we see that we need community that is actively discerning what the Holy Spirit is saying to us in order to help us obtain a fuller blessing and insight into the meaning of scripture. Progressive Christianity encourages a communal reading of scripture instead of a myopic, individualistic reading.[259] We embrace the "many minds are better than one" perspective. Christianity has long advocated the wisdom of reading and interpreting the Bible as a group experience. An example of this is seen in the Bible Studies and worship services in progressive congregations where the pastor is considered less as an expert and more as a guiding facilitator who helps people ponder the Word in small group settings. Roman Catholicism has always been wary of overly democratized readings of scripture and hold that priests do this best. Protestants, who believe in the "priesthood of all believers,"[260] suggest that priests and

---

[258] I.e., a hermeneutic approach that focuses on messages of love in the Bible.

[259] That said, a goodly number of progressive Christians aren't currently active with local church congregations. To the extent that they do discuss the Bible with peers, it tends to be via the internet.

[260] The priesthood of all believers was a central teaching of Martin Luther in the formation of Christian communities that would ultimately become the Lutheran Church. Rejecting the Roman Catholic sacrament of ordination or Holy Orders, Luther declared that, "we are all priests as long as we are Christians." [This is a doctrine

pastors shouldn't have a monopoly on the proper interpretation of scripture, but most major historical Protestant denominations embrace the role of church tradition as a guide in helping interpret the Good Book. Ironically, progressive Christians affirm the insight of Richard Rohr, a Catholic priest. His insight states that:

> *Mere literalism is always a decrease of meaning, not an increase. The very thing that fundamentalists protect is the lowest, most narrow level of meaning that is possible. When we read the Scriptures or receive a Sacrament with a contemplative mind, we will find 25 levels of meaning, and not feel the need to prove our "one and only" level of meaning. Mature spirituality does not throw out a very possible literal meaning; rather it includes all possible levels. We can agree to some good meaning on that first level, but we must strive to see things on other levels of the heart and mind. This was assumed for the first 1400 years of Christianity, taken for granted by the Church Fathers, mystics, and saints. In many ways we have gone backwards and limited the ways that God could speak to us. If Emerging Christianity is going to healthily emerge, we need to rise above and beyond the dualistic "desert" of literal thinking. All religious language is by necessity metaphor and simile, which leaves both the mind and the heart free to hear all that God might be telling us through a text.*[261]

As a progressive United Methodist, I work with John Wesley's suggested rubric for living out the Christian faith. Often referred to as "The Wesleyan Quadrilateral," the four factors of Scripture, Tradition, Reason, and Experience are all to be involved and engaged when doing theology, making moral choices, and interpreting the Bible. In practice, this means allowing scripture to interpret itself—seeing how other passages of the Bible speak to a given topic. It means discerning the historic teachings and

---

for most Protestant denominations]. http://protestantism.suite101. com/ article.cfm/the_priesthood_of_ all_believers#ixzz0wm7rsvEB

[261]   From his book, *Radical Grace*, Saint Anthony Messenger Press, 1995. Rohr is a Franciscan priest, and proof that progressive Christianity isn't solely a Protestant approach to the faith.

doctrines of the Church and allowing them to influence our interpretations. It means engaging our intelligence and rational minds. A valid interpretation ought to be reasonable and make sense. And it means testing one's potential interpretation by seeing how it correlates to one's experience of his or her individual and communal relationship with God and the world around them—which includes the insights of science.

Break it Down XII

The following is a letter that I published in the church newsletter for Delano UMC in Delano, MN in 1996, a few months after I started my first appointment as a pastor out of seminary:

Why My Fish are Kissing

As many of you know, I'm a person who notices bumper stickers when I'm out and about. I enjoy making mention of the more interesting ones in my sermons. It seems that there are some of you who enjoy this kind of thing as well—in fact a few of you have approached me and asked about the things that are stuck on the back of my car, namely, those two silvery "fish" emblems.

You've probably noticed that there are an increasing number of vehicles on the road with one of two symbols on their bumpers; 1) the Christian fish symbol, or 2) the fish with feet underneath it with the word "Darwin" in the middle (perhaps representing secular humanism). Lately I've been seeing more elaborate versions with the Christian fish aggressively swallowing the Darwin Fish or visa versa or even doing more interesting things to each other (I guess they're evolving).

It seems that there are two "competing truths" at war with each other. Either the literal interpretation of the biblical creation story is true (that God did everything "just as it says" in 6 days just 6,000 years ago) or else the truth lies in the evolutionary theory of the emergence of the species over many billions of years advanced by Charles Darwin.

To many of the unchurched folk in our society who see these bumper emblems on their daily commutes it would appear that *all* Christians are literal Creationists who ignore, and even attack, the fruits of critical thought and the contemporary sciences. And this troubles me.

This perception can become yet another reason for them to write off Christianity as "antiquated and irrelevant" and thus, they miss out on the richness of being involved with a community of faith—and possibly experiencing the deep joy of salvation and abundant life. et there are many millions of faithful believers who contend that being a Christian doesn't mean being oblivious to critical thought. We aren't called to turn off our brains when we enter a church, read the Bible, or let Christ into our lives!

As a United Methodist, I embrace John Wesley's "method" of fully utilizing the tools of Scripture, Tradition, Reason, and Experience. This means taking in as much as we can from all fields and disciplines as we discern meaning in our lives. It is for this reason that I subscribe to a wide range of magazines and have Minnesota Public Radio and a Christian radio station right next to each other as presets on my car radio. As a result, it seems quite reasonable to many Christians to perceive that the processes of evolution are employed in the unfolding of God's Creation. So, it's not necessarily an "either/or" situation, perhaps it's more of a "both/and"—these views of creation aren't necessarily contradictory or mutually exclusive. Perhaps God created human life through the means of evolution. In fact, it might even be idolatry to claim that God *didn't* do it that way as that'd be humans putting limitations on God.

There are truths that are essential to the faith: that the depths of Gods' mercy and love for us are uniquely manifest in the life of Jesus of Nazareth and that Jesus is Lord. Yet there are many things that are "non-essentials"—for example, our understandings of the virgin birth, the miracle stories, stances on sexuality, whether the Communion bread really becomes Christ's body, etc.—and this is one of them.

John Wesley spoke to this saying, *"In essentials, unity; in non-essentials, liberty; and in all things, charity."* And, *"Though we may not all think alike, may we not love alike? May we not be of one heart though we may not be of one opinion? If your heart is as my heart, give me thy hand."*

And so, I purchased both of these fish emblems, faced them toward each other, and show them "kissing" in order to convey to the world (both churched and unchurched) that there are other ways of being a faithful Christian. If nothing else, it might help shift things into a healthier way of playful dialogue. It's a small thing, but who knows? It might make a difference.

Evolving in Christ,
Pastor Roger

One of the key tools for progressive Christians is the use of what has come to be known as the "Historical-Critical" method of working with the Bible. This method is a branch of literary analysis that is based upon scientific methodology. Sometimes known as "higher criticism," this phrase refers to a large umbrella that includes a variety of tactics and strategies to help understand biblical texts—particularly, to discern the motivations and agendas the respective authors had; what specific situations they were likely responding to; what sources they drew from; and what rhetorical techniques they employed. These approaches seek to learn what we can about who wrote the texts, where they wrote them, when they wrote them, why they wrote them, and how they wrote them.

This approach has much in common with the deductive reasoning of the famed detective Sherlock Holmes. Some of the **Historical-Critical methods** include:

* **Source Criticism**—seeks to discover the various oral and literary sources that the authors drew from in writing their texts. Some of the insights from source criticism include: that the Ten Commandments were in part based upon the Babylonian *Code of Hammurabi*;[262] that Matthew and Luke likely had a copy of Mark on hand as they wrote their Gospels; that Mark may have followed some of the story line from Homer's *Odyssey* to help

---

[262] The Code of Hammurabi is one of the oldest known legal codes, predating the Ten Commandments by about 1000 years. It was cast in stone in Mesopotamia (the area we now call Iraq) around 1750 B.C. This stone currently resides in the Louvre museum in Paris. The code spelled out the fundamentals of contract law and human rights. The code included prohibitions against lying, theft, and murder. Hammurabi was the 6th king of Babylon and the 1st king of the Babylonian Empire.

convey his Gospel to the Hellenized Jews[263] of his day;[264] and so on.

* **Form Criticism**—takes the Bible and breaks it down into smaller units that stand on their own and then categorizes them according to genres such as prose, poetry, verse, parables, hymns, wisdom sayings, law, genealogies, etc. The form critic then seeks to discover the setting in which a given passage was composed and how it was used.

* **Redaction Criticism**—examines how an author wrote and presented his or her text; for example, the unique ways that each of the Gospel writers put their respective texts together and what they each emphasized, minimized, and appeared to have as their agendas that they sought to propel. Their agendas are noticed by their respective ordering of events, what they emphasized and elaborated upon, what they left out, and which words they tweaked or modified, etc.[265]

A key insights from the Historical-Critical approach is that the traditionally accepted notions about authorship and origins have turned out to be incorrect. Authors other than those attributed in the scriptures actually wrote many of the books of the Bible. These books were also written at later points in time than some people have assumed. Conservative Christianity tends to reject the Historical-Critical methods because of those insights. For many conservative Christians, the idea that the biblical books weren't

---

[263] *Hellenized* means that because of Israel's having been a subject state of the Greek Empire, they had become thoroughly exposed and participants in Greek culture. They spoke Greek, thought in Greek, and were familiar with Greek myths and stories. Hellen as the mythological patriarch of the Hellenes (Greek: Ἕλληνες), the son of Deucalion (or sometimes Zeus) and Pyrrha, brother of Amphictyon and father of Aeolus, Xuthus, and Dorus. His name is also another name for Greek, meaning a person of Greek descent or pertaining to Greek culture, and the source of the adjective "Hellenic".

[264] See: Dennis McDonald's, *The Homeric Epics and the Gospel of Mark*, Yale University Press, 2000.

[265] For more info see: http://www.participatorystudyseries.com/historical-critical_method.shtml

purely written by "who the Bible says" wrote them produces great anxiety. There is much fear that this notion undermines the authority of the Bible and the whole basis of their faith. For them, it makes the Bible seem more like a fallible and dismissible human creation and less of a unique and special revelation from God.

Progressive Christianity does not share that anxiety. Progressive Christianity isn't overly wedded to the scientific approach to scripture. Our postmodern sensibilities urge us to leave room for mystery, to accept the lack of definitive answers about the origins of the Bible, and to be at peace with the fact that our knowledge about biblical texts will never be fully accurate or "correct."

Another approach to the Bible that is employed by progressive Christians is referred to as the "canon within the canon." In literary terms, a *canon* (from the Greek, meaning "measuring stick") is an officially recognized collection of books that is thought to contain the best and highest examples of an author, composer, or genre. Historically, students majoring in English or philosophy read books from a list of texts chosen by academic experts as being ones that are deemed as the essential classics from those disciplines. They are considered to be the gold standards that truly represent the best of the tradition.[266] The canon of a religion refers to the officially recognized and established sacred texts that are deemed to be the ones that contain and best convey the essential truths and teachings of its founders. For Judaism, the canon is the *Bible* (Hebrew scriptures); for Muslims it is the *Qur'an*; for Taoists, it is the *Tao Te Ching* and the *I Ching*; for Buddhists, they are the *Tripitaka*, the *Sutras*, and Tantric texts; for Hindus they are the *Bhagavad Gita*, the *Vedas* and the *Upanishads* (among others); for Mormons, it is the *Book of Mormon* and the "Inspired Version of the Bible;" and for Christians, it is *The Holy Bible*.

Many progressive Christians have come to adopt a "canon within the canon" approach to interpreting scripture. This basically means that we view some of the biblical texts as being more authoritative and important than others. We therefore interpret those other texts through the lens of the teachings and values conveyed in the ones we consider as more authoritative.

---

[266] The "Great Works" approach.

This is not a new or radical development. Indeed, Jews have long considered the Torah, the first five books of their Bible, as being by far the most important texts in their canon. The Sadducees rejected the prophets[267] as part of their canon. This likely played a major role in Jesus' tensions and conflicts with the Sadducees. Jesus embraced the prophets as well as the Torah. In fact, it may well be argued that Jesus interpreted the Torah via the lens of the prophets and the values they championed. Jesus quoted from the prophets more often than any other Jewish texts—with Isaiah apparently being his favorite. Jesus chose to speak from the Isaiah scroll when he preached his first sermon. In fact, the majority of that sermon was quoting from Isaiah and then proclaiming those words had been fulfilled in the presence of the people gathered there to hear him that day (Luke 4:17). And Jesus and his early followers consistently linked the law and the prophets as belonging together.[268]

Progressive Christianity follows Jesus' example in lifting up certain books over others and reading all of them with a certain perspective: unconditional love, compassion, and mercy. For many of us, the prophets and the Gospels of Luke, Mark, and Matthew serve as the lens through which we read the rest of the Bible. Many of us would also include the letters of Paul, particularly, the ones that the majority of scholars agree that Paul wrote (not the pastoral epistles). Most of Paul's letters were written before the Gospels, so that gives them authority, as they are closer in time to the life of Jesus. Mark was the first of the Gospels written so that gives it credibility. Luke's Gospel is arguably the most in line with the teachings of the prophets, and since, the Prophets were largely "Jesus' Bible," this gives it authority. Though some of us might be wary of the Gospel of John, there are strong threads within it

---

[267] The Hebrew Bible includes two categories of prophets, the Major Prophets such as Isaiah and Jeremiah, and the Minor Prophets such as Micah. Prophets were people called by God to speak on God's behalf during the era when Israel was led by kings. They helped the people stay faithful and just. That often involved rebuking the monarchs and the elites of society for oppressing the masses.

[268] Matthew 5:17, 11:3, 16:16, Luke 24:44, John 1:45, Acts 13:15, Acts 34:14, etc.

that advocate self-giving, agape love, and an anti-imperial ethic as intregral to faithful discipleship.

Within all of that, many progressive Christians find the following passages of scripture to especially exemplify the heart of Christianity:

* "Love the Lord your God with all your heart and with all your soul and with all your mind and with all your strength.' [and to] 'Love your neighbor as yourself" (Mark 12:30-34)
* Micah's call "to act justly and to love mercy and to walk humbly with God" (Michah 6:8)
* he Beatitudes (the countercultural "Blessed ares . . ." that begin the sermon on the Mount, Matthew 5:3-12)
* The radical calls to a simple life-style of dependence upon God and non-violence in Jesus' Sermon on the Mount/ Plain (e.g., Matthew 6:21 and Luke 6:17-49)
* The call to show compassion to others in the parable of the Good Samaritan (Luke 10:30-37); the call to serve "the least of these" in the parable of the sheep and the goats (Matthew 25:31-46)
* Jesus' first sermon (Luke 4:14-30)
* Jesus' inquiring about the depth of John's love (John 21:15-19)
* "God is love" (1 John 4:8)
* The emphasis on doing good works in James 1-2
* And the call to "help and provide for others according to their needs" in Acts 2-4

Some Progressive Christians consider themselves to be "Red letter Christians."[269] Many versions of the Bible have highlighted in red ink the words attributed to Jesus. Hence, if one considers

---

[269] Many Christians over the years have referred to themselves as "red letter Christians," but starting in 2006, Jim Wallis and Tony Campolo (social justice oriented evangelicals) have been marketing that name to refer to "a new political movement that transcends left and right, and Democrat vs. Republican based upon the core values that Jesus taught. See: http://www.beliefnet.com/Faiths/ Christianity/2006/02/Whats-A-Red-Letter-Christian.aspx and also this book, *Red Letter Christians*, by Campolo, Regal, 2008.

those words to be the most direct links to Jesus, then it makes sense to use those words as the primary standard by which all other scripture is to be read and understood. Red letter Christians point out that Jesus said nothing about abortion or homosexuality so Jesus' followers would do well to "not go there" either, let alone devote so much time, energy, and money in God's vineyard on those tangential matters.

If one's primary exposure to Christianity is the Pastoral Epistles, certain portions of the Gospel of John,[270] and the Book of Revelation from the New Testament, along with Leviticus and Deuteronomy from the Old, then one is likely to adopt a form of Christianity that is judgmental, legalistic, exclusive, oppressive to women, anti-Semitic, homophobic, and prone to blessing the status quo of the powers that be.

While not dismissing those texts, progressive Christianity denies that those are the actual values that Jesus intended to teach and pass on—in fact, quite the opposite. Progressive Christianity suggests that one needs to interpret them via the lens of what we see as the more normative "canon within the canon."

Despite their tendency to quote, *"Everything in the Scriptures is God's Word. All of it is useful for teaching and helping people and for correcting them and showing them how to live"* (2 Timothy 3:16), when defending their notion that "all of the Bible is equally God's word and that Christians should be bound by all of it," in reality, conservative Christians also employ a canon within the canon approach, even if subconsciously. In my experience, conservative Christians preach from, quote from, and otherwise operate out of the following texts: certain portions of the Gospel of John; the Pastoral Epistles; Paul's

---

[270]   In all fairness, the Book of John, while lending itself to interpretations of substitutionary atonement and anti-Semitism, also contains the story of Mary being the first evangelist of the good news of the risen Christ, and there is a major focus on love in that text. Simply put, many progressive Christians have a love-hate relationship with that Gospel. More of us are coming around to loving John, however, due to recent scholarship which highlights its emphasis upon love and anti-imperialism; e.g., *John and Empire*, Warren Carter, T & T Clark International, 2008; and *Becoming Children of God: John's Gospel and Radical Discipleship*, Wes Howard-Brook, Wipf & Stock, 2004.

letters; Exodus (especially the ten commandments), Leviticus, and Deuteronomy. This is effectively their canon within the canon.

A challenge to their canon is to ask how those texts jibe with Jesus' over-arching teachings of unconditional love, non-judging, non-violence, and radical inclusivity. Whoever wrote 1st and 2nd Timothy didn't likely intend for those letters, or any of Paul's letters, or perhaps even the Gospels themselves (some of which hadn't even been written yet) to be considered as scripture. When Jesus or the writers of the letters in the New Testament referred to "the scriptures," they were referring to the Old Testament of the Hebrew Bible, not to any of their own writings or sayings. In time, the Gospels began to carry the weight of scripture for the early Christian communities. Several of the letters of Paul and others were considered as valuable classics, which help convey Christian teachings and the story of the origins of the Christian faith. After many years of ardent prayer and contentious politicking, the New Testament became adopted as part of the Christian canon.

It's been thousands of years since the books of the Bible were written and it is becoming increasingly difficult for high-tech suburban and city dwellers to understand the writings from foreign, ancient, rural peoples. Reading the Bible well takes a bit of work. Fewer and fewer people (Christians and atheists) today are willing to take the extra time that is needed to rightly read and interpret the Bible.[271] More radically progressive Christians may be receptive to "opening the canon." A closed canon means that no new books or letters are to be added to the existing collection.[272] Those who would open the canon generally want to maintain the Bible as primary, but supplement it with more contemporary stories from the Civil Rights movement in the United States. Perhaps it would include some of the late Rev. Dr. Martin Luther

---

[271] Ironically, atheists and fundamentalist Christians both read the Bible in the same, problematic, wooden, literal manner. The only difference is that the fundamentalists believe what they think they're reading.

[272] The Mormons have an open canon in that in addition to their "Inspired" version of the Bible, they have included *The Book of Mormon*, the *Book of Doctrines & Covenants*, and *The Pearl of Great Price*.

King's writings such as the *Letter from a Birmingham Jail*.[273] These persons might also want to include some of the documents that describe the struggle for the end of racial Apartheid in South Africa, or maybe even certain inspiring stories of truth and love from other world religions and their texts. I'm not one to call for opening the canon, but I am certainly in favor of augmenting the Bible with those sorts of inspiring materials! When I'm feeling down and glum about the future of the Church, reading from the Book of Acts along with the sermons and letters of Martin Luther King, Jr., always re-fans the flames for me to press on in faith. I have no doubt that King was just as inspired by the Holy Spirit when he wrote his letters as Paul was when he wrote his.

Progressive Christianity agrees with the Protestant assertion of *"sola scriptura"*—that the Bible contains all that is necessary for salvation.[274] However, that doesn't mean it's the only vessel of God's ways of communicating and conveying God's grace and wholeness. To say otherwise is *idolatry*—the sin of humans having the gall to limit God by making an idol of the Bible. As John Wesley noted, Church Tradition, Reason, and Experience are also helpful means for coming to a sense of salvation, and there are a lot of other spirit-filled books out there to be fed by. A protein, yogurt, fruit, and wheat grass smoothie, or perhaps a serving of quinoa, may contain all that is necessary for human life—but that doesn't mean other foods don't offer many of the same sorts of things as well. In fact, supplementing basic foodstuffs with other foods actually enhances how those "basics" are utilized by the body.

Progressive Christianity emphasizes orthopraxy (right practice) over orthodoxy (right beliefs). It affirms the classic saying, *"Take care in how you live your life. It may be the only Bible some people ever read."* In other words, namely Maya Angelou's, *"Each of us, famous or infamous, is a role model for somebody, and if we aren't, we should behave as though we are—cheerful, kind, loving, courteous. Because you can be sure someone is watching and taking deliberate and diligent notes."*

---

[273]   http://www.law.umkc.edu/faculty/projects/ftrials/conlaw/mlkjail.html

[274]   Though again, progressive Christians favor the passages that describe following Jesus and his way, and not the ones that focus on the shedding of his blood.

Gulp. I don't know about you, but that makes me want to read my Bible for some guidance in how to live that way!

———————

For more in depth treatments of progressive Christian approaches to the Bible, see: *The Good Book: Reading the Bible with Heart and Mind* by Peter Gomes; *Rescuing the Bible from Fundamentalism* by Jon Shelby Spong; and *Reading the Bible Again for the First time,* by Marcus Borg.[275]

———————

[275]   . . . respectively, Harper Perennial, 1998, HarperOne, 1992, & HarperSanFrancisco, 2002.

Chapter 9

Evil & Theodicy: The God Problem

Have we ever known tragedy or been close those who have been close to it? (paraphrased)
—*The Impression that I Get*, Mighty Mighty Bosstones

I'm writing a letter to God asking Him to help out because things aren't going well down here on Earth; the people God made are starving . . . I don't believe in you God.
(paraphrased)
—*Dear God*, Xtc

How long, O LORD, must I call for help, but you do not listen? Or cry out to you, "Violence!" but you do not save? Why do you make me look at injustice? Why do you tolerate wrong? Habakkuk 1:1-4

The world we live in is beautiful, wondrous, abundant, and awesome, yet it's filled with tragedy, heartache, and inexplicable suffering. Theodicy (literally, *"the God problem"*) is the attempt to explain God's goodness and power and reconcile these with the apparent evil in the created world. It's often put this way, "Why would an *all* good, *all* knowing, and *all* powerful God cause or allow such *horrible* things to happen to His people?" Since most theologians and religious philosophers in the West have assumed both God's "unconditional power" and God's "absolute goodness," the existence and persistence of evil are often held to be inexplicable/unexplainable. In recent centuries, the absence of a convincing or satisfying resolution to the issue of theodicy and the frequent theological resort to "Divine mystery" as an explanation have led many to atheism.

Atheistic arguments concerning the non-existence of God give serious challenge to the traditional theistic view of God as loving, all knowing, all-powerful, and everywhere present. If horrible things happen in the world—such as the Plague, the Nazi and Stalinist genocides, or the attacks in the U.S. on September 11, 2001—and if God knew about it in advance, and had the ability to prevent it; then, God couldn't be fully loving, or all-powerful, and/or all knowing. Or, the atheists are right: there is no God.

Many traditional Christians (and Muslims and Jews) facing this argument reply with something like, "We finite humans simply aren't able to fully fathom or discern the ways of God—it's God's will and it's a mystery." While I can appreciate that defense, it isn't fully sensible or satisfying. I recognize that the early Christian thinkers were greatly influenced by pagan Greek philosophical ideals (the omnipotent and omniscient notions)—influences that progressive Christians suggest didn't benefit Christianity. Instead, the theology that many progressive Christians resonate with holds that God is:

* all loving
* *very* powerful (largely persuasive rather than coercive)
* all knowing of everything that is possible to know—all that has happened in the past, all the possibilities in the present; and very perceptive about the various probabilities of our future.

This perspective stems from "process theology" by liberals or "openness theology" by evangelicals. Despite some people's concerns, the existence and integrity of God remains secure and sound with this understanding. This position is just as biblically grounded as the more traditional and popular one is said to be.

Certain people might reply that they "wouldn't want to worship a God who is only *very* powerful, and only *mostly* knowing." However, we believe that God created us in God's image in order to have real and authentic relationships. This means that part of how we were created in Her image is by being gifted with real free will. Hence, God cannot know all that we'll do from moment to moment. But God does actively try to influence all of us at every moment in order to lure and woo us toward opting to choose actions that are in sync with God's will. To the extent that we do this, our actions are Godly. To the extent that we deviate, they aren't—they're sinful. Yet, no matter what we do to deviate from God's intentions and make a mess of things, the promise remains that God's powers and abilities will redeem and transform things for the better, and ultimately bring about God's Kingdom "on earth as it is in heaven."

The following is the transcript of a brief chat-room instant message "whisper" discussion I had with someone in 2001 exploring these issues, particularly the matter of *theodicy* (why God allows bad things to happen to good people):

Her: I like to come in these rooms and listen to the different religions, I don't agree, but it's interesting . . . what do you say to people when they ask why God lets bad things happen to them?

Me: Well, I may not be a "typical" Christian in my thoughts on this matter. I lean toward what's known as Process theology (by liberals) and it's similar to Openness theology (an evangelical variation). It's also similar to the view promoted by Rabbi Harold Kushner.

Her: ??

Me: Essentially, this perspective suggests that God isn't responsible for acts of nature, like when a tree falls on someone, or when people die in floods or lightning, etc., as God has set creation up in such a way that the laws of physics (even the ones we don't yet know about) must apply; for example, if a rock falls off a cliff on earth, it must fall down, and it is just bad luck/timing if someone happens to be underneath it or in its path.

Now, when it comes to why human caused bad things happen, it is just that, HUMAN-caused. That is, God didn't cause someone to rape or murder someone else, it was simply that offending individual misusing and abusing his or her God-given free will. Now, some will say that "Since God is supposedly all powerful, all knowing, and all loving," then why wouldn't God stop someone from murdering someone else, or why wouldn't God have prevented the Holocaust or the tragedies on 9/11?

Her: Exactly, and they ask why did he create evil?

Me: For me, God is very powerful (but not able to actually catch nuclear missiles in the air should we decide to fire them); all loving, all present, and all knowing of that which is possible to know; i.e., God knows all of the past, all of the present, and the likely probabilities of what will happen in the future.

I don't personally feel that God created evil, but simply the possibility for it. When Adam and Eve (if one takes that myth/narrative literally) committed the first sin (an act/thought that is contrary to God's will), they did so using their free will. Once this happened the first time, it made things such that we're more and more likely to sin again. Sort of like how a drug user takes one hit, which leads to another . . . or like when a person gets frostbite on a toe, once that happens, it's more prone to having it happen again.

Does any of this make any sense?

Her: yes, perfectly

Me: Ultimately, most people of faith, when pressed, will resort to saying that we need to defer to the "Mystery" of God and God's ways; i.e., we puny humans can't understand it all. However, the way I've presented it above helps me make as much sense as possible for me.

Her: yeah . . . There's a website one of them showed me . . . "godlessamerica" or something like that . . . it had these horrible pictures of people in misery and asked where was God then? I just didn't know how to answer it

Me: Well, I'd say that God was very much there with those people! 1) God was working hard to try to sway the perpetrators from doing their evil acts, minimizing this as much as possible, and 2) God was suffering with those people, being there for them and with them, working to give them strength and hope.

Her: See, and that makes perfect sense to me, but it's so hard to get that through other people's heads!

Me: Yeah, like how when Rabbi Heshel was asked in a WWII German concentration camp by a fellow inmate, "see that little boy hanging by his neck from that rope on those gallows, where is your God now?" To which he replied, "He's there hanging upon those ropes."

Her: wow.

Me: Great acts of horror and tragedy are difficult for people to process—indeed, after WWII many of the world's Jews have become atheistic, agnostic and/or only minimally religious.

However, for me the real problem is that in popular Judaism & Christianity, God is made to be some kind of Superman hero who can do anything to stop bad things from happening, and hence, people are prone to having crises of faith when God "fails" to stop bad things from happening. I think we need to put aside that popular image of God and shift to a healthier one.

By the way, are you a person of any particular faith?

Her: I was told once that God lets things happen to bring people closer to him, and I just thought that was horrible . . . to put people in misery for your own good?

Her: yes, I'm a Christian

Me: Yes, I've heard many say that "there is a purpose to everything," or that "this happened so I could learn this lesson," "this happened to test my faith to make me stronger," etc. Such logic is odd and even offensive—especially if said to a victim/mourner soon after their tragedy.

However, I do feel that those are things that can be true in a way in that after the fact, looking back on it, people can often see how things have "worked out for them" since then. But this is quite different than saying that one was raped "in order to learn a certain lesson."

I'd say that if lessons are learned, or people become stronger, etc., then this is because God was working hard to do damage control (to help them dust off, move on, and maybe even help others) after the incident. But not that God caused it.

Her: that makes so much more sense

Me: Glad I could be of help! The question you raised is a biggie. It's called the issue of "theodicy" (literally, "the God problem") in theological circles—why would an all good, loving, and powerful God allow such bad things to happen to God's people? There are many takes on this matter, but I like this one.

Her: I think I like it too

Me: From my experience, Christians/Churches that come from a Calvinist perspective (conservative Baptists, Evangelicals, Fundamentalists) say that God did intentionally cause those acts of trauma, but that Christians/Churches that come from an Arminian perspective (Methodists, Episcopalians, liberals, etc.) embrace the concept of Free Will; i.e., evil is human caused—not God caused. Interestingly, both groups can point to various Bible passages to support their views.

Say, which churches, if any, have you been a part of?

Her: I was baptized in the Baptist church, but now attend the Methodist church

Me: How 'bout that, I'm a United Methodist myself!

Her: lol . . . its a small world after all

Me: Keep in mind that if you had whispered this matter to a more conservative Christian you would've likely gotten a very different answer.

Her: probably

Me: I have enjoyed this little chat with you. I remember your screen-name from a few nights ago in this chat-room. Good to "see" you again!

Her: LOL, I've just become really interested in the past few weeks . . . it's weird but I hope to "see" you again sometime.

Me: God be with you sister. Bye for now.

Her: Bye

The contemporary Christian perspectives known as process theology and openness theology—approaches embraced by many progressive Christians—respond to this issue in ways quite similar to that held by the famed Jewish Rabbi Harold Kushner, author of *Why Bad Things Happen to Good People*.[276] To help convey some

---

[276] The difference between process theology and openness theology is essentially a matter of degree. Process theology asserts that God cannot know the future and is incapable of coercive involvement in human affairs in the worldly realm whereas openness theologians would contend that God is capable of knowing the future and/

of the basic features of this line of thinking, I have written the following piece inspired by a document entitled "Theodicy" by John Cobb, Jr. and Truman G. Madsen.[277] The wording is mine, but I follow their helpful outline; i.e., their headers in capitalized bold type. Also included are my personal thoughts on these matters.

Break it Down XIII

The "Process/Openness" Perspective:

OMNIPOTENCE & SELF EXISTENCE—God's sovereign power is typically expressed with the concept of *omnipotence* ("all powerful"). This means that God can do anything—or at least anything that is "logically possible" (protecting God from the "Can God create a rock that He cannot lift?" dilemma). This is often linked to the doctrine that God created the universe *ex nihilo* ("from nothing"). The logical implication of this traditional line of thought is that all forms of evil (including that of the devil and/or demons) are directly or indirectly made by God.

Some logical challenges to this traditional line of thinking are that:

- Since God made everything that is, then God made guns, pollution, and nuclear weapons.

---

or of direct forceful involvement in the world but *chooses* to limit Himself—to effectively "put one arm behind His back" and restrain His capacity to directly intervene in the world in order to allow us to have true and real freedom. The process view is more satisfactory for many in regard to theodicy as the openness view leaves God open to the charge of being not all loving (and even a bit evil) as if God is good, and loving, and all powerful, and *is able* to intervene in the world then God is culpable and responsible when tragedies happen in the lives of good people—for if God is indeed capable of directly preventing a rape or a murder (or a genocide) from occurring, then it would be His fault that they happen as God could've done something to prevent them (or She'd at least be complicit and culpable).

277 "Theodicy," *The Encyclopedia of Mormonism*, Macmillan Publishing, 1992. See: http://eom.byu.edu/index.php/Theodicy. Cobb is a United Methodist and Madsen is a Mormon. Apparently there are some progressive Mormons (or at least one). Who knew?

- Since God made everything, then God made Hitler. Hitler caused the murder of 6 million Jews; therefore God is responsible for their slaughter. And, since this slaughter was a real thing, and since all things are God-made, then it follows that God "made" this genocide.

- Since God made everything, then God must've also made Satan/the devil & evil.

- Since God made everything, then this must mean that God is the cause/source of cancer, disease, famine, floods, droughts, earthquakes, wild fires, hurricanes, tsunamis, etc.

According to process thought, God isn't the only reality that is self-existent. Biblically, God isn't presented as a dictatorial creator who acts by arbitrary fiat. Instead, God is an amazing organizer and giver of life. "The pure principles of element" can't be created or destroyed. The foundations of eternal law, with certain bounds and conditions, co-exist with God. With this understanding, omnipotence means that God has "all the power that it is possible to have in the universe." Hence, God didn't create evil. We did as a result of our misuse of our free will; i.e., by our choices to not follow the leadings of God's Spirit in our lives. When it comes to disasters such as volcano eruptions, earthquakes, fires, etc., process thought contends that these events aren't ordained or caused by God—they aren't "acts of God." Instead, they're simply the results of the constant motion and shifting of the natural world that occur when natural forces (which follow the laws of physics) run their course. I disagree with the notion within process thought that God didn't create the principal elements of Creation. However, I agree with the conclusion that God isn't at fault if lighting strikes someone's home or if a tree falls on top of someone. Either way, God has established Creation in such a way that it is not able to defy the laws of physics. If someone dies as a result of a boulder falling on top of him, it's not an "act of God." It's an unfortunate tragedy of being in the wrong place at the wrong time.

APPEARANCE & REALITY—Traditionally, *omnipotence* is usually thought of as God being able to override or undo and erase all that other powers might do that interfere with God's agenda and His sovereign will. In this view, God isn't restricted by human will or bound by the laws of nature, gravity, physics, energy conservation, thermodynamics, etc. This view makes God responsible for everything that occurs, exactly as it occurs.

God just caused me to type this sentence in just this way! If God is truly good, then it follows that despite appearances, everything that happens must be good—no matter how horrible the "good" may seem to us. For example, "that brutal act of rape that just took place was actually good in God's eyes." "Evil" is therefore a mistaken interpretation of the human mind, or simply a matter of perspective. The conclusion that follows is that "this is the best of all possible worlds" and that "whatever is, is right" (to quote Leibnitz and the medieval thinker Alexander Pope from his famed *Essay on Man*; a work which Voltaire deftly satirized and lampooned in his even more famous Enlightenment era work *Candide*). However, the problem then remains, why doesn't God exercise His great power to simply remove the pain and suffering that arises from human dysfunction, waywardness, or misunderstanding?

In response, process thought contends that sin, mistakes, ignorance, dysfunction, disease, evil, and death are real. Because these things and their consequences continue to exist, and even increase, then even from God's perspective, this is a less than perfect world. Another, better, realm is conceivable where these evils have been overcome and are no more.

INVIOLATE FREEDOM—Certain perspectives suggest that God limits His/Her own power for the greater good. Usually this view is associated with insistence on the importance of human freedom (particularly in Arminian based theologies as opposed to Calvinist/determinist ones). According to these perspectives, character and personality can only develop if people are truly free. Similarly, God's love, if it's real, has to be voluntary.

Essentially, it is believed that God doesn't want to be a mere "puppet master pulling our strings" and controlling our thoughts and actions. God empowers us with free will with which we choose to either follow God's guidance and will, or ignore and go off and do our own thing (to sin and be alienated from God).

Openness and process thought believe that God would prefer to have Her people *freely* do Her will and freely love God in return because they *genuinely want and choose to*, instead of merely loving God and doing God's will because they *have* to and can't do any other. That would not be *real* love.

In this perspective, these "goods" are thought of as outweighing any evils that people commit in the world, even when the consequences of their evil are highly detrimental and destructive. Humans need to know the contrasts of both good and bad to help them increase in knowledge and in growth. According to openness theology, God's self-limiting (God "choosing to tie one arm behind His back") is essential to the attainment of God's purposes. However, according to process theology, God not only will not, but cannot, force humans to choose to do God's will. God can't prevent someone from shooting a gun, or stop us from blowing up the world if we're determined to do it. However, God attempts to employ persuasive power to woo and guide people toward better ends. This can include attempting to nudge other individuals to intervene in a situation. God can bring about good and positive transformation (resurrection) from experiences of evil that end up taking place if we align our will with God's will. In this cooperative mode, God can help all Her creatures to manifest the best they are capable of being.

NATURAL EVIL & THE NATURE OF POWER—Not all evil is caused by people. Tsunamis, floods, earthquakes, plagues, droughts, forest fires, and other natural disasters take place on this planet. In addition, some evils are caused, or aggravated, by human involvement, for example, acid rain, global warming, pollution, and war. Many natural and human-affected evils are so severe that they warrant Divine intervention. The threat of full-scale nuclear war is the epitome of this. While God has power and does seek to intervene, God's power and influence aren't coercive. God doesn't *control* us. Instead, God's power is liberating, empowering, and persuading. It is this "persuasive power" that God constantly exercises, even, and perhaps especially, in the midst of trauma and tragedy. As God's children we are called to emulate God's persuasive power as we interact with each other. God doesn't have or seek coercive power, and neither should we.

These understandings of evil, theodicy and God are well captured in the popular saying: *"When life hands you lemons, make lemonade!"* Christians understand that God's specialty is the transforming and redeeming of things that seem forever lost and broken. We see God as the head chef for making this restoring lemonade. This is one of the key themes of the biblical text and human life. Indeed, our hopes of eventual reconciliation, justice, restoration, and social harmony are grounded and based on God's promises. The ultimate basis for our hopes is God's resurrection of Jesus, rejected by the world and politically executed. That was a serious lemon turned into some powerful lemonade![278]

I close this chapter with a sermon that I wrote on human suffering from a progressive Christian perspective.

"Even our Moans and Groans"

Based on Job 1:1, 2:1-10 & Romans 8:18-27:

> *I consider that our present sufferings are not worth comparing with the glory that will be revealed in us. For the creation waits in eager expectation for the children of God to be revealed. For the creation was subjected to frustration, not by its own choice, but by the will of the one who subjected it, in hope that the creation itself will be liberated from its bondage to decay and brought into the freedom and glory of the children of God. We know that the whole creation has been groaning as in the pains of childbirth right up to the present time. Not only so, but we ourselves, who have the firstfruits of the Spirit, groan inwardly as we wait eagerly for our adoption to sonship, the redemption of our bodies. For in this hope we were saved. But hope that is seen is no hope at all. Who hopes for what they already have? But if we hope for what we do not yet have, we wait for it patiently. In the same way, the Spirit helps us in our weakness. We do not know what we ought to pray for, but the Spirit himself intercedes for us through wordless groans. And he who searches our hearts knows the mind of the Spirit, because the Spirit intercedes for God's people in accordance with the will of God.*

The great Apostle Paul was one of the most heroic and exemplary Christians who ever lived. His faith in God through Jesus Christ was as pure and solid as it gets! Through his convictions and his unwavering tenacity, Paul traveled thousands of miles, and founded lots of churches. Several of the letters that he wrote to these churches have become canonized as sacred scripture in

---

[278]   At its best, Christianity is part of that transformed lemonade. However, at its worst, it can be pretty sour stuff.

our Holy Bible. Today we read from Paul's letter to the Church that was founded in Rome. Scholars tell us that Paul wrote these words near the end of his life. This was probably one of the last letters that he ever wrote.

Now, we might expect such a successful and faithful person, writing at the peak of his career, to share about the many glorious and wonderful things that are involved with being a Christian! We might expect him to demonstrate that he's one of those "shiny happy people" who wants others to see how joyous he is in order to persuade others to join the Church and be just as upbeat and happy as he is! We might expect him to write about how if people come to Christ, then their lives will be magically blessed and nothing bad will ever happen to them again! And the more faith we have, the richer, and the wiser, and the happier we'll be!

But if we expect those things, watch out! Our bubbles are gonna burst!

Now we gotta notice this! In no way does Paul deny that life is hard! He says that "the creation has been subjected to frustration" and that "it has been groaning as in the pains of childbirth!" He even says that "we who have become believers in Christ, we who see that we are heirs to the Kingdom, that we also groan inwardly as we wait for the completion of God's promises."

Many of us gathered here today know the pains and struggles which life in this world has to offer. We know these pains too well. I'm a young man, and I consider myself to be fairly strong and healthy, yet I too have suffered painful illnesses and losses, and I know full well that I'll faces bumps and bruises and struggles of all sorts again! Some suffering comes to us in the form of broken relationships. We lose people whom we love because of death, or because they choose to break away from us. Either way, we feel loss and pain.

Doctors tell us that several kinds of mental disorders and illnesses can enter into our lives without notice and for no apparent reason. People of all ages can become chemically depressed and even begin to think about ending their lives. Others may begin to lose their memories and mental functions from the onset of Alzheimer's and other truly frustrating disorders. Our bodies are also subject to many kinds of trauma. People of all ages get into car crashes and other accidents where skin is burned and bones are broken. Hardly a day goes by without our hearing about some car, train, or plane crash somewhere in the world! This is real isn't it?!

We have heart attacks and strokes. We're susceptible to devastating addictions to gambling, drugs, and alcohol. We become victims of senseless acts of violence. And it would take several hours for us to name all of the known diseases that we could become stricken with! And the fact remains; we'll all die and end this life as we know it.

There's a young person I know, not even 30 years old, who was recently discharged from a hospital. The cancer that has been attacking her body has become so widespread that the highly trained doctors she's been working with can do no more. She was released last week to die at home in the presence of her young husband sometime in the next few weeks. Paul said that the "creation groans in agony" and he wasn't kidding was he?

So, what are our groans? What are our moans?

If we think about things that cause us the most pain, we sometimes find that it's hard to find words that can describe them. These are our aches that seem too painful to even name. Some of these pains are physical ailments that are difficult to accept. Some of us ache inside as we experience the aging process and we mourn for our youth. Some pains come from guilt and bitter conflicts with our friends and loved ones. Some pains may come from guilt or shame that we still carry from terrible things that we've done in our past—or things that were done to us. And other pains come from destructive things that we still find ourselves engaged in when we're not at our best, the things that we're ashamed to think about, to tell others about, or to even admit to ourselves.

I had a friend during my high school years who went to a rival school. I'm going to change his name here, and just call him "Jake." Jake was in my Scout troop. We were in the same patrol and we usually shared a tent together on camp-outs. Something that I noticed about him was that he always wrestled about in his sleep and at times, strange and tormented sounds would come from his side of the tent, like the sounds that I could picture coming from a man who'd been staked out in the desert and left to die.

Well, one day a few years after I'd graduated from high school, I came across Jake's younger sister working at a little shop in St. Paul. Because I'd been such a good friend with him, I'd gotten to know her pretty well too. She seemed interested when I told her that I was seeking to become more intentional as a follower of Jesus and how I was working for a crisis intervention center in Minneapolis.

She asked me to join her for a cup of coffee later on and we went to a little café down the street. And before I knew what hit me, she told me about how her brother used to sexually assault her when she was younger. She told me about how she'd been having a hard time sleeping at night, and that until that moment, she hadn't told anybody about this trauma in her life. She told me that she'd often find herself just crying, sobbing, and moaning as she struggled with how to cope with all that had happened.

After she shared more of her story, I told her that God loves her very much and that she'd already been asking for help even though she didn't think she had been. She asked me what I meant, and I told her "God hears all of our prayers, even our moans and groans! So, whether you know it or not, you've been praying to God when you've been curled up on the floor crying!" And then she began to cry, but it was a cry of relief.

Now since then, she's been active in a counseling program for survivors of sexual abuse and she's come to see that God has always been standing beside her just like God stood beside Jacob and Ruth when they ventured off into new and dangerous lands, just as God stood beside Job when he faced all of those losses and afflictions in his life. She's come to know that God constantly assures us that He will keep with us wherever we go, whatever we face, and bring us back safely into His arms whenever we stray.

And as I've been reflecting on all of this over the past week, I've come to think that when I noticed those moans and groans coming from her brother as he slept in our tent on those camp-outs, Jake was praying to God and asking for help in the only way that he knew how, even if he didn't know that's what he was doing!

In theological terms, one of the issues which we're talking about here is called "theodicy"—the issue of why an all good, all powerful, and all loving God would allow such terrible things to happen to His children? Paul was getting at this issue in this part of his letter to those believers in Rome.

When I was in college, one of my friends had a friend who became terribly sick with a severe illness. A group of students would go to his house to visit him and they'd often find him literally moaning because of his agony. They felt so badly for him. His father even complained about all his moaning!

Well, he got better. Sometime later on, I heard that some research has been done at university hospitals, where it's been observed that while many still died, patients who prayed and who were being prayed for oftentimes recovered more quickly, some almost miraculously!

I also heard that other studies were done where certain patients who moaned healed more quickly than those who didn't. The doctors thought that there must be some kind of bio-chemical changes that occur as the result of the resonating sound waves that are emitted by these moans. *"Oohhhhhh!"*

"Christian" or not, we still ache from the wounds that have been inflicted upon us in life. We still mourn and grieve the loss of loved ones. And we're still mortal beings who will continue to know suffering until the day we die. It's been said that in the early Christian churches, that there was much "weeping and wailing, moaning and groaning"—even during worship. In fact, loud and publicly expressed moans and groans were often a regular part of their worship services, and it's still common in some sectors of Black and Pentecostal churches here in the U.S.! *"I'm gonna moan when the Spirit says moan! . . ."*

In this passage, Paul describes the Holy Spirit as a Being Who advocates for us in a heavenly Court—a Spirit Who translates our groans, or maybe as a Spirit Who echoes them, just as we've uttered them. It could be that moans and groans are "the Cosmic and Universal language of prayer and suffering!"

Friends, because of Jesus, we know that God came to humanity to be with us in a unique way. While Jesus was alive on the earth, He was living a human life—with all of the joys and pains that go with it! This means our God was celebrating and suffering as a living human being!

Jesus Himself said to His disciples, *"I will ask the Father and He will give you another Counselor to be with you forever . . . The Spirit of*

Truth . . . The Holy Spirit Whom the Father will send in My name will teach you; My peace I give to you . . . Do not be troubled, don't let your hearts be afraid" (from John 14:1-27). And here, Paul is attempting to explain this to the people of Rome. He's saying that our pains and sufferings, even the ones we can't talk about, that our pains don't fall upon deaf ears to God! Instead, because of the life of Jesus, and because of the indwelling of the Holy Spirit, we know that God is with us. We know that God is suffering with us each time that one of us is hurting. God's Creation had to be blessed with freedom. Freedom for us to live lives with all the richness that life has to offer—including the freedom to suffer.

We know that God is not the cause of our pains or sufferings. Instead, God is our partner Who feels what we feel and offers us compassion and strength. And it is *here* that we can find our hope. It is here that we can find the strength to go on—in faith!

Church, we are assured that what we know now is incomplete. We've only begun to experience but a foretaste of the great heavenly banquet and blessed inheritance that we'll all enjoy in the future. But even here and now, we can know that God is with us—sharing the broken bread that makes us whole.[279] *Amen.*

---

[279] For a beautiful poem/hymn that speaks to how the Spirit hears our moaning prayers see "Through Our Fragmentary Prayers" by Thomas Troeger, p. 123, *Borrowed Light, Hymn texts, prayers, and poems*, Oxford University Press, Oxford, 1994.

Chapter 10

The End—or is it?

It's the end of the world as we know it—REM

When soldiers put down their weapons and monarchs step down, the messiah will be rescuing us, and that means sorrow no more. (paraphrased)
—*Sorrow*, Bad Religion (see Revelations 21:1-4)

It's over and not going further. (paraphrased)—*The Future,* Leonard Cohen

Waiting on the world to change—John Mayer

If by some miracle and all our struggle, the earth is spared, only justice to every living thing (and everything is alive) will save humankind. Alice Walker

No one knows about that day or hour, not even the angels in heaven, nor the Son, but only the Father. Jesus, Mark 13:32

Non-judgment Day is Near! | Jesus is coming look busy! | Come the Rapture can I have your car? bumper stickers

In 1999, many Americans were anxious about the potential end of the world because of Jesus possibly returning in 2000 and/ or because of the "Y2K" computer[280] glitch. I couldn't believe

---

[280] A calendar issue pertaining to IBM based computers.

how so many people were alarmed by what seemed clear to me to be superstition, mass paranoia and ignorance.

Around that same time, I was utterly dismayed that so many people in the U.S. were so enthralled with the *"Left Behind"* book series. I read the first book and didn't care for the retributive, "us versus them" theology and anti-intellectual arrogance it exuded. I couldn't relate to it and found its lack of compassion and love disturbing. The idea that people may've thought that they presented authentic Christianity is troubling.

Break it Down XIV

Jesus wasn't born in 1 A.D. When the Western world switched from the Julian calendar to the Gregorian one that we now use, the dating for when Jesus was thought to have been born was inadvertently altered by 4-6 years. In 525 A.D. a monk named Dionysius Exiguus, acting under the orders of Pope St. John I, retroactively set the start of the current era to 1 *Anno Domini* (meaning "year of our Lord")—the alleged date of the birth of Christ—but he made a mistake in doing so. He forgot to factor in that Jesus was born under the reign of King Herod and Herod is known to have died in what we now refer to as 4 B.C. *(B.C. is the English translation that means "before Christ").* If Jesus were born later than 5 B.C., he would have been too young to fit the Gospel of Luke's report that he began his ministry at about 30 years of age. Since there is no year zero, that means that the third millennium after the birth of Christ probably started in November or December 1996.[281] This also means that you need to add 4-6 years to whatever year it happens to be when you read this book; for example, if you read this book in 2011, it's actually 2015-2017!

Certain forms of Christianity have become so widespread in the U.S. that even the non-Christians among us have become absorbed by the drama of the notion of a "looming end of the world," based upon certain interpretations of the book of Revelation in the Bible. Bottom line: progressive Christians think

---

[281] See this article by David Briggs of the AP about Paul Maier, "Bible Scholar from WMU says the 2,000th anniversary of Christ's birth likely was last year," Sat. Jan. 11, 1997, *The Grand Rapids Press*

that those interpretations are misguided and based more upon fear than faith. Progressive Christianity doesn't make a priority of discussing these matters. I haven't come across any people who identify as progressive Christians who say much about the allegedly biblical end-time beliefs. I suspect that this is because Jesus had so little to say about them. It's the area of theology that we know the least about, and if Jesus didn't say much about it, why should we?

> *I tell you the truth, this generation will certainly not pass away until all these things have happened. Heaven and earth will pass away, but my words will never pass away.* "*No one knows about that day or hour, not even the angels in heaven, nor the Son, but only the Father. Be on guard! Be alert! You do not know when that time will come.* Mark 13:30-33

Jesus was able to be faithful without having an overly defined set of beliefs about "the end-times," and so can we. Jesus, however, did appear to believe in an ending of the oppressive ways of the world and in an ultimate fulfillment of the Kingdom of God on earth as it is in heaven:

> *As he was leaving the temple, one of his disciples said to him, "Look, Teacher! What massive stones! What magnificent buildings!" "Do you see all these great buildings?" replied Jesus. "Not one stone here will be left on another; every one will be thrown down." As Jesus was sitting on the Mount of Olives opposite the temple, Peter, James, John and Andrew asked him privately, "Tell us, when will these things happen? And what will be the sign that they are all about to be fulfilled?" Jesus said to them: "Watch out that no one deceives you. Many will come in my name, claiming, 'I am he,' and will deceive many. When you hear of wars and rumors of wars, do not be alarmed. Such things must happen, but the end is still to come. Nation will rise against nation, and Kingdom against Kingdom. There will be earthquakes in various places, and famines. These are the beginning of birth pains ...*
> *"Now learn this lesson from the fig tree: As soon as its twigs get tender and its leaves come out, you know that summer*

is near. Even so, when you see these things happening, you know that it is near, right at the door. I tell you the truth, this generation will certainly not pass away until all these things have happened. Heaven and earth will pass away, but my words will never pass away." No one knows about that day or hour, not even the angels in heaven, nor the Son, but only the Father. Be on guard! Be alert! You do not know when that time will come. It's like a man going away: He leaves his house and puts his servants in charge, each with his assigned task, and tells the one at the door to keep watch. "Therefore keep watch because you do not know when the owner of the house will come back—whether in the evening, or at midnight, or when the rooster crows, or at dawn. If he comes suddenly, do not let him find you sleeping. What I say to you, I say to everyone: 'Watch!'" Mark 13:1-8, 28-37 and

"Teacher," they asked, "when will these things happen? And what will be the sign that they are about to take place?" He replied: "Watch out that you are not deceived. For many will come in my name, claiming, 'I am he,' and, 'The time is near.' Do not follow them. When you hear of wars and revolutions, do not be frightened. These things must happen first, but the end will not come right away." Then he said to them: "Nation will rise against nation, and Kingdom against Kingdom. There will be great earthquakes, famines and pestilences in various places, and fearful events and great signs from heaven" Luke 21:7-11

It appears that Jesus truly believed that the end of the world would really happen soon. Certainly his earliest followers believed that too. It may be debatable if Jesus literally meant the end of the physical world would be ending soon, or if he meant *terra firma* (another way to say the Earth) would continue on, but that false powers and principalities would be no more and that the Kingdom of God would fully be realized. Either way, it's been over 2000 years and neither of those things has happened.

So then, what are we to make of this? The options are that either Jesus or those who wrote about him were wrong about his second coming, that it has been delayed, that it will take a lot longer than he or his first followers expected, or it means something different than what many have thought it to mean. We need to keep in mind that the Gospels and the Book of Revelation were written first and foremost for their original, specific, audiences over 2000 years ago.

Another possible option is to posit that that the world *as they knew* would end soon. This could actually be said to have happened on two levels. Jesus died around 33 A.D. and the Romans brutally quashed an Israelite uprising in 70 A.D., completely destroying the temple in Jerusalem (as Jesus had predicted: Matthew 24:1-2). No longer having the Temple and the Temple system form of worshipping God meant that the world of those ancient Hebrews was effectively turned upside down. Similarly, it wasn't too many years later that the Roman Empire itself collapsed. That empire was effectively the "known world" of West and it fell in 395, 476, or 603 A.D., depending upon what factors you consider. The early medieval era was known as the "Dark Ages" and one might argue that the end of the civilized world had taken place at that time. And yet, here we still are, in the early 21st Century and there are still oppressive empires and domination systems. It'd be hard for any one to say that we're already living in the fully realized Kingdom of God or that this is as good as it gets.

There are two basic responses within Christianity to this predicament—a conservative one and a progressive one. The conservative approach is essentially a "dominionist" one that holds that Jesus really will come back again, descending from the clouds, "just as it's written" (Revelation 1:7). It holds that Jesus will forcefully reclaim his rightful authority and dole out violent retribution on the false, un-godly, worldly "powers that be" and those who are aligned with them. He will judge the living and the dead. Those who are deemed worthy will dwell with him praising God forever. There are variances within that camp that concern which details happen in which order: a "rapture," an anti-Christ, a judgment day, a violent war, a 1000 year reign of peace, and souls being sent to heaven or hell.

Break it Down XV

The most popular of these "millennialist" perspectives is "pre-millennialism." The following is a helpful description of premillenialsim written by Wayne Jackson. [Bracketed remarks are mine]:

The premillennial concept is the result of literalizing a few symbolic verses in the book of Revelation, coupled with a considerable disregard for scores of Bible passages of clearest import. The word "premillennial" itself is derived of two components—"pre" signifies before, and "millennium" denotes a period of 1000 years. The theory thus suggests that Christ will return to the earth just prior to a 1000-year reign.

The premillennial theory is advanced in several different ways. It is, therefore, not an easy task to generalize regarding this system of doctrine. We will focus mainly on that branch of millennialism that is known as dispensational premillennialism. The following quotations are introduced to bring some of the main points into focus:

It is held that the Old Testament prophets predicted the re-establishment of David's Kingdom and that Christ himself intended to bring this about. It is alleged however, that because the Jews refused his person and work he postponed the establishment of his Kingdom until the time of his return. Meanwhile, it is argued, the Lord gathered together "the church" as a kind of interim measure (Kevan 1999, 352).

Pre-millennialists believe that shortly before the second coming the world will be marked by extraordinary tribulation and evil and the appearance of the Anti-Christ. At his coming, Christ will destroy this anti-Christ and believers will be raised from the dead. There will then follow a millennium of peace and order over which Christ will reign with his saints. At the close of this time, Satan will be loosed and the forces of evil will once again be rampant. The wicked will then be raised, and a final judgment will take place in which Satan and all evil ones will be consigned to eternal punishment (Harvey 1964, 151).

For centuries the Jews have been scattered among many nations. In preparation for the return of Christ and the beginning of the millennium, they are being gathered back to their own land, according to prophecy, in a national restoration. David's throne will be re-established at Jerusalem, and through these restored people as a nucleus Christ will reign with his immortal saints over the whole world (Nichols n.d., 279).

To summarize, the Premillennial view asserts that Christ came to this earth for the purpose of setting up his Kingdom. However, [he was rejected]. So, he postponed the Kingdom plans and set up the church instead—as a sort of emergency measure. When [Jesus] returns, he allegedly will raise only the righteous dead, restore the nation of Israel, sit upon David's literal throne in Jerusalem, and then reign for a span of 1000 years—after which comes the resurrection of the wicked and the judgment.[282]

. . . [And then, the wicked will go to hell, and, depending upon one's sub-theology, God will destroy hell itself, along with those in it, or hell will continue on and those in it will suffer eternally]

With that background in mind, another writer has provided the following description of how the pre-millennial perspective undergirds the *Left Behind* book series:

Fundamental to the spirit of the Left Behind *Series is the sense of vindication that "we" have been right all along. The not-so-subtle news headline that lies behind the entire series could well be, "Premillennial Dispensationalists Proved to Have Been Right All Along." The message of this series is unadulterated triumphalism.—You can forget the business of Christians taking up the cross in this series! Premillennial dispensationalists have admittedly gotten rough treatment in the modern world. From a modernist or secularist point of view, the claims of a pre-Tribulation rapture of the church, followed by seven years of Tribulation, followed by the thousand-year reign of Christ just seems too preposterous to be believed. Combine that with the fact that premillennial dispensationalists have been prone to set dates for the Second Coming of Christ—and the fact that their batting average so far has been zero—and that well-educated theologians as a whole pooh-pooh their ideas, and you quickly come to a point of eschatological frustration with the way things are. It is not the Lamb who has conquered in this series, but the*

282   Wayne Jackson, http://www.christiancourier.com/articles/322-examining-premillennialism

premillennial dispensationalists! "We win!" (4:247; 6:66; 6:179). Similarly, "You lose!" (9:179).

At the end of the day, this series is ultimately a rejection of the good news of Jesus Christ. I say this because it rejects the way of the cross and Jesus' call to obedient discipleship and a new way of life. It celebrates the human will to power, putting Evangelical Christians in the heroic role of God's Green Berets. In this story, premillennialist dispensationalism meets American survivalism. This is a story about so-called Christian men who never really grew up, who still love to play with toys and dominate others, and whose passions are still largely unredeemed. Love of enemies is treated as a misguided strategy associated not with the gospel, but with the Antichrist. Tim LaHaye and Jerry Jenkins have the right to offer any kind of interpretation of Christianity and of the end times that they wish. Ultimately, it is not their interpretation of the end times that troubles me so much as their interpretation of Christianity. It is devoid of any real theology, or substantial Christology, or any ethics that are recognizably Christian. This is a vision of unredeemed Christianity.—Loren Johns[283]

The perspective expressed in the *Left Behind* series is the exact same view that was the basis of Hal Lindsey's *The Late Great Planet Earth*—a book that was wildly popular 20 years beforehand. The thrust of that book was espousing the pre-millennial theory of Christ's second coming and interpreting present world political trends as signs of the imminent return of Jesus Christ. This end of the world mania has been with us for a while.

Another person who has made his career out of promulgating these ideas is Jack Van Impe. For years, he and his wife Rexella have hosted a TV program, *"Jack Van Impe Presents,"* which analyzes the headlines of the daily news and seeks to point out how they are "fulfilling prophecy." It is incredible and disturbing how his eyes light up and twinkle with delight when he describes various tragedies taking place around the world. To him, they

---

[283] http://www.ambs.edu/LJohns/Leftbehind.htm   used   with permission.

mean "Jesus is coming all the sooner!" I've even discovered a website that tracks and catalogs such alleged correlations of news headlines and "biblical prophecy."[284]

There is a sizeable percentage of the population that is highly attracted to the notion that Jesus will return as a vanquishing conqueror that kicks "bad guy" butt. However, that perspective contradicts the notion of Jesus' unconditional love[285] that he clearly espoused in the Gospels. Jesus taught against retribution. He championed non-violence, reconciliation and restoration.

There has never been any official gathering or council of Progressive Christianity that has met to declare an official position[286] on *eschatology* (the subset of theology that pertains to the *eschaton* (the end of the world and/or humanity). Again, this hasn't been a priority for progressive Christianity. Many believe that millennialism (of any variety[287]) advocates an escapist form of theology that leads to social apathy and moral quietude. If people are expecting to be "raptured up" into heaven soon, they're disinclined to be actively engaged in bettering the world here and now.

In my experience, progressive Christians tend to see Christ's return as something that happens every day. We see it when people minister to, and especially *with*, the "least of these" (Matthew 25:40). We see it when oppressed persons are liberated and when oppressive systems are put in check. An example that comes to mind is the end of Apartheid in South Africa and the notably nonviolent transition of power that occurred afterward. Few of us would say that God's Kingdom is fully realized and manifest here and now and we yearn for it. We share the evangelical notion that we live "in

---

284 http://www.raptureready.com/rap2.html

285 Even to the point of loving those who killed him.

286 Such a meeting for that sort of purpose wouldn't be a very progressive Christian thing to do.

287 In addition to Historical Premillennialism, there are Dispensational Premillennialism, Postmillennialism, Amillenialism. Preterism. Moreover Dispensational Premillennialism has rival subgroups including those who believe in a Pre-Tribulation Rapture, a Post-Tribulation Rapture, a Mid-Tribulation Rapture, a Pre-wrath Rapture, or in a Partial Rapture. Ack. see: http://www.religioustolerance.org/millenni.htm

between the what is, and the what will be"—when God's Will is fully done on Earth as it is in heaven.

Many progressives believe that Jesus "returns," and God's Kingdom is manifest, whenever we feed the poor, heal the sick, stand with the oppressed, seek to end their oppression, and love our neighbor. I might suggest that the return of Christ could be said to have "fully returned" and that the "fully realized Kingdom of God" could be said to have taken place when we eventually come to a place where a critical mass of the world's population comes around to thinking and acting in these ways.

Living "in Christ" and living in Kingdom ways doesn't make for an easier life. It is certainly far more challenging than merely making do while passively hoping for Jesus to come down from the clouds. In fact, this way of being Christian, intentional deep discipleship, may seem much more challenging. It creates yet another reason for many people to passively go along with the teachings of conservative Christianity. If we're not really meant to dwell on the earth, if we're really "just visiting" here, if what happens after we die is what really matters, then there's no need for us to be concerned about the environment or the wellbeing of future generations. There'd be no reason to notice the irony of America a supposedly "Christian nation" being the largest consumer of the world's natural resources and one of the top producers of the gases that contribute to aggravating global warming.[288] It's easier to just chalk it up to "God's will" than to do the work of grappling with the morality of our fiscal and national priorities.

An approach within progressive Christianity that seeks to address the challenging and demanding ways of Jesus in light of the Book of Revelation is what I call the **"radical discipleship view."**[289] This perspective asserts that the Book of Revelation is best understood as a handbook for authentic discipleship—how to remain faithful to the spirit and teachings of Jesus and avoid simply assimilating to

---

[288] This is ironic because Christians are supposed to practice good stewardship of the earth's resources, yet the U.S. is clearly not engaged in good stewardship of them.

[289] My addition to the entry on the Book of Revelation page on Wikipedia, http://en.wikipedia.org/ wiki/Book_of_ Revelation# Radical_discipleship_view

surrounding society. A premise for this view is that contrary to popular belief, Revelation wasn't written during a time of great persecution against Christians. It was written during a time of relative calm and affluent stability in the Roman Empire. The primary agenda of the book is to expose worldly powers that seek to lead people away from the ways of God, as imposters. The chief temptation for Christians in the First Century, and today, is to adopt the worldly values of empire (domination systems, nationalism, patriotism, materialism, consumerism, corporatism, fascism, civil religion,[290] etc.) and fail to hold fast to the anti-imperial, non-materialistic, and nonviolent teachings of Jesus. This perspective (which is closely related to Liberation theology)[291] draws on the approach of Christian activists such as Dorothy Day and Bible scholars such as Ched Myers, William Stringfellow, Richard Horsley, Daniel Berrigan, Wes Howard-Brook, and Jorg Reiger.

For a compelling progressive Christian understanding that is written from this "radical discipleship" take on eschatology, the end times, and the Book of Revelation, see: *Unveiling Empire: Reading Revelation Then and Now.*[292] It is the best resource I've encountered to help make the Book of Revelation understandable and meaningful.

Progressive Christians believe it when we say, *"Christ has died, Christ is risen, Christ will come again."*[293] Yet, rather than spending our time and energy waiting and planning for Christ's return, we think the world would be better served by reducing his level of disappointment when he does. Many of us share the view expressed in this assertion: *"I am not as concerned about when the moment will be as I am about the fact that the moment is coming. I want to encourage you to*

---

[290] for more about Civil Religion, see Appendix VI.

[291] Liberation theology suggests that Christianity should focus upon liberating economically oppressed persons because of God's "preferential option for the poor." Liberation theologians claim to be in sync with the Spirit of Jesus' first sermon and they seek to see it manifested (Luke 4:16-20).

[292] By Wes Howard-Brook and Anthony Gwynther, Orbis Books, 1999.

[293] A common litany that is part of the liturgy in mainline Protestant denominations.

get off the 'Planning' Committee and get on the 'Welcoming' Committee."[294]
We'd rather see ourselves as being on the street team (like promoting an upcoming band gig or theatre show). Instead of informing folks *about* Jesus with lots of information, we seek to simply *be* Jesus. We seek to be part of the incarnate, living Body of Christ—helping people experience his love and his Kingdom here and now.

Progressive Christians also resonate with the late Catholic Henri Nouwen when he said, *"Where will you find the Messiah?—He is sitting among the poor covered with wounds . . ."* as well as Emergent Christian pastor Brian McClaren's observation that *"The Gospel is a transformation plan, not an evacuation plan."*

We agree that our hope is in the future, but let's embrace and be present to the present moment.[295]

It's hard to embrace the present without a sense of hope for the future. As Christians, we believe that God is actively seeking to move Creation toward a beautiful goal. Like Paul, we have "our eyes on the prize"[296] and we "press on toward the goal to win the prize for which God has called us."[297] We sense deep in our bones that things will turn out okay—in fact, far better than we could ever imagine.

Progressive Christianity affirms Martin Luther King, Jr.'s remarks, *"I refuse to accept the view that [human]kind is so tragically bound to the starless midnight of racism and war that the bright daybreak of peace and brotherhood can never become a reality . . . I believe that unarmed truth and unconditional love will have the final word," "The moral arc of the universe is long, but it bends toward justice,"* and, *"Even if I knew that tomorrow the world would go to pieces, I would still plant my apple tree."*

Progressive Christians have hope in the conviction that somehow despite all sorts of evidence to the contrary, love wins.

---

[294]   James McDonald, http://blog.harvestbiblefellowship.org/?p=3699
[295]   I'm reminded of the song *Right here, Right now* by the British alternative rock band *Jesus Jones*. See: http://www.lyricsmode.com/lyrics/j/jesus_jones/right_here_right_now.html
[296]   Based on 1 Corinthians 9:24 and the Civil Rights era folk song, *Keep Your Eyes on the Prize*. See also my description of this at http://wiki.answers.com/Q/What_is_All_eyes_on_the_prize_definition
[297]   Philippians 3:14

Section II

Chapter 11

Love: the real Heart of the matter

Love is my religion, Ziggy Marley

"I grasped the meaning of the greatest secret that human poetry and human thought and belief have to impart: The salvation of man is through love and in love." Viktor Frankl

They will know we are Christians by our Love—Peter Scholtes

To love is to risk not being loved in return. And that's all right too. You love to love, not to get something back, or it isn't love.
Leo Buscaglia

I have found the paradox, that if you love until it hurts, there can be no more hurt, only more love. Mother Teresa

"Love is the only shocking act left on the face of the earth."
Sandra Bernhard

The moment we choose to Love, we begin to move toward freedom. bell hooks

Jesus said, . . . "Simon son of John, do you love me? . . . He answered . . . "Yes Lord, you know that I love you." Jesus said, "Feed my sheep." John 21:15-17

Religion that God our Father accepts as pure and faultless is
this: to look after orphans and widows in their distress and to
keep oneself from being polluted by the world. James 1:27

And now these three remain: faith, hope and love. But the
greatest of these is love.
Paul, 1 Corinthians 13:13

And so we know and rely on the love God has for us. God
is love. Whoever lives in love lives in God, and God in
him/ 1 John 4:16

The greatest lesson we can learn is simply to love and to allow
ourselves to be loved in return. (paraphrased)—Nature Boy,
Eden Ahbez, made famous by Nat King Cole

. . . Sensing a theme?

As the old Swing era hit put it, "'It don't mean a thing if it
ain't got that swing" and brother-sister, *love* is that swing. You can
meditate and pray, go to church, get baptized and take communion,
light candles and burn incense, read sacred texts, chant, fast and
do yoga, and even help out at soup kitchens, but if you aren't doing
them with love, it's all a bunch of vapid, empty horse apples. I
know what I'm talking about. I've got a shed full of them.

When I started writing this book I thought that the chapter
on salvation would be the most important, the most demanding,
and the one that I'd have the most anxiety about. But I'm finally
at this one and it occurs to me that *this* is the one that really
matters. The chapter on salvation puts me at risk for being called
a "heretic," (by those that go around doing that sort of thing) but
my discussion of how to put faith and love in action is what truly
matters. You see, as a follower of Jesus Christ, I have to care more
about what Jesus thinks than what Christians think.

On top of this theological realization, I'm forced to admit that
I feel somewhat handicapped in writing about love. I'm not very
good at loving. However, at this point in my life, I have received
and given enough love—and have failed to accept or give it—that
I just might have some things to say about it.

I'm someone who learns things the hard way, especially about love. And it didn't help me any to be living in a culture where Christianity has been reduced to legalistic dogmatism and schmaltzy, symbolic sentimentalism. Too often American Christianity has emphasized right beliefs, right positions, and right doctrines and dogmas. Too often American Christianity emphasizes the *symbols* of: wearing crosses (ironically, often made of expensive precious metals and blood diamonds), wearing Christian T-shirts (ironically, often made in sweatshops where the workers are exploited), owning a Thomas Kincade painting[298] or a shelf-full of porcelain *Precious Moments* figurines, spamming each other's email in-boxes with sappy Christian anecdotes, wearing WWJD? or "Live Strong" bracelets on our wrists, having "the Jesus fish" emblem on the back of our cars, and not using swear words. Too often, it's all just a bunch of futile exercises in missing the point. Too often, it's cultural religiosity that has the trappings and *appearance* of (what some claim is) Christianity, but none of the heart or soul.

People can go to church every week, serve as members of their congregation's board of trustees, have an encyclopedic knowledge of Christian creeds and orthodoxy, have the Bible entirely memorized, and even diligently visit someone in the nursing home and yet still be completely oblivious to the main point of the Gospel and Jesus' intention for their life because they miss the proverbial forest for the trees. As the apostle Paul put it,

> *If I speak in the tongues of men and of angels, but have not love, I am only a resounding gong or a clanging cymbal. If I have the gift of prophecy and can fathom all mysteries and all knowledge, and if I have a faith that can move mountains, but have not love, I am nothing. If I give all I possess to the poor and surrender my body to the flames, but have not love, I gain nothing.* 1st Corinthians 13:1-3

And as my friend Dave Swinton puts it, *"The quality of our faith will never exceed the quality of our love."*[299]

---

[298] (Ironic . . . er, no. He's actually paid pretty darned well for his work. Nevermind.)

[299] Those exact words were one of his status updates on Facebook.

This issue truly is the heart of the matter. It's where the rubber hits the road. It's what matters. In the words of Carlos Castaneda,

> "Any path is only a path, and there is no afront, to oneself or others, in dropping it if that is what your heart tells you . . . Look at every path closely and deliberately. Try it as many times as you think necessary. Then ask yourself, and yourself alone, one question . . .
> Does this path have a heart? If it does, the path is good; if it doesn't it is of no use."

Sadly, many members of my generation have asked that question and decided to drop Christianity because the forms of it they've encountered lacked heart, love, and compassion. I've decided to stick it out because I was fortunate to have been a part of more congregations and Christian gatherings that did have heart, love, and compassion than those that didn't. I've also discovered that the way of Jesus really is about those things. Anything else is a tragic imposter.

It isn't only today's generations that have looked at religion with a wary and discerning eye. Throughout human history, there has been a desire for spiritual paths to have integrity and yet be down to earth, relatable, and relevant to the needs of very real, hurting, and needy people who yearn to love and to be loved. For instance, Kahil Gibran said, "*Keep me away from the wisdom which does not cry, the philosophy which does not laugh and the greatness which does not bow before children.*"

And we don't want it to be overly heady, codified and legalistic:

> I have never united myself to any church, because I have found difficulty in giving my assent, without mental reservation, to the long, complicated statements of Christian doctrine which characterize their articles of belief and confessions of faith. When any church will inscribe over its altars as its sole qualification for membership, the Savior's condensed statement of the substance of both law and gospel, 'Thou shalt love the Lord thy God with all thy heart, and with all thy soul, and with all thy mind, and thy neighbor as thyself,' that church will I join with all my heart and all my soul.
> Abraham Lincoln (and he was a lawyer!)

A friend of mine recently had the following experience take place in his life. It's a story of the tragedy of what might be called "Christian religiosity" vs. authentic Christian faith:

As he was getting ready for church, a young woman came to the door and asked to use his phone. He listened as she explained to one friend after another that she had attended a party last night with friends, and those friends had left and she had no way home. He listened with dismay as one friend then the next excused themselves from coming to her aid because they "had to" go to church. He didn't make it to church that morning. Instead, he helped her collect her things and he drove her across town to her home. Which of those people truly worshipped God that day? That girl's friends who were "duty-bound" to go to a church building or this man who was a complete stranger to her? Which of them modeled authentic Christianity?[300]

The prophet Isaiah spoke to this human propensity for missing the point:

> "The multitude of your sacrifices—what are they to me?" says the LORD. "I have more than enough of burnt offerings, of rams and the fat of fattened animals; I have no pleasure in the blood of bulls and lambs and goats. When you come to appear before me, who has asked this of you, this trampling of my courts? Stop bringing meaningless offerings! Your incense is detestable to me. New Moons, Sabbaths and convocations—I cannot bear your evil assemblies. Your New Moon festivals and your appointed feasts my soul hates. They have become a burden to me; I am weary of bearing them. When you spread out your hands in prayer, I will hide my eyes from you; even if you offer many prayers, I will not listen. Your hands are full of blood; wash and make yourselves clean. Take your evil deeds out of my sight! Stop doing wrong, learn to do right! Seek justice, encourage the oppressed. Defend the cause of the fatherless, plead the case of the widow. Isaiah 1:11-17[301]

---

[300] Perhaps a contemporary version of Jesus' parable of the Good Samaritan (Luke 10:25-37)

[301] Jesus stated pretty much the same in several places including Matthew 6:1-8, see also what Jesus' brother says in James 2:14-18.

. . . in other words, *love!*

Break it Down XV1

The Ethic of Love: applying Biblical Principles to Life

On a related note, I contend that Jesus taught a form of ethical relativism in which the letter of the law took second place to the spirit of the law. An obvious example is Jesus' teachings regarding the Sabbath day. The religious leaders of his era maintained a rigid notion that Jews should not do any sort of physical work or exertion on the Sabbath whereas Jesus taught that a certain amount of work is okay if it is to provide for the necessities of life, gleaning wheat, healing the sick, etc. on any day of the week and that "the Sabbath was made for [humans], and not [humans] for the Sabbath" (Mark 2:27). Though this school of thought didn't exist until after Jesus' time, philosophically speaking, Jesus' teachings are a form of *principled consequentialism* where what is ethical is that which is most unconditionally loving, forgiving, merciful, and just. Sometimes what is most ethical transcends the letter of the law. Indeed, the apostle Paul follows suit in this manner when he taught that it is okay for Christians to eat anything in God's creation (including shellfish and pork) because of his ethical realization that what matters most is fostering loving relationships with people and so if someone serves you food that is on the "no-no" list for Jews according to the law, it's right to eat such foods for the sake of hospitality (Romans 14). Similarly, Peter had a vision where God told him not to consider anything in creation as being "unclean" (Acts 10). By the same token, if someone in the faith might fall astray by seeing you eating forbidden foods, it's better to refrain from eating such foods in their presence (Romans 14), even if you would otherwise be perfectly free to eat them. The Christian ethic comes down to doing what is most loving and affirming of your relationships in each unique moment and situation. In my experience, many women come by this pretty naturally. It's mostly men who need help in this department. Indeed, American culture has largely been one of ridding men of this relational ethic and concern. As a result, it's not an accident that there are more women in most churches than men.[302]

I understand that there is a current trend toward hyper-masculine, uber macho rhetoric and showmanship within certain mostly Calvinist ministries that are seeking to reach young men by appealing to their egos, testosterone

---

[302] Single straight men might want to ponder that piece of information.

and latent sexism.[303] I guess that's one approach, but it's not one that makes sense considering that Paul said that, "There is neither Jew nor Greek, slave nor free, male nor female, for you are all one in Christ Jesus" (Galatians 3:28). Why overly emphasize our differences when we are ultimately the same?[304]

So just what *is* love? I think answering that question may be above my pay-grade, but I'll take a crack at it. Love is ironically like a certain something else that Justice Potter Stewart described "I know it when I see it."[305] Here are some places where I've seen it. As I noted earlier in the book, the Bible indicates that, "God is love" (1 John 4:8). This is the origin and root of all love that we experience and know. Jesus emphasized a certain form of love, *agape*, unconditional, self-sacrificial, willing love. Almost all of the New Testament references to love are *agapao* or *agape*. This is the love that Christians are called to embrace, allow into our lives, and share with others. Jesus modeled this kind of love through

---

[303]   A prime example of this is Mark Driscoll's Mars Hill Church in Seattle, "Who Would Jesus Smack Down?" Molly Worthen, *New York Times*, Jan. 6, 2009, http://www.nytimes.com/2009/01/11/magazine/11punk-t.html

[304]   It's also interesting to note that the churches that overly emphasize the differences between the sexes and genders are the ones that speak out the most against homosexuality. It may be that people who attend such churches want defined roles because it is safer to have a "box" you belong to. Such people don't like the gray aspects of life. Defining those roles leads them to condemn the people outside those boxes, such as the LGBTI community.

[305]   Former U.S. Supreme Court Justice Potter Stewart, concurring with the decision in *Jacobellis v. Ohio, 378 U.S. 184 (1964)* Here's the exact "quote: "I shall not today attempt further to define the kinds of material I understand to be embraced within that shorthand description [hard-core pornography]; and perhaps I could never succeed in intelligibly doing so. But I know it when I see it, and the motion picture involved in this case is not that."

intentionally living and giving his life for others. The apostle Paul's famous poem about agape captures it pretty well:

> *Love is patient, love is kind. It does not envy, it does not boast, it is not proud. It is not rude, it is not self-seeking, it is not easily angered, it keeps no record of wrongs. Love does not delight in evil but rejoices with the truth. It always protects, always trusts, always hopes, always perseveres. Love never fails.* 1 Corinthians 13:4-7

Here's how Jesus responded when challenged by a group of religious leaders seeking to entrap him in matters of the law,

> *Hearing that Jesus had silenced the Sadducees, the Pharisees got together. One of them, an expert in the law, tested him with this question: "Teacher, which is the greatest commandment in the Law?" Jesus replied: "'Love the Lord your God with all your heart and with all your soul and with all your mind.' This is the first and greatest commandment. And the second is like it: 'Love your neighbor as yourself.' All the Law and the Prophets hang on these two commandments."* Matthew 22:34-40

Jesus elaborated further about agape love to his disciples saying,

> *"As the Father has loved me, so have I loved you. Now remain in my love. If you obey my commands, you will remain in my love, just as I have obeyed my Father's commands and remain in his love. I have told you this so that my joy may be in you and that your joy may be complete. My command is this: Love each other as I have loved you. Greater love has no one than this, that he lay down his life for his friends. You are my friends if you do what I command. I no longer call you servants, because a servant does not know his master's business. Instead, I have called you friends, for everything that I learned from my Father I have made known to you. You did not choose me, but I chose you and appointed you to go and bear fruit—fruit that will last. Then the Father will give you whatever you ask in my name. This is my command: Love each other.* John 15:9-17

And Martin Luther King, Jr. said this about love,

> *Love is creative and redemptive. Love builds up and unites; hate tears down and destroys. The aftermath of the 'fight with fire' method which you suggest is bitterness and chaos, the aftermath of the love method is reconciliation and creation of the beloved community. Physical force can repress, restrain, coerce, destroy, but it cannot create and organize anything permanent; only love can do that. Yes, love—which means understanding, creative, redemptive goodwill, even for one's enemies—is the solution.* (He was speaking about racial tensions but this transcends that situation)

This kind of love isn't the common variety, and it ain't easy. It requires practice, discipline, and a willingness to be vulnerable—even to sacrifice—and put the needs of another ahead of your own. We're not talking about trite and syrupy sentimentalism or romantic feelings (although *agape* can certainly be a part of healthy life partnerships). It's not an emotion, it's a radical commitment to give a damn about the wellbeing of others and then do something about it. It's not something that leads to feelings of being smitten that blindly lead us to not see any wrong in people. Instead, it's what enabled Jesus to put up with the thickheaded pettiness of his disciples for three long years. It's what empowered Jesus to constantly tend to the hordes of desperately needy, broken hurting masses. It's what allowed Jesus to not wring the necks of those who continued to squabble amongst themselves as to "which of them would be the greatest" in God's Kingdom and who demonstrated a complete discipleship "FAIL" when they pulled out a couple of daggers when Jesus sarcastically told them to go buy some weapons. They just had the last supper and were preparing to go to the Mount of Olives (the secret rendezvous point where Jesus would be betrayed and arrested) and since they were going to be perceived as radical bandits and outlaws by the religious and political leaders, Jesus essentially quipped that they may as well *look* the part! One can imagine Jesus rolling his eyes and dejectedly shaking his head when they said that they had two daggers. One can see him sighing with exasperation, "That's enough" or, alternatively, shutting them up by yelling, "That's *enough!"* . . . [*of that kind of foolishness! You knuckleheads still don't get it, but I'm still willing to be arrested and die for you guys anyway*].[306]

Agape doesn't necessarily involve high heroics, and it certainly doesn't involve syrupy sentiment. It's practical. It makes a difference. And it matters. It's evident when someone cooks a nutritious meal for his children after an exhausting day at work. It's seen when a mother takes on three or more jobs to do what it takes to keep her family clothed, housed, and fed. It's donating blood on a regular basis to the local blood bank. It's risking looking un-cool, and perhaps far more than that, by interrupting people as they're telling a racist or anti-gay joke. It's when someone decides to use the year end bonus that he received from his employer to repair the car of the struggling single mother down the street, or purchase a burial plot for someone without means, instead of buying that boat or motorcycle he's been wanting.

Agape happens when someone decides to forgive someone who wronged them instead of retaliating—and even to go out of their way to help him or her. It happens whenever people willingly decide to put the needs of others ahead of themselves; speak truth to power;[307] feed the hungry; clothe the naked; visit the imprisoned; release the captive; love the unlovable; forgive the

---

[306] My interpretation of Luke 22:35-38 based upon: a) Jesus' other teachings that consistently taught nonviolence, his own reference to his earlier teaching to go forth with few possessions simply trusting on God to provide—having swords in their possession would clearly be in direct opposition to simply trusting God to provide and protect; b) that just a few moments later, when Peter uses his dagger to slice off the ear of one of the people seeking to arrest Jesus, Jesus rebukes him and heals that man's ear; and c) as well as upon other places where Jesus employed sarcasm, for example, Matthew 15:21-28. I've just discovered that I'm not alone in this interpretation see: http://www.ecapc.org/articles/RensbeD_HS4_BuyASword.asp

[307] This phrase is either originally from a charge to Quakers/Friends in the 18th Century. http://www.quaker.org/sttp.html; or it is from a phrase written by a Quaker expression during the Civil Rights movement in the 1950s, http://www2.gol.com/users/quakers/living_the_truth.htm. It means boldly standing up to the powers that be (oppressive governments, etc.) and to proclaim God's truth—typically about the dignity of human worth and rights.

unforgivable; associate with the disreputable; and to eat and drink with the unsavory. As theologian Søren Kierkegaard observed, this is a rigorous kind of love.

Clearly, it doesn't come naturally. Or is that so clear? Children innately love. Their innate love is amplified if they receive love and witness loving parents and adults in their lives. Sure, there's always some rebellion. That's part of our nature, but I'd argue that loving is our intended way of being. The thing is, most of us have been so beaten down in life, desensitized, and numbed to it that we've come to perceive it as a threatening foreign object and our metaphorical white blood cells go out to reject it. Jesus ran into that. The following poem speaks to the difficulty we face in loving people:

ANYWAY[308]

People are unreasonable, illogical, and self-centered. Love them anyway.

If you are kind, people may accuse you of selfish ulterior motives. Be kind anyway.

If you are successful, you will win some false friends and true enemies. Succeed anyway.

The good you do today will be forgotten tomorrow. Be good anyway.

Honesty and frankness will make you vulnerable. Be honest and frank anyway.

What you spend years building may be destroyed overnight. Build anyway.

People need help but will attack you if you help them. Help them anyway.

In the final analysis, it is between you and God. It was never between you and them anyway.

There's no way around it. Agape love is radical. Loving people in this way, putting their needs ahead of yours, forgiving them, being

---

[308] I've come to understand that a Keith Kent originated this poem in 1968, and Mother Teresa placed it on her children's home in Calcutta in a slightly different version. As a result, many have attributed it to Mother Teresa.

patient with them, always seeking to reconcile with them . . . is demanding. A friend of mine responded to my describing this sort of love saying, "Everyone says that, everyone has heard about this. But you cannot "decide" to do something with "love" can you?" An understandable question, but I think one can, moment by moment.[309] Such decisions come more readily and easily when they become habits of the heart.

That is where spiritual practices come in. They help foster love and love helps enliven spiritual practices. Love is an active, constant commitment. It's a discipline. If it were easy, we wouldn't have needed Jesus to tell us to do it. If humans were incapable of loving in this way, Jesus would've unfairly been setting us up for failure. However, Jesus thinks we can do this. If left to our own devices, we humans may in fact be incapable of loving in this way—at least with any sort of consistency. We need help. Jesus, and his life, teachings, death, and resurrection are a huge part of that help, but Jesus also promised us that He'd send us another Counselor—the Holy Spirit:

> *"If you love me, you will obey what I command. And I will ask the Father, and he will give you another Counselor to be with you forever—the Spirit of truth. The world cannot accept him, because it neither sees him nor knows him. But you know him, for he lives with you and will be in you. I will not leave you as orphans; I will come to you. Before long, the world will not see me anymore, but you will see me. Because I live, you also will live. On that day you will realize that I am in my Father, and you are in me, and I am in you. Whoever has my commands and obeys them, he is the one who loves me. He who loves me will be loved by my Father, and I too will love him and show myself to him."*

---

[309] According to Dan Gilbert's book, *Mistakes Were Made, But Not By Me* (Houghton Mifflin Harcourt, 2007) research shows that when people do something nice for someone else, they then believe that the recipient was worthy of that, and it starts a positive cycle. In contrast, if they do something to hurt someone, they will then rationalize that that person somehow deserved it, to not have to hate themselves. We can fall down either side of the "pyramid" of decision.

Then Judas (not Judas Iscariot) said, "But, Lord, why do you intend to show yourself to us and not to the world?" Jesus replied, "If anyone loves me, he will obey my teaching. My Father will love him, and we will come to him and make our home with him. He who does not love me will not obey my teaching. These words you hear are not my own; they belong to the Father who sent me. "All this I have spoken while still with you. But the Counselor, the Holy Spirit, whom the Father will send in my name, will teach you all things and will remind you of everything I have said to you. Peace I leave with you; my peace I give you. I do not give to you as the world gives. Do not let your hearts be troubled and do not be afraid. (John 14:15-27)

Our basis for loving unconditionally lies first in God's love for us. It may seem cliché, but our evangelical and conservative Christian friends have it right when they emphasize John 3:16: *"For God so loved the world that He gave his only begotten son that whoever believes in him shall not perish, but have eternal life."* God loves "the world"—*cosmos*; i.e., all that is, the whole universe, including those who we have a hard time loving. God loves you, me, Sara Palin, Jimmy Carter, Ronald Reagan, Bill Clinton, George W. Bush, Bono, the Pope, Saddam Hussein, Barack Obama, Lindsey Lohan, Amy Winehouse, Osama bin Laden, Elton John, Pat Robertson, the billionaire executives of bailed out banks, old Mrs. Hernandez who lives down the street, and that malnourished child who's chained to a sewing machine in a sweatshop in Pakistan—*equally*! As Anne Lamott puts it, *"You want to know how big God's love is? The answer is: It's very big. It's bigger than you're comfortable with."* We're not comfortable because God's ability to forgive, extend grace, and love unconditionally far surpasses ours.

The basis of our ability to love rests in our status as loved, forgiven, and accepted Children of God. Evangelicals will say that we're only God's children because of what God did for us in having his only begotten son crucified on the cross on our behalf and because we made a conscious choice to accept that. Progressive Christians suggest that we are God's children because that's simply who human beings are, even before Jesus arrived on the scene. He just reminded us of it. Either way, when we come to accept this essential truth, and come to own that identity, we can't help but strive to *respond* by loving and liberating others as best we can, no matter how hard it is at times.

Jesus instructed us to "Love God . . . and to love our neighbors as ourselves" (Matthew 22:36-40).[310] When we aren't loving toward others, or ourselves, we haven't embraced that truth that we are loved, forgiven, accepted Children of God, nor integrated it into our identities. Christians are called to know ourselves fully, to realize that we are God's, to own that realization, and to live accordingly. As we do this we are called to take inventory of our inner lives, to make friends with our shadow sides, and to healthily incorporate them into ourselves as well. I am a loved, forgiven child of God, who isn't always lovable, who has much to be forgiven, and who behaves like a child at times. To know this—to accept, cherish, and integrate this into who we—is a major part of Christian spiritual development and discipleship. As Sydney J. Harris observed:

". . . quite a few believers, may find it easier to love other people than to love ourselves. And yet, Jesus' instruction to "love your neighbor as yourself" is only meaningful if a person loves his or her-self. And ultimately, our ability to love other people in our lives is proportionally related to the degree that we love ourselves. It's surprising how many people go through life without ever recognizing that their feelings toward other people are largely determined by their feelings toward themselves, and if you're not comfortable and loving within yourself, you can't be comfortable and loving with/towards others."[311]

Loving yourself

This concept of having difficulty loving oneself has been a rare one in most of the Christian tradition. The adage to "love your neighbor as you love yourself" takes it as a given that people love themselves. Jesus didn't command people to love themselves, it's

---

[310] Many Christians may not know this but Jesus wasn't saying anything new here, merely citing Leviticus 19:18. What Jesus did do was to radically expand what is meant by "our neighbor" to everyone, even those who society rejects. See his parable of the Good Samaritan, Luke 10:25-37.

[311] I came across this quote on the internet but can no longer find the source for it.

assumed. And for many of us, this is true. We were all created with a natural drive for self-preservation and self-fulfillment. We want to be happy and we want to live—and to do so in a way that is satisfying. We want shelter from the elements, a place to hang our hat, and enjoy the freedom to be ourselves. We want to be protected from violence and we want to fill our days with things that are pleasant and meaningful. We want a circle of friends who like and support us. And we want to have the sense that our life has purpose and matters. We yearn to increase our happiness and to reduce our suffering. We also seek increased self-acceptance; to make peace with the not-so-great things we've done to others or the help we failed to give others. All of this is self-love.

And yet, some people have difficulty with this. Some of us have a hard time establishing boundaries that would allow us to have the integrity to take care of ourselves and to ensure that we are safe and not being abused or victimized. Some of us beat ourselves up for not "being worthy."

When we find ourselves in such a state, we need to realize that we're not alone in such feelings, that it's pretty common,[312] and, we need to get over it. You and I are *amazing!* We *rock!* God created us in His image and She's blessed us with tremendous potentials, capacities, gifts and graces. It is a crime against God and the world whenever we fail to let our lights shine[313] and to bless others with our God-given wonderfulness. If you can relate to this phenomenon of not feeling good enough, or find it hard to love yourself, please believe that *I* believe in you. I believe in you because of my belief that God loves me, and if God loves *me*, I can assure you that God also loves you.

At my most worst, I have been selfish, petty, addicted, depressed, dysfunctional, self-loathing, and just plain 'ol grumpy and mean. Yet, in spite of that, God manages to love me anyway—just as I am—the wayward runt of the litter who sometimes poops inside the house and ruins shoes by chewing on them. Turns out, I'm actually fairly lovable. God did this for me, and God's doing it for you. I love you.

---

[312] ("all have sinned and fall short of the glory of God" Romans 3:23)
[313] *In the same way, let your light shine before others, that they may see your good deeds and glorify your Father in heaven.* (Matthew 5:16)

Now some of you may be saying, "If you *really* knew the *real* me, who I *really* am deep inside, that you wouldn't say that." Well, okay, if you're going to be *that* way about it. I guess if I squint *really* hard, you're right. Now that you mention it, you do sorta suck (though mostly, you rock!). That's okay. So do I. It takes one to know one. But I doubt if any of us has been a slave trader. I'm willing to bet that few of us have made our living displacing people from their homes and families in Africa, forcing them on board cramped ships where many of them would die en route, and then sold those who survived the voyages to the highest bidders in a land far away across the seas—to live out the rest of their lives treated as mules toiling in the hot sun picking cotton and tobacco. And yet, if we *had* done those things, guess what? We'd still be worthy of love. God would still love us anyway.

Want proof? That's exactly what happened to a fellow named John Newton. Newton was the captain of a slave ship and he helped to forcibly bring hundreds, perhaps thousands, of Africans over to America.

. . . . [O]n a homeward voyage, while he was attempting to steer the ship through a violent storm, he experienced what he was to refer to later as his "great deliverance." He recorded in his journal that when all seemed lost and the ship would surely sink, he exclaimed, "Lord, have mercy upon us." Later in his cabin he reflected on what he had said and began to believe that God had addressed him through the storm and that grace had begun to work for him. For the rest of his life he observed the anniversary of May 10, 1748 as the day of his conversion, a day of humiliation in which he subjected his will to a [God]. *"Thro' many dangers, toils and snares, I have already come; "tis grace has bro't me safe thus far, and grace will lead me home."*[314]

Because of his conversion—his personal experience of God's radical love John Newton left the slave trade and wrote what may be the most famous Christian hymn of all time—*Amazing Grace*.

Another key basis for loving ourselves is the awareness that God is in us and is part of us. Many progressive Christians embrace the

---

[314] "Amazing Grace, the Story of John Newton," http://www.texasfasola. org/biographies/johnnewton

mystical Quaker notion that each of us has a "inner light" that is of God, and/or the Hindu concept of *"namaste"*—which essentially means, that which is Divine in me greets that which is Divine in in you.[315] As Tom Skinner describes it, *"The Christian life is not your attempt to be like Jesus, rather it is Jesus being allowed to be himself in you."* There are several passages of scripture which support such a concept. Jesus' said "let your light shine before men" (John 8:12); "the Kingdom is within/among you" (Luke 17:21); and "whatever you did for the least of these brothers of mine, you did unto Me" (Matthew 25:40). Paul said "it is no longer I who live, but Christ who lives in me" (Galatians 2:20); and also "We know and rely on the love God has for us. Whoever lives in love, lives in God, and God in him/her" (1 John 4:16). If you love God, if you love at all, you should love yourself.

> *Love yourself—accept yourself—forgive yourself—and be good to yourself, because without you the rest of us are without a source of many wonderful things."*
>
> Leo Buscaglia

Loving Others:

Jesus instructed His followers to love each other and to love our neighbor as ourselves. The background behind this teaching is an ancient Middle Eastern teaching that carried over into the Judaism of Jesus' day—a negatively worded version of the Golden Rule. "Do not do unto others that which you would not want them to do to you."[316] Reminding people of the apparently obscure second half of a verse in Leviticus—*"Do not seek revenge or*

---

[315] It also means the place where we transcend our unique selves and recognize that we are one in union with each other and God.

[316] E.g. "Do to no one what you yourself dislike." Tobit 4:15; when Rabbi Hillel (an elder contemporary of Jesus') was asked to sum up the entire Torah, he answered: "That which is hateful to you, do not do to your fellow man. That is the whole Torah; the rest is the explanation; go and learn." Talmud, *Shabbat* 31a; "Recognize that your neighbor feels as you do, and keep in mind your own dislikes." Sirach 31:15

bear a grudge against anyone among your people, but love your neighbor as yourself," (19:18)—Jesus radicalized that teaching and took it to the next level, essentially saying, "Not harming others is the minimum and should be assumed."[317] What we really need to be doing, to love fully and act in a way that is pleasing to God, is to proactively go out of our way to *do* unto others as we *would* have them do unto us" (Matthew 7:9-12). It is possible to mistake the forest for the trees if one reads this too literally. If I happen to want people to bring me chicken noodle soup and *7-Up* when I'm sick, that isn't a solid basis for me to bring that to some other person when they're sick. They may far prefer beef broth and *Coke*—or to not have anyone come by at all. It's important to ask what *they* want! The bottom line is that we should try to treat others lovingly, with dignity and compassion. It is less about the specifics about how I'd like to be treated and more about gauging another person's actual wishes and needs.

In this spirit of radicalizing previous teachings and taking them to the next level, Christian mystic Pierre Teilhard de Chardin said, *"We are one, after all, you and I. Together we suffer, together exist, and forever will recreate each other."* With this concept in mind, if I love myself, and if you in some way are me, and if somehow God is in both of us, then I am loving myself by loving you. I'm also

---

[317] Jesus radicalized several other wisdom sayings that preexisted him, especially in his sermon on the mount: **"You have heard that it was said,** 'Eye for eye, and tooth for tooth.' **But I tell you,** do not resist an evil person. If anyone slaps you on the right cheek, turn to them the other cheek also. And if anyone wants to sue you and take your shirt, hand over your coat as well. If anyone forces you to go one mile, go with them two miles. Give to the one who asks you, and do not turn away from the one who wants to borrow from you. **"You have heard that it was said,** 'Love your neighbor and hate your enemy.' **But I tell you,** love your enemies and pray for those who persecute you, that you may be children of your Father in heaven. He causes his sun to rise on the evil and the good, and sends rain on the righteous and the unrighteous. If you love those who love you, what reward will you get? Are not even the tax collectors doing that? And if you greet only your own people, what are you doing more than others? Do not even pagans do that? Be perfect, therefore, as your heavenly Father is perfect. (Matthew 5:38-48)

loving God by loving you. Many progressive Christians embrace this mystical insight.

George Washington Carver once said: *"How far you go in life depends on your being tender with the young, compassionate with the aged, sympathetic with the striving, and tolerant of the weak and strong. Because someday in life, you will have been all of these."* This observation may just be stating the obvious, but humans have a long history for ignoring the obvious. When we're robust and healthy, it's easy for us to not care about those who aren't. That's where Christianity comes in. In many respects, following the way of Jesus is a call for those of us in the prime of our lives to go out of our way to give a damn about those who aren't doing as well—even if that means some inconvenience and sacrifice to ourselves. Jesus was in his prime, and look what he did for us.

As Catholic theologian Richard Rohr puts it,

> *Somewhere each day we have to fall in love, with someone, something, some moment, event, phrase, word, or sight. Somehow each day we must allow the softening of the heart. Otherwise our hearts will move inevitably toward hardness. We will slowly become cynical without even knowing it—that's where too much of the world is trapped.*[318]

Jesus didn't let his heart become hard or cynical, he sustained softness and love. In the next chapter (13) we'll explore some things we can do to help live this too.

People who would be Christians are called to follow Jesus' teaching to love our neighbors as ourselves. When asked, "who is our neighbor?" Jesus told his famous parable of the Good Samaritan (Luke 10:25-37)—with the moral that a neighbor is *anyone* who lovingly helps *anyone*. The author of 1 John puts it even more plainly, *"If anyone says, "I love God," yet hates his brother, he is a liar. For anyone who does not love his brother, whom he has seen, cannot love God, whom he has not seen"* (14:20). *The Message* (a contemporary version of the Bible) puts it,

> *If anyone boasts, "I love God," and goes right on hating his brother or sister, thinking nothing of it, he is a liar. If he won't*

---

[318] From *Radical Grace*, Saint Anthony Messenger Press, 1995.

love the person he can see, how can he love the God he can't see? The command we have from Christ is blunt: Loving God includes loving people. You've got to love both (verses 21-22).

And it was the keen student of Jesus' teachings, Mahatma Gandhi, who said, *"If you don't find God in the next person you meet, it is a waste of time looking any further."* Everyone around the world is our neighbor and we're called to love them in the same way that God loves us, unconditionally. We accept people not for the purpose of changing them. That's God's job. We lovingly accept and help people so we can display how much God loves them—just as they are. In my experience, conservative Christians often think they are accepting others, but then they undermine that alleged acceptance by saying that they, "Love the sinner, but hate their sin." Genuine empathy doesn't mean, "accepting" the person while criticizing everything about that person. As Thomas Merton put it, *"The beginning of love is to let those we love be perfectly themselves, and not to twist them to fit our own image. Otherwise we love only the reflection of ourselves we find in them."*

The Guy in the Booth

As I shared before, this unconditional loving stuff is hard for me. I write the following paragraphs from my booth at the local IHOP restaurant and I'm having a hard time loving the man sitting in the booth across from me. He's talking a mile a minute, really loudly, and blathering about any and all things which he is an expert on, which seems to be most everything. Seeing as though there are only three cars in the parking lot and there's only one that I don't recognize, I deduce that it belongs to him. It has bumper stickers all over it that promote the Tea Party and hyper-libertarian ideals. I happen to find those values to be contrary to Gospel values and since I'm thinking he's the owner of that SUV, I find myself disliking him and everything he stands for. He's rubbing me the wrong way and disturbing my tranquility. I'm also loathing whom I assume to be this guy's adult son, sitting across from him. The son is encouraging the man or least doing nothing to prevent these long tirades that his father is spouting out.

I have a choice. I can either keep hating on this man, or I can try to see him with the eyes of Christ. I can try to see this man's hurts and struggles in life. I can soften my heart and see in him a fellow child of God who is probably lonely and just trying to make it through life as best he can. I can try to practice Plato's wisdom of, *"Be kind, for everyone you meet is fighting a hard battle."*

Where his words and opinionated blatherings are clearly wrong (from my point of view), instead of wanting to get into an argument with him to set him straight, I can say inside "Father, forgive him for he knows not what he's saying." I can say, "Mother, help me to not be so judgmental." I can choose to humble myself knowing that he's really no different than me. I can be an opinionated, talkative, know-it-all, who gets on soapboxes and rubs others the wrong way.[319] I can embrace the wisdom of "it is better to be kind than to be right" and not choose this as a battle that's worth fighting. I can trust that others are at work in his life to help him be the best he can be. It doesn't depend on me to be the one to "change him." Heck, who says he needs to change at all? We're both fine—just as we are.

I've decided to get up, leave my table, give him a smile, and simply go outside and sit at a table on the patio, leaving that old man to enjoy some quality time with his son without the weird energy of someone judging him at the next table. They smiled back.[320]

Doubting Thomas

Here's another recent example of this personal struggle I have with loving unconditionally: Today, is Sept. 16, 2010, and I am having a hard time loving. For the past three nights I've allowed an indigent person named Thomas to sleep in the chapel I'm the pastor of. But I haven't done so out of love. It's been more out of

---

[319] I'm sure that not everyone has agreed with some of the bumper stickers that I've had on my cars over the years.

[320] These sorts of simple situations happen every day. They happen every day when I judge a car that is going "too slowly" or "too fast" down the road. Why is it that I always think that my speed is the correct one?

a sense of duty and obligation. This lack of loving on my part is probably a bit understandable.

I first met Thomas a couple of years ago when he called the chapel to see if we could help him out with his charges for the room he'd been renting at a local motel. I learned from the motel's manager that Thomas had been way behind on making payments and I could tell that Thomas had found a softie and a sucker in this manager. The manager warned me not to pay for too many nights or else I'd find myself being used. I paid for a few nights but that wasn't the end of it. Thomas kept stopping by and he is simply incapable of cutting to the chase and having a short conversation. And, he always finds a way to make another request or ask for another favor or loan. My shields went up and I learned to be short and direct with him. Coming from Minnesota, the land of "Minnesota Nice,"[321] I felt like I was being rude, but I was probably just being appropriate and establishing healthy boundaries.

At any rate, after a week or two of being flooded by contact with him, I didn't hear from him again until the next year, when the same thing happened again. I also learned that he'd been working a kindly man who was active in a church that's near mine. It was from this other fellow that I learned that Thomas had been diagnosed with lung cancer. That other fellow and his church helped pay for many of Thomas' medical bills. I learned a few months later that the cancer had been dealt with . . . and then after a few more months it had come back and there was nothing more that could be done. I heard that he was living in Chicago, and I figured that'd be the last I'd hear about him.

But then in late August 2010, Thomas called me saying he was back in Boulder for a weeklong visit. He didn't have any money to pay for a motel room and wanted to know if he could sleep in the chapel. I said yes, informing him of the times when he could arrive when the students are likely to be gone. I didn't ask much about him or his condition, or why he was back in Boulder, etc. I

---

[321]   There's a cultural phenomenon in Minnesota where, for the sake of peace and calm, people feign niceties with a "faux" civility. I guess it works, but it leads to grudges and resentments because people don't express their feelings in the moment.

didn't do anything other than help to put a roof over his head for a few nights. He had only asked to sleep one night, but I knew he'd be asking again for other nights. I'd have to set up some limits. Lo and behold, one night turned into about five. Yep, I had his number, and he had mine, the co-dependent dance of user and enabler. I felt the overwhelming need to break out of that pattern. I especially wanted to be released from pattern of treating him like a nuisance and as an *issue* to be dealt with instead of as a fellow human being—and probably a lonely and frightened one at that.

So, I made the choice to shift things. It required a surrendering of agenda on my part. I made the choice to love him just as he is—not for how I want him to be. I chose to try to see Jesus in someone I've been resisting that with. It was a time to practice what I preach. It was a time to love . . . dammit!

40 minutes after I made that choice, I discovered that I missed him. I was hoping to catch him in the chapel before he left for the day. He had led me to believe that he was going to be leaving town that day. I figured I must've missed my chance to live out this shift in my heart. I missed my chance and I felt horrible.

Then, later that day, I went over to that neighboring church where he had been seeking financial assistance and he wasn't there either. They said that he was still in town and they would have him call me when he stops by to get his backpack.

That night I spoke to him and learned he got money to stay at a motel so he wouldn't need to stay at the chapel that night. I arranged to meet him for coffee at a local coffee house the next morning.

We met up and, while I can't exactly say it was the most amazing conversation I've ever had with someone, he was noticing the shift that had taken place in my heart. He could tell that I'd been keeping him at bay and it turned out he needed someone to just spend time with him, more than he'd needed motel rooms to stay in.

In time, I cautiously asked about how he was doing with the bad news of his terminal situation. I could tell that it made him uncomfortable to "go there." He kept talking about the history of his various medical procedures—conveying information instead of feelings. Guys do that sometimes. Eventually, he set up his own boundary and said that he didn't want to talk about "that stuff."

Good for him. But he also said that he was glad that I was asking about him and showing that I cared. Good for me. I told him I'd pray for him and asked if he'd pray for me. The conversation then shifted to college football and life in college towns. As we got back to the chapel, he asked to stay here overnight again. Incredible. I thought he was leaving *that day!* Well, whatever. I said yes, but that time, I really meant it—with love.[322]

> *"Love many things, for therein lies the true strength; whosoever loves much performs much and can accomplish much and what is done in love is done well."*
> Vincent van Gogh

Loving enemies:

Loving "our neighbor" is one thing, but what if our neighbor hates us or does something to harm or attack us? What if they are our enemy? Jesus answered that question plainly. We are to forgive them "seventy times seven times" (Matthew 18:22) and to love them anyway.

> *Love your enemies and pray for those who persecute you.*
> Jesus, Matthew 5:44

> *Apparently Jesus thinks there are two kinds of people in the world: our neighbors who we are to love and our enemies who we are also to love.* Sara Miles

> *If we do not think it possible to love our enemies then we should plainly say that Jesus is not the messiah.* Stanley Hauerwas

It is possible. If Jesus could do it, so could Julio. The following is based on a story on the NPR news website.[323] Julio Diaz is a

---

322   It's now December and I've learned that he's still living in Boulder and that he's found a new church to lean on.

323   *A Victim Treats His Mugger Right*, produced for NPR's, Morning Edition by Michael Garofalo, March 28, 2008, http://www.npr.org/

social worker in New York. He takes the subway to commute to the Bronx every night. One evening, Julio stepped off the train to encounter a disruption of his daily routine. A teen-ager approached and pulled out a knife.

Diaz pulled out his wallet and told the boy, "Here you go."

The teen started walking away, but Julio called out to him, "Hey, wait a minute. You forgot something! If you're going to be robbing people for the rest of the night, you might as well take my coat to keep you warm!"

The teen was dismayed. He asked Julio, "Why are you doing this?"

"If you're willing to risk your freedom for a few dollars, then I guess you must really need the money. I mean, all I wanted to do was get dinner and if you really want to join me, you're more than welcome!"

Julio and the teen went into a diner and sat down. The manager, the dishwashers, and the waiters all came by to say hi to Julio (a regular there).

"You know everybody here?" asked the teen. "Do you own this place?"

"No, I just eat here a lot."

"But you're even nice to the dishwasher!"

"Well, haven't you been taught you should be nice to everybody?"

"Yea, but I didn't think people actually behaved that way!"

"What do you want in your life?"

A saddened expression appeared on the teen's face. He couldn't answer.

When they got the check, Julio said, "Look, I guess you're going to have to pay for this bill 'cause you have my money and I can't pay for this. So if you give me my wallet back, I'll gladly treat you."

The young man quickly gave Julio his wallet back, and Julio gave him $20.

Julio then asked for the teen to give him the knife, and he did.

Julio reflected about this experience saying "I figure, you know, if you treat people right, you can only hope that they treat you right. It's as simple as it gets in this complicated world."

If Julio can do it, so can we.

---

templates/story/story.php?storyId=89164759

But how?

The key to living and acting in this gracious way is to try to see other people as God sees them—as one of God's children, who has some quirks and characteristics that differ from me, and many more that are a lot like me. This involves a certain degree of faith. It also involves knowing one's own feelings, and being able to reflect upon one's experiences, values and biases. It involves developing a sense of empathy—to be able to imagine yourself in someone else's circumstance. The more one is in touch and comfortable with and able to express his feelings, the easier it will be for him to understand where another person is coming from, what their hopes and fears are, and what may be motivating them to act as they are. It is best to hear a person's feelings coming directly from them. It's been said, "an enemy is someone whose story you haven't heard."[324] To the extent that we really are God's children, it makes great sense to think of God as having full and complete empathy with each of us. Christians are those who see God through the life of Jesus, and Jesus clearly knew our stories and had empathy for God's children—the wealthy and the poor alike.

When I'm feeling at odds with another person, even to the point of seeing him/her as my "enemy," I try to take a time out to ponder how I am similar to that person. I list the things that I have in common with them and I even reflect on how I am similar to the parts of them that I don't care for. For example, if someone is hogging the conversation and talking way too much, I think about how I can be like that at times. If someone is being overly aggressive driving on the roads, I try to remember times when I've driven like that, and so on.

There's a wise adage that is often taught in seminaries and pastoral care trainings that goes, *That which we criticize most in others is that which we struggle with most ourselves.* That's a pretty offensive assertion and I resisted it when I was first introduced to it. But then, I got brave enough to look into that mirror and, yep, it rang profound bells of truth. This insight goes a long way in helping us make the mental and emotional shifts that are

---

[324] Source unknown, but perhaps by Rabbi Arthur Gross-Schaefer, Slavoj Žižek, Irene Butter, or Gene Knudsen Hoffman.

needed to make an enemy into a friend. I employed that sort of self-reflection in the passage I wrote above about the man sitting in the booth across from me at the restaurant. As a result, I was able to shift from an escalating combative mode to a friendly one. However, there may situations that will stretch our usual abilities to see ourselves in others. The following is an example of this for me. It's a blog I wrote from a politically liberal perspective. If I were politically conservative, I might have written about Michael Moore, Bill Clinton or Barack Obama:

I heart Dick Cheney: a true test of spiritual practice.[325]

> Dick. Cheney.
>
> That pairing of words causes hives to break out for many and anaphylactic shock to be induced in not a few. Associations with Hitler, The Grinch, The Architect from *The Matrix*, Darth Vader, or the Sith Lord from *Star Wars* are made in the minds of many who consider themselves to be "conscious, spiritually awake" persons and practitioners of numerous religious traditions. He's also a *gift*.
>
> You see this despised and hated man is now facing serious health problems. His heart is failing and his days are numbered.
>
> How one reacts to this news says a lot about where we're really at in our spiritual or yogic practice. It says volumes about the health of our own hearts. It's where things get real and where the proof may, or may not be seen in our pudding.
>
> Try taking "The Great Dick Cheney Empathy Test"[326] and see how you do.

---

[325] See my blog: http://www.elephantjournal.com/2010/07/dick-cheneys-heart-a-true-test-of-spiritual-practice/

[326] http://www.sfgate.com/cgi-bin/article.cgi?f=%2Fg%2Fa%2F20 10%2F07%2F16%2Fnotes071610.DTL see also, http://www.

I passed . . . but if I'm being honest, I had to cheat a little bit.

As John Wesley, the founder of the Methodist movement, once put it, "preach faith until you have it"—which was essentially the origins of "fake it till you make it." There's something to be said for that. Trying on and mimicking that which we aspire to become is in fact a tried and proven method for spiritual growth. This may well be one of those times for a lot of us.

Less judging. More unconditional loving. Less damning. More grace and mercy. Less vengeance. More forgiving. And less excluding. More reconciling—at least for this wanna-be follower of Jesus.

Thank you, Vice President Cheney for providing this mirror for us to gaze into and for this opportunity to check our spiritual pulse and our abilities to be compassionate.

May God's amazing, transforming, healing, strengthening, and comforting Grace, Peace, and Love be with you and your loved ones during this difficult time.

I (*gulp* . . . can't believe I'm saying this) love you.

{{Hug}}.

It is especially difficult for us to see an enemy as a fellow child of God, let alone as a friend. Even wording it that way takes away from our seeing someone as a unique individual—instead lumping them into a wider group of "*those* kind of people." Indeed, this dehumanizes people all together. This is why so many of the

commondreams.org/view/2010/07/16-6 (blog by Mark Morford)

parables that Jesus told dismayed and confounded the people who heard them. He humanized those that "the righteous" dehumanized. Jesus lifted up persons who were not fellow Hebrews as being fully worthy of God's grace and love, of being the heroes of the story, of being the ones who truly "got it" and lived in a godly and righteous way. And beyond his parables, Jesus upset the religious elites by associating with, and even breaking bread with, people whom that society considered "unclean" and was prejudiced against.

I've been prejudiced against people. When I was a youth I was fully steeped into the homophobia that is rampant among young males in our society. I reckon I told a few "fag jokes" back then. During my college and post college years, my biases began to soften as I began to know and interact with gays and lesbians—as well as bisexuals and a few cross-dressers. I discovered that they're pretty much like me. They pay bills and taxes, get in arguments with their lovers, get stressed out about their finances, are worried about the environment, have hopes, dreams, quirks, and habits. Nothing too scary (well, the worries about the environment are a bit scary).

During my years in seminary, my homophobia relaxed even further and I found myself on the streets urging voters in Colorado to not pass an amendment that would have allowed employers and landlords in that state to discriminate against gay people. My only remaining rigidity was that I was against lesbians (or straight women) self-impregnating and intentionally bringing a child into the world without a father in that child's life. "Why can't they just adopt a child?" But, even that bias dissolved as I realized that a number of the people I knew and loved had grown up in homes effectively without a male in them. They turned out just fine. I realized that my fear about how children would grow up in such situations was just that—my fear. Fear is a lack of faith. I had to ask myself—who am I to question God's ability to bring about loving families in the world?

During my last semester of my seminary graduate studies I was involved in monitoring the proceedings at the General Conference of the United Methodist Church (effectively, the "Congress" of the denomination that meets every four years to adopt and revise rules and regulations) that happened to meet in Denver that year.

Like many mainline churches, the UMC has been in a state of
turmoil regarding whether or not to allow for the full inclusion of
GLBTQI[327] persons. Here's what happened at the conference one
day:

Cookies of Love

As I got off the bus downtown and approached the Denver
Convention Center, I could see a bunch of people holding signs.
They didn't seem like fellow United Methodists and they didn't
appear friendly. As I got closer, I could read the signs and realized
that this was a group of outside interlopers who were crashing
our convention with their messages of hate. The signs read,
"Methodists Repent! Don't become a Gay Church!", *"Homosexuality is
an Abomination! (Leviticus 18:22)"*, and the like.

The closer I got to them, the more my blood pressure raised. I
could feel the adrenaline pumping through my veins. I was getting
into attack mode. I went up to the dude holding the sign quoting
from Leviticus and said, "Do you eat shrimp?"

"What?"

"Do you eat shrimp or crab meat? Because if you do *that's* an
abomination—Leviticus 11:12!"

"Well that's different!"

"Oh really? Say, is that a polyester-cotton blend shirt that
you're wearing? *That's* against the law too! What do you think
you're doing picking and choosing verses from the Bible and then
being such a *hypocrite?!*"

It was on. The shouting match took off and it was a truly epic
match of tit for tat proof-texting each of us proving how we were
right and the other one was wrong—and an ass.

In the midst of this nasty melee, I felt a breeze against the
back of my legs. I turned and saw a tall man in a suit reaching
in between us with a large cookie in his hand, saying, "Have a
cookie!" The guy with the sign and I looked at each other, then
at him, and then we took the cookie being offered. We broke it in
half and started to enjoy the cookie. The guy in the suit walked off
hardly breaking stride at all. We found ourselves still arguing, but

---

[327]   Gay Lesbian Bisexual Transgendered Queer Inter-Sex

our volume level went way down and we somehow shifted into a more civil mode of slightly more rational debate. Eventually, we honored each other as being fellow Christians. We shook hands and pledged to pray for each other.

Later that day, I came across that strange man in the suit and went up to him and thanked him for offering that cookie to us as a means of grace and transformation.

He replied, "What are you talking about? I was trying to put something in that guy's mouth so he'd shut up and let *you* speak!"[328]

I learned a lesson that day, the Holy Spirit can work even through people who aren't aware of it—and who even have a different agenda all together. In fact, I think She may've even done it through me a few times. The other lesson was that the line between enemy and friend is not a rigid one. The concept of "enemy" is only there to the extent that we want and allow it to exist.

The shopper who rocked my world

I realized this one day when I was grocery shopping during my second year of seminary in Denver. I made my purchase and started to walk with my bags (probably filled with ramen noodles, bananas, and cans of tuna fish as that was what my diet largely consisted of at that time) across the parking lot toward my car. As I got near my car a middle-aged woman hurriedly approached me and said, "Can you lay hands on me brother? I need a healing in Jesus' name!"

I would love to have seen the expression on my face as I tried to comprehend what I was hearing. There I was, this scholar-in-training attending one of the most liberal and academically rigorous schools of theology in the country, and yet here was this person who didn't fit into any of the boxes that I was being trained to deal with. I had no idea how to respond to this woman, let alone to minister to her. My prejudices were inclined to lump her into the category of "crazy, fundamentalist, charismatic, lunatic;" i.e., the sort of person who I don't particularly want to associate with because she "makes Christianity look bad."

---

[328] Rev. Chuck Schuster, currently at First UMC Ft. Collins, CO

In an instant, I let go of all of my biases and my seminary blinders. This wasn't a time to for judging. This wasn't a time for arguing theology. This was a time for compassion and action. I felt a strange, empowering feeling flow through me that allowed me to say, "Sure." I placed one hand on her forehead and the other on her shoulder. With as much holy boldness as I could muster, I said, *"I lay hands on you in the name of our Risen Christ. May the Lord touch you in the way that you need. God, You know her brokenness. You know her pain. Help her to feel Your love. Holy God, give this sister a dose of Your transforming power so she can be the most wonderful vessel of Your love in this world. Be with her now and always. In the name of your Son, Jesus Christ our Lord. Amen!"*

She then opened her eyes, said thank you, smiled, and gave me a hug. Then we parted ways each heading off in our different directions.

That woman blessed me more than I blessed her. That encounter forced me to be less rigid about the theological boundary lines I'd created in my mind. It was a lesson in getting the hell out of my head, and providing heaven out in the world.

Whether we're liberals, conservatives, progressives, intellectuals, fundamentalists, or mystics, we need to get over ourselves and to meet people where they're at. If that means doing things in a *really* outside the box sort of way, so be it. As Paul put it, "I will be all things to all people" (1 Corinthians 9:19). The churches I lead will probably attract certain types of folks with certain sensibilities and perspectives, while other pastors and ministries will draw those from other views, notions, and perspectives. God is at work in it all.

What we need is more openness and tolerance within the Church family.

Augustine and Wesley each proclaimed, *"In essentials, unity; in non-essentials, liberty; and in all things, love."* Progressive Christians affirm that, and we suggest that the primary essentials are unconditional love and compassionate living. Progressive Christianity celebrates the power in seeing Christ in the person right in front of us. Christians from across the theological spectrum can resonate with this. Paul and James were leaders of the early Church and they disagreed on many things. They disagreed on so much so that they decided to "be together" in different places (there's some wisdom in that). However, they agreed on one thing—the importance of caring for the poor in Christ's name.

Historical writings about the early Church tell us that non-Christians often remarked of Christians *"See how they love each other!"* These were written during a time of such a lack of love in Roman society that any show of love or joy[329] set Christians apart from the rest of the crowd. People could sense something different about Christians. That difference was radically inclusive love and compassion. That difference made Christianity worthy of consideration.

Could the same be said of us today? Could people look at us and be able to say, *"See how they love?"* It's such a simple thing to have said of us, but it's the highest compliment of behavior we can possibly receive. It's certainly better than, *"See how nice their buildings are,"* or *"See how big their church is."* It was simply, *"See how they love!"* It's not by accident that some Christians are demonstrating and manifesting this sort of love. It's because they've worked at it. The next chapter shares how.

---

[329] Let alone the sort unconditional love that had them going out of their way to ensure that the poor people of Rome received proper burials.

Chapter 12

Progressive Christian Spiritual Practices: "The Push-ups of Love"

Have a talk with God—Stevie Wonder
Run in such a way as to get the prize. Everyone who competes
in the games goes into strict training. They do it to get a crown
that will not last, but we do it to get a crown that will last
forever. 1 Corinthians 9:24b-25

As profoundly powerful, transforming, and life-changing as *agapé* love is, it certainly isn't easy to love everyone this way at all times. It is difficult to sustain. We cannot live and love in this way without a lot of help. The people who were involved in the non-violent and transforming Civil Rights movement in the U.S. would have burned-out early on if they hadn't engaged in certain practices which helped to keep them inspired, unified, and on board with the path of non-violence and loving their enemy.

They met frequently for church meetings. They worshipped the God who loves them unconditionally. They studied the Bible to remind them of Jesus' teachings. They sang songs to help drive home the message of nonviolence into their bones. They practiced not retaliating when people lashed out at them. They participated in "hassle lines" and role-playing exercises[330] to prepare them

---

330   I learned about this from Dr. Vincent Harding when I was a student at Iliff. Harding, a Quaker, was one of MLK's speech-writers and advisors. He helped prepare a group of us for how to protest

for how to behave non-reactively when they would attempt to order food at the segregated lunch counters at *Woolworth's*. They simulated situations where they might normally be inclined to react with aggression and to instead employ actions and behaviors that would defuse and de-escalate tensions. Even simple things like smiling, focusing on breathing and counting to 100 inside their minds were used.

Let's explore some of the spiritual practices that can help feed souls and nurture love. A spiritual practice is only good to the extent that it helps us be more loving. Feel free to experiment with and try these with that in mind. Spiritual practices and disciplines are actions or activities that we can engage in to help us experience the Divine. If you do them more than once, they have the potential to become habits—and starting new habits is scary. As Orison Swett Marden said, *"The beginning of a habit is like an invisible threat, but every time we repeat the act we strengthen the strand, add to it another filament, until it becomes a great cable and binds us irrevocably, thought and act."* Knowing this is daunting but if we practice healthy habits, the beautiful lives we weave will be worth it.

Jesus was a practicing Jew. He honored the Jewish customs, rites, and rituals on his own terms. He did them because he *wanted* to—not because he felt he *had* to. When Jesus went to the synagogue in his hometown to preach that first sermon, he did so because it was his custom, his habit. *"He went to Nazareth, where he had been brought up, and on the Sabbath day he went into the synagogue, as was his custom."* (Luke 4:16) That approach should be ours as well—not to do spiritual or religious things because we "have to," but because we want to, and because they've become part of who we are. The following are some practices that can foster and nourish unconditional love:

Shift from believing to having faith Believing in something is an intellectual exercise. It means I accept that a certain assertion

---

against Colorado's infamous "Amendment 2." Sadly, the majority of voters had passed and it allowed discrimination against GLBTQ persons. Happily, Colorado's Supreme Court eventually overturned it as unconstitutional. You can read more about hassle lines here: http://www.yesmagazine.org/issues/finding-courage/the-time-for-nonviolence-has-come

is true. Saying that one "believes in" God, that Jesus is God's only Son and that Jesus is our Savior, is a far cry from actually trusting and relying on God. Beliefs aren't the same things as truly depending upon God and Her grace. Faith is putting your trust and reliance upon God. People can have deep faith in God and not be able to articulate and state their beliefs very well. However, people can state all sorts of things that they believe and not have much faith at all. Faith trumps belief.

While conservative Christians generally agree with what I stated above, in practice, it seems that some of them also hold the opposite perspective. Seeking to "get prayer back into public schools" and having the Ten Commandments posted in public places is more about getting the masses to believe certain things. But, if our nation has the world's largest stockpile of nuclear weapons and spends more on our military than nearly all of the rest of the world's nations do on their militaries *combined*, whom do we really put our faith—our trust and reliance upon? Not God.

Having faith means recognizing that there is a God, that you need God, and that deep down, you know that things will be okay because you trust that God is at work to bring about good. That inner trust and assurance matter far more than do believing "the right things" about God.

Practice referring to yourself (and others) as "a person of faith" or as a "follower of Jesus" instead of as "a believer." When people ask you if you believe in God, practice answering about how you trust and rely upon God in life.

Hold things loosely Shift toward being more concerned about the larger Truth that your beliefs (or practices) *point to*, rather than the beliefs themselves. Beliefs and practices aren't God.

Many heated family arguments and wars have been waged because one or more persons were holding their beliefs too rigidly. It is a shame that people are willing to shun or even kill fellow humans, even members of their own families, merely because they don't agree with views of God and religion. This is the supreme example of persons entirely missing the point of their own religion. I happen to believe that Jesus was resurrected, that Jesus is Lord, that God is triune (a trinity of three persons), and that it's okay to consider Jesus as God. There is, however, no godly reason for me to need for other people to share those beliefs. Why on earth does anyone *need* others to think the way they do about religion? Such a need comes from a place of insecurity and anxiety, not faith. And, it is most unbecoming.

People of faith attract far more people to consider their way of thinking when they speak with humility, grace, and love. This is particularly true if they engage with others while keeping an open mind and a willingness to have some of their thoughts changed or modified because of their encounters with others. People can tell if we're being rigid, or if we're being relaxed and flexible. It's hard for people to have an authentic encounter with someone who is entrenched in her beliefs. To the extent that progressive Christianity has resolute firmness about beliefs, it comes from a sense of our ongoing participation in a covenant with God—one that we assess, reassess, and recommit ourselves to on a daily basis. The root of that covenant is the belief that God loves us. If you're going to be rigid about anything, be rigid about being loving above all else. If you do, it may soften you so that you aren't rigid and unloving.

Prayer This one may be a challenge for a few of us. Some people like the idea of God being real, and of God "being there," but the idea of actually being able to *communicate* with God seems impossible to them. There may also be some who believe that it is possible but that doing so would be too assuming on our part, as, "Who are *we* to have the gall to try to tell God what to do?" Or, perhaps, more frequently, there are many who somehow don't feel worthy of God's time and attention. But, Christians are called to pray, "without ceasing" (I Thessalonians 5:17).

There are many different forms of prayer. One can even say that anything from traditional prayers to playing the piano to gardening, rock-climbing, surfing, and riding a motorcycle through the mountains is "prayer." For the purposes of this book, we'll limit the discussion of prayer to some basic forms—as I include those other sorts of activities in other spiritual practices that I'll discuss.

The traditional forms of prayer that Christians have engaged in over the years boil down to three concepts, "Thank you" "I'm sorry," and "Help!" That's pretty much it, and it doesn't really have to be more complicated than that. Nevertheless, let's take a brief look at each of them.

Gratitude: Meister Eckhart, a famed Christian mystic, said, *"If the only prayer you ever say in your entire life were 'thank you,' it would be enough."* I'm inclined to agree. After Jesus healed ten lepers and sent them on their way to the priests to show them that they'd been restored and made clean, only one of them came back to say thank you

> *One of them, when he saw he was healed, came back, praising God in a loud voice. He threw himself at Jesus' feet and thanked him—and he was a Samaritan. Jesus asked, "Were not all ten cleansed? Where are the other nine? Was no one found to return and give praise to God except this foreigner?" Then he said to him, "Rise and go; your faith has made you well."* (Luke 17:15-19)

Those who are outside the Church may be the ones who more readily get this. It was the secular *Five Man Electrical Band* who sang those wonderful lines at the end of their song *Signs* about someone seeing a church with a sign that said something like 'Everyone's welcome, come on in and pray.' He went in, enjoyed the service, but because he didn't have any money, he made his own little sign, a note that he put in the offering plate simply thanking God for thinking about him and letting God know that he's doing okay![331]

It may be that many of us in the Church have come to take God's many blessings in our lives for granted. Theologian Dietrich Bonhoeffer said, *"How can God entrust great things to one who will not thankfully receive from Him the little things?"* It is during the times that I am most appreciative of what God is doing in my life that I am inclined to be the most loving. Try making a list of things you are grateful for and saying thank you for each of them. Try doing it weekly or even daily. However, we'd also do well to ponder these words by Johannes A. Gaertner, *"To speak gratitude is courteous and pleasant, to enact gratitude is generous and noble, but to live gratitude is to touch heaven."* I'm not entirely sure what it means to "live gratitude," but I invite us to try.[332] God and the world will be blessed by our efforts.

---

[331] http://www.lyricsdepot.com/five-man-electrical-band/signs.html
[332] I think part of it may be being more gracious, compassionate, and understanding with others. I think it may be giving more to help people in need.

Praying to express our sorrow and regret and to seek forgiveness. While progressive Christianity doesn't encourage people to overly dwell on our failings and shortcomings, it does call us to be real. As social creatures, humans have a need to express regret and remorse. Even though we try to openly admit that we aren't perfect, we have a basic need to apologize to others, God, and ourselves.

The confession portion of the medieval prayer liturgy for the Close of the Day, *Compline*, meets this need well:

> *Leader: Holy and gracious God,*
>
> *People: I confess that I have sinned against You this day. Some of my sin I know—the thoughts and words and deeds of which I am ashamed—but some is known only to You. In the name of Jesus Christ I ask forgiveness. Deliver and restore me, that I may rest in peace.*
>
> *Leader: By the mercy of God we are united with Jesus Christ, and in Him we are forgiven. We rest now in His peace and rise in the morning to serve Him.*

Expressions of confession almost always help me to feel like I have a fresh start. It's hard to love yourself or others if you're still weighted down by guilt and regret. When followers of Jesus offer such expressions, they do so trusting in God's unconditional love and amazing grace. *"Therefore, if anyone is in Christ, he is a new creation; the old has gone, the new has come!"* (2 Corinthians 5:17). When we accept forgiveness, we are free to love and forgive others.

Intercessory prayer is praying for God to intervene and provide some assistance or transformation for you or others, for example: "God, please help Lisa to deal with this time of challenge;" "Help Juan to know that you are there and working to provide the strengthening assurance that he needs now;" "Lord, I'm powerless over this addiction and I need you to help me break free;" "God, help my son's brain swelling to subside;" "Spirit, give me wisdom to help me make a good choice;" "Lord, help me to get over that relationship;" "Help me to be more loving;" and "God please help the leaders around the world work toward peace!." I can't say that this form of prayer always "works" in the way that I'd like, or that things turned out the way that I would have wanted them to go, but I can say that I have felt better after saying such prayers. In hindsight, I can see how something good played out—oftentimes far better than what I had originally hoped for. Jesus modeled for us that we are worthy to connect to God. We should name and share our requests, but we should let God be God and not prescribe the potential answers. As Jesus put it, "Father, not my will, but yours, be done" (Luke 22:42).[333]

Asking for help is a powerful way of loving yourself and others. Which of us, when our house is on fire, wouldn't contact our neighbors to seek some help? Which of us when our neighbor's house is on fire, wouldn't also seek some help and maybe even help ourselves? I cannot say that every time people pray that houses are always prevented from burning down and that lives are always saved. I can tell you that it makes a difference.

God works with the world as it is. When there are prayers happening, that is a different world than one where they aren't. When people pray, God has more to work with—more intentions, more feeling, and more expression of need. Perhaps most importantly, this means more people with their "God radars" tuned in so that they can more effectively receive God's nudges for how they can be of loving service in the world.[334] Praying for

---

[333] Note: I'm not talking about God's will in a Calvinistic way where God has pre-determined certain intentions and outcomes. I mean instead, that God's will isn't fixed for all time but is capable of changing based on how circumstances, events, persons, attitudes, words, actions, deeds coincide at every new moment.

[334] Notice: from our previous discussion about God in Chapter 3, a direct result of God's ability to change is seen in the area of prayer. A God who cannot change cannot respond to prayer. If God has already decided before He even created the world how things will turn out, then there is no reason to pray. With that logic drawn to its fullest extension, the God of traditional theism (at least some strands of it) is neither personal nor responsive to His creation. On the other hand, progressive Christianity's emphasis that God does change, implies that God responds to your prayers and requests. She is more interactive. As openness theologian (similar to process theology) Greg Boyd puts it, some of the future truly depends on prayer. Hence, "this translates into people who are more inclined

yourself and for the needs of others is one of the best ways to love.

On a related note, not all of our prayers have to be articulate or even worded at all. According to Romans 8:26-27,

> *In the same way, the Spirit helps us in our weakness. We do not know what we ought to pray for, but the Spirit himself intercedes for us with groans that words cannot express. And he who searches our hearts knows the mind of the Spirit, because the Spirit intercedes for the saints in accordance with God's will.*

It may be said that **moans and groans** may be the universal language of prayer. Anyone can do it, and most of us do from time to time (even if merely when we're sick or in pain). In fact, moaning and groaning has been a prominent part of many African American Christian worship services. It's an equalizer that strips away human degrees, articulateness, and status and goes straight to the source. Perhaps moaning with others, or being present to their moaning, is a powerful way to love them.

Pray in a humble manner. As Jesus instructed,

> *"when you pray, do not be like the hypocrites, for they love to pray standing in the synagogues and on the street corners to be seen by men. I tell you the truth, they have received their reward in full. But whenever you pray, go into your room, close the door, and pray to your Father who is hidden. And your Father who sees from the hidden place will reward you.*
> Matthew 6:5-6

If Jesus were walking around in the U.S. as a human today would he show up to Promise Keepers[335] rallies or National Day of Prayer breakfasts, and the like? I'm currently leaning toward, no.

---

to pray with passion and urgency." (*God of the Possible*, p. 95) For more on this understanding of how intercessory prayer works, see: *In God's Presence*, by Marjorie Hewitt Suchocki.

[335] The Promise Keepers movement is a nation-wide, evangelical men's movement started by a former University of Colorado football head coach, Bill McCartney in 1990. They meet in stadiums and arenas

It is not the case that progressive Christianity has a better hold of this than conservative Christianity. More than a few pastors and lay people from both perspectives have been known to turn a prayer into a longwinded, politicized, sermon. There is a certain form of prayer that is currently more common in progressive Christian circles than conservative ones—**Centering Prayer.**

Centering prayer is a form of prayer that is more about nurturing a daily connection with our maker. In centering prayer, there are no words that we utter to God. Instead, we simply sit in silence. It's basically "quality time with God." Centering prayer originates from the "Desert Fathers and Mothers" in early Christian history.[336] Those early mysticism-embracing hermits felt called to live life detached from the world with a focus on simply being present to God and to grow in godliness and holiness. They created the monastic tradition that influenced all subsequent monastic traditions including the Order of St. Benedict, to Eastern Orthodoxy, German Evangelicalism, European and American Pietism, and the Methodist movement. One of the key practices they developed was *Hesychasm* (Greek for "stillness, rest, quiet, silence"). It's the practice of "interior silence and continual prayer." They developed what might be called "Christian meditation." This is a contemplative practice where one simply seeks to be present to God and to enjoy God's presence. It's a way for God to enjoy Her children.

To do centering prayer, you set aside 25-45 minutes during the day (alone or with others) to simply sit still (often-times cross-legged on a cushion on the floor) and just be. It's a practice of being a human *being* not a human *doing*. It's based upon Psalm

---

and seek to reactivate the faith lives of nominally Christian men by appealing to their love of sports, heroes, Jesus, and, being men. In many ways, I support their efforts, but I do have issues with their appeals to machismo and teaching men that they are "the spiritual heads of their households." From what I can tell, they hold a very conservative view of homosexuality. I experience "PK" as seeking to help men become more Christian by appealing to their fragile egos and their need to feel important, and superior to women. They of course would dispute this.

[336] Around 260-350 A.D. in Egypt and Syria.

46:10 where it says, "be still and know that I am God." You choose a "prayer word" (for example, *God, Abba, Love, Grace, Spirit, Peace*) to say in your mind. You gently utter it under your breath to bring yourself into awareness of God's presence as you begin the session. Use that same word to bring yourself back to simply being present to God whenever your mind gets distracted.[337] Centering prayer is a practice that helps people to experience God's unique grace and love for them as an individual child of God. It has helped me tremendously in experiencing and believing that God loves me—just as I am. I have also found that my "God radar" and my ability to be calm, cool and collected are notably heightened on days that I've done centering prayer.

One specific prayer that speaks to the hearts and souls of many people is the prayer that has become known as *The Serenity Prayer.* Theologian Reinhold Neibuhr wrote it in 1943. It has become a central staple for people in Twelve Step addiction recovery programs but it speaks to all of us.

> *God, grant me the serenity to accept the things I cannot change; courage to change the things I can; and wisdom to know the difference.*
>
> *Living one day at a time; Enjoying one moment at a time; Accepting hardships as the pathway to peace; Taking, as He did, this sinful world as it is, not as I would have it; Trusting that He will make all things right if I surrender to His Will that I may be reasonably happy in this life and supremely happy with Him in the next. Amen.*

The first portion of it is probably more familiar than the full prayer—perhaps because there are more Christian beliefs assumed in the second half. This prayer has helped millions of people to be at their best and to release the stresses and worries that have led them to self-medicate or worry so much. I'm not part of the addiction community, but I've certainly had my seasons of obsessing, worrying, stressing, and even self-medicating (in a broad sense of that term). This prayer works.

---

[337] For more on centering prayer, see Appendix V.

Many progressive Christians also affirm the prayer that Jesus taught his disciples: **"The Lord's Prayer"** (based on Matthew 6:10-14 & Luke 11:2-4)

> *Our Father [Mother], Which art in heaven, hallowed be Thy name;*
> *Thy Kingdom come; Thy will be done, on earth as it is in heaven.*
> *Give us this day our daily bread.*
> *And forgive us our trespasses (debts/sins), as we forgive them*
> *   that trespass (sin) against us. (our debtors)*
> *And lead us not into temptation; but deliver us from evil.*
> *For Thine is the Kingdom, the power, and the glory, forever.*
> *Amen.*

The Lord's Prayer, contains all of the elements that are needed to communicate with our Creator: praise to God; a call for God's Kingdom to be fully manifest on earth (including social justice); a request for having our daily sustenance provided; asking for forgiveness (and an admission that we screw up and are sorry); an appeal for help in forgiving other people; a request for protection from powers and forces which would lead us astray; and a reminder to ourselves that God is great and that it's going to be okay.

Perhaps you're saying, "I don't have time to do all of this praying!" No one said we *have* to. You can live a fine life without doing it. But, it is hugely beneficial to make some time to connect and commune with God. I can think of no instances where I have said to myself, "Gee, I should've been doing this instead of spending time in prayer." Indeed, as Martin Luther and Mother Theresa have put it, "The busier I am, the more I pray."

Participating in relationships If God is truly immanent in all of God's creatures, then God is in each of us and we're able to experience God in one another. Non-human animals are arguably purer channels of this. If you've ever owned, or even hung-out much with a dog, you've felt God's unconditional love. The bumper sticker that reads, *"Lord, help me to be the person that my dog thinks I am,"* has it right. Dogs have a way of assuming the best and forgiving the worst. They also teach profound spiritual truths such as loyalty, patience, assuming the best in others, "Wag more, bark less," "Don't bite the hand that feeds you," and only resort to violence as a last resort and then, no more than is needed.[338]

But, if you really want to grow spiritually, nothing beats the crucible and womb of being in a deep relationship with a fellow human being. This doesn't necessarily have to be a romantic one. People are complicated enigmas with capacities for amazing love and charity, monstrous cruelty, and incredible grudges, pettiness, fears, foibles, and hang-ups. If you can love and be loved by a human, you can love and be loved by anything.[339]

I'm hardly a walking success story when it comes to relationships, but I have learned a few things. One practice that works well is **listening.** *Really* listening. The kind of listening to another person where you are truly tracking what someone is saying without thinking about what you'll say next. As one Bible passage puts it, *"be quick to listen and slow to speak"* (James 1:19). And as theologian Paul Tillich put it, *"The first duty of love is to listen."* When people are heard in that way, they notice and bonds are formed. A profound question to ask someone is "how is it with your soul?" But only ask that sort of thing if you are willing to truly listen. In fact, it will likely take several encounters with people where they experience you being a good listener before they will even consider answering such a question, other than superficially. You'll need to develop a sense of mutual trust first.

A related practice is to engage in **shared silence** with another person. When you meet with someone, who says you have to talk the whole time or even at all? We do. We talk this way because it is scary to simply be quiet and have silence. We even call it "awkward silence." That is a judgment that we impose on things. Perhaps just being with someone is what matters most and filling the air with talking is what is awkward. This need to chatter comes from a fear of intimacy. You can tell a lot more about someone by sharing space with them in silence than you can by hearing them chat away. Likewise, we reveal more about ourselves when we're

---

[338] As I understand it, most animals don't fight fellow members of their own species to the death. Most clashes resolve quickly with one party submitting or retreating.

[339] And similarly, as was discussed in Chapter 12, if you can love yourself, you can love anyone.

just quietly being ourselves than we do when our lips are flapping. We are known by how we "do" silence. I think deep down we know this, and it is scary, so we fill the air with talking. Ironically, the more we share about ourselves, the less we reveal. It comes from a fear of being known, because if we are known we might be rejected, and rejection is scary. A practice then is to try to not fill the air with quite as much talking when we meet with people. Perhaps try only answering questions asked of you and to keep those answers as brief as possible. Or perhaps ask questions of others and then really listen to their response with no expectation of being asked the same question by them.

This practice of sharing silence with fellow humans is heightened when you're with someone who is hurting. It is tempting to help them rationalize their suffering. To help them put things into context, to philosophize, to solve their problem, and to suggest why this happened or where God might be at work in it.

But as the biblical story of Job makes clear, sitting in silence is what helps the most. After Job suffered through his many losses, he sat for three days with his friends. For three days his friends simply sat quietly with him. They "held space" for him to just be and feel. They shared their *compassion* (com-passion means "suffering with"), solidarity, and love by metaphorically "sitting in the fire" with him in silence for seven days and seven nights (Job 2:11-13). Eventually they couldn't sustain this silence and (probably out of their own anxiety) started blaming him for his plight and waxing philosophical and theological. In so doing, they made unhelpful nuisances of themselves.

Our human capacity to communicate with words is phenomenal and it'd be poor stewardship of those around to not make use of this gift. One way this can take place is **"mirror holding and gazing."** It is a way to help each other through mutual accountability. It's a chance to learn how others experience you. It's an opportunity to notice your growing edges and to celebrate your strengths and recent growth. Relationships force you to explore the questions: What are my triggers? What are my buttons? How do I engage, or not, in conflict?

One of the best things that people in relationship with another person can do is to overtly name and express the love they have. It is an amazing practice to convey your feelings to the ones you love as if each day is the only day you and those around you might have. **Name and share the specific things you love about another person. Give thanks each day** for each person you love. **Saying, "I love you"** is perhaps the most powerful spiritual practice that there is. However, if your actions don't match your words—it can be a destructive practice.[340]

Practice empathy Practice wondering what another person is thinking, feeling, or needing. Ponder what it would be like to be in their shoes if you were in their circumstances.[341] Ask yourself, what would be the best way to love such a person? Then, do that. Your actions will speak louder than your words. A place where things get tricky is when someone expresses something like "I thirst." It may be that they want you to bring them a glass of water, or they may simply yearn for a fellow human to honor and validate their feeling by saying something like, "I know this feeling. I have thirst too."[342] This is where it's important to ask them what they need from you and not to assume.

Another key practice when relating to others is **forgiveness**. It's not a matter of *if* people will let you down, but when. When they do, how you respond matters. You can either respond by widening the divide or seeking to narrow it. That choice is yours. If you forgive them, how they respond is their choice. You can't control that, but you can choose to forgive.

---

[340] I'm speaking here of *agape* love, but this is especially true with romantic love. People rush to say "those three words." It's not that we don't all love each other, but that particular type of love can be such a pressured thing that it's said too soon, when it's not really true. Once we utter those words, it's hard to go back. So when it comes to that type of love, it's best to wait until the right time instead of rushing into it.

[341] It's good to remember that you really *could* be in that other person's shoes, not just wondering what it would be like. You would do well to recognize with humility that you could be that person who is homeless, poverty-stricken, filled with grief, afraid, etc. None of us is "above" anyone else and that, based on a series of random circumstances, we could be on the other side of the equation. Most Americans are only 1-2 paychecks away from being homeless.

[342] Apologies to the movie *White Men Can't Jump.*

Why forgive? Well, for those who are seeking to follow Jesus, because He *said* to—and because he practiced what he preached. As Jesus was dying on the cross, he cried out, "Father, forgive them, for they know not what they do!" (Luke 23:34) Before he died, he predicted that Peter, the one whom he'd chosen to take over and lead the Church when he departed, would betray him and deny him three times. According to the story, Peter did in fact deny that he even *knew* Jesus—three times. Yet, Peter was forgiven and served well as the leader of the early church. If God can forgive Peter, who are you to say that God can't forgive you or the people who've wronged you? Think about it.

Even beyond Jesus' instruction to forgive, it is simply the case that forgiving others helps relationships. When I was young my dad was a bit too heavy handed in his parenting style. I perceived him as being a tyrant at times and as a volcano that I didn't want to see explode. As I've aged, and experienced him as a fellow adult, I've come to embrace him, including his foibles and needs. I realize that he never meant to be scary or intimidating. He had some unresolved stuff from his childhood and had a few of those glitches and hang-ups that humans have. I forgave him because he "knew not what he did."[343] Our relationship is transformed because of it. I also realized that I'd be a hypocrite if I didn't forgive him as I have a few hang-ups too and I'm not always the father that I want to be to my son. I pray my son forgives me someday.[344]

Important note: forgiving does not mean "forgetting." And it doesn't mean condoning what happened. As Rabbi Michael Lerner says, *"One must be compassionate and forgiving toward others with whom we disagree on ethical issues, but forgiveness does not require us to stop struggling against the policies and institutions that wounded people have created to dominate our lives, and against their oppressive beliefs and behaviors."*

Human life is not a solo journey. We are social creatures and we can only thrive fully if we're in relationship with others. This is especially true for people who choose to follow Jesus. It's been said,

---

[343] Luke 23:34
[344] "Family of origin work" (working on the baggage and hang-ups we acquire during our childhoods) could be said to be a spiritual practice, but in my opinion, it really comes down to forgiveness.

"Christianity isn't a religion, it's a relationship." It's both, but there is much to be said for emphasizing the relational aspect of the faith. First of all, one can't "love thy neighbor as thy self" or "forgive others seventy times seven times" unless one relates to others. As John Wesley put it, *"'Holy solitaries' is a phrase no more consistent with the gospel than holy adulterers. The gospel of Christ knows no religion, but social; no holiness but social holiness."* He called upon the Church to maintain social holiness, meaning we were to be connectional and responsible for each other's moral and spiritual life and growth. We *are* our brother's keeper (Genesis 4:9 & Matthew 25:40)—indeed, we are our brother's brother (or sister).

Jesus' teachings about forgiveness and loving others aren't easy. They are counter-cultural and radically different from the ways of the world.[345] So much so, that we need to learn how to follow them. We've been so steeped in the domineering, competitive, vindictive, and oppressive ways of the world that we need to be deprogrammed and re-trained. We need to practice our training in the "Kingdom" ways of living. It's especially difficult to try to "live in the world, but not of it"—engaging in the world without falling back into worldly ways.

Cohorting or Church Participation This may sound like the last thing that some of you might want to do, but it works. It doesn't have to be meeting on Sundays in a traditional church building, let alone joining the institution of a church by becoming an official member. It can mean getting together with a cohort of like-minded and like-spirited people at a coffee shop, or in someone's apartment. The main thing is to find a group of Jesus-oriented people who pledge to intentionally be there for each other and to be "for" each other as they live their lives. Being involved in a *healthy* Christian congregation or community is sort of like being at a military boot camp—but for being trained in how to love instead of how to kill. A healthy cohort will offer experiences where people have the opportunity to rub up against the lives of other fellow believers and to put into practice what they're learning about. This can even involve people buying a

---

[345] Biblically, *the world* means dominating human created systems, powers and principalities. Hence, the ways of the world refer to dominating, oppressive ways. For more see Appendix IV.

home and living together in intentional Christian community, sharing their possessions, and life in general, with others (like the early Christians did, see Acts 2 and 4).

Doing activities and ministries teaches more than any sermon or book ever could. As primates, we humans learn best by doing and watching others who've been at it longer than we have.[346] People can say they are Christians even though they aren't active with a church or Christian community. However, a person who meets on a regular basis with fellow believers will be far more effective as a worker in God's Kingdom than someone who doesn't. When we are active in a Christian community we get the benefits of hearing the Gospel, studying the Bible, being inspired to do God's work, engaging in sacred rituals with others, praising God together, participating in community projects, mutual support and accountability, opportunities to serve and lead, and practicing the ways of Jesus.

Similarly, people can say that they are football players. Yet, if they only workout on their own and never train with the team, they won't learn new plays and practice drilling them. They won't be able to learn from players who are more seasoned and better than they are. And, if they will never show up for the games . . . well, you do the math.

Christians are by definition members of the living Body of Christ, which is the Church universal. Being active with a local church or Christian community is our way of being on the team. Your teammates are your fellow ministers, the ones who help you grow in the faith and with whom you worship, celebrate, grieve, play, pray, learn, and serve God. Proverbs 27:17 says, *"As iron sharpens iron, so one person sharpens another"*. Being active in a local church or Christian cohort involves rubbing up against other living, breathing people who are struggling along and living life as best they can. Sometimes we offend and hurt each other. Those are moments to cherish. They are the crucible that tests and refines us. In the safety of this cocoon of grace and love we can practice forgiveness and reconciliation, loving and being loved.

---

[346] Learning really is largely "monkey see, monkey do." French Philosopher René Girard (and Aristotle before him) calls this process *mimesis*.

As Jane Redmont put it in her Open Letter to Anne Rice[347]

> *"What I am writing to tell you is that there's no such creature as a lone follower of Jesus. You can't be a Jesus-person away in a corner. Even hermits pray in Communion with a larger tradition, a church beyond themselves in a world which is the place where God becomes incarnate."*

The following parable[348] is a bit hokey but it does convey the value of being active with a local church or Christian ministry:

> *The story is told of a man named John who had once been faithful to attend his church regularly, but had grown lackadaisical recently. The Pastor knew that he hadn't seen the gentleman in a while, so he went for a visit. John greeted the Pastor and welcomed him in, directing him to the chair beside the fireplace. The pastor didn't mention anything about his concern about not having seen him in awhile, instead he simply said, "So, what's up with you these days? How are you doing?" As John started responding, the pastor listened. After John had finished talking. The pastor casually grabbed the fireplace tongs, picked up a hot coal from the fire, and set it away from the fire, out on the hearth. Both men then watched the coal. While the fire roared on, the coal that had been red hot began to lose its heat. It gradually lost its red color, and then cooled off so that it became cool to the touch. The Pastor picked up the coal, and handed it to John for a moment . . . neither man said a word. Then the Pastor reached out and took the coal back from John, and returned it to the roaring fire . . . and in just a few short moments, the coal once again glowed red hot, as the pile of flaming coals caused it to heat up again. The pastor then got to his feet, put his hat on,*

---

[347] Anne Rice is a popular author who famously became a Christian and then in the summer of 2010, "quit Christianity for the sake of Christ" due to her frustrations with hypocrisy and various tendencies and stances within the Catholic Church. This is from a blog called The Episcopal Café, August, 2010, http://www.episcopalcafe.com/daily/episcopal_church/the_only_thing_that_makes.php

[348] Source unknown.

and shook John's hand. At that point, John looked at the pastor and said, "You know, I think you might start seeing a bit more of me in church again."

There are a lot of you who are probably feeling a bit resistant to the idea of visiting church—let alone joining one. Some of you have felt burned by members of the Church when they weren't at their best. Maybe you've seen them at their worst. You see them as a bunch of hypocrites. Fair enough. I'm not going to try to talk you out of your experience. What happened to you happened. It shouldn't have. On behalf of the Church, we are sorry.

But I would like to share the following dialogue that took place on someone's Facebook page:

> **Original poster:** Spencer and Heidi and Stephen Baldwin calling themselves "Christians" was more than enough evidence to convince me that that's a "club" I definitely DO NOT want a membership in.

> **Somebody else:** "If there's a hypocrite standing between you and God, it's only because they are closer to God than you are."

> **Roger Wolsey:** It's unfair to judge an entire group based upon its weakest members. In my experience, most people who come to church have some part of them that is seeking/wanting to change, to become more Christ-like. There are always a few who are there because someone dragged them, or because they want to "keep up appearances," etc. but most come because they want to change for the better—even if they have a long way to go.

> **Original poster:** "I don't care to belong to a club that accepts people like me as a member."
> —Groucho Marx

> **Roger Wolsey** . . . and getting to that observation, and choosing to join that club *anyway*, is precisely what

Christianity is all about; i.e., it's about accepting grace even if we don't feel worthy or that we merit it—and extending the same to others who we think don't deserve it either. It's about focusing more on the common ground that we share than on the things that might divide us. It's about making space for people to be "real."

Now, all of that said, the other reason why you should be a part of a congregation or intentional Christian community isn't because it will change you—it's because you will change it. Your presence and participation will change, and help create, the Church of the future. You'll be a new fish in the fishbowl and the fishbowl will have to adjust and grow. Come on in. We need you to stir the pot!

Worship Luke reports that it was Jesus' custom to worship God at synagogues on the Sabbath day. The Sabbath day is a day set apart for simply resting and being especially present to God. In the Jewish tradition, worship services often center on reminding people that they are God's chosen people. Hearing reminders from the scriptures about the covenant they have with God and how God promises to continue to be there for them are part of that. Jesus didn't go to synagogue because he felt he had to, but because he wanted to. This should be our attitude and approach to worship too. It's is a good habit to bring into your life.

I could point to recent studies that people who are active in local churches live longer and happier lives,[349] but those aren't the reasons I have in mind. For Christianity, the goal isn't longevity or happiness. Our aim is to be *faithful* and to experience joyful, abundant lives as humble servants who have a sense of joy in God's Kingdom. As Jesus, the early Christian martyrs, and Martin

[349] One academic study suggested that churchgoers—Methodist ones in England—live up to 7 years longer than the rest of the population, http://www.telegraph.co.uk/news/newstopics/religion/7855002/Methodists-live-more-than-seven-years-longer-than-rest-of-population.html; see also this article about a Duke study showing that churchgoers "live longer, enjoy better health, and gain better job prospects, "http://www.creationtips.com/christianadvantage.html

Luther King, Jr. demonstrated, this doesn't necessarily mean living a long time or being especially happy.

I think that the Sunday Church experience among the progressive and conservative Christian churches have more in common than not. They're usually on Sundays,[350] they typically last 1-2 hours, and there is often a time of shaking hands and "passing the peace." Songs are sung, the Bible is read, and a sermon is preached that attempts to make that Bible passage relevant to our lives today and to challenge and inspire us. There are times for prayer, people are invited to contribute financial gifts to support the work of the church, and occasionally, people participate in the sacraments of Baptism and Holy Communion.

There are some differences in the content of the lyrics of the songs and hymns, what is prayed for and how, the content of the sermons, and the frequency and understanding of the sacraments.[351] But both conservative and progressive churches seek to offer a space and an environment that allows people to connect, commune, offer thanks, offer praise, and to stretch, and grow. Worship and the various things that happen in churches on Sundays provide many people with opportunities to share their gifts and graces and serve. It isn't just paid staff that does the work of ministry. Sunday worship helps provide a weekly touchstone for people to take stock, reassess, remember the best of who they are, seek forgiveness for their failings during the previous week, and to be inspired, equipped, and empowered to boldly face the next week in faith and with a sense of purpose.

Both progressive and conservative Christian worship services differ from *two other* forms of worship that operate under the

---

[350] Though the earliest Jewish Christians worshipped on Saturdays, at some point a decision was made to switch to Sundays. The logic for this shift is that Sunday is the first day of the week and Sunday is the day Jesus was resurrected. This reminds us of the fresh start that we have in Christ. I think the shift also may've taken place as the Church became more dominated by gentiles and they sought to distance themselves from the Jews.

[351] Not all Christian worship services include singing, public prayers, or sermons. The "unstructured" (non-churchy) sort of Quakers mostly sit in silence together for an hour—with perhaps a few respected elders sharing brief insights afterward.

guise of Christianity—the **"gospel of wealth and prosperity"** and **"churches of positive thinking."** Those sorts of ministries have a large presence on the television. When pastors in $1000 suits preach, "God wants you to have financial success in your life"; "How well you're doing financially is a sign of how close you are to God and shows God's favor and blessings for your life;" "The more money you send in to support their ministry, the more God will bless you in your life;" or, "If you give $10, God will send you $100!" that is the false gospel of wealth and success, not the Gospel of Jesus Christ.

When preachers smile all the time and tell you warm and fuzzy, feel-good messages that only seek to inspire and entertain you, that isn't the real Gospel. When pastors preach sermons that never challenge you with the radical demands and challenges of following Jesus and his sacrificial way of the cross, that isn't the real Gospel. When sermons never address the darker, sadder parts of life, that isn't the real Gospel. Those are ministries are based more upon the teachings from Norman Vincent Peale's book *The Power of Positive Thinking* (1952) than they are on the Bible.[352] The "Hour of Power" TV ministry aired worships services from Robert Schuller's Crystal Cathedral in Garden Grove, CA. Schuller's messages were based upon Peale's book. The Lakewood Church in Houston, TX is the platform for Joel Olsteen's popular TV ministry that draws from this same source.[353]

Some of the largest ministries in the U.S. focus solely on the superficial, the "light and fluffy," and make no room for the very real down times and struggles of life. They make no allowance for being real. Their sermons are only about bellowing sails but never about what happens when we hit a sandbar or when the winds snap our masts. Authentic Christian ministry honors those times—without simply chalking it up to "God's Will." Humans need to lament. We need some dirges. We need some blues. We need some country. We need some adagios. We need some punk, emo and grunge. We need messages and music that recognize and

---

[352] That book was written in the early years of the "new thought" movement that has become new-agey Christianity, and is arguably similar to the Unity Church, Christian Science, and The Course on Miracles.

[353] See: http://www.spiritwatch.org/firebehindsmile3of4.htm

honor those parts of life too. In my experience, churches that lean toward progressive Christianity embrace more of this balanced, fullness of life.

Perhaps like how some people are drawn to *Twinkies*, *Hostess* fruit pies, and lottery tickets, both the gospel of wealth and prosperity and the power of positive thinking ministries are attractive to many in this country—just as they are equally off-putting to many others one. Please know they are not what Christianity is all about.

One unique aspect of Christian worship is the celebration of the sacraments of Holy Communion and Baptism—things you'll never see on the major TV ministries. Words such as these are what pastors typically say when leading Communion: *On the night before Jesus was betrayed, he gathered his disciples together in the upper room of a dwelling and they had a meal together. In the course of that meal, He took bread, raised it to God and gave thanks, and then he broke that bread saying, "Take, eat, this is my body broken for you." Then he took a cup and raised it to God and gave thanks, and then he said, "Take, drink, this is My blood, my life-force, shed for the forgiveness of sins. Me. For you. It's the wine of the new covenant, for you and for many. Do this in remembrance of Me."* To my mind, the real power of the experience isn't in the bread or the juice/wine themselves. The power is when the people come forward to partake and to serve each other with reasonably common intent and purpose—even if that purpose is as vague as "somehow participating or communing in God's grace and love." Some Christian traditions celebrate Communion every week.[354] Others do it once a month, and some less frequently. Most progressive Christian congregations offer Communion at least once a month as part of their worship services, with many offering it every week.

We don't become more holy by receiving Communion more frequently—at least not merely due to ingesting the bread and the juice or wine. None of God's grace that comes to us through the Holy Spirit in the sacraments is "magically medicinal" in a literal sense (that would be superstition). What makes the sacraments holy is our *participating* in them. They are rituals that are practiced among a certain community—the intentional community of

---

[354] I understand some Catholic ministries offer Communion every day of the week!

fellow believers, who pledge to help each other to strive to be faithful and to be the best we can be and the best that we can become. The sacraments are rituals to help us re-commit and re-pledge this intention to each other and to deepen our bonds of intentionally Christian fellowship, discipleship and authentic relationship. In these sacred rituals, God's presence and grace are uniquely experienced and woven into our lives. In them, we transcend time and space, and commune. We find solidarity with all Christians, past, present, and future—across the globe (and even outside of Earth's orbit).

There is a certain seriousness in the sacraments (with Communion symbolically[355] remembering Jesus' unjust death and baptism symbolically participating with Jesus in dying to our former selves and rising up as new creations) progressive Christian ministries emphasize *celebrating* them. They are joyous occasions for claiming the truth that we are loved, forgiven, and accepted children of God. They aren't times for dwelling on our failings and beating ourselves up for not being worthy.

My personal take on Communion is that we celebrate how the early disciples discovered the risen Christ in their midst as they journeyed on the road to Emmaus after Jesus was executed. The spirit of the living Christ was made known to them "in the breaking of the bread" (Luke 24:13-35). This was the supreme "*A-ha!*" moment of all time. In my opinion, that moment had less to do with a physically resurrected Jesus than it did with people finally "getting" who Jesus was and what he was about. That meant they got who God is and what God is about. And that translates into knowing who they were and what they could be about! When we participate in Holy Communion, we celebrate Jesus' modeling and manifesting the epitome of his message of self-giving, unconditional love. "Me, for you." We celebrate his offering of his entire self, including his very life, and his willingness to give his whole *being* to help us know God's love for us.

---

[355] The Roman Catholic tradition differs in that for them, Communion isn't symbolic but transsubstantive; i.e., they believe that when the priest says the words of institution, the bread and wine actually become Jesus' flesh and blood and that Jesus is physically present in those elements.

As Lutheran emergent pastor Nadia Bolz-Weber puts it "In the moment when the bread and wine become other, something is made whole, and we take it, hoping it is us." That is Jesus' prayer for us.

It is not enough to merely participate in the sacraments of grace. We are called to live a life that is sacramental, demonstrating to the world those outward and visible signs of inward and invisible grace. Our worship of God should extend beyond the walls of a church or house church "Therefore, I urge you, brothers, in view of God's mercy, to offer your bodies as living sacrifices, holy and pleasing to God—this is your spiritual act of worship" (Romans 12:1).

Many progressive Christian churches eclectically incorporate a vast array of worship elements—picking from mostly Christian traditions that are centuries old as well as quite contemporary. This has sometimes been called a "Celtic" approach to worship. Aside from the aforementioned elements of passing the peace, singing songs, reading scripture, hearing a sermon, praying and the sacraments, progressive Christian worship may also weave in centering prayer, walking a labyrinth,[356] Taize[357] worship, small group discussions, making art, and more. It may also be less clergy-centered and driven.

Even though progressive Christian worship is Christ-centered, it is open to practices from other religious traditions, perhaps including, yoga, meditation, songs, and certain prayers as valid

---

[356] A labyrinth is a large maze-like path built into or painted on a floor where worshippers prayerfully walk in silence to help sense the Divine. It's a contemplative practice and it's a form of moving meditation. Labyrinths were first built on the stone floors of cathedrals in Europe during the Middle Ages. Christians were encouraged to make a pilgrimage to the Holy Land (Israel/Palestine) at least once in their lives. But few people could actually do this so walking labyrinths served as a proxy. They remind us of Jesus' "stations of the cross," and they help us take stock of where we're at in our larger spiritual journeys.

[357] *Taize* worship is that form of worship that was started by the Taize community in France (an ecumenical Protestant mystical young people's movement). The Taize style of worship involves following a simple liturgy that involves lots of chant/mantra-like songs, often in Latin, and no sermons.

expressions of genuine faith. Progressive Christians are unafraid to borrow and adapt from other sources,[358] for example, from Gaelic runes,

> *"Deep peace of the running wave to you. Deep peace of the flowing air to you. Deep peace of the quiet earth to you. Deep peace of the shining stars to you. Deep peace of the infinite peace to you;"*

And from the Hindu *Upanishads,*

> *"Lead me from death to life, from falsehood to truth. Lead me from despair to hope, from fear to trust. Lead me from hate to love, from war to peace. Let peace fill our heart, our world, our universe. Peace, peace, peace."*

That some Christians would deny that such expressions are Godly seems most stubborn to those of us from the progressive Christian perspective.

Sacrificial giving Second only to teaching about the Kingdom of God, the topic that Jesus spoke most often about was money and our relationship to it. Jesus said, "For where your treasure is, there your heart will be also" (Matthew 6:21) and that we "cannot serve both God and money" (Matthew 6:24). Many progressive Christians consider national and corporate budgets, as well as our personal checkbooks, to be moral and spiritual documents. They show what our true priorities are and what we really worship. In the case of the U.S. budget, it would seem that we put our trust and reliance upon our military might. In the case of many Americans, aside from food, housing and health care, the lion's

---

[358] Borrowing and adapting from extra/non-Christian sources doesn't mean *syncretism.* The term syncretism is used to refer to the practice of bringing together two or more distinct sets of beliefs to create an entirely new one. Most progressive Christians wish to be Christians, not create some sort of new hybrid religion. Syncretism also refers to people from a majority group capriciously and disrespectfully attempting to engage in rituals, customs, and traditions of minority groups. Progressive Christians seek to avoid that.

share of our discretionary spending may be in memberships to country clubs, entertainment, fashion, and their pet animals.[359] It's ironic that many Christians in the U.S. consider our country to be a "Christian nation" yet the overwhelming majority of American churchgoers don't tithe 10% of their income. Instead, they donate only a paltry 2.5% of their income to their churches. Many put less in the offering plate than they spend on one cup of coffee at a coffee shop. Studies have indicated that poorer congregants give a higher percentage of their income than wealthier members do. As Jesus put it, "It is easier for a camel to go through the eye of a needle than it is for a rich man to enter the Kingdom of God" (Matthew 19:24). This is related to the seventh of Gandhi's "Seven Deadly Sins of Today,"[360]

> *Wealth without Work*
> *Pleasure without Conscience*
> *Science without Humanity*
> *Knowledge without Character*
> *Politics without Principle*

---

[359] I'm not seeking to guilt-trip us. Unless we're feeling called to be monks or nuns we aren't called to take a vow of poverty. There's nothing wrong with enjoying some of the nice things in life such as opportunities to travel if we keep those things in perspective: 1) Material items are just stuff—stuff that could be taken from us at any time. It's good to remember that who we are isn't defined by the car we drive or the size of our TV sets. To quote the movie Fight Club, "You are not your pants!"; 2) if we choose to buy things that enhance other people's lives (e.g. items that are Fair Trade certified), then we're "doing good" by providing needed income for others; 3) Having beauty in our homes contributes to a happy, uplifting environment; 4) It's fun to get dressed up sometimes, and that's OK, too (though I've gotten to be pretty savvy at finding cool clothes at thrift stores). Moreover, we don't want people to lose their homes because they are tithing instead of paying the mortgage. Giving needs to take into account our survival needs. The same thing goes for medical debt—an increasing problem for many citizens.

[360] This listing is found in many sources, including, http://www. deadlysins.com/features/gandhi.htm

Commerce without Morality
Worship without Sacrifice

Don't those words ring huge bells of truth? Don't they tell it like it is? A lot of young progressive minded adults like to quote various sayings of Gandhi. It's cool to quote Gandhi. But what would it mean take seriously and act on the things that he wrote and said? One of the implications is that true worship involves a sense of sacrificial giving. Giving to a church or charity that helps others should be a higher priority in our lives than it is. That can mean not purchasing all season passes for skiing or sports teams; switching to renting movies instead of paying to see them in theatres, or simply drinking one less cup of coffee at the local coffee house per week. The point is that when our giving involves sacrifice, this helps us realize our dependence upon God—and that leads to spiritual growth.

John Wesley instructed the early Methodists to *"Earn all you can, save all you can, to give all you can."* For Wesley, money is a powerful tool for doing good in the world. It is only useful and blessed to the extent that we use it in that way. Wesley practiced what he preached, and as his income grew because of the heavy publication of numerous books and journals, he made a point to maintain the same humble standard of living. He gave away to the poor what he did not need. He said that if he died with more than ten pounds to his name, he could be called a liar. He died with less.

We aren't all called to be single, itinerant preachers. Some of us have mouths to feed and bodies to clothe. We are motivated in part to perform well in our work because of the hope of reaping the fruits of our labors. Rather than legalistically insisting that people tithe 10% of their income, progressive Christianity encourages people to give in response to their awareness of God's presence and blessings in their lives. We're invited to give because God first loved us. For some people, that may mean 1% of their income, but for others, it may mean 5-10%, or much more. I contend that many progressive pastors don't stress giving *enough* as many of their churches are struggling financially. It's easier to avoid talking about these matters with their flocks for fear of turning off people who are already wary of the Church. However, it is my experience that young adults who are seeking to grow spiritually, and who seek to follow Jesus, yearn to have their faith taken seriously. They have a need to support and give to ministries that authentically share Jesus' loving message with the world. They just need to be asked.

Work Theologian Frederick Buechner says, *"Vocation is where your gifts, and the world's needs, meet."* I like that. I realize that during times of economic downturns, simply having a job, any job, may be the best that many of us can do. There is usually some degree of choice involved however. Even if it is the choice of others who notice us and invite us to work for them based upon what they see in us. God made each of us unique individuals and we each have different personalities, temperaments and aptitudes. Some of us are more introverted, some more extroverted, some more intuitive, others more sensing, and so on. Some people thrive as mechanics, some as accountants, others as teachers, others as artists, etc. It's frustrating for people with one set of gifts and graces to work in settings that aren't natural for them and where they can't shine as God intended. As poet Maya Angelou says,

> *"You can only become truly accomplished at something you love. Don't make money your goal. Instead, pursue the things you love doing, and then do them so well that people can't take their eyes off you."*

There are, however, times in the course of our working lives where many of us do have to put in some time performing tasks that we aren't well suited for. It's a great blessing to society that so many of us have had stints of working as custodians, street cleaners, waiters, dishwashers, and the like. This broadens our perspectives, and teaches us humility, empathy, and compassion. There is dignity in all work and certain people feel called and well suited to some of those menial tasks. However, when we find ourselves working jobs that we aren't suited for, we'd do well to heed the words of theologians Thomas Merton, and A.W. Tozer, respectively:

> *"Do not depend on the hope of results . . . your work may seem worthless and achieve no result at all, or results opposite to what you expect. As you get used to this idea, you start to concentrate not on results, but on value, rightness, truth of*

the work itself. You struggle less and less for ideas and more and more for specific people. In the end, the reality of personal relationship saves everything."

"It is not what a man does that determines whether his work is sacred or secular, but why he does it."

Work for the cause of love.

Reading the Bible The Bible is our primary source of information about God, Jesus and our ancestors in the faith. It's a good idea to pray before you read it to seek the guidance of the Holy Spirit to help you interpret it. It's helpful to consult study aides to help you learn about the background of those texts and to learn what they may have meant to their original audiences. The use of a good Study Bible and Bible Commentary are incredibly beneficial (especially if you use several to seek different perspectives). *Lectio Divina* ("Divine reading") is an increasingly popular approach to pondering the scriptures in progressive Christian circles. It shares similar roots with centering prayer. It's a contemplative, mystical, approach where one hears a passage read aloud three times, each time being invited to hear through a different lens or intention. Each time, seeking the gift that God may have in store for you at that moment. This is usually done in a group setting but it can be done solo.

It is best to read the Bible with a loving attitude, seeking to discern how God is speaking through those texts to love you and to urge you to love others. Many progressive Christians also read passages from various spiritual giants of the faith along with the Bible (for example, the remarks and writings of Luther, Wesley, Gandhi, Dorothy Day, Oscar Romero, Mother Theresa, Rumi, Thomas Merton, and Martin Luther King, Jr.). Spirit knows spirit, light knows light, and love knows love.[361]

---

[361] Many Christians also spend time reading from a "Daily Devotions" booklet. There are subscriptions to monthly devotional booklets, *The Upper Room* being a popular example. These booklets will often have a brief Bible passage, a relevant quote from a famous person, and then a short reflection written by someone. They may also include a question or two to ponder and a short prayer to pray

Being present to the present moment You may be familiar with the saying, *"Yesterday is history. Tomorrow is a mystery. Today is a gift, that's why it is called the present."* It may seem trite but it is quite profound and packs a wallop. It conveys the deep spiritual truth that what matters is the now. It is really all that we ever have. Yet, it is so easy for us to become stuck in the past, or made impotent in the present because of anxiety about the future. From a Christian perspective, Fulton Oursler said "Many of us crucify ourselves between two thieves—regret for the past and fear of the future." Having residue and influence from our past can't be avoided. It's part of the air we breathe. The same is true with concern about what's next. Regret and fear cannot be avoided. There are those who are crippled by fear, and robbed of any sense of contentment, peace or fulfillment.

The apostle Paul spoke to our tendency to be overly defined by our past when he said, *"Therefore, if anyone is in Christ, he is a new creation; the old has gone, the new has come* (2 Corinthians 5:17). Jesus spoke to human anxiety about the future when he said

> *"Therefore I tell you, do not worry about your life, what you will eat or drink; or about your body, what you will wear. Is not life more important than food, and the body more important than clothes? The birds of the air; they do not sow or reap or store away in barns, and yet your heavenly Father feeds them. Are you not much more valuable than they? Who of you by worrying can add a single hour to his life?*
>
> *"And why do you worry about clothes? See how the lilies of the field grow. They do not labor or spin. Yet I tell you that not even Solomon in all his splendor was dressed like one of these. If that is how God clothes the grass of the field, which is here today and tomorrow is thrown into the fire, will he not much more clothe you, O you of little faith? So do not worry, saying, 'What shall we eat?' or 'What shall we drink?' or 'What shall*

---

as you start your day; e.g., http://www.upperroom.org/devotional/ Another option is one of the "Read the Bible in a Year" guides that are available online; e.g., http://www.oneyearbibleonline.com/ & http://www.biblegateway.com/resources/readingplans/

we wear?' For the pagans run after all these things, and your heavenly Father knows that you need them. But seek first his Kingdom and his righteousness, and all these things will be given to you as well. Therefore do not worry about tomorrow, for tomorrow will worry about itself. Each day has enough trouble of its own. (Matthew 6:25-34)

I have found that engaging in practices such as meditation, centering prayer, and yoga immensely helpful in becoming more attuned to the present moment. Taking walks with my dog helps too. Animals live far more readily in the present. Do the things that help you to trust that God has forgiven the past and will take care of the future.[362] We can only fully love others when we're embracing the present moment.

Living simply also helps foster an ability to love in this world. The more property and assets we own, the more stuff that we have, the more distracted we are from what matters—other people. We become less available to our fellow human beings if we're concerned about material goods. I'm not calling for you to sell all of your possessions and give them to the poor. I certainly haven't done it. But Jesus makes that call (Luke 12:33) and we'd do well to consider moving toward it.[363] Living simply applies not only

---

[362] My friend Cynthia Beard would qualify this, saying: "The only thing I struggle with, in this concept, is that suffering still happens—sometimes great, deep suffering. I think of those who were imprisoned in concentration camps. God did not take care of most of them in the way that we tend to say we'll be taken care of. This also gets back to Jesus' final words on the cross: 'Why have you forsaken me?' Because he taught that we will be provided for, and yet maybe he felt abandoned in those final moments. That's the most abject type of suffering—feeling abandoned in that way. So maybe there will indeed be times when the future won't be taken care of. Maybe children in Africa will continue to get raped. Maybe human rights violations of all kinds will continue to occur. This becomes the primary reason that *we* must be advocates." I fully agree. See also the previous discussion about suffering and theodicy in Chapter 9.

[363] See also, "But will it make you happy?" Stephanie Rosenbloom, http://www.nytimes.com/2010/08/08/business/08consume.html?_r=2

to material things but also to how we "live" our lives. Minimize the drama. Don't date people who make things more complicated than they need to be. Try to keep the peace as much as possible. Avoid conflict unless it's absolutely necessary. Use naturally based cleaning products instead of ones containing bleaches, anti-bacterials, ethylene-based glycol, chlorine, phosphates, and the like. When possible, eat whole; natural, organic foods (instead of proceed ones) and slow cook them. Consider not having the TV on while you eat. As Henry David Thoreau put it, *"As you simplify your life, the laws of the universe will be simpler; solitude will not be solitude, poverty will not be poverty, nor weakness weakness."*

Fasting Intentionally avoiding and not partaking in things that we see as good seems counterintuitive. It certainly goes against the culture of selfish hedonism. Many Christians don't like the idea of it either. Think about it, how many Christians in America fast? Not many. Sure, there are a handful of folks who abstain from red meat on Fridays during Lent (mostly Catholics), but other than that? It isn't an accident that our population is the most obese citizenry in the history of the world. Somehow Christianity in America sanctions and blesses the pursuits of "the American dream" of having a large house in the suburbs with 2.5 cars, children, and pets; and subscriptions to cable TV, the Internet, cellphones, and so much more (most of which contribute to obesity). We often think of fasting as avoiding food or drink. That is a powerful form of it. Limiting our intake of food reminds us of our utter dependence upon God—and that a lot of people around the world do not have enough to eat. One can also benefit by taking intentional timeouts from sex, masturbation, shopping, television, the news, and more. In fact, for many of today's overly plugged-in, excessively multi-tasking young adults, taking fasts from our incessant use of Facebook, and from our cell phones and MP3 players might do us a world of good. Times of fasting can help us to hear the God who loves us and who urges us to love others—speaking "in a still small voice" (1 Kings 19:12)—that we often drown out.

Doing good in the world Jesus expanded the age-old, trans-cultural value of not harming other people to teaching us to doing unto others, as we'd have them do unto us. That was a radical development. Historically, people took take of their own, not others.

It's not that other religions don't care about other people. However, what makes Christianity unique is its making active concern for others *central* to the faith. It is the very heart of our religion.[364] As Nicolai Berdyaev put it, *"Bread for myself is a material concern, but bread for my neighbor is a spiritual concern."* John Chrysostom said, *"This is the rule of most perfect Christianity, it's the most exact definition, its highest point, namely, the seeking of the common good. For nothing can so make a person an imitator of Christ as caring for [their] neighbors."* And John Wesley said, *"Do all the good you can; by all the means you can; in all the ways you can; in all the places you can; at all the times you can; to all the people you can; as long as ever you can."*

Without going so far as to call it a *sacrament*, Wesley considered performing good deeds and acts of compassion to be a *means of grace*—a way for humans to connect directly to God and to experience God's saving love and presence. It's been said that one discovers whom their true friends are by who shows up to help them move. Be that friend.

This can range from random acts of kindness to participating in more organized community service projects and volunteerism. As Mother Theresa put it, "Kind words can be short and easy to speak, but their echoes are truly endless" and, "As one person I cannot change the world, but I can change the world of one person."

If the efforts of several people are banded together, even more significant change can take place. As anthropologist Margaret Mead famously put it, *"Never doubt that a small group of thoughtful, committed citizens can change the world. Indeed, it is the only thing that ever has."*

This brings us back to our previous discussion of the biblical value and importance of *hesed*, which means "loving-kindness." It's about not living in ways that exclude, oppress, mistreat, or alienate others.[365] It's about actively giving a damn about the needs of others and seeking to meet those needs.

---

[364] Jesus didn't invent that concept however. He merely helped the Jews recall a concept that had apparently been minimized or made dormant from their own tradition; i.e. Leviticus 19:18.

[365] *Hesed* is about not living inhospitably as the people of Sodom did. *"Sodom and her daughters never did what you and your daughters have done. She and her daughters were arrogant, overfed and unconcerned; they did not help the poor and needy. They were haughty and did detestable*

Hesed can happen on large scales by helping build houses through Habitat for Humanity or repairing cleft lips in developing countries through Doctors Without Borders. It can also take place on a small scale—by having a healthy attitude. It's been said, "Being kind is more important than being right." I think there's wisdom there. In other words, be as right as you like, but unless you are also being kind then please keep your rightness and correctness to yourself. As Maya Angelou puts it, "I've learned that people will forget what you said, forget what you did, but never will forget how you made them feel." And as James Barrie put it, "Always be a little kinder than necessary." And as Plato put it long before, "Be kind, for everyone you meet is fighting a hard battle." Doing good deeds may not get you to heaven, but it sure won't hurt. Who knows? It may be just the thing to allow God to mold you and nudge you toward the next stage in spiritual growth—perhaps, doing all that you do in love.

Advocating for Social justice Personal conversion and transformation is ultimately for the purpose of social transformation. Christianity isn't about getting to heaven. It's about doing all that we can to help others get there—and to experience as much of it as possible here and now. This means following Jesus' teachings—to put the needs of others ahead of your own. As Nelson Mandela puts it, "to be free is not merely to cast off one's chains, but to live in a way that respects and enhances the freedom of others." There are worldly powers and systems in place that actively oppress others and we are obliged to try to end such oppression. This may mean letters to encourage Congress to have the U.S. meet its financial pledges for the Millennium Goals to end global poverty. It may mean participating in the lobbying efforts of organizations such as Bread for the World. It may mean being an advocate for Fair Trade products. It may mean doing what you can to put an end to human slavery, to seek to end warfare, and to be an advocate for the environment. In all of these things, what matters is doing them out of love—the kind of love God showed in "For God so loved the world . . ." (John 3:16).

---

things before me." Ezekiel 16:48-50 The men of the town also acted inhospitably (to an extreme) toward the three angels God sent to visit them; i.e. they wanted to rape them.

Self-reflection In our hectic, go-go-go, overly "plugged in", multi-tasking lives, many of us have come to be uncomfortable just being alone with ourselves—let alone quietly. Many people these days can't just spend a morning or an evening alone in their homes, or even just exercising, without some background noise on (TV, computer, music, etc.). If we don't spend time in stillness and quiet, it makes it difficult for us to notice coincidences and patterns or to ponder and reflect upon our interactions with others during the day. It also greatly handicaps our ability to pray. One of the things that make us unique among the many other species on our planet is our ability to be aware of ourselves, and our mortality. We have a profound capacity to be self-reflective and it is a profound tragedy that so few of us spend adequate time doing it.

> *Carl Jung recounts a story of a clergyman who had been working fourteen hours a day and was suffering from emotional exhaustion. Jung's advice was that he should work eight hours a day, then go home and spend the evening alone in his study. The clergyman agreed to follow Jung's advice precisely. He worked eight hours, and then went home and to his study, where he played some Chopin and read a novel by Hesse. The following day he read Thomas Mann and played Mozart. On the third day he went to see Jung and complained that he was no better. "But you didn't understand," Jung replied, on hearing his account. "I didn't want you with Hermann Hesse or Thomas Mann or even Mozart or Chopin. I wanted you to be all alone with yourself." "Oh but I can't think of any worse company," answered the clergyman. Jung replied, "And yet this is the self you inflict on other people fourteen hours a day."*[366]

We need quiet time to ponder. "How is it with my soul? What is God up to in my life? Where am I seeing God at work in the world? What would help my relationships be healthier and more solid?" Many find that writing a journal helps immensely with this process. I use blogging as one of the ways to meet this need in my life. It also helps that I no longer watch television and I no longer have a need to have the radio on.

---

[366] from *Experiencing God* by Kenneth Leech, Harper Collins, 1989.

I've been in a process of getting to know myself. While there are some parts of me I'm not thrilled about, on the whole, I sort of like me and I'm increasingly comfortable just being with me. Do the things that help you to be more self-reflective. Your loved ones will love you for it.

Shadow work According to Jungian psychology, we all have metaphorical masks that we wear and images (our *personas*) that we seek to put forth in the world for how we'd like to be seen and known. The more that we focus on those idealized images, the more we repress the opposites of whatever our preferred images may be. If I want to be known as "nice, sensitive person," I stuff and hide away the mean, insensitive, jerk parts of me. But, when we try to minimize those darker shadows, we *increase* their power. Unless we do something to embrace and integrate those darker parts of ourselves, they grow and fester until they erupt—sometimes in embarrassing, even career-ending, ways. We need to make friends with our shadows[367] and allow them to communicate and vent on our terms. If we don't, they will speak their peace and they'll do it on their terms. I want to be seen as a "nice guy," so I repress my feelings when people offend or wrong me. When I do that too long, my anger eventually erupts in destructive ways on hapless people who inadvertently trigger me. Usually, what they did was something petty and the damage control is awkward. I prevent this by practicing sharing my feelings of being wronged or slighted in the moment, or at least as close as possible to the event, rather than stuffing it. It scares the hell out of me each time I do this but it really does prevent the volcano from mounting. Spending time pondering how we'd like people to view us and pondering how we don't want them to view us is time well spent.

Shadows thrive on being kept secret. A healthy thing to do is admit what they are and tell people about them. This seems like it would be the *last* thing you'd want to do, but shining some light on them and openly talking about them reduces their power considerably. It may endear you to the people you disclose them to.[368]

---

[367] See: *Make Friends With Your Shadow*, by William Miller, Augsburg Fortress Publishers, 1981.

[368] There are some times when there are practical reasons for *not* disclosing certain aspects of ourselves. This is where a therapist/

This kind of sharing shows that you're a fellow human being who is trying to be authentic. Yep, talking about your dark side makes you more attractive to people than keeping them hidden. It takes some time and practice to get your mind around this, but it's true.

Again, a sage truth is, *"That which we criticize most in others is that which we struggle with most ourselves."* A powerful bit of shadow work is to think about the people in your life who irritate you and rub you the wrong way—the people who you simply can't stand. Then, think about how *you* are *like* those people. Consider how you share some of the same qualities and tendencies that you loathe in them. What you discover may be most revealing. Consider what you can learn from your shadow(s). What are they trying to tell you? You can come to see them as a gift—a gift that can help you be a more gracious and effective vessel of God's love in the world.

Noticing coincidences and patterns One of the ways that humans can sense what God might be up to in our lives is to pay attention to the "God-incidences" where two or more things that are obviously, but unexpectedly, related catch our attention. There may be signs along the way that jump out at us and cause us to pause and wonder. It may be details around meeting people, or happenings and circumstances that are too odd and laden with meaning to be purely random. But everything isn't "a message from God." Discernment is important. As Freud put it, "sometimes a cigar is just a cigar."

Reassessing This is my term for revisiting some of the negative experiences that we've encountered in the past and thinking about them anew. Are there are any lessons that we can take from them? Are there any hidden blessings or gifts that they ended up providing for us? Reassessing at one month, six months and one year after such experiences may be helpful. Just because we may come to see some potential or even actual goodness that may have come from bad stuff, doesn't mean that God intended those bad things to take place. It is often hugely transformative to notice how God may be at work doing damage control and making the best of a negative situation.

Getting Raw and Real Embrace the fullness of your humanity. Sometimes church-going Christians get into the mode of only showing happiness. An REM song describes such persons as

counselor and/or having a confidant can be really useful.

"Shiny, Happy People." But who wants to go to a church where the only feeling that seems to be condoned or allowed is happiness? We need to remember that Jesus modeled a fully human life. He felt the full range of emotions and he showed them. Jesus grieved. He wept. He got angry. He felt forsaken, and more! Indeed, Jesus showed us that it's okay to yell at inanimate objects (his cursing a fig tree) as well as knocking over tables and making a scene—but only if we're prepared to accept the potential consequences.

Not all of us are free with our emotions (except maybe for anger) so engaging in activities that help you to feel deeply and to stretch yourself beyond your comfort zone may be useful. I have found that participating in workshops in red nose clown[369] and butoh dance[370] do this extremely well. I don't take these workshops in order to prepare me to perform them however. Those classes force me to be vulnerable and to expose that vulnerability before others in the class. Similarly, workshops that help us to become more comfortable with intimacy can be a huge blessing. For instance, workshops in Tantra teach deep gazing, and help you to grow in your capacity of seeing and being seen, and being known, accepted and loved just as you are—and loving others just as they are.

Awe & Amazement As Rabbi Abraham Heschel beautifully says, *"Our goal should be to live life in radical amazement. Get up in the morning and look at the world in a way that takes nothing for granted. Everything is phenomenal; everything is incredible; never treat life casually. To be spiritual is to be amazed."* A popular church hymn captures this well, *"O Lord my God when I in awesome wonder consider all the worlds you have made. I see the stars I hear the roaring*

---

[369] "Studying red nose clown is about clearing the way. Your clown is you—you at your most open, vulnerable, sensitive, human and ridiculous. In this workshop we will discover your clown and the enormous pleasure to be in the spotlight, to be complicit with an audience and not shy away. These workshops are not just for actors but also for anyone interested in exploring the beauty of being present and the pleasure to play."—Philippe Gaulier, http://www.rednoseclown.net

[370] Butoh is a form of contemporary dance that originated in post WWII Japan. It embraces an "anti-aesthetic" and is hard to define. It seeks to express the grotesque, angst, and full range of emotions of the human condition.

thunder . . . how great Thou art!" There is so much for us to be nurtured, inspired, and otherwise wowed by in the world around us. It can come to us through noticing the words and behaviors of our co-workers or our neighbors (even our Samaritan ones). It can also happen through nature—a waterfall or the moon's effect on the tides, the beauty of a sunset, the glory of a sunrise, the stunning heavenliness of the Milky Way in a clear night sky, the stubborn "yes!" to life in an animal giving birth in the dead of winter, and the hope of a tree growing out of a rock or a weed busting forth through a cement sidewalk. Such observations on our part are often humbling and result in us taking stock of our improbable, and yet noble, place in the universe. They give us a chance to put things into perspective and they can help to diffuse any excessive emotion, hook, or hang-up that we may be feeling about some conflict or concern in our life. Most of the things that we get hung up about are really no big deal. They're quite inconsequential cosmically speaking. Being aware, awed and amazed at what's around us can help us to shift away from anxiousness and toward the things that matter—namely, love.

Creating and self-expressing Part of how we're created in God's image is that we have the capacity to creatively introduce new things into the world. It's part of our purpose as a species. Humans have an innate need for creative self-expression. Sadly, we sometimes allow that part of ourselves to go dormant. Perhaps it's because our lives get too busy, but I think it's partly because we overly judge the quality of what we create. Since we suspect it's somehow inferior, we don't do it very much (I spoke to this tendency in the poem at the end of Chapter 5). Yet, we need to do this. God and the world crave our efforts to convey what we feel and to creatively express ourselves. As writer Shel Silverstein inspirationally put it

> *"Draw a crazy picture, Write a nutty poem,*
> *Sing a mumble-gumble song, Whistle through your comb.*
> *Do a loony-goony dance, 'Cross the kitchen floor,*
> *Put something silly in the world, That ain't been there before."*[371]

---

[371] http://www.goodreads.com/quotes/show/17041

Playing or listening to Music Many people feel spiritual when they are engaged with music. It touches and affects us in ways that sermons and lectures never can. David soothed King Saul by playing his harp (1 Samuel 16:23); Psalm 150 encourages us to *"Praise him with the sounding of the trumpet, praise him with the harp and lyre, praise him with tambourine and dancing, praise him with the strings and flute, praise him with the clash of cymbals, praise him with resounding cymbals. Let everything that has breath praise the LORD Praise the LORD."* The apostle Paul instructs us to *"speak to each other with psalms, hymns and spiritual songs. Sing and make music in your heart to the Lord"* (Ephesians 5:19). Many younger people feel spiritually connected when listening from a spiritual place, and with spiritual ears to Christian praise and worship songs, as well as the music of U2, Coldplay, The Fray, Xavier Rudd, Sarah McLachlan, Enya, Mary Gauthier, Ben Harper, Keb Mo, Michael Franti, Israel Kamakawiwo'ole, Bob Marley, Eva Cassidy, and so many more. I often play the piano or my trumpet as a form of prayer—expressing the yearnings of my heart in ways that are hard to put words to—and as a way to love God by giving Her a personal recital. I highly recommend music as a spiritual practice. You're probably already doing it. Do it more.

Celebrating and moving our bodies A popular saying in Gnostic-influenced new age circles is "We are spiritual beings having a human experience." I'd say that humans are spiritual *and* physical beings who are having a human experience—that is both physical and spiritual. Too many people are not "in their bodies" (not comfortable and at ease in them). Horses are born to run, birds are born to fly, and humans are born to boogie. Unfortunately, certain forms of Christianity have largely frowned upon paying attention to, let alone, celebrating our bodies. Some Gnostic, anti-flesh values seem to have been woven into their theologies. Or perhaps it's residue from the prudish Victorian era. In either case, it is sad. Some Christian denominations officially condemn dancing and the president of Southern Baptist Seminary just issued a statement that Christians shouldn't practice yoga.[372]

---

[372] "Avoid yoga, it's not Christianity, says Baptist leader," Dylan Lovan, AP, Oct. 7, 2010, http://newsok.com/avoid-yoga-its-not-christianity-says-baptist-leader/article/3502205

Good grief. The kind of yoga that is largely practiced in the West isn't Hinduism or Buddhism, and it isn't anti-Christian (though I suppose some yoga instructors could be, but the same is true with doctors, postal carriers, opera singers, and lawn care professionals). At its best, as T.K.V. Desikachar put it; "Yoga is the practice of observing [and accepting] yourself without judgment." But frankly, most yoga classes in the U.S. are simply exercise classes and most Americans could stand more of that.[373]

Progressive Christianity encourages us to be good stewards of our bodies—our "temples" (1 Corinthians 3:16 & 6:19) and exercise supports that. This includes dancing and walking or biking to work as a way to love the earth. In fact, the more that we take care of our bodies, the better able we are to be effective vessels of love for God to work through in the world. A combination of strength and cardio training is probably best. This improves balance, posture, and stamina and makes it easier for us to do perform physically demanding volunteer or mission work.[374] When we exercise, we love others by demonstrating healthy living and self-love. We set a healthy example for others to follow. Many of the times when I go out for a trail run or do some rock climbing I do so as a form of prayer and a way of communing with God. I also feel more alive, vital, energized and focused on the days that I exercise. Those who say that, "moving our bodies doesn't bring us closer to the Divine" don't know what they're missing.[375]

Repenting When we sin against someone, our primary sin is against God. Repentance is choosing to turn our hearts and minds to God, to confess to God, to cease to sin against God, and resolving to live according to the ways of God. We admit our guilt and resolve not to repeat the offense. It often includes

---

[373]   . . . a pet-peeve of mine as yoga isn't primarily a form of exercise, it's a way of being that encourages a balance of grace, strength, power and flexibility in how we live our lives on and off the mat.

[374]   Not to mention that exercise (especially combined with good sleep and healthy eating) lowers blood pressure and resting heart rate, improves breathing and our oxygen efficiency. This makes us more productive because we are able to think more clearly and make better decisions.

[375]   And they likely could stand to lose a few pounds.

an attempt to make amends.[376] Ultimately, we know that there's nothing we can do to fix something we broke, hurt, violated, or betrayed. Though we are assured that God forgives us, we need to **apologize to the person we wronged, and surrender to the possibility of being forgiven by them.**

Reconciling As discussed earlier, relationships characterize our earthly lives. How we relate matters. When real people are in real relationships, they will bring out the best and worst in each other. At times, they will step on each other's toes, ruffle each other's feathers, and otherwise offend or wrong each other. How we respond to and handle those moments, matters. We can respond from our baser selves and react by retaliating, or by allowing the relationships to become estranged. The ministry of reconciliation is arguably what was most important to Jesus. It's certainly what he did most. Jesus engaged in conflict. He started and resolved conflict. On behalf of his Father, Jesus was an agent of reconciliation. Jesus has given us the ministry and the message of reconciliation in order to further and continue his passion for unity and restoration in this broken world.[377] As Paul put it, *"All this is from God, who reconciled us to himself through Christ, and gave us the ministry of reconciliation"* (2 Corinthians 5:18).

Sometimes people tell me they would love to reconcile with someone they are estranged with, but they can't unless the other person who wronged them, first comes to them apologizing and seeking forgiveness. Jesus didn't put the onus on the person who did the offending, but really on the person who was wronged or offended. As Lewis Smedes put it, *"To forgive is to set a prisoner*

---

[376] This spiritual practice can be misused if the person doing the repenting goes far beyond what is reasonable in terms of making amends. Admitting guilt is important, but this has to include forgiving oneself and moving on. Getting stuck in a cycle of guilt-amends can be harmful if the one who did something wrong and the one who was wronged don't approach the situation with love and a willingness to move on.

[377] Jesus' reconciling extends beyond the individual, inter-personal level, to reconciling people groups of differing beliefs, customs, classes, sexes, ages, and races.

free and to discover that that prisoner was you.[378] Jesus teaches us to "forgive seventy-seven [or seventy times seven] times" (Matthew 18:22). This isn't about forgiving that exact number of times. The point is to do so lavishly as our default way of life. In Jesus' parable of the prodigal son, though the son was not coming back home to apologize and seek familial reparations (instead, merely to work as a common worker on his father's estate), when the father saw the son coming toward him in the distance, he ran out to him with arms wide open and embraced him back into his proper place in the family (Luke 15:11-32). With this in mind, we should ask ourselves, "Do I need to be hurt by what someone said or did? Do I need to carry that grudge? Does it need to become a wedge between us?" Between the values and implications of this parable, and Jesus' Sermon on the Mount, and his lived example, when someone has wronged us, we should realize that we should try to reconcile with the one who wronged us. We share our sadness and our yearning to be reconciled. If there's some small part of the altercation that we did that was less than ideal, we say we're sorry about it. This may nudge the person with whom you're estranged to offer his or her own apology.[379] It's following the example of striving to be like the father who graciously made the first move to reconnect with his wayward son.

Such efforts on our part may or may not work to become restored with someone. We can't control that. Seeking to reconcile and make peace is more important than being right. Sometimes our pride causes us to say "It's the principle of the matter" and that keeps us from seeking to seek to reconcile with someone. That's the wrong principle. The principle that matters is love. Love seeks reconciliation.[380]

---

[378] Note: this approach does not apply to persons who are being abused by someone. In such cases, forgiveness may take place, but the need to get away from the person who is doing the abusing is paramount. That is an important act of self-love. You can still forgive an abuser, but from a safe distance.

[379] This said, when you converse with that person you might discover that the whole thing was all a simple misunderstanding. Often times we over-react and make mountains out of mole-hills.

[380] Attempting reconciliation involves taking risks. We risk being rebuffed and rejected. This is vulnerable stuff and we need to

It's hard to fathom principles like the one just stated above and that leads many of us to hold back from fully taking the leap of faith. Some of the ways of God, and the ways that it would seem God wants us to act, are beyond reason and beyond our perceived capacity to live out. And so, we doubt. It's been said by some that doubt is the opposite of faith—or is at least incompatible with it. Progressive Christianity suggests otherwise.

Doubt I think it's fair to say that we are more often than not people of doubt who have faith, than we are people of faith who have moments of doubt.[381] As André Gide so aptly puts it, *"Believe those who are seeking the truth. Doubt those who find it."* It is best not to suppress or deny doubt. Instead, it's best to honor doubt and give it some breathing room. Once doubt is expressed, many times it seems small in comparison to the potential hope that might be at hand. That alone diffuses it. But there is no need to try to diffuse it or to hurry it along. Why be anxious about it? Let it be. Faith that is real and mature has seasons of doubt—sometimes long ones. Mother Theresa struggled with her faith—for years.[382] If someone you love is doubting, it's okay. All is well. Really.

As a pastor, I've had the honor of leading numerous confirmation classes over the years. I'd like to think that all of the students who've participated in them increased their understandings about Christianity, God, Jesus, and the Church. Pastors get kudos for the number of people who join the church by making professions of faith. But I have a special place in my heart for the few young people who made the choice not to declare that they wanted to become a confirmed member of the church or an intentional follower of Jesus. You'd think I might've done all that I could to try to convince them to join the church with the rest of their peers. One 14-year-old girl simply couldn't get her mind around a God

---

recognize that we might get hurt further in the process. Do it anyway.

[381] I thought I coined those words myself, but I think I heard them uttered by one of the 21 speakers at the "Christianity 21" Conference held in Minneapolis, MN in October, 2009.

[382] "Mother Theresa's Crisis of Faith," David Van Biema, Time Magazine, August 23, 2007, http://www.time.com/time/world/article/0,8599,1655415,00.html

who would love us so much. In her experience, humans are more unlovable than not. My response to her was, "Yeah, that is pretty incredible. In fact, it's preposterous. Just know that there are some of us who do believe that God loves us this much even though we aren't always particularly lovable. For now, just know that we love you and we'll always be here for you." If that young woman ever does decide to join up with the Church, it'll be because she does so on her terms (not due to peer pressure), and she'll be one who brings a mature faith.[383]

The bottom line is this, *when in doubt, do that. God can handle it.* God wants us to be authentic. God wants real relationship with real people. While you're busy doubting, you can still lean on the faith of other people who aren't, currently, in a season of doubt. Vicarious faith is still faith.

Remembering The ancient Hebrews went through many times of doubt. There were times when they felt that God was absent or had abandoned them. They knew this was part of the deal—that it goes hand in hand with being people of faith. They made a point to remember how they'd seen God be active in the past, how God had brought them out of captivity in Egypt, and into the Promised Land. Like those ancient Hebrews, I too have seasons of doubt and remembering ("re-visiting") the instances in my life where I know for sure that God was present and active greatly helps me get through the times when I feel abandoned. I highly recommended re-visiting and cherishing your own spiritual experiences.

Radiating love This may sound a bit flakey perhaps (or like I've lived in Boulder too long), but when I do it, something happens. It's always something good. It's loosely inspired by

---

[383] Conservative Christianity sometimes endorses a "blind faith" approach and makes it difficult for anyone to have doubts or questions. However, it is by doubting that we really know whether something is "real" or authentic. If we blindly accept everything that we are told, we aren't using our analytical skills fully, and this can be really dangerous when it comes to things outside of religious faith. It's being gullible. Examination and reflection include doubt—and it's only through doubt that we can really explain why we believe something (in more than a superficial way).

Jesus' instruction to *"Let your light shine before men"* (Matthew 5:16) and Jesus' shining when he was "transfigured" on a mountaintop (Matthew 17:1-13). I can be somewhat intense at times and not as "chill" as I'd like to be. So one of the practices that I engage in is simply being and trying to be a channel and vessel of God's amazing love. I started doing this when I was promoting the free yoga classes at Wesley Chapel out in front of the student union building at the University of Colorado. At first I'd assertively yell out, "Free Yoga!" and hand little cards to people as they walked by. Over half of them ended up in the trash or recycle bins. I then shifted to a more passive, but far more effective, approach. What I do now is to just stand there with a gentle smile on my face—as calmly and serenely as possible. I allow myself to simply beam out and radiate sunshine, light and love. I hold the flyers in my hands, and one by one, people come to me because they are drawn to the love I send out. They come to me smiling even before they can read what it says on the cards. I don't say a word unless they ask me a question. Few of those flyers get thrown away. It's manifesting the best of what yoga and Christianity offer—unconditional acceptance and breathing gently and non-anxiously in the midst of this chaotic world. It's allowing the message and the medium of conveying it to be one.

Evangelism and witnessing Some of you have just been triggered upon seeing those words. After you recover from wheezing and hyperventilating please read on. Even though progressive Christianity doesn't claim to be the one and only truth nor the only way that God is working in the world, we do have something good to offer. The world would be handicapped if we kept our faith to ourselves. Simply put, if we've been fed, healed, and inspired by something, wouldn't we want others to know about it? In fact, it could be said that we wouldn't be very good friends to our friends and loved ones if we kept this goodness to ourselves. It'd be being selfish. However, unlike the aggressive tactics employed by more conservative brands of Christianity, progressive Christians engage in this in a more humble way. Instead of trying to *scare* people into believing, progressive Christians think that *loving* people into the Kingdom is far more effective.

We're inspired by words such as *"always be prepared to give an answer to everyone who asks you to give the reason for the hope that you have. But do this with gentleness and respect"* (1 Peter 3:15*)*; *"Let your light shine before men, that they may see your good deeds and praise your Father in heaven"* (Jesus, Matthew 5:16); St. Francis of Assisi's famed teaching, *"Preach the gospel always, use words if necessary"*; and Roger McClellan's, *"Telling someone about Christ is a cheap substitute for showing them Christ."* If you're doing some of the things mentioned in this chapter, you're on your way to doing just that. I'll end with an ironic observation noted by Raymond Rivera, *"We try to be more spiritual—and God, became flesh."*

Chapter 13

Peace & Justice: Creating Beloved Community

*Our goal is to create a beloved community and this will
require a qualitative change in our souls as well as a
quantitative change in our lives.* Martin Luther King, Jr.

*Christianity is not called to conservation, but to change. Jesus
came into the world, not to conserve the system that was, but
to change the world into what it ought to be.* Tony Campolo

*A church that does not join the poor in order to speak out from
the side of the poor against the injustices committed against
them is not the true church of Jesus Christ.* Oscar Romero

*It is impossible to have a man sit by you as your brother and
let him go hungry while you feed. Therefore as a usual thing
we do not let him sit by us or we deny that he is our brother.*
Walter Raushenbush

*The Earth provides enough to satisfy every man's need, but
not every man's greed.* Gandhi

*All life is interrelated—somehow we are caught in an inescapable
network of mutuality—tied in a single garment of destiny.
Whatever affects one directly affects all indirectly. Injustice anywhere
is a threat to justice everywhere.* Martin Luther King, Jr.

When I feed the poor, they call me a saint. When I ask why the poor have no food, they call me a communist. Dom Helder Camara

"The Spirit of the Lord is on me, because he has anointed me to preach good news to the poor. He has sent me to proclaim freedom for the prisoners and recovery of sight for the blind, to release the oppressed, to proclaim the year of the Lord's favor." . . . "Today this scripture is fulfilled in your hearing."
Jesus, Luke 4:18-21

Thy Kingdom come, Thy will be done on Earth as it is in Heaven! Jesus, Matthew 6:10

I write this chapter in the summer of 2010, a summer of discontent. President Barack Obama's honeymoon with the nation has long passed and his support is dwindling. The past few months have seen a vehement backlash against progressive politics and a time of harsh criticism of social-justice oriented Christianity. This started during the 2008 presidential campaign with criticism of the African American liberation theology[384] preached by Rev. Jeremiah Wright, Obama's former pastor in Chicago. It has grown into a full fledged schism whereby Christians on both sides of the divide have been referring to each other as "heretics," "Socialists," "Marxists," and "fascists."

Nowhere have these fireworks been more dramatic than in the highly covered interactions between Rev. Jim Wallis (a progressive, evangelical leader and founder of the Sojourners Community and *Sojourners* Magazine) and Glenn Beck (a politi-tainment personality on FOX News and proponent of the "Tea Party" movement). Earlier in the year, Glenn Beck told his viewers to leave their churches if their pastors preached about

---

[384] Liberation theology suggests that Christianity should focus upon liberating economically oppressed persons because of God's "preferential option for the poor." Liberation theologians claim to be in sync with the Spirit of Jesus' first sermon and they seek to see it manifested. (Luke 4:16-20)

social justice.[385] Wallis countered by asking Americans to stop watching Glenn Beck.

Later in the summer, on August 28, 2010, Beck hosted a rally at the Lincoln Memorial on the 47th anniversary of Martin Luther King, Jr.'s famed "I have a dream" civil rights speech in which he championed the uniquely American, hyper-individualistic and anti-social notion of salvation. Beck later retracted his earlier remark that Obama is a racist by sidestepping the matter and introducing a new one—an attack upon liberation theology and collective understandings of salvation. The following is Wallis' response to Beck's event:

Break it Down XVII

An Open Letter to Glenn Beck by Jim Wallis 09-02-2010

Dear Glenn,

I think we got off on the wrong foot. I listened to your speech last Saturday and heard a lot of things that we agree on. In fact, I have used some of the same language of our need to turn to God, and the values of "faith, hope, and charity" (love). What I would like to find out, and others would too, is what you mean by that language. Until last weekend, you have consistently described yourself primarily as an entertainer, and the public has known you as a talk show host. But last Saturday, you sounded more like an evangelist or revivalist on the steps of the

---

[385] See: "Glenn Beck Urges Listeners to Leave Churches That Preach Social Justice," David Sessions, March, 2010, http://www.politicsdaily. com/2010/03/08/glenn-beck-urges-listeners-to-leave-churches-that-preach-social/ Moreover, "social justice" is not code for communism, socialism, and whatever other "isms" Mr. Beck has fantasized about. It's an established part of mainstream denominations like the United Methodist Church (the denomination that George W. Bush and Dick Cheney claim membership in). And wouldn't you know it, on December 19, 2010, Judson Webb, the founder of the Tea Party Nation, called for the end of the United Methodist Church in his blog, "My Dream: No More United Methodist Church," http://www. tngovwatch.org/2010/12/my-dream-no-more-methodist-church/ see also: http://www.nashvillescene.com/pitw/archives/2010/12/21/local-tea-partier-no-more-methodist-church

Lincoln Memorial. I know we disagree significantly on many issues of public policy, but you said that people can disagree on politics and still agree on basic values and try to come together. Maybe we should test that. Instead of my being up on your blackboard and a regular target of your show's rhetoric, why don't we finally have that civil dialogue I invited you to months ago? Your speech on the Mall suggested and even promised a change of heart on your part, so why don't we talk? Here are a few things I think we could talk about.

First, I've been asked by people in the media if it matters that you are a Mormon. I unequivocally answer, no, it does not. We don't want more anti-Mormon bigotry any more than we want the anti-Muslim bigotry now rising up across the country. By the way, you should speak to that (against it). On Saturday you talked about the fact that our nation has some scars in our past. I think one of those scars is the historical persecution and bigotry that many Mormons have faced, as well as Catholics, Jews, and Muslims. But, as you said, instead of dwelling on the bad things of the past, we need to learn from them and look to the future. The best way to do that is to make sure we all stand for religious liberty and tolerance, and are careful not to denigrate anybody else's faith tradition, experience, or language. If you are ever in need of an evangelical Christian to speak out against anti-Mormon sentiment directed at you or others, I am here to help.

In an interview the day after your rally you said that you would like to "amend" your statement in which you accused President Obama of being a racist and said he had a deep hatred in his heart for white people. I commend you for that. But a simple and straightforward apology would have been better. All of us say things we shouldn't sometimes, but you have consistently mischaracterized the President's faith. You also said in that interview that you would like to have a conversation about it. I'd like to do that.

I also think it would be a good thing to stop attacking people and churches you label as "social justice Christians," not just because I'm tired of being on your blackboard, but because I think you genuinely don't understand the concept and how central it is to biblical faith, and how essential to the whole gospel. I am sure there are those who have misused the term, just as there are those who will co-opt any good label that exists. If "social justice" were truly code for Communism or Marxism or Nazism, as you have suggested, I would be right beside you in condemning it.

In his opening sermon at Nazareth, Jesus gave his own mission statement when he declared, "The Spirit of the Lord is upon me, because he has anointed me to bring good news to the poor, he has sent me to proclaim release to the captives and recovery of sight to the blind, to let the oppressed go free, to proclaim the year of the Lord's favor." Those were his very words, Glenn, including the stuff about releasing captives and freeing the oppressed—language you have been pretty critical of. In fact, the end of Jesus' famous sermon in Luke 4, about proclaiming "the year of the Lord's favor," was a direct reference, according to most biblical scholars, to the "year of Jubilee" in the Hebrew scriptures, which called for a periodic freeing of slaves, cancelling of debts, and returning land to original owners. It was written into the Torah as legal code and not just left up to individual charity. It was about "social justice" and even "redistribution"—two of the least popular words on your show. You regularly criticize other people's "versions" of Christianity. How about Jesus' version of Christianity?

I thought you might be changing your own mind a bit when I heard you lifting up the legacy of Dr. Martin Luther King Jr. and associating yourself with him on the 47th anniversary of his eloquent "I Have a Dream" speech, given from the very place you stood on Saturday. I was encouraged by that because Dr. King was the archetypal social justice Christian and the primary teacher for many of us on the social implications of biblical faith. His personal faith led him to fight for racial and economic justice—social justice. I hope you read many of his words before you spoke on the anniversary of his great speech, because we can't claim the mantle of King without also embracing his message. You seemed to affirm King's assertion that racism was not simply a private moral issue but one that required response through federal action and legislation. I'd like to talk with you about the rest of King's dream. If King was right about racism, could he have also been right about poverty and war? I didn't hear much about King's words on either of those issues in your speech on Saturday.

And let's talk about salvation. You have emphasized that you believe strongly in personal salvation, as opposed to "collective salvation." As an evangelical Christian, I also believe deeply in personal salvation—it is the foundation of my faith. But we need to ask ourselves, what are we saved for? Is salvation just about getting a pass into heaven? Is it just for us? Or is it also for the world, and being a part of God's work and purposes in the world today? When I read a passage like Matthew 25 or Amos 5, I believe it's clear that God won't hear my prayers if I don't care for the least of these, or I refuse justice to those in need. You spoke about charity at your rally on Saturday. Throughout the Old Testament it is clear that God requires compassion and charity from individuals, but God also requires justice from society. We agree that personal charity is important, but the God of the Bible is also a God of justice. His prophets regularly challenged the priorities, policies, and behavior of kings, rulers, employers, judges, and any leaders (including religious ones) who practiced injustice and robbed the poor of their dignity and rights. The leaders of his day were so upset with Jesus' challenge to their status quo that they killed him. Would they have been so threatened if Jesus was just asking people to be better persons and volunteer more often? Jesus announced the Kingdom of God, which would change everything—personally, spiritually, socially, economically, and even politically—not with a new government or program, but with a new way of living that included both love and justice.

Before, I thought you were just another cable news talk show host. But now, you are using the language of a spiritual and even a religious leader. You acted as though you now want people to look to you for that kind of spiritual leadership. But to invoke the name of God and the vocation of a spiritual leader has consequences. It brings with it a whole new level of responsibility and accountability. It will require a more civil and even humble tone than you are used to. It will likely mean saying some different things and, certainly, saying many things differently than you have in the past. Pundits and talk show hosts say things that divide, create conflict, and get good ratings. They appeal more to fear than to hope. But spiritual leaders try to avoid vitriol and bombastic language, and to rather seek to find common ground and bring people together to find real solutions to real problems. So let's talk about that too.

You said your rally day was the start of the nation turning to God. Many people in this country have already done that and, in fact, try to do it every day. But maybe it was the start of Glenn Beck becoming a different kind of public voice than you have been before. I hope so. And one good way to demonstrate that is to agree to an honest and civil conversation with somebody you have often attacked. How about it, Glenn?[386]

This article first appeared on Sojourners' God's Politics blog: blog.sojo.net. For more information, visit www.sojo.net.

It will come as no surprise that progressive Christians lean toward one side of that debate. As we see it, Wallis rightly interprets the social justice implications of Jesus' first sermon at that synagogue in Nazareth. The Year of Jubilee ("the year of the Lord's favor") that Jesus prophetically proclaimed had "come about again in him" *does* in fact involve the redistribution of wealth (Luke 4:16-20). It does mean liberation of those who were enslaved to debt. It does mean a relinquishing of lands by those who had amassed them over the past 50 years and the returning of those lands to their families of origin. This is based upon the Levitical laws that Jesus was referencing.[387] It is because Jesus began his ministry by delivering this message that progressive Christians claim this speech was of paramount

[386] http://blog.sojo.net/2010/09/02/an-open-letter-to-glenn-beck/ used with permission.
[387] Leviticus 25:8-12

importance. It established who Jesus was and what he was about. We regard it as being Jesus' "mission statement"—or maybe even as his "manifesto." Those words speak far more to social justice and collective salvation than they do to an understanding of salvation that is reduced merely to the individual. Because we believe Jesus was primarily focused upon collective salvation here and now, and building a "new Kingdom," progressive Christianity emphasizes those goals as well. According to the Gospels, Jesus spoke the most about proclaiming and describing the imminent and immanent collective Kingdom of God. The second most frequent topic of Jesus' teachings was money and our relationship to it. If salvation and the Kingdom are collective and communal, then so should be our relationship to money.

When conservative Christians assert that "Christianity is about *personal* transformation and being saved from our *personal* sins—and that those sins are primarily sexual in nature, progressive Christians respond by noting that

> . . . *All told, [there are] 258 verses [in the Gospels] about mercy, forgiving enemies, not judging others, loving all people, helping the poor and woe to the wealthy vs. nine verses that mention adultery or fornication in any way, and 19 more saying divorce isn't good. Oddly enough, Jesus didn't say a single word against homosexuality or masturbation or abortion or birth control, although if you listened to some of our conservative friends, you would think he was obsessed with those topics. Those ratios are pretty daunting. About 14 to one on class war vs. sex. Almost four to one on just the simple idea of not judging others as compared to all the mentions of sex sins. If you combine all the things Jesus said about sex and divorce, and compare it to all the stuff he said about helping the poor and how the rich should give away everything they own, you get close to a five to one. And if you combine all the stuff about sex and divorce vs. all the stuff about social justice, it's more than nine to one in favor of us social justice lefty types.*[388]

---

[388]   "Sex and Social Justice," Mike Lux, The Huffington Post, Sept. 20, 2010, http://www.huffingtonpost.com/mike-lux/sex-and-social-justice_b_731447.html

Because the authors of *Daring to Speak in God's Name: Ethical Prophecy in Ministry*[389] did such a marvelous job of presenting the reasons for a collective, social, and communal notion of salvation as being essential to Christianity, I share my paraphrased outlining of the first two chapters of that fine work:

Foundational Premises & Bases of Progressive Christian Justice & Peace:

Our personal identities are shaped communally. One becomes a mature person only in community. Full personhood happens only in community. There is no *me* without *we*. *I* am because *we* are. We are individuals-in-community. Humans are only *fully* human when in *relationship* to others. Whatever happens to one of us happens to all of us. Our own individual welfare depends upon how well the others are doing.

Oral events, especially narrative/story, help form community. Bible study and preaching inform the communal identity of the hearers who hear as a group. We develop our sense of right and wrong in community. No community, no moral life. No moral life, no society worth living in! Yet, without communities, people's self-formation suffers. Each person becomes less of a person.

Christianity is a social/relational community that is based upon a specific communal story. There is no such thing as a solo or "lone-ranger" Christian. The Christian faith isn't a private one. It's about the *Body* of Christ—not a fingernail of Christ.

"P&J Christians" (Peace and Justice) are ones who seek to help the Church remember and reclaim the relational aspects of our faith. We seek to correct the Church's tendency to be accommodated to Western culture's tendency toward hyper-individualism.

---

[389] by Mary Allice Mulligan & Rufus Burrow, Jr., Pilgrim Press, 2002.

Who *we* are is based upon Who *God* is. The God of Christianity is *not* a rugged lone individual. Instead, our God is a *relational* God Who is relational within Himself (the Trinity).

The Christian God is infinitely loving and always faithful. God wants *all* of His children to share a meaningful life, in all its fullness, here and now. God has created *each* person as "fearfully and wonderfully made" in Her image. We *each* have a Divine spirit within us. Each one of us is precious to God. Our lives have dignity and are sacred.

The Christian God, the Holy One of Israel, the God of Jesus of Nazareth is One Who demands an ethical-prophetic life response. God demands righteous conduct.
Because God loves us, we are obligated to love God back and to love the rest of His children. By loving and respecting our sisters and brothers, we exhibit our love for the God Who cares about each of us. We are able to love because God loves us and because each of us was created in love.

While God loves all of His children, He has a *particular* love and concern for those who are struggling and suffering the most in this world—for the "least, the last, and the lost." Hence, we should also have particular love and concern for those whose pain God feels most.

Christians are called to make God's love manifest in the real life situations of those who are hurting the most, those who are the weakest and most vulnerable among us. God's good news of salvation is intended for all, but it is *especially* life giving and liberating to the poor and the suffering huddled masses—those at the lowest ranks of society. This good news may feel like *bad* news to those who are at the top of the humanly constructed social pecking order.

Jesus' human life points to God's nature, character, and priorities. Jesus made it clear in His inaugural address in Luke 4:18-19 that He came to proclaim good news to a specific group of people—the poor and suffering. This implies that God has a special concern for these persons.

At the heart of the Gospel of Jesus Christ is the fundamental dignity and sacredness of all persons, the total liberation, and empowerment of oppressed peoples and the envisioning and living-into the Reign/Kingdom of God. Life on Earth is transformed into the harmony of heaven—a fellowship of equality, compassion, justice, and love.

Christianity is about making healthy life possible for all persons in order to establish an ideal world community, where all humans can be united by the will and love of God.

Not all of us are called to be actual prophets, but *all* Christians are called to be *prophetic* in word and action, especially in the face of injustice. I am for the God of Amos, Isaiah, Jeremiah, Micah, and Jesus, or I'm for idolatry. That's what it comes down to. Fence sitting isn't acceptable. We're called to say *Yes* to all that God desires for humanity and *No* to every act of injustice and dehumanization. We're called to be faithful to God's faithfulness here and now—not tomorrow or some other day, but now. There's a sense of *urgency*. Justice delayed is justice denied.

We need to notice and tend to the condition of those who are dearest to God—the weak, the poor, and the alienated. Societies are judged based upon how they treat these persons.

Christianity calls us to a way of life that motivates us to remake the world in ways that are more consistent with God's Kingdom, God's ideal community of love. Martin Luther King, Jr. referred to this as "the Beloved Community."

We can't be genuinely Christian and be indifferent to injustice, to be knowingly complicit in it, or to be a perpetrator of it. We're called to *repent* of all of that and to live life in a *new* way—Jesus' sacrificial Way of the Cross.

God has initiated loving concern for all persons. Our ministry must always rest on the assurance of God's Divine faithfulness, which has no end. It's only because of God's faithful compassion for suffering that we're able to band together in our faith communities to pursue an end to suffering, oppression, and despair.

Without God's faithfulness, our efforts couldn't succeed. Because of God's faithfulness, we too can be faithful. God's Kingdom *will* come!

(an abbreviated and paraphrased summary I created of the first two chapters of *Daring to Speak in God's Name* by Mary Allice Mulligan and Rufus Burrow, Jr., with certain adaptations of my own woven in)

I offer a detailed description of some of the key qualities of the liberating Kingdom of God (the "beloved community" in Appendix IV and show how it dramatically differs from the oppressive ways of the world).

Another basis for Christian commitments to collective social justice is the over-arching sense of Divine-Human covenant that we see ourselves as participants in. There are seven major covenants described in the Hebrew Scriptures. They essentially state Who God is, who the Jews are as God's chosen people, and how God and Her people are to relate to each other. It's largely encapsulated in the promise God made, "I shall be your God and you shall be my people."[390] From the "Ten Commandments," a system of 613 laws was established in order to help the Hebrews to

---

[390]   Exodus 19:5

live out their covenant. Many of those laws dealt with matters that we today would call "social justice." This included issues such as workers rights, debtors rights, the charging of interest, land use and ownership, and the just treatment of aliens, immigrants, and strangers in their midst.

Jesus later introduced the notion of a "New Covenant" that states that the essence of all of the law is "that God is one, to love God with all your heart, soul and mind" (the *Shema*)[391] with the added call "to love our neighbors as ourselves."[392] Jesus also shifted the covenant from being a cumbersome burden that causes people to stumble by introducing the idea that "the burden should be light."[393] It's more about following the spirit of the law instead of the letter of it. Paul described this as a "circumcision of the heart"—a metaphor for a new mindset and lifestyle—instead of a legalistic judicial code. Paul described how Gentile believers in Jesus have been "grafted" into the Jewish covenantal relationship as full-fledged children of God, who are called to honor and relate to God by following Christ. This was more explicitly stated by Jesus in Luke 22:20-30, where he symbolically said during his last supper *"This cup is the new covenant in my blood, which is poured out for you . . ."* Historically, many Christians would say that Jesus actually shedding his blood on the cross then ratified this new covenant. Again, conservative Christians focus more upon the blood whereas progressive ones emphasize the symbolism of the blood as "the life force"[394] of Jesus—and his motivation, teachings, and example. Even though Jesus said, "his burden is easy and light," he also made it clear that there are real, radical, and challenging demands and costs of following him. Among them are the demands for social justice, *including* the redistribution of wealth (Luke 18:18-23 & 14:25-34).

It is those aspects of Jesus' life and teachings that the early Christian community started following upon the creation of the church. They actually sold all they had and shared their possessions in collective community as a significant part of their

---

[391] Deuteronomy 6:5
[392] Matthew 22:39
[393] Matthew 11:25-30
[394] "Life force" being the meaning of the word blood in Hebrew.

way of discipleship. They understood that being the Church meant that they were part of "the living Body of Christ"[395] and the in-breaking Empire of God in the world.[396] Immediately, upon the Pentecost experience (Acts 2:1-41), the first Christians are reported to have:

> . . . *devoted themselves to the apostles' teaching and to the fellowship, to the breaking of bread and to prayer. Everyone was filled with awe, and many wonders and miraculous signs were done by the apostles. All the believers were together and had everything in common. Selling their possessions and goods, they gave to anyone as he had need. Every day they continued to meet together in the temple courts. They broke bread in their homes and ate together with glad and sincere hearts, praising God and enjoying the favor of all the people. And the Lord added to their number daily those who were being saved.* (Acts 2:42-47)

> *All the believers were one in heart and mind. No one claimed that any of his possessions was his own, but they shared everything they had. With great power the apostles continued to testify to the resurrection of the Lord Jesus, and much grace was upon them all. There were no needy persons among them. For from time to time those who owned lands or houses sold them, brought the money from the sales and put it at the apostles' feet, and it was distributed to anyone as he had need. Joseph, a Levite from Cyprus, whom the apostles called Barnabas (which means Son of Encouragement), sold a field he owned and brought the money and put it at the apostles' feet.* (Acts 4:32-37)

It is clear that Jesus and his early followers lived communally and shared their resources in a communitarian manner. Sharing our wealth and giving to people as they have need is part of following the Way. This is not easy for some people to do. As Jesus rightly

---

[395] Colossians 1:24

[396] "Empire" is in many ways a better translation for the Greek word *baselia*, usually translated as "Kingdom." Hence, we're talking about the *Empire* of God versus the Empires of this world.

observed, "It is easier for a camel (or a *rope*, in the Aramaic) to go through the eye of a needle than for a rich man to enter the Kingdom of God."[397] People like Glenn Beck apparently dismiss the actions of these early Christians as being a bunch of "Pinko, Commie, Marxist, liberationist, social justice hippies."

This is not an either/or situation. It isn't *either* personal salvation *or* social justice. Employing careful analysis of the Gospel of Mark, Progressive Christian authors John Dominic Crossan (a Catholic) and Marcus Borg (an Episcopalian) end their book *The Last Week*[398] concluding that that Christianity must give equal weight to the daily cross/crucifixion and to transformation/resurrection. Without each of these components they do not consider any form of Christianity as being authentic. They argue that Christians must non-violently struggle for social justice in the face of the "domination system." They claim that Christians must undergo personal transformation from non-follower/non-believer to intentional disciple of Christ.

Progressive Christianity fully affirms Bishop Gregory V. Palmer's words in his inaugural speech before the Iowa Annual Conference of the United Methodist Church in June 2000,

> *"I don't want to be part of a church that doesn't care about the conversion and transformation of individuals into being personal followers of Christ. And I don't want to be part of a church that doesn't care about the social justice demands of the Gospel. I want to be part of a church that does both! A church that has both oars in the water and rows!"*

I close this chapter by sharing a sermon on social justice from a progressive Christian perspective that I wrote and delivered to the people of Heritage UMC, the church I was serving in 2004 in Littleton, CO. The statistics mentioned are dated. Tragically, many of them are far worse now. [Note: The section that addresses fair trade coffee draws from a sermonette written by Rich Aronson[399]

---

[397]   Matthew 19:21
[398]   *The Last Week*, HarperOne, 2007
[399]   "Building a Better World one Sip at a Time," http://gbgm-umc.org/umcor/fairtrade/buildingabetterworld.cfm

and portions of the last few paragraphs are paraphrased from the last chapter of Jim Wallis' book *The Call to Conversion*].[400]

"Peace With Justice: Band-Aids Aren't Enough!"
Amos 2:6-7a; 4:1-2; 5:7, 10-12; 6:1, 3-7, 12b & 5:24

It's been said that a Christian pastor's job is to "comfort the afflicted and to afflict the comfortable" and well—as our friends from Texas might put it—I'm fixin' to do a little bit of *both* of those things this mornin'!

It seems like my 3-year-old boy Andrew needs Band-Aids all the time! I'm tellin' ya, the kid has *lots* of boo-boos and owies! Nearly one a day! And it's almost always due to him wiping-out in the driveway on the green plastic scooter that a *certain* set of grandparents bought him!

I could just keep putting those Band-aids on him day after day, or I could do something to prevent those injuries from taking place in the first place! I could try to find him some little toddler-sized kneepads. I could buy him some private green plastic scooter lessons! I could try to make a new rule not allowing him to ride it anymore—*Yeah, right!* Or, I could "accidentally" forget where that green plastic scooter is one night and then "accidentally" back over it with our minivan the next morning! *Pretty tempting!*

The point is, there're all kinds of options, and I don't really have to keep on putting those Band-aids on him if I can prevent him from having all of those accidents to begin with!

It reminds me of a parable I know. A man from a village was standing by a river and he saw a baby floating in the water. He let out a yell, dove into the water, swam out, grabbed the child, and swam back to shore. The next day another villager also retrieved a baby from the river. By the end of the week, the villagers had pulled dozens of babies from out of the water. It was hard work. It was exhausting work. And it never seemed to end. One day, the man who found

---

400   *The Call to Conversion*, Jim Wallis, HarperSanFrancisco, 1981.

that first baby started to run up a path—*not* to the river. The people yelled, "Where are you going? We need everyone available to help out!" He said, "I'm going upstream to see who keeps throwing these babies into the river and try to stop him!"

Powerful story. It's about the difference between charity and justice. Charity is like committing those "random acts of kindness." It's those isolated acts of mercy that respond to certain specific needs, things like giving a warm blanket to a homeless person on the street or serving a meal to a person whose hungry. Justice is more of a systemic thing. It's about reforming the societal context and conditions in order to more fairly correct things when the decks are stacked against certain kinds of people.

Metaphorically, charity is like giving Band-aids to people after they've had a trauma.
Justice is seeking to prevent those traumas from happening in the first place. And over the years, faithful Jews and Christians have leaned toward each of those two things. People like Florence Nightingale and Mother Theresa excelled in personal acts of charity and mercy, and people like Isaiah, Jeremiah, Amos, Micah, and Martin Luther King, Jr. focused on prophetic calls for social justice and transformation.

I happen to lean toward the "prophetic justice" side of things and in the spirit of those great persons before me, let me ask us exactly **how just is our world today?**

Well, here are some facts and figures that suggest some answers to that question:

* Every day, approx. 29,000 people in the world die of hunger, or hunger related diseases.
* 80 million children between the ages of 10-14 work for low wages in often dangerous conditions to supply inexpensive products for citizens of wealthier nations to consume.
* 100 million children from 6-11 years of age are receiving no education and they will likely soon join the 900 million adults who are illiterate round the world.

* 1 billion children do not have clean water or sanitary waste disposal (that's 1/6th of the world's population, and that's just the children!)
* The wealthiest 345 people in the world possess the wealth equivalent to that held by the poorest 40% of the world's people—that's over 2 billion people!
* If we were to join the ranks of the 1.5 billion people, half of them children, who are constantly hungry, our diets would consist of 2 oz. of rice a day.

Okay, I know. That's overwhelming! It's hard for us to comprehend those things. So, let's just focus on the country that we happen to live in.

Here's some truths that we Americans need to know about: The United States has but 5% of the world's population and yet we consume over one third of the world's natural resources and we generate 19% of the world's waste.—E Magazine Jan/Feb 99

A *USA Today* snapshot feature this past week stated that the U.S. gives the highest amount of aid for development assistance around the world. (Fri. June 18, '04, 1A) But what that article didn't mention is that the U.S. is # 20 among nations in the percentage of our national income (GNP) that we give to other nations. We're currently giving less than 1/10th of 1% of our national income (GNP) to humanitarian aide. Luxemburg is # 1 at $352/person—while for the U.S., it's just $23 per person! (http://www.finfacts.com/biz10/worldstatistics.htm) Yet we're the wealthiest nation in the world! In fact, we're the wealthiest nation in the *history* of the world. It's inexcusable that we're giving so little. In fact, for just one penny per American per day, the U.S. could cut hunger in Africa in half by 2015. We could cut it in *half!!* But, we don't, and we aren't.

Our domestic scene has problems too. Though, there's been improvements, female workers in America still earn about 80 cents to every dollar earned by males—I guess it's even *worse* at Walmart!

31 million Americans live in households that experience hunger or the risk of hunger.

It's been reported that requests for emergency food assistance in 26 major cities increased for the 15th year in a row, by an average of 18%. 2/3 of all adults requesting assistance were employed. They're known as "the working poor." And that "gap between the haves and the have-nots" is growing. Our rich are getting richer and our poor are getting poorer and more numerous. The gap in the U.S. between rich and poor families with children is the largest among 18 industrialized nations and our social programs for the poor are less generous.

Most tragic of all, some 40 million Americans—9 million of whom are children—aren't covered by any form of health insurance. I can't even imagine what it'd be like to raise my son without health insurance!

On a different front, our nation's criminal justice system is more of a criminal *in*justice system. In most every state, the criminal justice institutions have given up on the notion of rehabilitation and the focus is simply on retribution and punishment. But, from the Christian point of view, the focus of justice should be restorative not retributive. As a wise student of Christianity, Mahatma Gandhi, put it, "An eye for an eye makes the world blind." Christian justice is about restoring wholeness to the souls of both victims and offenders and the goal is restoring both to abundant life in community. Now this is a high ambition to be sure, but restoration and reconciliation is a *major, major* theme in our New Testament.

Some individuals have very hardened hearts or have hard to treat mental illnesses that mean that they really do need to be kept locked away from society, but the *goal* should always be to seek as much restoration as *possible*.

This is why the UMC is opposed to capital punishment as there can be no restoration if you kill the person whom you're estranged with. There can be no healing of souls, no transformation of lives.

As a denomination we think that God doesn't want us killing any of the people that God created in God's image. We think it's a bit strange for the State to be killing people to teach people that killing people is wrong!

On top of all of those more important reasons 1 out of every 4 African-American males between ages 15-40 are caught up in the criminal justice system—either awaiting trial, incarcerated in jail or prison, or on parole or probation. A disproportionately high percentage of the people on death rows across this nation are poor people of color!

Let's face it. We've got a lot of social problems. Now I realize that there are legitimate philosophical differences that various people have with one another. Some folks prefer to raise taxes and spend those tax monies to provide for governmental programs and services, and some of us would rather reduce taxes and allow churches and other religious groups to provide for the social needs of our society,

That's all fine and well. Frankly, there are so many severe problems that need to be addressed that we need to be supporting both governments *and* churches a whole lot more than we are!

But there's *another* group of people who want to cut taxes and cut governmental social programs, and who merely *say* that they want the churches to take care of things. I'm talkin' about the folks who don't want to pay taxes *and* who don't want to give to their churches either!

The average American churchgoer doesn't tithe 10% of their income to their local church. They don't even give 5%! The average American churchgoer gives but 2.4% of their income to their church—and a whole lot of folks give a lot less than this! If any of those are people who want to cut taxes and yet *claim* that they want the *churches* to do things, they don't really want to help! They don't want to help anyone! They just want to hold on to their money! *Hmmpphh!!*

Today's Peace with Justice Sunday happens to fall at a time when our nation is at war.

We're a nation at war, and we're at war on several fronts. From a worldly perspective, it's made sense for us to retaliate against al-Qaeda and to engage in Afghanistan as we have. But from a Christian perspective, most of the Christian Church and denominational leaders—including our own—have contended *the way and manner* we waged war with Iraq failed to meet the criteria for a Just war. Now we don't have to agree with them, but that's what they said.

As I understand it Christians are called to be pacifists.[401] However, we happen to live in a country that has a Department of Defense, and supposedly it's the best in the world! It'd be *surprising* if it wasn't, as the U.S. spends as much on our Defense Department as nearly all of the other nations in the world do—*combined!*

To the extent that the U.S. is a "Christian nation," what about having a Department of Peace? Seems like we ought to be spending far more time and energy beefing up our negotiation and diplomacy skills and procedures than we do. Seems like any wars that we fight ought to be waged only after all other means have been fully explored and attempted. But we can't really explore or attempt those ways and means if we don't devote power, prestige, and resources to them!

I think that a fella who was a whole lot brighter than I'll ever be may've had it right when he said, **"You cannot simultaneously prepare for war and for peace."** That was Albert Einstein, but I don't think it takes a *rocket scientist* to see the truth in that!

Another simple truth is seen in Martin Luther King, Jr.'s observation that **"Peace is not just the absence of war, it is the presence of justice."** It reminds me of a photo I saw in the paper this past

---

[401]   Despite his actions, even Deitrich Bonhoeffer agreed with that. He was a theologian who was part of a plot to try to have Hitler killed with a bomb.

March of someone holding a sign at one of those peace rallies that took place. The sign simply said, "No justice. No peace." It was powerful. It's similar to the Roman Catholic teaching, "If you want peace, work for justice." This isn't a liberal catch phrase. It's not the rallying cry of leftist or socialist rabble-rousers. It's simply a stated truth. If there is no justice, there can be no peace. I'd like you to think about that for a minute. If governments in places like El Salvador or in the Middle East deny their people, *especially* their poorest people, justice, the people will be resentful and troublesome. Perhaps, like the early American colonials suffering under the injustice of George the Third, the people will take to arms and revolt. No, unless there is justice in the land, peace will not follow.

All right, this sermon's been a bit heavy this morning. It's been a bit heavy on issues and concepts that are frankly *huge* and hard for us to get our minds around.

So I'd like to break it down to something that's truly more down to earth and practical. Let me focus on one bite sized—or *sip*-sized—tangible issue. (I take a sip of coffee) Amos talked about those people who asked their spouses to fetch them "something good to drink," well, here's something *really* good!

In today's world, there's perhaps no greater barrier to the building of God's Kingdom than the willingness of the few to profit at the expense of the many. All around the globe, millions of our brothers and sisters toil in conditions we can't even imagine, and they work for wages that fail to provide any measure of stability or security. As Christians, it is God's expectation for us to live in solidarity with these exploited workers by speaking out against this injustice.

We're also called to use the wealth that God has placed in our care to bring about positive change on their behalf. The exploitation of workers in the developing world has become standard operating procedure in the new global economy. Nowhere is this problem more acute than in the coffee industry.

Second only to oil, coffee is the most heavily traded commodity in the world. It originates from plantations that are traditionally run and owned by wealthy landowners, or small family-run operations that are primarily owned by impoverished farmers. These small farmers frequently live in isolated communities, and rely on middlemen in addition to processors, creditors, exporters, and brokers to buy their coffee. Fluctuating market prices make it difficult for farmers to plan for the future, and prices are often set below the cost of production. So, the way the system's set up, coffee farmers just aren't able to get a fair return for their labor! When we purchase most of the coffees that we find in our grocery stores, we're actually participating in this system that traps so many coffee growers and their families in the developing world in cycles of poverty.

Throughout the developing world, hundreds of thousands of small coffee farmers and workers have lost their jobs due to the current coffee crisis. In many situations, farmers must choose between starvation and growing coca, which is used to make cocaine.

And yet, in spite of all this gloomy darkness, there's light at the end the tunnel for the world's small coffee growers! That light's coming from an alternative economic model that doesn't adhere to the premise that "good business" and "the common good" are opposed to each other. This system is called "Fair Trade." The international standards of Fair Trade work to ensure that the people who grow the things we consume are paid a fair wage for their labors by having consumers buying directly from the co-ops that the farm workers own and govern themselves.

The United Methodist Book of Discipline states that *"Consumers should exercise their economic power to . . . avoid purchasing products made in conditions where workers are being exploited . . . [and] we call upon consumers, including local congregations . . . to organize to achieve [this] goal."* (¶163D)

In response to this call, The United Methodist Committee on Relief has developed the UMCOR Coffee Project. UMCOR's partner in this project is the employee-owned fair trade organization Equal Exchange. In 1991, Equal Exchange became the first company in the United States to adopt internationally recognized fair trade standards. Today, the organization remains one of the few companies committed to these standards on 100% of its coffee, tea, and other products.

We've got some of this coffee here today, and so this morning, during the fellowship time after worship, think of the coffee that you're drinking as more than just a great way to get your day started. Think of it as a *Just* way to get your day started and think of it as building God's Kingdom—one sip at a time!

Okay, my coffee sales-pitch is over now. But I need to close with the *real* sales-pitch that's the basis of all of these calls to peace and justice. It's the sales pitch for the Gospel of Jesus Christ.

The basis for the Christian concepts of peace and justice is God's forgiveness of sins. Yes, God does have high expectations and standards for us to live up to. And yes, God does call us to account for them. But the Christian yearning for peace and justice is possible. It's a natural fruit of lives converted to the Gospel and Kingdom that are ushered in and made possible by the life, death, and resurrection of Jesus Christ.

Our social action is centered in our own experience of God's mercy for us. As it says in 1st John 4:19, "We love because God first loved us." We're merciful because God is merciful to us. And if we accept that Gospel Good News, then we need to follow the ways and teachings of Jesus, the One Who called us not to be peace *lovers*, but peace *makers*.

As Jim Wallis put it in his book *Call to Conversion*, we don't all need to be sign-carrying protesters shouting for "justice!" The challenge for us is to listen to the still small voice of God in our hearts, Who *isn't* shouting "Justice!" but instead whispering, "Were you fair to your brother? Did you hurt your sister's feelings?" And then to be open to the subtle nudging of the Holy Spirit reminding us that there will be no peace until we make it right.

We need to know our failings and where we fall short, but we are much more than our sin. We're beings of infinite worth, capable of incredible beauty and meaning. And yet we all blow it—we sin.

But we aren't defined by our sins. We're much more than that! We have the ability to sin, and to repent; the power to hurt, and to heal; the ability to offend, and to say, "I'm sorry;" the capacity to be hurt or offended, and the power to *forgive*; the power to make justice, and the power to make peace! God has given us the capability to change our ways.

Because of Jesus, we are able to shift our loyalties and allegiances from the ways of the world to the ways of God's Kingdom; to turn away from being cogs in the warring worldly systems and toward being followers of *The* Way—the peace-making way of Jesus Christ.

Christians are called to be peacemakers and evangelists of the Christian Gospel of the forgiveness of sins. Christians are also called to be justice-makers—people who do what they can to create a world where there will be as few sins and transgressions committed as possible! For we know that there'll be less to forgive if there are fewer sins and offenses committed! And we know there'll be much less of a need for bandages in a world where *"justice rolls on like a river, and righteousness like a never-failing stream!"* (Amos 5:24) And all God's people said? *Amen!!*

A nation that continues year after year to spend more money on military defense than on programs of social uplift is approaching spiritual doom. Martin Luther King, Jr.

Every gun that is made, every warship launched, every rocket fired, signifies in the final sense a theft from those who hunger and are not fed, those who are cold and are not clothed. Dwight D. Eisenhower

Gonna lay down my sword and shield Down by the riverside Down by the riverside Down by the riverside Gonna lay down my sword and shield Down by the riverside Ain't gonna study war no more. American Spiritual

Postlude

What I have presented as progressive Christianity isn't new. I haven't invented something from out of the blue. Several other authors have described approaches similar to the one I've presented here.[402] It's just as biblically based as other Christianities that are out there in the marketplace of ideas. I should make it clear that progressive Christianity goes far beyond the notions and ideas presented in this book. It's a diverse and eclectic approach and no single text can capture all of its variances.

Progressive Christianity is about loving more deeply and living more meaningfully. It's about following Jesus' invitations for practicing radical compassion and loving-kindness, living-out Jesus' Kingdom values, and experiencing a fuller, more profoundly connected and meaningful life. You don't have to believe in any of the theologies about God that have been used to damn, judge or exclude people. You don't have to believe in Satan or the Devil. You don't have to believe in heaven or hell. You don't have to believe in a virgin birth, or that someone walked on water, or that Christianity is the only way that God is at work in the world (though certain progressive Christians believe several of those things). Instead, it's about cultivating a sense of appreciation for what God has done for the world though Jesus. It's about nurturing direct experience with the Divine and practical actions to inclusively live in right relationships and make a positive difference in the world in the name of Christ—without denying that God is at work in the world in other ways.

Both conservative and progressive Christianity feed people's souls. Both are "bread"—even if they're on different ends of the

---

[402] Marcus Borg is perhaps the most prominent. See Appendix VIII for a listing of books similar to mine.

table.[403] It's not an either/or situation, and they aren't necessarily mutually exclusive. Both perspectives have their strengths and they each have certain dangers. The risk of conservative Christianity is that it reduces things to shallow sentimentalism and symbolism or depicts a God who is too harsh, demanding, exclusive, and mean—a god whom many can't worship. The risk for the progressive approach to Christianity is that it might reduce things to overly cerebral universalism or depict an impotent, amorphous, fuzzy sort of God who doesn't seem to be worthy of worshipping. I'd like to think that depiction of progressive Christianity is unfair and that the theology presented in this book is more robust, specific, and compelling. This will be up to each reader to determine for him or herself.

A mature progressive Christianity acknowledges that God works in many ways and that no one perspective can claim to have the corner on the truth. Jesus said that people who come to him with a child-like faith are okay (in fact more than okay), and we're pretty sure he's okay with those who approach him through other ways too. People are saved and come to God in different ways. A man who's drowning doesn't care who tosses him a rope! There's nothing wrong with a simple, concrete, "Jesus said it, I believe it, that settles it" sort of faith, and there's nothing wrong with an intellectual approach to the faith. There's also nothing wrong with a contemplative, mystical take on things. And there's nothing wrong with a charismatic, Pentecostalist approach to the faith (I've even heard of "progressive Pentecostalists").[404]

Progressive and conservative Christianity share common ground in that we all place our hope in something greater than ourselves. We hope in a God Who loves, cares, and intervenes on our behalf, and we hope in a God Who loves us enough to show us an alternative way of connecting and living. So it's not

---

[403]   To remind us, that there are "other" (moderate) Christianities "in the middle of the table." The range from Conservative to Progressive is a continuum. The continuum involves some "picking and choosing." It's not just a matter of us marking a spot "on the line," it's a fluid process and where we locate ourselves will shift.

[404]   http://pewforum.org/Christian/The-New-Face-of-Global-Christianity-The-Emergence-of-Progressive-Pentecostalism.aspx

conservative vs. liberal. It's not "Right vs. Left." Perhaps it's *combined* Left *and* Right = *L-IGHT*, and does this world ever need more of that. Amen?

In the non-dualistic, paradox-embracing words of Brennan Manning, a contemplative-minded Catholic priest:

> *"If we maintain the open-mindedness of children, we challenge fixed ideas and established structures, including our own. We listen to people in other denominations and religions. If we are open, we rarely resort to either-or: either creation or evolution, liberty or law, sacred or secular, Beethoven or Madonna. We focus on both-and, fully aware that God's truth cannot be imprisoned in a small definition."*[405]

Perhaps this could be part of the meaning of one of U2's songs: *Two Hearts Beat as One.*[406]

I'm going to guess that the progressive Christian understandings of God and Jesus described in this book probably sound a bit different than what many of you have heard before. I'm also going to guess that certain "bells of truth" might be ringing in your ears. Perhaps some of what I've shared is what you've been thinking for years but never heard anyone say before and you're feeling validated, maybe like you've "come home." If this is you, we are kindred spirits—fellow progressive (*"Kissing Fish"*) Christians, followers of the Way of Jesus. Blessings to you brothers and sisters.

> *For all who see God, may God go with you.*
> *For all who embrace life, may life return your affection.*
> *For all who seek a right path, may a way be found,*
> *And the courage to take it, step-by-step.*
> Robert Mabry Doss

> *May God bless you with discomfort at easy answers,*
> *half-truths, and superficial relationships, so that you*

---

[405]   http://www.goodreads.com/quotes/show/4242

[406]   see this link for the lyrics: http://www.metrolyrics.com/two-hearts-beat-as-one-lyrics-u2.html, click here to hear it: http://www.youtube.com/watch?v=uIuAFBRyjj4.

*may live deep within your heart.   May God bless you with
anger, at injustice, oppression, and exploitation of people, so
that you may work for justice, freedom, and peace.   My God
bless you with tears, to shed for those who suffer from pain,
rejection, starvation, and war, so that you may reach out
your hand to comfort them and turn their pain to joy.
And may God bless you with enough foolishness, to believe
that you can make a difference in this world, so that you can
do what others claim cannot be done. Amen.*
A Franciscan Benediction

*And yet many of us who revere that same Jesus who was
crucified on a cross for the crimes of 'sedition' and 'blasphemy'
are all too guilty of sacrificing bodies on the altar of orthodoxy.
May we learn to grant each other the same grace that we
ourselves are saved by.*
The Progressive Christian Alliance

*Forgive me my nonsense, as I also forgive the nonsense of
those that think they talk sense.*
Robert Frost

Appendix I

A Progressive Christian Easter Sermon

based on Matthew 21:1-17; 27:11-26 & 28:1-28
Rev. Roger Wolsey
(first preached at Wesley Chapel, Boulder, CO Easter, 2007)

It's been said that the world is a tough place to live and parts of it are *really* tough. Places like Antarctica, the top of Mt. Everest, deserts, the oceans with their tidal waves, hurricanes . . . places like these are inhospitable to human life. But it's not just these extreme places that are hard to live in. The regular parts of the world are tough too! We learn this as children. We start learning to walk and right away what happens? We trip and fall down on the sidewalk and bump our heads on rocks! We bang up against things and it hurts! *Ouch!* Yet God created this world and God said it was *good* when She created the oceans and the land, and all the rocks and creatures in it. God hopes we'll love it and think it's good too.

But what God *didn't* create and what God doesn't love is the ways that we run our societies. God doesn't love that we've created a world where we live by the law of the jungle, where "might makes right," where we compete and hoard, where powers and domination systems place the overwhelming majority of humanity into abject poverty and misery.

The first major, massive scale instance of this kind of human created system of power was the world's first territorial empire, the Roman empire. Rome conquered many nations through the means of military, political, economic, and ideological exploitation and domination. They imposed a *Pax Romana*—a "Roman peace"—that meant there was peace unless a nation dared to resist them—and then they'd be brutally squashed back into submission! When Octavian defeated Anthony and Cleopatra, he changed his name to *Augustus* and the Roman Empire took things to an even higher level than ever before. The Romans had just gone through 20 years of civil war and Augustus ended it. He brought peace—*40 years* of peace! The people responded "Thank God! Thank Augustus! He must be Divine!" And then the Roman "Emperor Cult" was born which was the heart and soul of the Roman Empire. It created a unifying ideology that asserted that Caesar was *God*, that he was *Son of God*, that he was *Savior, Redeemer, and Lord!* And Rome expected all of its subject nations to call him those things too!

Well, God had quite enough of that! So when the next Caesar was in power, a certain *Yeshua* of Nazareth arrived on the scene! And this Yeshua, this "Jesus," had the gall to take on and resist that arrogant Roman ideology!

All of this is a bit like the story line in the movie *The Matrix*. In *The Matrix*, humankind has been relegated to serving as cogs in a machine that they're powerless to do anything about. They are nourishment for a world run by machines. And yet there was a prophecy that a messiah would come along to liberate humanity from their oppressed state! And that savior came in the form of *Neo*, "the One," Neo *Anderson*—meaning "Son of Man."

It's no accident that that's the same title that Jesus referred to Himself as being! But unlike Neo, Jesus' way wasn't about fighting back and becoming even better at wielding deadly martial arts and the ways of the world than anyone else in the world. Instead, the way that Jesus taught was of rejection of any powers that be, any powers or principalities that dare to usurp God's power in God's world! Those false powers were the ones who *really* had the gall—the gall to create systems that put all of the property and farms into the hands of a few. They oppressed the masses by turning them into tenant farmers or sharecroppers who ended up beholden to debt collectors. They created a system where women had no voice or legal standing, but were instead treated as the property of men; and where humans were enslaved to other humans. They justified oppressing and exploiting the poor, and forcing young people to fight in wars of expansion. They said worldly leaders and worldly powers are god instead of God Himself!

But Jesus' way was a nonviolent way. He didn't fight fire with fire. He didn't use the world's ways against the world. He simply said that the worldly powers are impotent. They have no power. The real power is with God and in the Kingdom of God! And then Jesus *demonstrated* that power by reaching out to the people who society had rejected. He told people to repent. He told them to change their way of thinking and living so that they could break free from ways that collaborated with the empire so that they could start living freely and abundantly in deep community and Communion with one another. He taught them to share all that they have and turn away from the domination system that sought to oppress them!

Then He went into the belly of the beast, right into the Temple in Jerusalem that had been collaborating with Roman dominance and said NO! He condemned the corrupted Temple system that had been blessing the unjust status quo and cooperating with the Roman Empire! He knocked over the tables in the courtyard and boldly confronted the powers and exposed them as frauds. He took back that house for God's purposes—not Rome's!

And then, the "empire struck back." The domination system conspired against him and they doled out the worst they could do, they had him arrested, beaten, and executed. One thing the powers that be can't tolerate is being rejected and so they rejected him! They killed him. As they say in Communist China, "the nail that rises up gets hammered back down." Take that! End of story. And with that, Jesus' disciples (at least the men) hid away in fear.

But then, something extraordinary happened. God said, "Uh, No . . . that *isn't* the end of the story!" And though He was indeed good and dead, God amazingly and graciously resurrected Jesus *back* to life! Jesus of Nazareth, who had been delivered up by the chief priests and executed by Romans under Pontius Pilate, was alive again! A man who died had been raised from the dead!

The guards who'd been posted at the tomb ran to tell the chief priests what had happened. Their very lives were at stake for failing to prevent the tomb from being opened. To break the Roman seal that had been placed at the entrance to the tomb was against the emperor's law and punishable by death. So Jesus' resurrection was an act of civil disobedience! God was breaking Roman law!

And then Jesus showed Himself to those disciples of His who had run away in fear. When they saw Him and recognized the nail marks on His hands, they came out of hiding! Until they saw Jesus, they viewed the world the way others did.

The central reality of their lives had been the power of the system and their own powerlessness. But when they saw Him risen and alive, they unlocked the doors, came out, and began turning the world upside down! At last, they were finally converted! They knew another reality that was bolder, truer, and stronger than the powers that had been paralyzing them with fear. Jesus had risen! And *Jesus* is Lord—not Caesar!

They saw that all that their rabbi had been teaching them about the Kingdom of God and how it's ways are better than the world's ways is true! They realized that no matter what, even if the worldly powers dish-out the worst they can, even if they end up getting killed too, that even death has lost its sting! Even death can't stop the truth of God in God's world! They took-off and proclaimed the Gospel Good News of the Life, Death, and Resurrection of Jesus the Christ!

Yes, the Empire tried hard to stifle their efforts—and thousands of Christians ended up dying on crosses, lit up as street torches, or eaten by lions or killed by gladiators in Roman coliseums. But the more they were persecuted, the more their movement spread! And it spread like wildfire! Until, eventually, Christianity became the official religion of the Roman Empire, and the empire itself was dissolved!

Today, the living resurrected Jesus stands in our midst. Jesus knows us and He knows our fears. We're afraid of weak economies. We're afraid of debt. We're afraid of running out of oil. We're afraid of increasing CO_2 and global warming. We're afraid of the unregulated power of multi-national corporations. We're afraid of racial tensions and the ever-growing gulf between the rich and the poor. We're afraid of the hurt between white and black, men and women, between people of different nations, and we're afraid of endless war. We fear for our loved ones and ourselves.

Like those first disciples, we're afraid of the power of the systems of the world with their armies, their courts, their prisons, and their threats. Like them, we fear our own sense of powerlessness. We're insecure. We're frightened by our emotions. And we're afraid to trust one another. We feel the guilt of our sin and the vulnerability of our broken places. And, we fear pain, suffering and death.

Like those first disciples, *we're* hiding behind locked doors and are afraid to come out. Friends, Jesus knows our fears and he wants us to know the power of His resurrection. Jesus says, "Go, tell my disciples that I have risen and that I'm going before them!" He tells us not to fret but to believe! Jesus died for our sins, our struggles and our fears. God raised Him from the tomb to show us His victory over them and to set us free from their power. And now, Jesus calls us to pick up our crosses and *follow* Him! Yeah, that's right. He wants *us* to follow Him into harm's way! But he wants us to do so knowing that no matter what, God'll be with us every inch of the way and She'll make things right in the end!

What do we make of all of this? Do we still doubt that Jesus' way of love, that His "way of the cross" makes much sense in today's cutthroat, dog eat dog world? Do we think that that kind of suffering servant-hood can make a difference or transform our world of overwhelmingly powerful systems and institutions? Well, those early disciples felt overwhelmed by the powers and forces that ruled their day, but they were converted! They had become people of the resurrection! They began living transformed lives filled with the fruits of conversion. They began living in the power of the resurrection! Friends, we too can know the power of Christ's resurrection! Like those first disciples, we need to come out of hiding and see the risen Lord! We need to get out into the world and put our faith, trust, and reliance upon Jesus and follow Him. The resurrection exposes the bogus powers and restores our communities. It restores us to who we really are! I'm not "Roger: a slave to the system!" I'm *Roger—free in Christ!* Liberated to serve God's people and meet their needs—and nothing's gonna stop me! And the same is true for you!

Every time we proclaim Jesus as Lord—instead of Caesar, every time we follow Jesus' teachings, we demonstrate His victory! Every time we refuse to be controlled by political or economic systems; every time we refute the absolute authority of nations; every time we embrace Christ's freedom over our fear; tear down the walls of class, race, sex, gender, and orientation; every time we love our enemies; advocate for the poor; forgive those who've wronged us, and resist violence by making peace, we're demonstrating Christ's victory in the world! Jesus' victory is present wherever it is proclaimed and acted upon. Brothers and sisters, let's dedicate the rest of our lives to claiming and acting upon this victory! Jesus Christ *is* risen today! *Alleluia! Alleluia! Amen!*

> *A message inspired by "The Last Week" by Marcus Borg and John Dominic Crossan*[407] *and a few paragraphs at the end are adapted from the last chapter of Jim Wallis' book, The Call to Conversion.*[408]

---

[407] *The Last Week*, HarperOne, 2007
[408] *The Call to Conversion*, HarperSanFrancisco, 1981

Appendix II

Progressive Christian Beliefs

The following are selected descriptions and statements of Progressive Christianity from several sources. You will notice some similarities and differences. There is no one official description of progressive Christianity. There are certain recognizable familial associations. I'd like to think that what I've written in this book is simpatico with the majority of them.

"The 8 Points of Progressive Christianity" according to The Center for Progressive Christianity www.tcpc.org

Point 1 By calling ourselves progressive, we mean that we are Christians who have found an approach to God through the life and teachings of Jesus.

Point 2 By calling ourselves progressive, we mean that we are Christians who recognize the faithfulness of other people who have other names for the way to God's realm, and acknowledge that their ways are true for them, as our ways are true for us.

Point 3 By calling ourselves progressive, we mean that we are Christians who understand the sharing of bread and wine in Jesus' name to be a representation of an ancient vision of God's feast for all peoples.

Point 4 By calling ourselves progressive, we mean that we are Christians who invite all people to participate in our community and worship life without insisting that they become like us in order to be acceptable.

Point 5 By calling ourselves progressive, we mean that we are Christians who know that the way we behave toward one another and toward other people is the fullest expression of what we believe.

Point 6 By calling ourselves progressive, we mean that we are Christians who find more grace in the search for meaning than in absolute certainty, in the questions than in the answers.

Point 7 By calling ourselves progressive, we mean that we are Christians who form ourselves into communities dedicated to equipping one another for the work we feel called to do: striving for peace and justice among all people, protecting and restoring the integrity of all God's creation, and bringing hope to those Jesus called the least of his sisters and brothers.

Point 8 By calling ourselves progressive, we mean that we are Christians who recognize that being followers of Jesus is costly, and entails selfless love, conscientious resistance to evil, and renunciation of privilege.

Their Original Version:

1. Proclaim Jesus Christ as our Gate to the realm of God.
2. Recognize the faithfulness of other people who have other names for the gateway to God's realm.
3. Understand our sharing of bread and wine in Jesus' name to be a representation of God's feast for all peoples.
4. Invite all sorts and conditions of people to join in our worship and in our common life as full partners, including (but not limited to): believers and agnostics, conventional Christians and questioning skeptics, homosexuals and heterosexuals, females and males, the despairing and the hopeful, those of all races and cultures, and those of

all classes and abilities, without imposing on them the necessity of becoming like us.

5. Think that the way we treat one another and other people is more important than the way we express our beliefs.

6. Find more grace in the search for meaning than in absolute certainty, in the questions than in the answers.

7. See ourselves as a spiritual community in which we discover the resources required for our work in the world: striving for justice and peace among all people; bringing hope to those Jesus called the least of his sisters and brothers.

8. Recognize that our faith entails costly discipleship, renunciation of privilege, and conscientious resistance to evil—as has always been the tradition of the church.

Here's another helpful description of Progressive Christian beliefs created by a Josh Magda that I came across on the Facebook page for the **Progressive Christian Alliance** in May, 2010 (I edited it slightly):

Progressive Christianity **rejects** what some might call **the "seven deadly doctrines" of modern "conservative" Christianity**:

1) Biblical literalism
2) Substitutionary atonement and other violent atonement theories
3) Religious exclusivism
4) Patriarchy and Homophobia
5) Belief-centered, dogmatic faith heavily reliant upon propositional argumentation and condemning those holding alternate views
6) The notion of eternal hell/damnation
7) Emphasis on the miraculous/supernatural, after-life oriented evangelism.

Similarly, the positive **affirmations** of Progressive Christianity are the converse of each of those previous propositions:

1) Non-literal, critical and yet spiritual approaches to biblical interpretation

2) Nonviolent atonement theologies (*Christus Victor*, Moral Influence, others)

3) Religious inclusivism or pluralism

4) Egalitarianism and inclusion in matters of gender and orientation, etc.

5) Action-centered, contemplative, reason-infused, yet mystery and paradox embracing, faith

6) Afterlife teachings that do not include eternal torture;

7) Emphasis on building God's Kingdom in our own lives and world in this lifetime here and now. I believe that the above is actually the authentic voice of the Christian tradition, with "progressive" being something of a misnomer, although a necessary one in a climate when Christian thinking is often associated with the seven deadly doctrines.

Belief Statement of the **Progressive Christian Alliance:**[409]

Jesus' central message is about radical inclusion, thus we welcome anyone to participate in our fellowship without judgment or forcing them to conform to our "likeness" or affirm our creeds in order to be accepted. We invite and offer *all* a place at the table—**no** exceptions.

> Faith is not about concrete answers, religious absolutes, creeds, or dogma. Faith is about the search for understanding, the raising of important questions, the open honesty of having doubt, and the realization that no one has it all completely right nor does any human hold all the answers. We seek to follow the advice found in 1st Thessalonians 5:21, which is to "seek truth out in all things and hold firmly onto that which is good." Religious absolutes of dogma, legalism, and strict doctrine become stumbling blocks and "litmus tests" for who is "in" and who is "out" of the circle of God's grace. These false tests that Jesus never required get in the way of truly following Jesus and his teachings.

---

[409] http://www.progressivechristianalliance.org/Blog/about/

Following Jesus is counter-cultural, radical, and disrupts the status quo. The good news of the gospel is intentional in its inclusion of those who are traditionally marginalized and refused by Mainline Christianity.

The words of Jesus found in the gospels; i.e., what he states are the greatest commandments: "Love God with all of your essence and love your neighbor as you should love yourself"—are to be the focus for any disciple of him. We submit the rest of Scripture to the position of "sacred commentary."

Recognition and affirmation of the differing belief systems of others, whose faiths offer a way into relationship with God and call upon them to further God's love and grace on the earth, is crucial. Jesus revealed this path in the acts and works of the *Gospel According to Matthew*, Chapters 5-7; and demonstrated this inclusion on many occasions—including in his witnessing and affirmation of the Samaritan woman, whose culture and people were looked down upon for worshipping God in a different way (*the Gospel According to John* 4:1-42). As Jesus taught and revealed through example, any "spiritual" or "non-spiritual" person adhering to this way of life are indeed furthering the Reign of God and God's message of radical love and inclusion here on earth. As Jesus said, "Anyone who is for us cannot be against us" (*the Gospel According to Mark* 9:39-41).

Creating fellowships and communities that are dedicated to lifting up, affirming, and equipping one another for the work the Spirit of God has called us to in *Micah* 6:8: active peacemaking, striving for justice and equality of all people and nations, loving those who are labeled by our government, society, and—at times—ourselves, as "enemies," caring for God's creation, and bringing hope to the poor and poverty-stricken.

God created humans with a brain capable of discovery and reason. God does not require us to "check our brains at the door," along with our coat and hat in order to be a part of the faith. Faith and Science are not in conflict; they are in harmony. The Bible is not a Science textbook and should never be taken as such. We affirm that if God is truth, then any discovery we make about ourselves, our origins, or the way the universe was created has come from God and should not be viewed as heresy.

The Church is not simply a four-walled institution, but a ministry without walls that surrounds and encompasses everything, everywhere we go. Our brothers and sisters are not only those who label themselves as "Christian," but are everyone we meet. Ministers and adherents of the Progressive Christian Alliance recognize that their ministry does not begin only when they are behind a pulpit or that their witness is only conveyed through spoken word; but their ministry extends to all places and their witness is conveyed by their actions.

Here are the personal reflections about progressive Christianity from Rev. David Gillespie, an ordained minister in the Progressive Christian Alliance: Tuesday, October 12, 2010 http://david-gillespie.blogspot.com/ (used with permission)

WHAT I MEAN BY "PROGRESSIVE"

I seem to have this ongoing debate with myself: what do I mean when I call myself a "progressive" Christian. The fact of the matter is, that adjective, "progressive" is a hard one to pin down. Lots of folks use it; lots of folks mean different things by it. Often I'm asked by friends or colleagues what I mean when I call myself thus. So I've tried to put down some thoughts on what it means, or what it doesn't mean, for me to self-identify as a progressive Christian.

POLITICS/ETHICS

Self-identifying as a progressive Christian does not mean that I am a Democrat. But then, on the other hand, neither does it mean

I am a Republican. It does not mean that I am a socialist or a libertarian; a communist or a capitalist.

Self-identifying as a progressive Christian, however, means that I understand the ultimate "political" division to be between Christ and Caesar; between the alternative way of being in the world as taught by Jesus and his disciples (beginning with a recognition of humankind's dependence upon God) and that of the "world's" way of being in the world (beginning with a self-deceiving notion of autonomy). It means I need to carefully discern between those teachings found in Scripture which are directed at this alternative community and those which have broader, universal implications.

Self-identifying as a progressive Christian does not mean I have to accept, in terms of my ethics, any particular "liberal" or "conservative" stance on issues.

Self-identifying as a progressive Christian, however, does seem to me to require my pro-life stance to be much broader than is usually conceived of: to speak prophetically against all practices in society and culture which demean, degrade or threaten dignified human existence.

THEOLOGY/PHILOSOPHY

Self-identifying as a progressive Christian does not mean I have to accept what is typically called a "Postmodern" view of things; that is, while Postmodernism might be a useful tool for understanding contemporary human existence and for critiquing modernism, it does not provide an adequate basis for knowledge.

Self-identifying as a progressive Christian means that I reject outright the "fundamentalism" of the "left" and the "right;" that I should not check my intellect at the door; that I should not engage in sloppy or meaningless discussion or debate; that I should not force alleged facts to fit my theory; that I should not reject an argument simply because it does not fit my theory. However, that does not mean I cannot recognize that we all have a starting point, we all have fundamental presuppositions about the way things are, about God, ourselves and the universe.

Self-identifying as a progressive Christian does not mean that I have to reject what might be called a "high" view of the Christian scriptures (aka, the Bible; aka, the Hebrew and Christian holy writings). Neither does not mean that I have to understand God to be something other than the infinite-personal God who brought all that is into existence, who is independent of the universe but acts in it, and who is self-revealing. While I can appreciate the work of various scholars of the Hebrew and Christian scriptures and early Christian origins, being progressive does not mean I have to uncritically accept their conclusions.

Self-identifying as a progressive Christian does not mean that I have to understand Jesus to be anything less tha[n] God incarnate and God's loudest, clearest word to humankind.

Self-identifying as a progressive Christian does not mean that I must try to downplay or reject outright the concept of sin as the willful rebellion of the creature against the Creator resulting in broken relationship with the Creator and death in an individual and cosmic sense.

Self-identifying as a progressive Christian does not mean that I reject Christianity's historic understanding, first developed by Paul in his letters to Christians in the years immediately following the execution of Jesus, of the cosmic significance of that execution in redeeming, restoring and reconciling the world with its Creator.

Self-identifying as a progressive Christian does not mean that I have to reject the bodily resurrection of Jesus. Even as a progressive Christian I can both believe and trust this to be true, to be an objective reality. As a progressive Christian, however, for the word "Christian" to have any meaning, I must see Jesus as much more than simply a profound man or revolutionary prophet or ethical teacher—that is, to understand the bodily resurrection of Jesus to be an essential part of the core of genuinely Christian faith.

Self-identifying as a progressive Christian does mean, however, that I am willing to question myself, to question my theology, to allow my theological and philosophical reflections to be informed by other sources of truth. After all, all truth is God's truth. Given that, it means that the ultimate expression of God's truth is in the person, teaching and redemptive work of Jesus as Christ and all other claims to truth must be assessed in light of that ultimate truth. I find that ultimate truth expressed in the gospel, as recounted in Scripture and testified to by the Church throughout the ages.

Self-identifying as a progressive Christian does not mean that I have to see the story of humankind as one of "progress" necessarily; that is, while the body of humankind's knowledge may be expanding, there is no definable goal toward which we are making progress—and neither is that to be necessarily expected. The one constant throughout the history of humankind is the human heart which possess the capability for great evil and often expresses that evil. In other words, being a progressive Christian doesn't mean I have to think that the world is getting better and better. It does mean, however, that I am called to live out, by God's grace, the gospel as I understand it in my day by day living and encounters with others, always reflecting that grace, and allowing the world to see that I am indeed of Christ by the love which I share with His other disciples.

FINAL THOUGHTS

When we start applying adjectives to the noun, Christian—such as "born again" or "evangelical" or "progressive" or "emergent" or whatever—we are invariably narrowing the definition. Sometimes that's unavoidable; sometimes it's helpful. But sometimes it can be arrogant, especially, for example, when a small group appropriates for itself the label, "orthodox." Orthodoxy is not defined by a small group of Christians who feel threatened by the theological explorations of others. Orthodoxy is not, for example in my own Communion of the Evangelical Lutheran Church in America, what a small group who interpret a scattered few passages about sexual activity. To disagree about the interpretation of a couple of passages does not constitute an example of unorthodoxy. We could say the same thing about certain groups within The Episcopal Church or Anglicanism as a whole.

The same thing applies to the word progressive. I have many friends who would accept the word, "evangelical," as a part of their identity. Notice I said "part." Those same friends often exhibit those characteristics which we might include in the word "progressive." Those two terms, progressive and evangelical, are not mutually exclusive terms. Yet there are those self-identified evangelicals and those self-identified progressives who want to make us think the words are mutually exclusive. Like with the word orthodox, we need to be careful about how much ownership we want to claim over it.

Ultimately, being a "progressive" Christian means for me welcoming all who would come; maintaining an open mind and being willing to change it when I'm shown a better, more convincing way of understanding; of always being willing to question myself; to not engage in the three "R's" of the world—retaliation, revenge, repayment; to always remember that I serve Christ, not Caesar; to maintain that of which I'm convinced by Scripture and reason while at the same time realizing that others of good faith disagree.

Appendix III

Progressive & Conservative Christianity Typology Chart

Differing Emphases within Christianity:

Note: these are merely differing emphases, not different religions. The chart is admittedly reductionistic and overstated in order to show distinctions. (Most of us are a mixture of both of these perspectives)

Progressive	Conservative
Christianity is described more as the following of Jesus' radical Way of life than upon agreeing with certain truth claims.	Christianity described more as believing certain "essential" truth claims, dogmas & doctrines.
Emphasis more upon the religion "of" Jesus. Comfortable with ambiguity, doubt & questioning. Comfort with science. Social reform & liberation.	Emphasis more upon the religion "about" Jesus. Comfort in known definitions & boundaries. Wary of science. Praise and evangelism.
Leans toward subjective flexibility.	Leans toward legalism.

God

Focus on God's immanence	Focus on God's transcendence
Spirit—loving, merciful Persuasive power	Male person—wrathful, judging Sovereign/coercive power
Limits own power or limited power	Omnipotent
Free will given to humans	Predestination, God's will rules

Jesus

Teacher, guide, trailblazer, prophet, moral example, radical revolutionary, holy man,	God; 2nd Person of the Trinity; Miracles; Perfect; sacrificial lamb; proxy for our punishment
Emphasizes Jesus' humanness	Emphasizes Jesus' divinity
Understand titles of *Son of God, Lord, Savior,* etc. as political counters to the imperial claims of "Caesar."	Treat titles as theological only. God incarnate (enfleshed)
Unique manifestation of Christ	Exclusive manifestation of Christ
Fully open to God working through Him, thus making him Divine and godly.	Exclusive way to God/salvation

Salvation

Here and now	Later, after we die, in heaven
Wholeness	Removal of sins; escape from punishment
Social/collective & personal via Jesus' life and following it	Personal/individual via Jesus' death

Sin

Focus on social, systemic sins esp. oppression.	Focus on personal sins, esp. sexual.
The focus of personal sin is on when we act to outside of love.	Focus on social sin is often limited homosexuality and abortion.

Heaven

Emphasis upon Kingdom of God on earth.	Emphasis upon the after-life (later, someplace else, when we die)
Eternal life understood as abundant thriving on earth.	Eternal life = infinite duration of time

Hell

Focus more upon various "hells on earth." A state of being whereby one is alienated and disconnected from God and from whom one really is.	Literal place, fiery, eternal physical torment and punishment

The Cross

The means of Jesus' execution by empire.	Blessed gift to humanity.
The worst that the worldly powers could dish out. Consequence of following Jesus' radical way.	The means by which salvation was made available to us. Instrument of sacrifice for our sins.

Bible

Interpretive, metaphorical, scholarly reading	Literal reading
Inspired co-creation of God & humans	Only & exclusive revelation from God
Gospels, esp. Matthew & Luke, the Prophets, Sermon on the Mount, the Beatitudes	Pastoral Epistles, Paul's letters, John, Revelation, Torah, The 10 Cs

Humans

Essentially good or neutral in nature	Essentially bad, sinful, wretched

Moral Concerns

Greed, consumerism, materialism, exploitation of the poor, increasing gap between haves and have-nots.	Lust, homosexuality, sloth laziness, personal responsibility
Restorative justice.	Retributive justice
Capital punishment, unjust wars	Abortion
Stewardship of God's creation/ environment	Good citizenship in one's nation
Challenge social status quo	Maintain societal status quo

Worship

Communing/connecting with God (God & "we")	Praising God (God & "me")
Social challenge emphasized	Personal comfort & healing

2nd Coming/Eschatology

See Christ's return every day
esp. when in ministry to and with
oppressed persons.
Fully realized when God's will is
done on Earth as it is in heaven.

Physical "rapture"
"Beam me up!"

Rewards or punishment

Other Religions

Open to all other Christians and
other religious traditions.

Not accepting of certain Christians
or other religions.

Appendix IV

Which World would you rather live in?

(Which world would you want your *children* to live in?)

Ways of the World:	Ways of God's Kingdom:
Violent	Peaceful
Unjust	Just
Coercive	Persuasive
Oppressing	Empowering
Binding	Liberating
Hierarchical	Egalitarian
Alienating	Relational
Power over	Power with
Exploitive	Fair/Equitable
Commodifying	Humanizing
Greedy	Satisfying
Lustful	Content
Escaping	Engaging
Idolatrous	Faithful
Privatizing	Sharing
Woman-rating	Woman-appreciating
Scarce	Abundant
Fearful	Assuring
Retributive	Restorative

Conforming	Transforming
Blind Sheep	Seeing sheep
Seducing	Inviting
Pseudo-culture (*most* fashion, pornography, pro sports, gambling, pop music, TV, movies, video games . . . though there are forms of those things that are meaningful and life enhancing . . . fun is still allowed in the Kingdom, just not getting obsessed by those things!)	Kingdom-culture (genuine expressions of love, grace, truth, and beauty)
Isolating	Fellowshipping
Pacifying (as in subduing and making passive)	Emboldening (empowered for peace making and nonviolence)
Depressing	Inspiring
Dividing	Uniting
Desensitizing	Sensitizing
Numbing/Distracting	Awakening/Engaging
Destructive	Constructive
Surviving	Thriving
Hurting	Healing
Arrogant	Humble
Self-centered	Other-centered
Leads to Death	Leads to Life—*abundant and eternal!*

For more on the World's Ways vs. God's Ways see: Matthew 16:24-26; John 15:18-19; Romans 12:1-2; 1 Corinthians 1:18-25; 2:12-16; 3:18-19; 4:8-ff; 2 Corinthians 10:3-5; James 2:5, 4:4; & 1 John 2:15, 5:4

Worldly "Wisdom":	Godly Wisdom:
Get them, before they get you!	"Love your neighbor as yourself." (Mark 12:31)
Hate your enemies.	"Love your enemies." (Matthew 5:44)
It's a dog eat dog world!	It's a brother/sister help brother/sister world!
Pull yourself up by your own bootstraps!	We get by with a little help from our friends! (James 2:14:17)
It's survival of the fittest!	It's salvation for the faithful! (John 3:16) *And besides, it's not about surviving, it's about thriving!*
Do unto them before they do unto you!	"Do unto others as you would have them do unto you!" (Matthew 7:12)
He who dies with the most toys wins!	"S/he who lives and dies knowing and living like they know God and God's Son are saved." (Matt. 26:31-46)
Self-esteem comes from: winning, success, good looks, achievement, popularity, etc)	Self-Worth comes from knowing you are a Loved, Accepted, and Forgiven Child of God, *Who made you fearfully and wonderfully!* (Psalm 139:14)
Eye for an eye!	Forgive those who wrong you. (Matthew 6:38-42, 18:22)

People who do wrong should be killed.	Those who are without sin may cast the first stone. (John 8:7)
Everyone should own their own stuff.	Everyone should share what they have. (Acts 4:32-35)
People should keep up with the Joneses.	People should be grateful for the blessings that they have.
It isn't cheating, if you don't get caught.	Even if you merely think about cheating, you are guilty of it. (Matthew 5:28)
Might makes right!	Truth and love make right.
The Greatest are the greatest.	"The Greatest are the least!" (Mark 9:35)
The cup is either half empty or half full.	"The cup runneth over!" (Psalm 23:5)
Truth is relative.	Truth is true and eternal.
Blessed are the rich, proud, and powerful!	"Blessed are the poor, humble, and meek!" (Matthew 5:1:11)
Faith is foolish.	God's foolishness is wiser than human wisdom." (1 Corinthians 1:25)

Appendix V

Ways to Pray:

A Common Christian approach:

1. Talk to God as you would an intimately close friend.
2. Give *thanks* for things in your life and in the world that are going well.
3. Ask for God's involvement in the lives of *other* people who need God's healing touch.
4. Ask God how *you* might be able to make a difference by letting God work through you.
5. Boldly ask for *forgiveness* for doing what you shouldn't do and for failing to do what you should. Accept God's assurance of pardon and ask God to help you repent and reorient your mindset and your life toward healthier ways of living.
6. Ask for God's assistance in *your own* life and circumstances.
7. *Thank* God for spending this time with you.
   Say *Amen!* (meaning "may it be so!")

Centering Prayer:

* Set aside 25-45 minutes in a quiet place. Sit comfortably, perhaps cross-legged on the floor, and maybe light a candle.
* Sit still and just **BE** with God.
* Don't think of things to say or ask, just sit quietly in God's presence and enjoy each other's company.

* If your mind starts to wander or become distracted, don't fight it. Acknowledge the distraction, let it run for a bit if you'd like, then say a "prayer word" in your mind to bring back to center (e.g. "Jesus," "Peace," "Grace," "God," etc.).
* Just—*be still and know that I am God."* (Psalm 46:10)

(learn more at **http://www.centeringprayer.com**)

The Serenity Prayer
GOD, grant me the serenity to accept the things
I cannot change, courage to change the things I can, and the
wisdom to know the difference.

The Lord's Prayer

(a prayer Jesus taught His disciples—
many Christians learn this one by heart)

Our Father [Mother/God], Who art in Heaven, hallowed be
Thy name.
Thy Kingdom *come,*
Thy will be *done,* on *Earth* as it is in Heaven.
Give us this day our daily bread, and forgive us *our* trespasses
(debts/sins) as *we* forgive those who trespass against *us;*
And lead us not into temptation, but *deliver* us from evil; for
Thine is the Kingdom, and the Power, and the Glory Forever!
Amen!

Appendix VI

Civil Religion:
A common concern

(first referenced in Chapter 10, this is a common challenge to both progressive & conservative Christianities)

Key Person or Founder, Date, Location:

The "founding fathers" and head leaders of one's nation; the early American colonies; and esp. Philadelphia, PA; July 4, 1776.

Key Writings:

Chartering documents such as Declarations of Independence, Constitutions; famous speeches and letters, etc. Often included are idealized myths describing the creation of one's nation.

Who is God:

A generic concept of God is embraced. This God is usually Deistic and has a special love for one's particular nation. In extreme forms, one's nation is equated to being God.

Who is Jesus:

Jesus is not a part of this religion but references and allusions to some of His sayings, usually out of context, are sometimes employed.

Who is the Holy Spirit:

The Holy Spirit is not a part of this.

How to be Saved:

In the case of the U.S., salvation is typically understood as achieving a certain level of material wealth, success, and status—"the good life." This is said to be attained through rugged individualism and "pulling one's self up by one's bootstraps."

What Happens After Death:

Death is usually denied but those who die serving one's nation—especially in the military—are honored and venerated on special holidays. People who die such deaths are remembered and it is assumed that God has a special place for them.

Other Beliefs or Practices:

National anthems, pledges of allegiance, and vague blessings are shared at public events. The hymns and prayers of other religions are often co-opted and altered as well. Flags, national birds, crests, etc. are the primary symbols. Blindly supporting the policies of the current national leaders is expected. Dissent is discouraged.

It may be that this is more of a threat to Christianity (both progressive and conservative) than atheism could ever be. Civil religion secularizes, waters down, and makes generic the specificity of any religion. It spins, distorts, and renders impotent authentic Christianity. The following is from an email I received:

Civil Religion: The 500 Pound Gorilla by Norman B. Bendroth (with permission)

This past Christmas Vice President Dick and Lynne Cheney sent out what is certainly the most brazen Christmas card I have ever heard of. It read: "And if a sparrow cannot fall to the ground without His notice, is it probable that an empire can rise without His aid?"

This is not the first time a power broker has co-opted the name of God to baptize the agenda of the empire, Pax Americana or otherwise. One thinks of Emperor Constantine's soldiers, whose armor was inscribed with the words In Hoc Signo Vinces ("In This Sign You Will Conquer"); and the banner of the Crusaders, Deus Vult ("God wills it"), as they swashbuckled their way through the Holy Land; and, in the last century, the slogan Gott Mit Uns ("God with us") which adorned the belt buckles of the Nazis.

Late last year, Lt. General William Boykin gave new meaning to the song "Onward Christian Soldiers" when he spoke of America's "Christian army" waging a holy war against the "idol" of Islam's false god, and the "spiritual battle" we're fighting against "a guy named Satan" while pursuing Muslim terrorists.

Even President Bush used an old gospel song to describe American vigilance. In his State of the Union Address on January 29, 2003, he said, "There is power, power, wonder-working power in the goodness and idealism and faith of the American people." Those who know their hymnody remember the original as, "there is wonder-working power in the blood of the Lamb." To exchange the salvific work of Christ for the "goodness" of the American people is sacrilege. Even Democratic candidates have waded into these murky waters, with Howard Dean declaring that the book of Job was his favorite New Testament book (oops!).

What is going on here? It is called American civil religion. Sociologist Robert Bellah coined the term in a groundbreaking article in 1967 to describe the set of rituals, doctrines, and allegiances that develop around nation-states and which become the sacred myth that binds citizens in common allegiance. The myth bestows a sacred canopy over the origins, destiny, and purpose of the State.

Daniel Marsh of Boston University has pointed out, in his book Unto the Generations: the Roots of True Americanism, the similarities between biblical history and American history. America's book of Genesis is the Mayflower Compact. Its exodus is the Declaration of Independence. The book of the law is the Constitution and the Bill of Rights. Its psalms include the "Star Spangled Banner" and "God Bless America." Lincoln's Second Inaugural address is its prophetic denouncement. (Congressman Tom DeLay has even gone so far to tell an audience at the Christian Coalition's Road to Victory Conference that American democracy is a perfect governmental expression of an inerrant Bible).

Rituals include saying the pledge of allegiance in our schools, singing the "Star Spangled Banner" at sporting events, having parades and ceremonies honoring the war dead, and invoking the blessing of some higher power at political events. The virtues of democracy, individual liberty, the right to private property, family, free enterprise, and a commitment to faith are part of its doctrines. Faith in this system of thought is vague and undefined. It is best exemplified in President Eisenhower's statement, "This country was founded on faith and I don't care in what."

Civil religion provides religious means and modes for the expression of patriotism. Civil religion and Christian religion can look deceptively similar, so much so that it is easy to merge the two into one, like many American churches do on the Sunday near the Fourth of July. It is not a state religion, but rather a set of practices and beliefs that renders sacred national values, national heroes, national history, and national ideals.

While there is nothing inherently wrong with civil religion (it often functions as a civic "glue"), it should not be confused with Christian faith. What makes American civil religion distinctive from other nations' is that we have always believed that we are special and have a "manifest destiny" (as the Pilgrims put it)—a sacred and noble cause bestowed from above. The Pilgrims saw themselves as a "New Israel" making an exodus from Europe to freedom and plenty in a new Promised Land. From the outset, we have seen ourselves as God's chosen people with a special (if not divine) mission to export liberty and light to the world.

Some have defended Gen. Boykin or the religious language that embellishes President Bush's speech, accusing their critics of being "anti-Christian" or "politically correct." While that may or may not be true, more fundamentally it is just plain bad theology.

To equate the Kingdom of God with the United States of America is idolatry of the highest order. The commonwealth of God is a global community that transcends all nation states and embraces all peoples. Rather than endorsing any imperial power, it calls all such pretensions to power into question.

The Cheneys' greeting card was sent during the season when churches read Mary's Magnificat, which promises that in the Messiah God "has brought down the powerful from their thrones, and lifted up the lowly" (Luke 1:52). During World War II, American theologian Reinhold Niebuhr was quick to remind us that the Axis powers were not entirely evil, nor were Allied actions entirely good. To cast the American struggle against terrorism as solely a "conflict between good and evil" is to miss the log in our own eye (Matthew 7:3). This is not asserting a moral relativism that equates American overreaching with terrorism. It is to say that sin is never privileged to any particular people or nation, but runs right through the center of every human heart—including every American heart.

Because of the danger of confusing civil religion with Christian faith, Christians must be careful what kinds of symbols are present in their churches as well. When Christians participate in worship on Sunday mornings, they are gathering to proclaim their first allegiance and to acknowledge that all of life is lived under the government of God. Consequently, the symbols we display there point to our ultimate loyalties, what is truly real: the cross, the baptismal font, the open Bible, the altar, the bread and cup, to name a few.

Why then do we display the American flag in our sanctuaries when Scripture teaches that all nations will come under the judgment of a righteous God (Psalm 2:1-5) and we are part of a worldwide Communion of faith? My Canadian Christian friends are amazed when they find American flags in our sanctuaries. The flag is a national symbol, not a religious one. As Christians, we are called to transcend national divisions. Baptism, not the flag, affirms our unity as God's people throughout the world.

By carelessly endorsing the religion and the policies of the State (read: empire), Christians forfeit their prophetic role to be critics-in-residence and to call the State to its highest principles. Martin Luther reminded the pastors of his day that one of their tasks was to "whisper the Law of God into the magistrate's ear." There's a 500-lb. gorilla called American civil religion sitting in the middle of most American sanctuaries and they are not even aware of it.

The challenge for Christians and all people of faith today is this: Will we prescribe to a national religion in service of empire, or will we follow the Lord of the nations in service of Shalom?

(Norman B. Bendroth is currently interim pastor at St. John's United Church of Christ in Grand Rapids, MI.)

For more on civil religion see: *The Myth of A Christian Nation*, Greogry Boyd, Zondervan, 2005 and "Civil Religion in America" by Robert Bellah, 1967.

Appendix VII

Progressive Christian Resources

(progressive oriented, or progressive leaning, Christian magazines, websites, blogs, songs, progressive congregations, etc.)

The Center for Progressive Christianity	http://www.tcpc.org
The Progressive Christian Alliance	http://www.progressivechristianalliance.org
The Center for Process Studies	http://www.ctr4process.org
Beliefnet	http://www.beliefnet.com
Religious Tolerance	http://www.religioustolerance.org
Re: Progressive Christianity	http://www.religioustolerance.org/int_rel22.htm

The Interfaith Alliance   http://www.interfaithalliance.org

Founded in 1994, The Interfaith Alliance (TIA) is a non-partisan, clergy-led grassroots organization dedicated to promoting the positive and healing role of religion in the life of the nation and challenging those who manipulate religion to promote a narrow, divisive agenda. With more than 150,000 members drawn from over 70 faith traditions, 47 local Alliances and a national network of religious leaders, TIA promotes compassion, civility and mutual respect for human dignity in our increasingly diverse society.

Faithful America   http://www.faithfulamerica.org

Faith In Action: Free action alerts & inspiration. FaithfulAmerica.org is an online community of people of faith who want to build a more just and compassionate nation. It aspires to be an online wing of a powerful, new progressive faith movement, like the ones that fought for independence, abolition and civil rights. FaithfulAmerica.org believes in the common good and in community—local, national and global. We reject a go-it-alone culture that reduces our politics and our personal lives to selfishness and fear. We accept the separation of church and state, but not the separation of moral principles from politics.

Church Folks for a Better America   http://www.cfba.info

A project of the Peace Action Education Fund, educational arm of the Coalition for Peace Action, 40 Witherspoon Street, Princeton, NJ 08542

Fellowship for Reconciliation (FOR)   http://www.forusa.org

The Fellowship of Reconciliation seeks to replace violence, war, racism, and economic injustice with nonviolence, peace, and justice. We are an interfaith organization committed to active nonviolence as a transforming way of life and as a means of radical change. We educate, train, build coalitions, and engage in nonviolent and compassionate actions locally, nationally, and globally.

American Friends Service Committee   http://www.afsc.org

(the political activist arm of the Quaker Church) 1501 Cherry Street, Philadelphia, PA 19102

Every Church a Peace Church   http://www.ecapc.org
Bread for the World   http://www.bread.org

Churches for Middle East Peace   http://www.cmep.org

110 Maryland Ave NE, #311, Washington, DC 20002
Telephone (202) 543-1222 Fax: 202-543-5025
(special focus upon Israeli-Palestinian conflict)

Pax Christi   http://www.pcusa.org & http://www.paxchristiusa.org

(an unofficial peace & justice wing of the Roman Catholic Church)

The Catholic Worker Movement   http://www.catholicworker.org
(another unofficial peace & justice wing of the RCC, founded by the late Dorothy Day)

Interfaith Worker Justice   http://capwiz.com/nicwj
1020 W. Bryn Mawr Ave., 4th Fl., Chicago, IL 60660
Ph: (773) 728-8400 Fx: (773) 728-8409

Sojourners Magazine   http://www.sojo.net
(a progressive evangelical journal, community, and advocacy group)

Locating a progressive Christian church can be challenging but congregations that lean in that direction are fairly common among the mainline Protestant denominations. If you visit their websites, you can use their **"find a church/congregation locator"** functions to find those close to you. See: United Methodist Church, www.umc.org; United Church of Christ, www.ucc.org; ELCA Lutheran, www.elca.org; Disciples of Christ, www.disciples.org; Quaker, www.quaker.org; Sojourners, www.sojo.net; The Center for Progressive Christianity, www.tcpc.org; and Progressive Christian Alliance, www.progressivechristianalliance.org. Moreover, many, but not all, congregations that announce that they are a "reconciling congregation" or a "welcoming and affirming" church (code for LGBTQI friendly) embrace progressive Christian theology.

Appendix VIII

Progressive Christian Books
(or at least progressive-leaning)

A New Christianity for a New World, John Shelby Spong, Harper SanFrancisco, 2001

An Emergent Manifest of Hope, Doug Pagitt and Tony Jones, eds., Baker Books, 2007

Announcing the Reign of God: Evangeliziation and the Subversive Memory of Jesus, Mortimer Arias, Fortress, 1984

Becoming Children of God: John's Gospel and Radical Discipleship, Wes Howard-Brook, Wipf & Stock, 2004

Blue Like Jazz: Nonreligious Thoughts on Christian Spirituality, Thomas Nelson, 2003

Christianity for the Rest of Us, Diana Butler Bass, Harper SanFrancisco, 2006

"Come Out My People!": God's Call Out of Empire in the Bible and Beyond, Wes Howard-Brook, Orbis, 2010

Daring to Speak in God's Name, Mary Allice Mulligan & Rufus Burrow, Jr., Pilgrim Press, 2002

God of the Possible: a Biblical Introduction to the Open View of God, Gregory Boyd, Baker Books, 2000

Good Goats: Healing Our Image of God, Dennis Linn, Sheila Fabricant Linn, Matthew Linn, Paulist Press, 1993

"Homosexuality and the Bible," Walter Wink, http://www.soulforce.org/article/homosexuality-bible-walter-wink

How to be an Open-minded Christian without Losing Your Faith, Jan Linn, Chalice Press, 2002

Hunger for Justice: the politics of food and faith, Jack Nelson, Orbis, 1980

In God's Presence: Theological Reflections on Prayer, by Marjorie Hewitt Suchocki, Christian Board of Publication, 1996

Jesus and Empire: The Kingdom of God and the New World Order, Richard Horsley, Fortress, 2002

John and Empire, Warren Carter, T & T Clark International, 2008

Meeting Jesus Again for the First Time, Marcus Borg, Harper One, 1995

Most Moved Mover: A Theology of God's Openness, Clark Pinnock, Baker, 2001

Open Christianity: Home by Another Road, Jim Burklo, Rising Star Press, 2000

Process Theology: A Basic Introduction, Don Compier, Chalice, 1993

Reading the Bible Again for the First Time: Taking the Bible Seriously But Not Literally, by Marcus Borg, HarperSanFrancisco, 2002

Rescuing the Bible from Fundamentalism, Jon Shelby Spong, HarperOne, 1992

Resident Aliens, Stanley Hauerwas and William Willimon, Abingdon, 1989 (See also: *Where Resident Aliens Live*, Abingdon, 1996)

Stages of Faith: The Psychology of Human Development and the Quest for Meaning, James Fowler, HarperSanFrancisco, 1995

Ten Things I Learned Wrong from a Conservative Church, John Killinger, Crossroad, 2002

The Call to Conversion, Jim Wallis, HarperSanFrancisco,1981

The Emerging Christian Way, Michael Schwartzentruber, ed., CooperHouse, 2006

The Good Book: Reading the Bible With Heart and Mind, Peter Gomes, Harper Perennial, 1998

The Heart of Christianity: Rediscovering a Life of Faith, Marcus Borg, HarperSanFrancisco, 2003

The Last Week, Marcus Borg and John Dominic Crossan, Harper One, 2007

The Myth of A Christian Nation, Greogry Boyd, Zondervan, 2005

The Nonviolent Atonement, J. Denny Weaver, Eerdmans, 2001

The Powers That Be: Theology for a New Millennium, Three Rivers Press, 1999

Traveling Mercies: Some Thoughts on Faith, Anne Lamott, Pantheon, Random House, 1999 (See also: *Plan B: Futher Thoughts on Faith*, Riverhead, 2005)

Unveiling Empire: Reading Revelation Then and Now, Orbis, 1999

What a Progressive Christian Believes, Del Brown, Seabury, 2008

Made in the USA
Middletown, DE
25 September 2021